LEARN JAPANESE
NEW COLLEGE TEXT

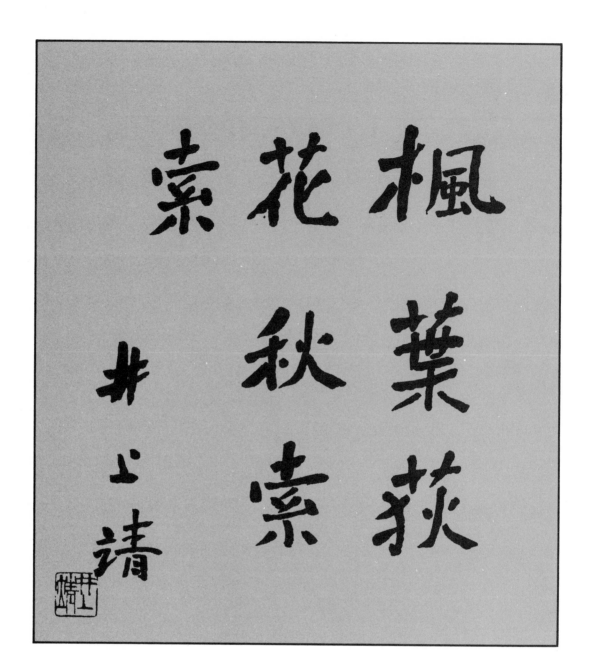

「楓葉荻花秋索索」　井上　靖

    written by Mr. Yasushi Inoue, who was born in 1907 and is one of the elders of the Japanese literary circle. He has received the ''Bunka Kun-shō,'' an imperial award to distinguished men of letters. He is the president of Japan PEN and has hosted the Forty-seventh International PEN Congress in Japan.

LEARN JAPANESE

NEW COLLEGE TEXT   VOLUME IV

John Young and Kimiko Nakajima-Okano

Published for
University of Maryland University College

University of Hawaii Press
Honolulu

This volume is another in a series of Japanese language text-books prepared by the Asian Division of the University of Maryland University College and published by the University of Hawaii Press.

Library of Congress Cataloging in Publication Data
(Revised for volume IV)

Young, John, 1920–
  Learn Japanese.

  Includes indexes.
  1. Japanese language—Text-books for foreign
speakers—English. I. Nakajima-Okano, Kimiko.
II. Title.
PL539.3.Y64   1984   495.68′3421   83–18060
ISBN 0-8248-0859-2 (v. 1)
ISBN 0-8248-0881-9 (v. 2)
ISBN 0-8248-0896-7 (v. 3)
ISBN 0-8248-0951-3 (v. 4)

CONTENTS

ACKNOWLEDGMENTS

The authors are deeply indebted to the Japanese language faculty and administrative staff members of the University of Maryland's Asian Division and of Seton Hall University who assisted in the preparation of this book. We would like especially to express our sincere gratitude to Dr. T. Benjamin Massey, chancellor of the University of Maryland University College, for his resolute decision to push this revision project through and to thank Dr. Ray Ehrensberger and Dr. Stanley J. Drazek, two distinguished chancellors emeritus of the University of Maryland, for their more than two decades of friendship.

We would like also to mention the following people whose assistance was most valuable: M. Yoshiko Andō, who assisted us in preparing the text and enriched it with her practical and valuable suggestions. Mr. Keiichirō Okutsu, who reviewed our notes, gave us his valuable suggestions, and gave us permission to use freely and adapt the content of *Learn Japanese—Pattern Approach*.

Urayama no
Yuuhi ni utsuru
Tsurara kana
　　—Seien—

Back mountain icicles
Transcendent in the setting sun;
Splendid—ephemeral.

INTRODUCTION

This is the fourth volume of *Learn Japanese: New College Text*. In this volume, a total of 129 *kan'ji* characters with 158 different readings are introduced. Altogether in Volumes I through IV, 329 *kan'ji* characters with 405 different readings plus one *kan'ji* mark 々 are introduced. Any *kan'ji* that has appeared in a previous lesson with a different reading or any compound *kan'ji* whose reading is especially derived as a result of a combination is introduced with the number with which it was originally introduced. Such *kan'ji* with different readings are assigned numbers (such as 後 2.6.a) that distinguish them from those numbers (such as 頼 2.6.l) assigned to newly introduced *kan'ji*. Most of the *kan'ji* first appear in presentations and dialogs, but there are some that first occur in notes or drills. They are identified with an asterisk.

In addition to the *kan'ji* for "active" learning, we have introduced *kan'ji* for "passive" learning. We have attached *furigana*—reading of the *kan'ji* in small *hiragana*—to these passive *kan'ji*. The student is required to identify and possibly reproduce the active *kan'ji*, but the passive *kan'ji* need not be memorized until they are introduced as the *kan'ji* for active learning. *Kan'ji* appearing in Lesson 14 are also for passive learning.

In many traditional *kan'ji* dictionaries, *kan'ji* are classified according to 214 *bushu*, or radicals. This kind of arrangement has generally been discarded by modern dictionary compilers because many simplified or modern *kan'ji*, as a result of the language reform measures taken since 1945, do not fit the various radicals. For example, the Agency for Cultural Affairs' *Dictionary of Chinese Characters for Foreigners* classifies *kan'ji* into 5 categories, namely, 丶, 丨, 一, 丿, and 乛 and 247 subcategories called elements. In this text the term "classifier" refers both to radicals of traditional dictionaries and categories/elements of reformed dictionaries. The traditional classifiers appear in parentheses after the reformed classifiers. For example: Vol. 2, 1.6.6 六 (3) classifier 亠 (八). The following popular dictionary is used in determining classifiers: Kikuya Nagasawa, *Meikai Kan'wa Jiten,* 1959, San'seidoo, Tokyo. Other reformed dictionaries might have different ways of grouping *kan'ji*, however.

Although an introduction to the speech levels has been incorporated into Lesson 1, it is not the authors' intention at this time to ask the student to practice the various levels, which have been listed there for cognitive or passive learning purposes.

Lessons 2 through 4, 6 through 9, and 11 through 13 constitute the main text, while Lesson 14 is only for the passive study of *kan'ji*. Lessons 5, 10, and 15 are review lessons. The Mike Harrison Series, as in Volume III, is included in review lessons for passive learning purposes to help the student develop aural comprehension skills through application conversations in a variety of situations. A new section called reading comprehension has been added to main lessons.

LESSON 1

1.1 GENERAL INTRODUCTION TO SPEECH LEVELS

Generally speaking, a speech style is determined by the speaker's relative status relationship with the listener. Therefore, only the relationship between the speaker ① and the listener ② is involved. A speech level, on the other hand, is determined by the speaker's evaluation of the relative status relationship of the subject-person with the object-person involved in the speaker's talk. Thus, only the relationship between the subject (person) ⓧ and the object (person) ⓧⓧ is involved.

As described in Lesson 1 of Volume III, the following symbols and abbreviations have been used here:

⓪ no person involved		↑ P promotion of ⓧ	} level
① the speaker, the first person		↓ D demotion of ⓧ	
② the listener, the second person		→ F more formal or polite	
③ the third person or persons		← I more informal, familiar, plain or less polite	} style
ⓧ the person referred to by the speaker as the subject			
ⓧⓧ the person referred to by the speaker as the object			

Thus, styles and levels can be described in a form of two axes with the speaker placed at the center.

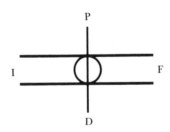

1.2 FORMULATIONS

Promotion or demotion levels, some deferential and some humble, are ordinarily formulated in three ways:

1. special lexical items:

    いらっしゃる、おっしゃる、くださる、なさる、ござる、いたす、もうす、おる、まいる、ぼく、きみ、etc.

2. affixing:

    山田さん、ごかぞく、お考え、etc.

3. special structural forms:

お考えになる、お持ちする、ごらんなさいます、ごせつめいください、

ごしょうかいします、ごぞんじです、教えてくださいます、行かれる、行ってやる、

おたのみいたします、etc.

1.3 PROMOTION LEVELS

There are nine types of promotion levels:

1.3.1 Type P12.... promotion of (1X), resulting in the downgrading of (X2X)

Example: 君に やったよ。

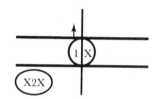

1.3.2 Type P13.... promotion of (1X), resulting in the downgrading of (X3X)

Example: あいつに やったよ。　　　　あいつに やりました。

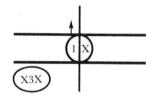

1.3.3 Type P20.... promotion of (2X), without involving any specific object-person or persons (0)

Example: （あなたは） きのう めしあがりましたか。

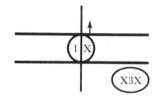

お読みになる

お読みなさる

お読みです

お読みでいらっしゃいます

読まれます

1.3.4 Type P21.... promotion of (2X), resulting in the downgrading of (X1X)

Example: （あなたは） 私に そう おっしゃいましたね。

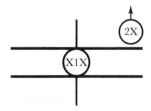

1.3.5   Type P23 .... promotion of (2X), resulting in the downgrading of (X3X)

Example:　一郎に　やったか。　　　　　　　　一郎に　やりましたか。

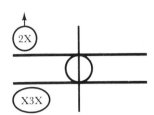　　　　　　　　　　　　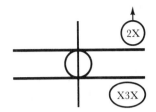

1.3.6   Type P30 .... promotion of (3X), without involving another object-person (0)

Example:　先生は　大阪へ　　　　　　　　先生は　大阪へ　いらっしゃいましたね。

　　　　　いらっしゃったね。

　　　　＊ *Sen'sei* is the third person.

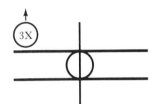　　　　　　　　　　　　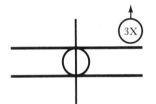

1.3.7   Type P31 .... promotion of (3X), resulting in the downgrading of (X1X)

Example:　社長が　ぼくに　そう　　　　　社長が　私に　そう　おっしゃいました。

　　　　　おっしゃった。

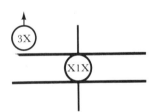　　　　　　　　　　　　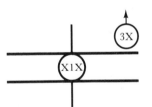

1.3.8   Type P32 .... promotion of (3X), resulting in the downgrading of (X2X)

Example:　先生が　君に　そう　　　　　　先生が　あなたに　そう

　　　　　おっしゃったね。　　　　　　　おっしゃいましたね。

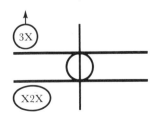　　　　　　　　　　　　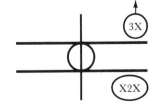

1.3.9 Type P33....promotion of one third person ③X, resulting in the downgrading of another third person or persons (X3X)

Example:　田中先生が　学生に　　　　　　　田中先生が　学生に　おっしゃいました。
　　　　　　おっしゃった。

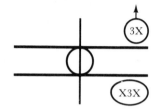

1.4　DEMOTION LEVELS

There are nine types of demotion levels:

1.4.1 Type D12....demotion of (1X), resulting in the upgrading of (X2X)

Example:　あした　お持ちいたします。

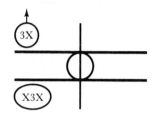

1.4.2 Type D13....demotion of (1X), resulting in the upgrading of (X3X)

Example:　あした　田中先生の　所へ　まいります。

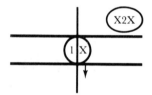

1.4.3 Type D20....demotion of (2X), without involving another object-person (0)

Example:　おまえも　くったのか。

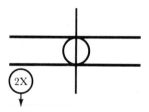

1.4.4 Type D21....demotion of (2X), resulting in the upgrading of (X1X)

Example: こっちへ　まいれ。　　　　　　早く　もうせ。

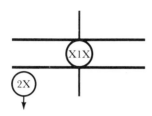

1.4.5 Type D23....demotion of (2X), resulting in the upgrading of (X3X)

Example: お父さんに　よろしく　もうしあげてください。

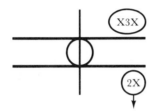

1.4.6 Type D30....demotion of (3X), without involving another object-person (0)

Example: 木村君は　もう　食べたよ。　　　木村君は　もう　食べましたよ。

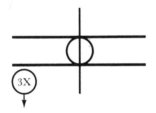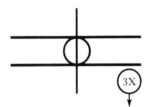

1.4.7 Type D31....demotion of (3X), resulting in the upgrading of (X1X)

Example: あいつ、まだ　（おれの　所へ）　まいらんか。

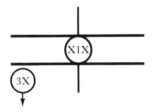

1.4.8 Type D32....demotion of (3X), resulting in the upgrading of (X2X)

Example: 一郎が　あなたに　さしあげたいと　言いましたよ。

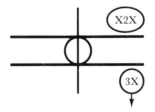

1.4.9 Type D33....demotion of (3X), resulting in the upgrading of another third person or persons (X3X)

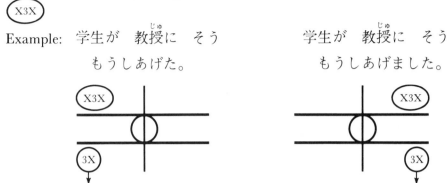

Example: 学生が　教授に　そう
　　　　　もうしあげた。

学生が　教授に　そう
もうしあげました。

1.5 CLASSIFICATION OF LEVELS

In conclusion, it can be said that style is determined mainly by sentence endings such as *desu*, *-masu*, and the like, and level is determined mainly by the nature of the Predicate.

When the Predicate involves promotion or demotion expressions such as *yarimasu*, *mairimasu*, the level then is either "promotion" or "demotion." When the first person is the referred-subject, however, then the referred-object-person must also be involved in order to be considered as either "promotion" or "demotion."

When the Predicate does not involve promotion or demotion expressions, the level is "neutral" unless the third person carrying either "promotion" or "demotion" expressions such as *Yamada kun* is the referred-subject.

Vague expressions, indirect expressions, reverse expressions, overlapping, offsetting, strengthening, and in-groupness which affect the level or degree of level study have not been dealt with here.

In summary, the eighteen types of levels may be described as follows:

P / d		XX			
P		0	1	2	3
↑ X	1			P12	P13
	2	P20	P21		P23
	3	P30	P31	P32	P33

D / u		XX			
D		0	1	2	3
X ↓	1			D12	D13
	2	D20	D21		D23
	3	D30	D31	D32	D33

P = promotion　　　D = demotion　　　d = downgrading　　　u = upgrading

It may also be summarized as follows:
1. Predicate contains P-D expressions.
2. Utterance contains referred-object-person.
3. Referred-subject-person contains P-D lexicon.

Then (1X) must have (1) and (2); (2X) must have (1); and (3X) must have either (1) or (3) for the purpose of "level" analysis.

1.6   VOCABULARY (for passive learning)

(行か)れる	(ika)reru	......	Dv	honorific Derivative (see 2.4.12)
あいつ	aitsu	......	N	that guy; he; she (slang)
めしあがる	meshiagaru	......	V	honorific equivalent of *taberu* or *nomu*
おまえ	omae	......	N	vulgar equivalent of *anata*
くう	kuu	......	V	eat (slang)
まいる	mairu	......	V	humble equivalent of *kuru, iku*
もうす	moosu	......	V	humble equivalent of *iu*
もうしあげる	mooshiageru	......	V	more formal equivalent of *iu*
おれ	ore	......	N	vulgar equivalent of *boku*
教授	kyooju	......	N	professor

1.7   DRILLS

1.7.1   Drills on *taberu, nomu, meshiagaru,* and *itadaku.*

1. おすしを　食べますか。

   A: おすしを　めしあがりますか。

   B: はい、いただきます。

2. あの　方は　おさけを　飲みますか。

   A: あの　方は　おさけを　めしあがりますか。

   B: はい、めしあがります。

3. たばこを　のみますか。

   A: たばこを　めしあがりますか。

   B: はい、いただきます。

4. もう　ご飯を　食べたんですか。

   A: もう　ご飯を　めしあがったんですか。

   B: はい、いただきました。

5. どんどん　食べてください。

   A: どんどん　めしあがってください。

   B: はい、いただきます。

6. 石井さんは　おかしを　食べましたか。

   A: 石井さんは　おかしを　めしあがりましたか。

   B: はい、めしあがりました。

7. コーヒーを　飲みませんか。

    A:　コーヒーを　めしあがりませんか。

    B:　はい、いただきます。

8. 飲んでね。

    A:　めしあがってね。

    B:　はい、いただきます。

1.7.2　Change *iu* into *moosu* or *ossharu*:

1. 先生が　そう　言ったよ。　　　　　⟶　先生が　そう　おっしゃったよ。

2. 父が　だめだと　言っています。　　⟶　父が　だめだと　もうしています。

3. 私は　鈴木（すず）と　いいます。　　⟶　私は　鈴木（すず）と　もうします。

4. できるだけ　ていねいに　　　　　⟶　できるだけ　ていねいに　おっしゃって
　　言ってください。　　　　　　　　　　　　ください。

5. なぜ　そんな　ことを　言うんですか。⟶　なぜ　そんな　ことを　おっしゃるん
　　　　　　　　　　　　　　　　　　　　　　ですか。

6. 主人は　たばこを　買ってくれと　　⟶　主人は　たばこを　買ってくれと
　　言いました。　　　　　　　　　　　　　　もうしました。

7. わたしは　あしたで　いいと　　　　⟶　わたしは　あしたで　いいと　もうし
　　言いましたけど。　　　　　　　　　　　　ましたけど。

8. あなたは　そう　言いませんでしたね。⟶　あなたは　そう　おっしゃいません
　　　　　　　　　　　　　　　　　　　　　　でしたね。

1.8　EXERCISES

1.8.1　次の　文(sentence)の　中の　ことばを　普通（ふつう）の　ことば使いに　書き変えなさい。

    Example:　山田さんに　<u>やる</u>よ。　⟶　山田さんに　<u>あげる</u>よ。

  1. あした　社長さんの　おたくへ　うかがうつもりです。

  2. 私は　石井（い）と　もうします。

  3. ここで　ちょっと　待っていてくれ。

  4. どなたに　お聞きしましょうか。

  5. どんな　日本料理（りょうり）が　お好きでいらっしゃいますか。

  6. 学長は　あしたの　朝　六時に　東京駅に　おつきに　なるそうです。

  7. 原（はら）先生の　おく様が　電話で　お知らせくださいました。

8. 中村部長の　お子さんは　今　会社に　つとめていらっしゃいます。

9. 伊藤さんが　うちへ　いらっしゃって、父に　お話しくださいました。

10. あの　方に　よく　説明していただきましょう。

11. もっと　はっきり　言おう。

12. 友だちに　ラジオを　買ってやりました。

13. どなたが　事務所に　いらっしゃいましたか。

14. 私が　すぐ　持ってまいります。

15. 食べ物は　何に　いたしましょうか。

16. あした　ひまだったら、うちへ　あそびに　いらっしゃらない?

17. あなたの　ご家族は　どこに　住んでいらっしゃいますか。

18. 君に　この　本を　やろうか。

19. 好きな　時に　れんしゅうなさってください。

1.9　SITUATIONAL AND APPLICATION CONVERSATION

1.9.1 Mrs. Katō: Kodomotachi wa moo min'na gohan ga owarimashita. Desu kara, doozo goyukkuri.

Mrs. Kimura: Soo desu no. Dewa.

Mrs. Katō: Saa, doozo meshiagatte kudasai.

Mrs. Kimura: Itadakimasu.

Mrs. Katō: Kore mo doozo meshiagatte kudasai.

Mrs. Kimura: Ee, itadakimasu. Totemo oishii wa.

1.9.2 Buchō: Kon'ban shachoo ga Oosaka e irassharu kara, kimitachi ni mo Tookyoo eki made kite hoshii n da ga.

Shain A, B: Hai, mairimasu.

Shachō: Watashi wa juuji no shin'kan'sen de iku kara ne. Oono kun, ... kara tanomu yo.

Buchō: Haa? Nan to osshaimashita ka?

Shachō: Iya, ii n da. Jaa, tanomimasu yo.

1.9.3 Okusan: Saa, minasan, doozo meshiagatte kudasai.

Shain A, B, C: Hai, jaa itadakimasu.

Buchō: Kon'ban wa takusan non'de.

Shain A: Buchoo wa meshiagaranai n desu ka?

Buchō:	Watashi mo nomu yo.
Shain B:	Kyoo wa okosan wa irassharanai n desu ka?
Okusan:	Iie, imasu kedo, ima ofuro ni haitte iru n desu yo.
Shain C:	Buchoo, shachoo wa moo Amerika e irasshatta n desu ka?
Okusan:	Ara, soo datta n desu ka? Shujin wa kaisha no koto wa mooshimasen no yo.
Shain A:	Kachoo mo okusan ni ossharanai soo desu yo.

LESSON 2
いろいろな 表現

2.1　PRESENTATION

　日本語では、　人に　ものを　頼む[1]時や　命令する　時に、　いろいろな　表現を
使う。　たとえば、　英語の　''Don't open it''という　文は、　「開けないでください」、
「開けないでくれ」、「開けないで」、「開けるな[2]」などと　表現することが　できる。

2.2　DIALOG

部長の
おくさん　「もしもし、　安藤の　かないでございます[3]が、　主人　おりますか[4]。」

秘書　「部長[5]の　おく様[6]でいらっしゃいます[3]か。　部長は　今　山田課長[5]と
　　　　お話を　なさって[7]います。　しょうしょう[8]　お待ちくださいませ[9]。」

···

部長　「もしもし。」

おくさん[17]「あ、あなた[17]。　るすの　間に、　あなたから　電話が　あったって
　　　　聞いたんですけど、　何の　用ですの[14]?」

部長　「じつは、　急に　きょうから　二日まで　大阪へ　出張しろ[10]という
　　　　命令が　出たんだ[11]。　本当は　社長[5]が　行かれるはずだった[12]んだけど、
　　　　ほかの　会に　出られる[12]ことに　なったんだ[13]よ。」

おくさん　「まあ、　そう。　それで、　一度　うちへ　帰っていらっしゃるの[14]?」

部長　「うん、　着がえが　いる[15]ので　帰るけど、　ゆっくりしている　ひまが
　　　　ないんだ。　だから、　いる　物を　黒い　かばんに　入れておいて
　　　　くれないか[16]。」

おくさん　「黒い　かばんですね。　ひつような　物　用意しておきます。　出発は
　　　　何時ですか。」

部長　「午後二時の　飛行機なんだけど、　うちには　一時前に　つくと　思うよ。」

おくさん　「わかりました。」

部長　「じゃあ、　頼むよ。」

頼む	開けないでください	おく様	用
黒い	用意	午後	飛行機

2.3   PATTERN SENTENCES

2.3.1

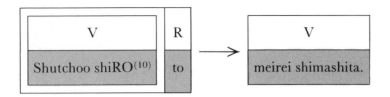

2.3.2

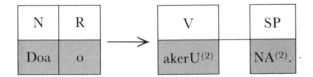

2.3.3

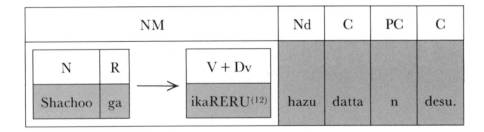

2.4   NOTES

2.4.1   *Mono o tanomu* is an idiomatic expression used in the meaning of "ask someone to do" or "ask a favor of someone." *Mono* in this expression has no particular meaning like "thing."

Japanese heteronomy is again revealed in language behavior in the expression *tanomu*. This expression carries two meanings, "ask" and "rely on." The actual meaning of this expression as used, however, is somewhere in between.

If, in asking someone to do something for you, you specify what the something is, the discretion is not left to the other person since it is included within the specification. On the other hand, if you rely on others, then you are leaving the discretion to others and are giving the least direction to them. The word *tanomu*, by carrying these two meanings, on the one hand seeks others' service, but on the other hand leaves discretion with the other by relying on the other.

Heteronomy is revealed here in the sense that the one who asks actually leaves maximum discretion to the one who is asked, thereby showing that the asker is at the mercy of, and dependent on, the other. This type of dependency is not at all shameful in Japan, and is viewed as a sign of sophistication. The "other-directed" inclination is obvious here.

2.4.2 *Akeru na* means "Don't open it." The Sentence Particle *na* used after the Dictionary form of a Verb carries the meaning of prohibition—prohibiting someone's doing something. In conversation this is always used by men as a negative command to their inferiors or sometimes to peers. At the same time, notice boards are sometimes written using the expression *Shibafu ni hairu na* "Keep off the grass," *Sakana o toru na* "No fishing." The Sentence Particle *yo* may follow *na* in conversation. As mentioned before, the imperative carries different degrees of politeness. *-te kudasai*, as opposed to *-te kure*, and *-naide*, as opposed to *na* (in the sense of a negative command), must be used according to the relative status of the speaker.

Dictionary form of Verb + *na*

Doa o shimeru na yo.	"Don't shut the door."
Kotchi ni kuru na.	"Don't come here."
Au jikan o wasureru na yo.	"Don't forget the time to meet."

2.4.3 *An'doo no kanai de gozaimasu* means "I am Mrs. Andō," and *Buchoo no okusama de irasshaimasu ka?* is "Are you Mrs. Andō?" (literally "Are you the wife of the department head?") Both *de gozaimasu* and *de (i)rasshaimasu* are the copular expressions which are used after a Noun in very polite or honorific situations. *De gozaimasu* is normally used for the speaker's or his in-group's being such and such, while *de (i)rasshaimasu* is used to refer to someone else's being such and such. *De gozaimasu* may be used also for inanimate objects for politeness.

Compare:

Donata de irasshaimasu ka?	"Who is it, please?"
	"May I have your name, please?"
Nakamura de gozaimasu.	"I am Nakamura."
Watakushi, buchoo no hisho de gozaimasu ga, buchoo san irasshaimasu ka?	"I am a secretary to the department head. Is he there?"
Hyakuen de gozaimasu.	"It costs a hundred yen, sir."

2.4.4 *Shujin orimasu ka?* means "Is my husband there?" *Orimasu* is a formal equivalent of *imasu* "be," and is often used in formal situations. *Oru* is normally used to refer to the speaker's or his in-group's being in a place, while *irassharu* refers to someone else's being in a place.

Compare:

Moshi moshi, Tomoko san irasshaimasu ka?	"Hello, is Tomoko there?"
Hai, orimasu. Shooshoo omachi kudasai.	"Yes, she is. Please wait for a minute."
Kinoo wa ichinichijuu uchi ni orimashita.	"I was at home all day yesterday."
Uchi ni irasshatta n desu ka?	"Were you at home?"

2.4.5 Many Japanese companies are organized and operated in ways which strongly contrast with their American counterparts. In the first place, the company system is rather paternal. Employees do not shift frequently from one company to another, and within the company structure employees enjoy a great deal of job and material security, including fringe benefits which are unheard of in the United States. For example, it is extremely uncommon for an employee to be fired by his employer; therefore, he will probably stay with one company for his entire life. In addition, larger companies provide, at a minimal cost to their employees, company housing, commissaries, medical care, and vacation resorts.

The result is that employees display a great deal of loyalty toward their company. Since the company is in many ways a large family, there is strong group solidarity with a seniority system prevailing. Modern trade unionism has begun to undermine this company solidarity somewhat; however, at present most unions are companywide rather than tradewide. This demonstrates a conflict between two types of groups in modern-day Japan; between the vertical concept of a companywide union and the more horizontal concept of a tradewide union. Although the two types are still competing with each other, the vertical arrangement is still very strong, demonstrating that hierarchical groupism is still much stronger than horizontal solidarity.

2.4.6 It should be noted that the secretary uses *buchoo no okusama* rather than the equivalent of "Mrs. Andō." This is another instance of the use of a title both to show politeness and to avoid direct address. The title in this case means "the wife of the division head."

2.4.7 *Ohanashi o nasatte imasu* means "someone is talking." *Nasatte* is the TE form of *nasaru* "do," which is often used to show politeness toward someone whom the speaker respects. *Nasaru*, *irassharu*, and the like are Verbs of politeness, showing respect. *Oru* "be," *itasu* "do," and the like are Verbs of modesty.

Kinoo nani o nasaimashita ka?	"What did you do yesterday?"
Sen'shuu ryokoo o itashimashita.	"Last week I took a trip."

2.4.8 *Shooshoo* functions here as a softener and carries no serious meaning. It is more polite and formal than *chotto* or *sukoshi*.

2.4.9 *Omachi kudasai* is a more polite equivalent of *Matte kudasai* "Please wait." The formulation is as follows:

o + Stem form of Verb + *kudasai*

Ohairi kudasai.	"Please come in."
Oagari kudasai.	"Please step up."
Oki-o-tsuke kudasai.	"Please be careful." "Please watch out."
Oyasumi kudasai.	"Please rest."

The verbal Derivative *-mase* is the imperative form of *-masu* and is used in very polite situations. However, the *-mase* form occurs only with the following Verbs or Extenders: *kudasaru*, *nasaru*, *ossharu*, *irassharu*, become *kudasaimase*, *nasaimase*, *osshaimase*, *irasshaimase*. In less polite expressions, as you have learned so far, the forms without *-mase*—*kudasai*, *nasai*, *osshai*, *irasshai*—occur.

Ohairi kudasaimase.	"Please come in."
Soo nasaimase.	"Why don't you do that?"

2.4.10 *Shutchoo shiro* is the imperative form of the Verb *shutchoo suru* "take a business trip." The imperative forms of Verbs are constructed in the following ways:

1.   Vowel Verb ..... Stem form plus *-ro*

shimeru	$\longrightarrow$	shimero	yameru	$\longrightarrow$	yamero
taberu	$\longrightarrow$	tabero	oriru	$\longrightarrow$	oriro
iru	$\longrightarrow$	iro	ki-o-tsukeru	$\longrightarrow$	ki-o-tsukero
akeru	$\longrightarrow$	akero			

2.   Consonant Verb ..... Base form plus *-e*

tomaru	$\longrightarrow$	tomare	tanomu	$\longrightarrow$	tanome
iku	$\longrightarrow$	ike	yobu	$\longrightarrow$	yobe
dasu	$\longrightarrow$	dase	isogu	$\longrightarrow$	isoge

3.   Irregular Verb

suru	$\longrightarrow$	shiro	kuru	$\longrightarrow$	koi

The imperative form of a Verb is normally used by men and is a direct affirmative command. In this sense this form makes a pair with the negative command (*suru*) *na*. The Sentence Particle *yo* may follow the imperative form to soften the directness of a command.

Akero. "Open it." $\longrightarrow$ Akeru na. "Don't open it."

Kaban o motte koi yo. $\longrightarrow$ Kaban o motte kuru na yo.
   "Bring a bag with you."   "Don't bring a bag with you."

Motto nome yo. $\longrightarrow$ Son'na ni nomu na yo.
   "Drink more."   "Don't drink so much."

Hayaku okiro.   "Get up early."

Motto ben'kyoo shirotte chichi ga iu n   "My father tells me to study harder."
   da.

Aka wa "tomare" to iu imi de, midori wa   "The red (signal) means 'stop,' the green
   "itte yoi," kiiro wa "ki-o-tsukero" to iu   means 'can go' and the yellow 'be
   imi desu.   careful.'"

2.4.11 *Deta n da* is a plain-style equivalent of *deta n desu* and is typical of men's informal speech. The plain forms of the Copula normally do not occur at the end of a sentence in women's speech. The Sentence Particles such as *yo* and *nee* may follow the *da* ending. (See Note 1.3.2A, Vol. III.)

Compare:

Soo da yo.   "That's right." (said by men)
Soo yo.   "That's right." (said by women)

Shizuka da nee.   "It's quiet!" (said by men)
Shizuka nee.   "It's quiet!" (said by women)

2.4.12 *Ikareru* is an honorific equivalent of *iku*. *Ikareru* is the combination of the Pre-Nai form of the Verb *iku*, namely *ika*, and the verbal Derivative *-reru* that adds the honorific meaning to the Verb. The person who performs an action represented by the verbal expression with *-reru* cannot be the speaker, because of its honorific function. The verbal Derivatives -reru and -rareru conjugate as a Vowel Verb does:

(mi)rareru   (mi)rareta   (mi)rarete   (mi)rarereba etc.
(yasuma)reru   (yasuma)reta   (yasuma)rete   (yasuma)rereba etc.

Depending upon the type of Verb, either -reru or -rareru is used:

1. Vowel Verb ..... Stem form plus -rareru

deru   ⟶   derareru   kiru   ⟶   kirareru
taberu   ⟶   taberareru   oriru   ⟶   orirareru
iru "exist"   ⟶   irareru   yameru   ⟶   yamerareru
ki-o-tsukeru   ⟶   ki-o-tsukerareru

2. Consonant Verb ..... Pre-Nai form plus -reru

uru   ⟶   urareru   yobu   ⟶   yobareru
iku   ⟶   ikareru   isogu   ⟶   isogareru
dasu   ⟶   dasareru   matsu   ⟶   matareru
tanomu   ⟶   tanomareru   iu   ⟶   iwareru

3. Irregular Verb

suru   ⟶   sareru   kuru   ⟶   korareru

Other functions of -reru and -rareru are presented in Lessons 3 and 4.

Gakubuchoo wa moo dekakeraremashita.   "The dean has already left."

Dochira made ikareru n desu ka?   "Where are you going?"

Maiban nan'ji goro ni neraremasu ka?   "About what time do you go to bed every
                                               night?"

Note that the verbal expression with -reru or -rareru may be used where the o- plus Stem form of Verb plus *ni naru* expression is used. (See Note 13.4.12, Vol. III.)

2.4.13 *Hoka no kai ni derareru koto ni natta n da yo* means "It has been decided that he attend another meeting." The plain imperfect tense form of a Verb plus *koto ni naru* carries the connotation "it is decided that ..." or "an original intention or plan has been changed and another decision is made."

plain imperfect tense form of Verb + *koto ni naru*

Rainen watakushi wa Furan'su e ikanai koto   "It has been decided that I am not going to
  ni narimashita.   France next year."

Oosaka e shutchoo suru koto ni natta n da yo.   "My official trip to Ōsaka has been decided
                                                 on."

Tsugi no kai wa raishuu hiraku koto ni nari-   "It has been decided that the next meeting
  mashita.   will be held next week."

Some scholars have pointed out that in Japanese there is a tendency to use ~*ni narimashita* "became" instead of ~*ni shimashita* "did." The latter requires decision-making, whereas the former does not.

2.4.14 *Uchi e kaette irassharu no?* means "Are you coming back home?" *Irassharu* can be used after the TE form of a Verb and functions as an Extender. Extender *iku* means "go away from the speaker," and *kuru* means "come to the speaker."

The *no* is a sentence ending used mainly by women or children. It may be a question or a statement, depending upon the intonation with which it is said. If it is said with rising intonation, it is a question. When it is a statement, the Sentence Particles such as *yo* and *ne* often follow *no*.

Nan no yoo desu no?	"What do you want with me?"
Doko e iku no?	"Where are you going?"
Eiga ni iku no yo.	"I'm going to a movie."

In the Japanese language quite a few commonly used Verbs such as "eat," "drink," "go," "come," "be," and "say" carry shared polite versions. For example, *irasshaimasu* is the shared very polite version referring to the second or third person for *ikimasu* "go" and *kimasu* "come" as well as *imasu* "be." Referring to the first person's going or coming, *mairimasu* is the humble version of both *ikimasu* and *kimasu*, while *orimasu* is the first-person humble version of *imasu* "be."

Likewise the more polite version of both "eat" *tabemasu*, and "drink" *nomimasu*, is *meshiagarimasu*, referring to a second or third person within a hierarchy, whereas *itadakimasu* refers to the first person's eating or drinking. *Mooshimasu* and *osshaimasu* are words to mean "say" with differing connotations. The former shows the speaker's humbleness, and the latter his politeness. *Orimasu* in *Shujin orimasu ka?* (see Note 2.4.4) and *nasaimasu* in *Ohanashi o nasatte imasu* (see Note 2.4.7) are also very polite Verbs.

2.4.15 Intransitive Verb *iru* here means "need." Something which is needed is followed by the Relational *ga*, and the person who needs something is followed by the Relational *wa*.

Noun (person) + *wa* + Noun (object) + *ga* + *iru*

Yamada san wa okane ga iru soo desu.	"I heard that Mr. Yamada needs money."
Nani ga irimasu ka?	"What do you need?"
Kitte wa doo desu ka?	"Do you want stamps?"
Iie, irimasen.	"No, I don't need them."

There is another Verb *iru*, which means "exist" or "be." It conjugates differently however.

iru "need" $\longrightarrow$ irimasu $\longrightarrow$ itte $\longrightarrow$ iranai
iru "be" $\longrightarrow$ imasu $\longrightarrow$ ite $\longrightarrow$ inai

2.4.16 *Irete oite kurenai ka?* is a man's expression used to peers. Women would use *Irete oite kurenai?* to peers. Both men and women would say *Irete oite kudasaimasen ka?* to superiors or persons requiring more formal expressions.

2.4.17 The wife of the division chief used *de gozaimasu*, the more polite version of *desu*, as well as *orimasu*, the humble version of *imasu*, when talking to the secretary. This usage immediately establishes her and her husband as an in-group, and the secretary as an out-group. The secretary, on the other hand, used very polite forms, for instance, *de irasshaimasu ka?* (very polite version of *desu ka?*) and the ending *-mase*. All of these usages demonstrate hierarchical groupism.

The conversation between Mr. and Mrs. Andō is much more intimate and less formal. This is shown particularly by the frequent use of Sentence Particles, such as *yo*, *no*, and *ne*. Comparison of their respective forms, however, demonstrates that the husband used the plain form constantly, while his wife always used the more polite form. It must be noted here that this kind of distinction in the use of speech levels has become less obvious with young couples in Japan today.

wife to husband	husband to wife
(Aa,) anata.	
(Nan no yoo) desu no?	
	(Meirei ga deta) n da.
	(... ni natta) n da yo.
(Uchi e kaette) irassharu no?	
	(Hima ga nai) n da.
	(Irete oite) kurenai ka?
(Kuroi kaban) desu ne.	
(Yooi shite) okimasu.	
	... hikooki na n da kedo,...
	(... ni tsuku to) omou yo.
Wakarimashita.	
	Tanomu yo.

Mr. Andō uses a different level of speech when referring to the president of his company. *Ikareru* and *derareru* are, in fact, honorific equivalents of *iku* and *deru*.

2.5   VOCABULARY

Presentation

ひょうげん 表現	hyoogen	......	N	expression
めいれい 命令する	meirei suru	......	V	order; give a command; direct
たとえば	tatoeba	......	SI	for example
文	bun	......	N	sentence

| な | na | ...... | SP | means "prohibition" when used after the Dictionary form of a Verb (see 2.4.2) |
| 表現する (ひょうげん) | hyoogen suru | ...... | V | express |

Dialog

安藤 (あんどう)	An'doo	......	N	family name
でございます	de gozaimasu	......	C + E	copular expression used for honorific purposes (see 2.4.3)
おります	orimasu	......	V	humble equivalent of *iru* (normal form of *oru*) (see 2.4.4)
秘書 (ひ)	hisho	......	N	secretary
でいらっしゃいます	de irasshaimasu	......	C + E	copular expression used for honorific purposes (see 2.4.3)
なさって	nasatte	......	V	TE form of *nasaru* – do (polite equivalent of *suru*) (see 2.4.7)
しょうしょう	shooshoo	......	Adv.	formal equivalent of *chotto* "a while"; "a little" (see 2.4.8)
ませ	-mase	......	Dv	imperative form of *-masu* (see 2.4.9)
用	yoo	......	N	business to do; things to do
急	kyuu	......	Na	urgent; sudden
出張しろ (しゅっちょう)	shutchoo shiro	......	V	imperative form of *shutchoo suru* – take an official trip (see 2.4.10)
出張 (しゅっちょう)	shutchoo	......	N	official trip; business trip
命令 (めいれい)	meirei	......	N	order; command
出た	deta	......	V	TA form of *deru* – come out; is issued; appear; attend
(行か)れる	(ika)-reru	......	Dv	Derivative used to show politeness and/or respect (see 2.4.12)
会	kai	......	N	meeting
(出)られる	(de)-rareru	......	Dv	Derivative used to show politeness and/or respect (see 2.4.12)
着がえ	kigae	......	N	spare clothes
いる	iru	......	V	need (intransitive Verb) ("need ～" is ～ *ga iru*) (see 2.4.15)
用意して (い)	yooi shite	......	V	TE form of *yooi suru* – prepare; get ready for
用意 (い)	yooi	......	N	preparations
出発 (しゅっぱつ)	shuppatsu	......	N	departure; setting out

出発する しゅっぱつ	shuppatsu suru	......	V	depart; set out

Notes

しばふ	shibafu	......	N	grass; lawn
けいかん	keikan	......	N	policeman
いたす	itasu	......	V	do (humble equivalent of *suru*) (see 2.4.7)
しぬ	shinu	......	V	die
みどり(いろ)	midori(iro)	......	N	green
ひらく	hiraku	......	V	hold (a meeting); open

2.6   KAN'JI

2.6.1   頼   (1) *tano(mu)*   (2) ask; request   (3) classifier 頁 [head]

(4) ﾖ 市 未 東 軒 頼 頼   (5) 頼んでみましょう

2.6.2   開   (1) *a(keru)*   (2) open; hold   (3) classifier 門 [gate]

(4) 丨 冂 冃 冃 門 門 門 開   (5) 開けてもいいですか

(6) 开 ← 幵 [hands]

2.6.3   様   (1) *sama*   (2) Mr.; Mrs.; Miss (polite suffix)   (3) classifier 木

(4) 木 术 栏 样 栐 様 様 様

(5) 井上様、お客様、おく様、田中様
いのうえ   (6) homonym YOO 様、羊、洋

2.6.4   用   (1) YOO   (2) business; use   (3) forms the classifier 冂 （用）

(4) 冂 冃 月 用   (5) 用があります、当用漢字、用事 [something to do]、急用、用意する
い

2.6.5   黒   (1) *kuro(i)*   (2) black   (3) forms the classifier 里 （黒）

(4) 日 甲 里 黒 黒 黒 黒   (5) 黒い、黒田さん、黒服
ふく

(6) 灬 represents fire and 里 indicates that the chimney is sooted

2.6.6   午   (1) GO   (2) noon   (3) classifier 𠂉 （十）

(4) 丿 𠂉 二 午   (5) 午前、午後
ぜん　ご   (6) homonym 御

2.6.a   _{13.6.5, Vol. III} 後   (1) GO   (2) after   (5) 午後、戦争後、その後
せんそう

2.6.7   飛   (1) HI   (2) fly   (3) forms the classifier 飛

(4) 乁 乁 飞 飞 飞 飞 飛 飛 飛   (5) 飛行機、飛行場
き　　じょう
[airport]   (6) the shape of a flying bird

2.6.8 機 (1) KI (2) loom; machine (3) classifier 木

(4) 木 朾 椣 椣 椣 椣 機 機 機

(5) 飛行機、機械 [machine]、ジェット機 [jet plane]、機長
[captain; pilot]、せんたく機 [washing machine]

(6) homonym 幾

2.6.9 赤* (1) *aka(i)* (2) red (3) forms the classifier 赤

(4) 土 尹 赤 赤 赤 (5) 赤ちゃん、赤い紙

(6) 大 (太) big + 火 fire → red

2.6.10 閉* (1) *shi(meru)* (2) close; shut (3) classifier 門

(4) 門 門 閉 閉 (5) まどを閉める

2.6.11 白* (1) *shiro(i)* (2) white (3) forms the classifier 白

(4) ノ ⺊ 白 白 白 (5) 白い車

*4.6.10, Vol. II

2.6.b 金 (1) *kane* (2) money; metal; gold (5) お金、金持ち [the rich]

(6) ノ 人 △ 仝 全 全 金 金

2.7　DRILLS

2.7.1　Transformation Drill

1. ドアを 開けなさい。 ⟶ ドアを 開けろ。
2. くすりを 飲みなさい。 ⟶ くすりを 飲め。
3. あの 赤い 車に 乗りなさい。 ⟶ あの 赤い 車に 乗れ。
4. 英語で はっきり 話しなさい。 ⟶ 英語で はっきり 話せ。
5. すぐ いしゃへ 行きなさい。 ⟶ すぐ いしゃへ 行け。
6. もっと 急ぎなさい。 ⟶ もっと 急げ。
7. もうすこし 待ちなさい。 ⟶ もうすこし 待て。
8. 大阪へ 出張しなさい。 ⟶ 大阪へ 出張しろ。
9. 早く おとうとを 呼びなさい。 ⟶ 早く おとうとを 呼べ。
10. 気を つけなさい。 ⟶ 気を つけろ。
11. こっちへ 来なさい。 ⟶ こっちへ 来い。
12. もう一度 言いなさい。 ⟶ もう一度 言え。

2.7.2　Transformation Drill

1. まどを 開けないでください。 ⟶ まどを 開けるな。

2. ドアを　閉めないでください。　　　　　⟶　ドアを　閉めるな。

3. うちへ　来ないでください。　　　　　　⟶　うちへ　来るな。

4. 学校に　おくれないでください。　　　　⟶　学校に　おくれるな。

5. ここに　すわらないでください。　　　　⟶　ここに　すわるな。

6. ぼくに　命令しないでください。　　　　⟶　ぼくに　命令するな。

7. いぬに　食べ物を　やらないでください。　⟶　いぬに　食べ物を　やるな。

8. さけを　飲みすぎないでください。　　　⟶　さけを　飲みすぎるな。

9. 気に　しないでください。　　　　　　　⟶　気に　するな。

10. しばふに　入らないでください。　　　　⟶　しばふに　入るな。

2.7.3　Transformation Drill

A. 1. 安藤の　かないです。　　　　　　　⟶　安藤の　かないでございます。

2. 私は　メリーランド大学の　　　　⟶　私は　メリーランド大学の　学生で
　　学生です。　　　　　　　　　　　　　ございます。

3. 出発は　午後　二時です。　　　　⟶　出発は　午後　二時でございます。

4. この　お茶は　中国茶です。　　　⟶　この　お茶は　中国茶でございます。

5. ここが　社長室です。　　　　　　⟶　ここが　社長室でございます。

6. 主人の　かばんは　みどりです。　⟶　主人の　かばんは　みどりでございます。

7. 課長が　お呼びです。　　　　　　⟶　課長が　お呼びでございます。

B. 1. もしもし、山田さんですか。　　　⟶　もしもし、山田さんでいらっしゃい
　　　　　　　　　　　　　　　　　　　　ますか。

2. あなたの　お父さんは　銀行員　　⟶　あなたの　お父さんは　銀行員で
　　ですか。　　　　　　　　　　　　　いらっしゃいますか。

3. あの　方は　加藤さんの　おく様　⟶　あの　方は　加藤さんの　おく様で
　　です。　　　　　　　　　　　　　いらっしゃいます。

4. 石川さんは　会社の　重役です。　⟶　石川さんは　会社の　重役で
　　　　　　　　　　　　　　　　　　　いらっしゃいます。

5. 中村さんは　秘書ですか。　　　　⟶　中村さんは　秘書でいらっしゃいますか。

6. こちらは　高木さんの　　　　　⟶　こちらは　高木さんの　ごりょうしんで
　　ごりょうしんです。　　　　　　　　いらっしゃいます。

7. 先生は　何の　専門ですか。　　　⟶　先生は　何の　専門でいらっしゃい
　　　　　　　　　　　　　　　　　　　ますか。

2.7.4 Transformation Drill

1. 社長は　どの　飛行機に　<u>乗りますか</u>。 ⟶ 社長は　どの　飛行機に　<u>乗られますか</u>。
2. おく様は　買い物に　出かけません。 ⟶ おく様は　買い物に　出かけられません。
3. 部長の　むすこさんが　大学に　入りました。 ⟶ 部長の　むすこさんが　大学に　入られました。
4. 小山先生が　事務所へ　来ました。 ⟶ 小山先生が　事務所へ　来られました。
5. 松本さんが　そう　命令しました。 ⟶ 松本さんが　そう　命令されました。
6. ムーアさんは　この　ホテルに　とまります。 ⟶ ムーアさんは　この　ホテルに　とまられます。
7. お客様は　もう　出発しました。 ⟶ お客様は　もう　出発されました。
8. ご主人は　よく　出張しますか。 ⟶ ご主人は　よく　出張されますか。

2.7.5 Transformation Drill

1. もうすこし　<u>待ってください</u>。 ⟶ もうすこし　<u>お待ちください</u>。
2. どうぞ　休んでください。 ⟶ どうぞ　お休みください。
3. もう一ぱい　飲んでください。 ⟶ もう一ぱい　お飲みください。
4. タクシーに　乗ってください。 ⟶ タクシーに　お乗りください。
5. すぐ　うちへ　帰ってください。 ⟶ すぐ　うちへ　お帰りください。
6. 電話で　知らせてください。 ⟶ 電話で　お知らせください。
7. 白い　紙に　所を　書いてください。 ⟶ 白い　紙に　所を　お書きください。
8. たばこは　やめてください。 ⟶ たばこは　おやめください。

2.7.6 Transformation Drill

1. まどを　<u>開けてくれない?</u> ⟶ まどを　<u>開けてくれないか</u>。
2. あした　うちへ　来てくれない? ⟶ あした　うちへ　来てくれないか。
3. ニューヨークへ　出張してくれない? ⟶ ニューヨークへ　出張してくれないか。
4. 石川君に　話してくれない? ⟶ 石川君に　話してくれないか。
5. 会社へ　行ってくれない? ⟶ 会社へ　行ってくれないか。
6. 電話を　かけてくれない? ⟶ 電話を　かけてくれないか。
7. 新しい　ことばを　使ってくれない? ⟶ 新しい　ことばを　使ってくれないか。
8. 秘書に　そう　頼んでくれない? ⟶ 秘書に　そう　頼んでくれないか。

2.7.7 Substitution Drill

A. ぼくは　来年　ヨーロッパへ　行くことに　なりました。

   1.　課長は　あしたから　出張する　……　課長は　あしたから　出張することに　なりました。

   2.　研究の　ために　もっと　お金が　いる　……　研究の　ために　もっと　お金が　いることに　なりました。

   3.　忙しいので、あなたにも　手つだってもらう　……　忙しいので、あなたにも　手つだってもらうことに　なりました。

   4.　わたしが　先生に　会って、話す　……　わたしが　先生に　会って、話すことに　なりました。

   5.　安藤さんは　飛行機で　行く　……　安藤さんは　飛行機で　行くことに　なりました。

   6.　わたしたちは　新しい　仕事を　しない　……　わたしたちは　新しい　仕事を　しないことに　なりました。

B. 社長は　ほかの　会に　出られることに　なったんです。

   1.　ほかの　会に　行かれる　……　社長は　ほかの　会に　行かれることに　なったんです。

   2.　大阪へ　帰られる　……　社長は　大阪へ　帰られることに　なったんです。

   3.　会社を　やめられる　……　社長は　会社を　やめられることに　なったんです。

   4.　東京へ　出張される　……　社長は　東京へ　出張されることに　なったんです。

   5.　この　事務所へ　来られる　……　社長は　この　事務所へ　来られることに　なったんです。

   6.　青い　自動車を　買われる　……　社長は　青い　自動車を　買われることに　なったんです。

2.7.8 E-J Substitution Drill

父は　おとうとに　行けと　言いました。

   1.　don't go　……　父は　おとうとに　行くなと　言いました。

   2.　come　……　父は　おとうとに　来いと　言いました。

   3.　don't come　……　父は　おとうとに　来るなと　言いました。

4. drink it　　　　　　……　父は　おとうとに　飲めと　言いました。

5. don't drink it　　　……　父は　おとうとに　飲むなと　言いました。

6. prepare it　　　　　……　父は　おとうとに　用意しろと　言いました。

7. don't forget it　　　……　父は　おとうとに　わすれるなと　言いました。

8. walk　　　　　　　……　父は　おとうとに　あるけと　言いました。

2.7.9　Transformation Drill

1. 田中さんは　今　お話を　<u>して</u>います。　⟶　田中さんは　今　お話を　<u>なさって</u>　います。

2. 午後の　飛行機で　出発しますか。　⟶　午後の　飛行機で　出発なさいますか。

3. 先生は　運転しますか。　⟶　先生は　運転なさいますか。

4. これから、どう　するつもりですか。　⟶　これから、どう　なさるつもりですか。

5. 外国へ　出張したことが　ありますか。　⟶　外国へ　出張なさったことが　ありますか。

6. 着がえや　かばんを　用意して　ください。　⟶　着がえや　かばんを　用意なさって　ください。

7. どんな　ことを　したいと　思いますか。　⟶　どんな　ことを　なさりたいと　思いますか。

2.7.10　Response Drill

1. もしもし、山田さん<u>でいらっしゃい</u>ますか。　……　<u>はい、山田でございます。</u>

2. お父様は　銀行員でいらっしゃいますか。　……　はい、銀行員でございます。

3. 中村さんは　秘書でいらっしゃいますか。　……　はい、秘書でございます。

4. みな様　元気でいらっしゃいますか。　……　はい、元気でございます。

5. ご主人は　おるすでいらっしゃいますか。　……　はい、るすでございます。

6. 安藤さんの　おく様でいらっしゃいますか。　……　はい、安藤の　かないでございます。

7. 出発は　午後でいらっしゃいますか。　……　はい、出発は　午後でございます。

26

2.7.11 Response Drill

1. もしもし、ご主人 <u>いらっしゃい</u>
   <u>ます</u>か。　　　　　　　…… <u>はい</u>、<u>おります</u>。しょうしょう　お待ち
   　　　　　　　　　　　　　　　　ください。

2. もしもし、<u>主人</u>　<u>おります</u>か。　…… はい、<u>いらっしゃいます</u>。しょうしょう
   　　　　　　　　　　　　　　　　お待ちください。

3. もしもし、かない　おりますか。　…… はい、いらっしゃいます。しょうしょう
   　　　　　　　　　　　　　　　　お待ちください。

4. もしもし、おく様　いらっしゃい
   ますか。　　　　　　　　　…… はい、おります。しょうしょう　お待ち
   　　　　　　　　　　　　　　　　ください。

5. もしもし、おにいさん　いらっしゃい
   ますか。　　　　　　　　　…… はい、おります。しょうしょう　お待ち
   　　　　　　　　　　　　　　　　ください。

6. もしもし、あに　おりますか。　…… はい、いらっしゃいます。しょうしょう
   　　　　　　　　　　　　　　　　お待ちください。

7. もしもし、お父さん　いらっしゃい
   ますか。　　　　　　　　　…… はい、おります。しょうしょう　お待ち
   　　　　　　　　　　　　　　　　ください。

8. もしもし、父　おりますか。　…… はい、いらっしゃいます。しょうしょう
   　　　　　　　　　　　　　　　　お待ちください。

2.7.12 Response Drill

1. 電話<u>な</u>さいますか。　　　　　…… <u>はい</u>、<u>いたします</u>。
2. きのう　日本語を　れんしゅうなさいましたか。　…… はい、いたしました。
3. 私から　電話いたしましょうか。　…… はい、なさってください。
4. きのう　出張なさいましたか。　…… はい、いたしました。
5. 夕方　出発なさるんですか。　…… はい、いたします。
6. 毎日　お料理を　なさいますか。　…… はい、いたします。
7. すぐ　出発いたしましょうか。　…… はい、なさってください。

2.7.13 Transformation Drill (Transform the given sentence into both male and female utterances.)

1. とても　忙しかったんですよ。　　⟶ とても　忙しかったんだよ。
   　　　　　　　　　　　　　　　　とても　忙しかったのよ。

2. 来月　外国へ　出張することに
   なったんです。　　　　　　⟶ 来月　外国へ　出張することに
   　　　　　　　　　　　　　　　　なったんだ。

来月　外国へ　出張することに

なったの。

3. あの　方は　この　会社の　重役なん　　　——→　あの　方は　この　会社の　重役なん

です ね。　　　　　　　　　　　　　　　　　だ ね。

あの　方は　この　会社の　重役なのね。

4. 十時の　飛行機に　乗らなければ　　　　　——→　十時の　飛行機に　乗らなければ

ならないんです。　　　　　　　　　　　　　ならないんだ。

十時の　飛行機に　乗らなければ

ならないの。

5. 課長の　山田さんに　用を　頼んだん　　　——→　課長の　山田さんに　用を　頼んだん

ですよ。　　　　　　　　　　　　　　　　　だよ。

課長の　山田さんに　用を　頼んだのよ。

6. あの　子どもたちは　えいがを　見た　　　——→　あの　子どもたちは　えいがを　見た

ことが　ないんですねえ。　　　　　　　　　ことが　ないんだねえ。

あの　子どもたちは　えいがを　見た

ことが　ないのねえ。

2.8　EXERCISES

2.8.1　次の　英語を　四つの　日本語の　文に　変えなさい。

Example: Open it.　(1)　開けてください。　(2)　開けてくれない(か)。　(3)　開けて。

(4)　開けろ。

1. Bring some milk to me.
2. Don't eat too much of it.
3. Try to do it once more.
4. Don't play in the street.

2.8.2　ていねいな　ことば使いに　変えなさい。

Example: 山田先生が　うちに　来ました。　——→　山田先生が　うちに

来られました。

1. 社長は　京都の　旅館に　二日間　とまったと　思います。
2. きょうの　昼ごろ　お客様が　二人　家に　来るはずです。
3. ご主人は　いつ　部長に　なったんですか。
4. 安藤さんの　ごりょうしんは　先週　外国へ　出かけたそうです。
5. 父は　今　うちに　いません。
6. ご主人は　会社員ですか。

28

7. 私は　社長の　秘書です。

8. おく様は　旅行の　用意を　しましたか。

9. どうぞ　こちらに　入ってください。

10. 私が　大阪へ　出張しましょうか。

2.8.3　文を　作りなさい。

1. 本当は　来月　オーストラリアへ　行くはずでしたが、

＿＿＿＿＿＿＿＿＿＿＿＿＿ことに　なりました。

2. 私は　＿＿＿＿＿＿＿＿＿＿＿ことに　なったのですが、

＿＿＿＿＿＿＿＿＿＿＿＿＿たくないんです。

3. 卒業後　銀行か　会社に　つとめたかったんですが、

＿＿＿＿＿＿＿＿＿＿＿ので、＿＿＿＿＿＿＿＿＿ことに

なりました。

2.8.4　次の　会話を　ふつうの　会話に　変えなさい。

1. —出かけるのかい。

—ええ。ちょっと　スーパーまで。

—ゆうびん局へ　行って、この　手紙を　かきとめで　出してくれないか。

—ええ、いいわ。かきとめね。

—それから、たばこ　買って来てくれないか。

—わかったわ。たばこは　何が　いいの?

—ホープを　頼むよ。わすれるなよ。

2. —どなたでいらっしゃいますか。

—吉田でございます。

—ああ、課長さんの　おく様でいらっしゃいますね。

—はい。主人　おりますか。

—課長は　今　ほかの　へやへ　行かれましたから、こちらで　しょうしょう

お待ちくださいませ。

2.8.5　Change the following into a more polite expression.

1. ちょっと　待ってください。

2. 「お父さん　いますか。」　「父は　今　いませんが。」

3. とても　きれいな　はんがを　ありがとう。

4. 「もしもし、鈴木さんですか。」　「いいえ、吉田ですが。」

2.8.6 ひらがなを　漢字に　変えなさい。

1. <u>ごご</u>の　<u>ひこうき</u>で　<u>でかける</u>ことに　なっています。

2. <u>なん</u>の　<u>よう</u>ですか。

3. お<u>きゃくさま</u>の　かばんの　<u>なか</u>に　お<u>かね</u>は　ありませんでした。

4. <u>あか</u>、<u>あお</u>、<u>しろ</u>、<u>くろ</u>、みどりなど、いろいろな　<u>いろ</u>の　くるまが　あります。

5. ドアを　<u>しめて</u>、まどを　<u>あけて</u>ください。

6. <u>ひと</u>に　ものを　<u>たのむ</u>　<u>とき</u>は、ていねいに　<u>たのま</u>なければ　なりません。

2.8.7 次の　漢字を　読みなさい。

1. 聞、開、閉
2. 百、白
3. 午、牛
4. 用、田
5. 様、機
6. 会、金

2.8.8 Discuss some reasons why there exists in Japanese companies a lifelong employment system, i.e., why an employee is rarely fired.

2.8.9 Describe the difference between the tradewide union and the companywide union system.

2.8.10 What would be the effect of a vertical society on its language usages?

2.8.11 In a classroom situation, while speaking to a teacher, which expression would be appropriate for a student to use?

1. Boku wa hatachi da yo.
2. Boku wa hatachi desu.
3. Watakushi wa hatachi de gozaimasu.

2.8.12 In what situation and to whom would you use each of the following?

1. Ashita, uchi ni imasu ka?
2. Ashita, uchi ni iru?
3. Ashita, uchi ni irasshaimasu ka?

2.8.13 When would each of the following expressions be used?

1. Hayaku shiro.
2. Hayaku shinasai.
3. Hayaku shite ne.
4. Hayaku shite kurenai kai.
5. Hayaku shite kudasaimasen ka?
6. Hayaku shitamae.

2.8.14 Which is correct?

  1. Shitsurei desu ga, (anata wa) Tanaka san de gozaimasu ka?
     Shooshoo matte ne.
  2. Shitsurei desu ga, (anata wa) Tanaka san de irasshaimasu ka?
     Shooshoo omachi kudasai.

2.8.15 Which is formal?

  1. Totemo rippa na uchi da nee.
     Taihen rippa na uchi desu nee.
  2. Ashita issho ni konai?
     Ashita issho ni kimasen ka?
  3. Chotto takasugiru ne.
     Shooshoo takasugimasu ne.

2.9 SITUATIONAL AND APPLICATION CONVERSATION

2.9.1 At school.

An American student who is studying Japanese tells his friend that Japanese is difficult. For example, there are many ways to say "Don't write it in *rōmaji*," he says.

His friend asks him to say them.

The student expresses the command in four ways that he has just studied.

The friend says he is very surprised.

The student tells his friend that his study is getting difficult rapidly, but it's also getting interesting.

2.9.2 At the president's room.

The president of a business firm tells his secretary to call a department chief, Mr. Yamamoto, and a section chief, Mr. Ōkawa, to the president's room for an urgent meeting he wants to hold.

The secretary says she will do so right away.

The president adds that he wants the secretary to attend the meeting also.

The secretary answers she will attend the meeting after making a telephone call to a bank.

The president orders the secretary to bring sheets of paper and pencils with her.

2.9.3 Make a polite telephone call to a business firm or to someone's residence inquiring if the person you want to talk to is in.

2.9.4 Hisho: Buchoo wa kyuu ni Oosaka e irassharu koto ni narimashita.

Okusan: Soo desu ka? Itsu soo natta no?

Hisho:　　Kesa desu.

Okusan:　　Katoo san wa irassharanai no?

Hisho:　　Hai, watakushi wa Tookyoo ni orimasu.

2.9.5　Okusan:　　Moshi moshi, An'doo desu ga. Shujin orimasen ka?

Yamada:　　An'doo san no okusama de irasshaimasu ka? Goshujin irasshaimasu. Shooshoo omachi kudasai.

2.9.6　Ane:　　Moshi moshi, watashi, Katoo Keiko no ane desu ga, imooto orimasu ka?

Tanaka:　　Katoo san no oneesan desu ka? Shooshoo omachi kudasai.

Imōto:　　Moshi moshi.

Ane:　　Keiko san, watashi.

Imōto:　　Oneesan, shibaraku nee.

2.9.7　(Ane ga imooto no uchi e den'wa shita toki)

Ane:　　Moshi moshi, Yoshiko da kedo. Shujin sochira ni iru?

Imōto:　　Ara, oneesan? Oniisan iru wa yo. Chotto matte.

2.9.8　Wife:　　Moshi moshi. Anata desu ka?

Husband:　　Aa, soo da. Nan no yoo?

Wife:　　Kon'ban massugū kaerimasu ka?

Husband:　　Soo da ne. Mada wakaranai kedo, tabun kyoo wa hayaku kaeru yo.

2.10　READING COMPREHENSION

2.10.1

　家族や　したしい (close)　友だちの　間では、"Shut it" は「閉めてくれない？」、「閉めてくれないか」、「閉めてくれ」、「閉めて」、「閉めろ」などと　表現する。このうち、男の人だけが　使うことが　できる　表現は　「閉めてくれないか」と「閉めてくれ」、「閉めろ」で、その　ほかは　男も　女も　使うことが　できる。

　ていねいに　話さなければならない　時には、上の (the above)　表現は　使ってはいけない。　この　場合は (in this case)、「閉めてくださいませんか」、「閉めてくれませんか」、「閉めてください」と　言う。この　ほか、「閉めていただきたいんですが…」や　「閉めてもらいたいんですけど…」なども　よく　聞く　表現である。

2.10.2

小山　「もしもし、山本教授(Professor)の　おたくでいらっしゃいますか。」

山本　「はい、山本でございます。」

小山　「私、秘書の　小山でございますが…」

山本　「あ、小山さん、いつも　主人が　お世話に　なって…」

小山　「いいえ、こちらこそ　お世話に　なっております。先生、いらっしゃいますか。」

山本　「きょうは　ちょっと　出かけているんですよ。」

小山　「何時ごろ　帰られますか。」

山本　「夕方には　帰ることに　なっていますけど。どんな　ご用ですか。」

小山　「先生が　書かれて、私が　タイプすることに　なっていた　手紙の　ことで　お電話
　　　　したのですが、夕方　もう一度　お電話いたしますから。」

山本　「そうですか。それでは　そう　おねがいします。」

LESSON 3
病気[1]

3.1　PRESENTATION

　日本の　医学が　かなり　はったつしていることは　よく　知られている[2]。　しかし、
病院[3]、かんご婦などの　数は　まだまだ　たりない。　また、　病人が　安心して
病気を　治すことが　できる　社会保障制度も　完全ではない。

3.2　DIALOG

—— 斉藤医院で ——

かんご婦　「次の　方[4]、　どうぞ。」

広田　　　「はい。　あ、　どうも、　先生[4]。」

医者　　　「やあ、　広田さん[4]。　どう　したんですか[5]。」

広田　　　「けさから、　頭が　いたくて、　どうも　気分が　よくないんです。　かぜを
　　　　　　ひいたらしいんです。」

医者　　　「のどを　見ましょう。…赤くなっていますね。　かぜですね。」

広田　　　「やっぱり　そうですか。　きのう　つかれていたのに、　課長に　頼まれて[2]、
　　　　　　夜　おそく[6]まで　残業したんです。　その　うえ、　帰り[7]には　雨に[2]
　　　　　　ふられて[2]、　すっかり　ぬれてしまったんです。」

医者　　　「おやおや。　夕べは　かなり　ザーザー[8]　ふりましたからね。　（かんご婦に）
　　　　　　では、　山口君[4]、　広田さんの　熱を　はかって[4]。」

かんご婦　「はい。…三十七度二分[9]です。」

医者　　　「ああ、　そう。　熱が　低いから、　心配は　ないですね。　注射を
　　　　　　しておきましょう。　それから、　薬を　あげますから、　一日に　三回
　　　　　　飲んでください。」

広田　　　「どうも　ありがとうございました[4]。　いつも　かないに　働きすぎ[7]だと
　　　　　　言われています。　今度こそ[10]　ゆっくり　寝ることに　します[11]。」

医者　　　「それが　一番ですね。　お大事に[12]。」

病気	医学	数	病人	安心	治す
医院	次	医者	頭	夜	山口
低い	薬	三回	寝る		

3.3   PATTERN SENTENCES

3.3.1

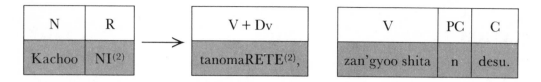

3.3.2

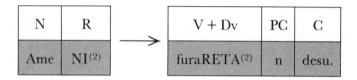

3.3.3

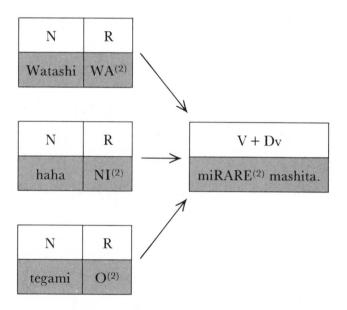

3.4   NOTES

3.4.1   Previously, illnesses (*byooki*) such as tuberculosis predominated in Japan. The prevalence of this type of illness can be attributed to the premodern diet and living conditions. Today Japan approaches the Western pattern in its high incidence of heart attacks and car accidents. Despite the emergence of these two as Japan's top "killers," however, life expectancy of both men and women now exceeds seventy-four, a tremendous improvement over earlier times.

3.4.2   *Yoku shirarete iru* means "it is well known." *Shirarete* is the TE form of *shirareru*, which is the combination of *shira*, the Pre-Nai form of *shiru*, and the verbal Derivative *-reru*. As already introduced in Note 2.4.12, the verbal expressions with *-reru* or *-rareru* are formulated as follows:

1. Vowel Verb ..... Stem form plus -*rareru*

taberu	⟶	taberareru	"is eaten"
miru	⟶	mirareru	"is seen"
kariru	⟶	karirareru	"is borrowed"

2. Consonant Verb ..... Pre-Nai form plus -*reru*

shiru	⟶	shirareru	"is known"
toru	⟶	torareru	"is taken"
butsu "beat"	⟶	butareru	"is beaten"
naosu	⟶	naosareru	"is corrected"
iu	⟶	iwareru	"is said"
nusumu "steal"	⟶	nusumareru	"is stolen"
tanomu	⟶	tanomareru	"is asked"
kaku	⟶	kakareru	"is written"
hiraku	⟶	hirakareru	"is held; is opened"
shinu	⟶	shinareru	"is affected by someone else's death"
yobu	⟶	yobareru	"is called"

3. Irregular Verb

suru	⟶	sareru	"is done"
kuru	⟶	korareru	"is affected by someone else's coming"

In this lesson only the passive functions of the Derivatives -*reru* and -*rareru* are discussed.

In Japanese there are two types of passive, namely direct passive and indirect passive. Note that the Japanese passive differs from the English passive in some points. Study the following:

1. Direct passive. This is similar to English passive. Only transitive Verbs that require the direct object Relational *o* may be transformed into the verbal expressions with -*reru* or -*rareru* of this passive. In a passive sentence of this sort the object of the original active sentence, which is followed by *o*, changes into the subject of the passive sentence and is followed by *ga* or *wa*. The subject of the original active sentence, if expressed, is followed by the Relational *ni* "by" as the actor of the passive. When a Verb of the active sentence is closely related with the Relational *ni* of the indirect object and the like, the use of *ni* "by" may cause an ambiguity. In that case the Relational *ni* "by" may be replaced by the Relational *kara* or *ni yotte* to distinguish an actor from other parts with *ni*. (The use of *ni yotte* is further explained in Note 12.4.2.) Do not think that all the English passive expressions are also passive in Japanese. There is a limitation in the use of the direct passive.

Noun 1 + $\left\{ \begin{array}{l} \textbf{\textit{ga}} \\ \textbf{\textit{wa}} \end{array} \right\}$ **+ Noun 2 +** *o* **+ transitive Verb**

⟶ **Noun 2 +** $\left\{ \begin{array}{l} \textbf{\textit{ga}} \\ \textbf{\textit{wa}} \end{array} \right\}$ **+ Noun 1 +** *ni* **+ Verb(-*reru* or -*rareru*)**

Isha *o yobimashita.*　　　　　　　⟶　Isha *ga yobaremashita.*
　"[We] called a doctor."　　　　　　　　"A doctor was called."

Atarashii gakusei *o shookai shimasu.*　⟶　Atarashii gakusei *ga shookai saremasu.*
　"[He] will introduce a new student."　　　"A new student will be introduced."

Sen'sei *ga* watashitachi ni atarashii gakusei *o shookai shimashita.*
"The teacher introduced a new student to us." ⟶ Sen'sei *kara* watashitachi ni atarashii gakusei *ga shookai saremashita.*
"A new student was introduced to us by the teacher."

(Hitobito *wa*) Nihon no igaku ga hattatsu shite iru koto *o* yoku *shitte iru.*
"They know well that medical science in Japan has progressed." ⟶ Nihon no igaku ga hattatsu shite iru koto *wa* (hitobito *ni*) yoku *shirarete iru.*
"It is well known that medical science in Japan has progressed."

Doroboo *ga* okane *o nusumimashita.*
"A thief has stolen the money." ⟶ Okane *wa* doroboo *ni nusumaremashita.*
"The money has been stolen by a thief."

2.   Indirect passive. This indirect passive is different from the above direct passive. First of all, the subject of this indirect passive is rarely inanimate, and it is the recipient of an action performed by an actor. Second, the Verbs used in this indirect passive can be either transitive or intransitive. When intransitive Verbs, such as *iku* "go," *shinu* "die," and (*ame ga*) *furu* "rain" change into their corresponding passive forms, the student may have difficulty in understanding the situations where they are to be used. When someone goes to you, when your family member or your in-group member dies, when you are caught in a shower, and so on, you are the recipient of the effect of those actions or happenings. Those actions or happenings may be favorable or unfavorable; they may be a mere description of the fact of receiving someone else's action or they may be said with an unpleasant or annoyed feeling. It all depends on the Verbs used, the situations under which they are said, or other elements to stress one's reaction to them.

Noun 1 + $\begin{Bmatrix} ga \\ wa \end{Bmatrix}$ **+ Noun 2 +** *o* **+ transitive Verb**

⟶ **Noun 3* (animate recipient)** $+ \begin{Bmatrix} ga \\ wa \end{Bmatrix} +$ **Noun 1 (actor)** **+** *ni* **+ Noun 2 +** *o* **+ Verb(*-reru* or *-rareru*)**

Noun 1 + $\begin{Bmatrix} ga \\ wa \end{Bmatrix}$ **+ intransitive Verb**

⟶ **Noun 3* (animate recipient)** $+ \begin{Bmatrix} ga \\ wa \end{Bmatrix} +$ **Noun 1 (actor)** **+** *ni* **+ Verb(*-reru* or *-rareru*)**

*Noun 3, the recipient of an action performed by someone else, may or may not occur in the original sentence.

Tomodachi *ga* shashin o *totta.*
"A friend took [my] picture." ⟶ Tomodachi *ni* shashin o *torareta.*
"[My] picture was taken by a friend."

Doroboo *ga* kanai no okane o *nusumimashita.*
"A thief stole my wife's money." ⟶ *Kanai wa* doroboo *ni* okane o *nusumaremashita.*
"My wife had her money stolen by a thief."

Ryooshin *ga shin'de,* kono kodomo wa kawaisoo desu.
"I feel pity for this child since his parents died." ⟶ Ryooshin *ni shinarete,* kono kodomo wa kawaisoo desu.
"I feel pity for this child since he was affected by the death of his parents."

Kinoo no yoru osoku kyaku *ga kita* n desu.
"A visitor came to see me late last night." ⟶ Kinoo no yoru osoku kyaku *ni korareta* n desu.
"I had a visitor late last night."

Ame *ga futte*, taihen datta deshoo.		⟶	Ame *ni furarete*, taihen datta deshoo.

Ame *ga futte*, taihen datta deshoo.
   "Since it rained, you might have had a
     hard time."

⟶   Ame *ni furarete*, taihen datta deshoo.
     "Since you were caught in the rain, you
      might have had a hard time."

Note that when the original active sentence has a Predicate of a Verb plus an Extender such as *tabete iru, mite shimau*, and the like, its passive is made by transforming the Verb into the passive form.

tabete iru   ⟶   *taberarete* iru
mite shimau   ⟶   *mirarete* shimau

There are cultural points which should be considered in connection with the passive.

The first point is that in Japanese one can combine something which has happened and the influence of that something on the speaker. For example, the speaker's baby has died and therefore the speaker is in a state of sorrow. The passive form of "death" is used to indicate this, with the result that the Japanese statement would be literally translated as "I was died by my baby," or, to put it another way, "I was cried by my baby." This type of passive form may be called affective passive, and is unique to Japanese. It provides a very convenient way for the speaker to inform others that he or she was affected by something, while leaving the exact nature of the effect vague. Moreover, it is for this reason that many intransitive Verbs can be used in the passive in Japanese, for example, *Ame ni furarete, kaze o hikimashita*.

The second point to be noted is that the Japanese always avoid inanimate subjects for passive Verbs. Therefore, when your book has been stolen, the literal translation of a Japanese statement to that effect would be "I was robbed of my book." This structure makes the subject as animate as possible, and emphasizes that it is the object which was acted on. It also allows, in part, the frequent omission of the subject in Japanese. This feature conforms to the Japanese tendency of not repeating "I" through omission of the subject.

3.4.3   The "integrated hospital" system operates in Japan, meaning that the hospital covers a number of functions. Hospitals, for instance, are obliged to act as centers for the training of interns and the further education of nurses and medical assistants in addition to their functions as a medical center.

3.4.4   Throughout this dialog, the relationship between the doctor, the patient, and the nurse is revealed in the language used. Because medical care is viewed as the giving of a favor, patients address doctors and nurses accordingly. The doctor and sometimes the nurse are superior to the patient, although the doctor, whose position makes him superior to the nurse, addresses the nurse as an inferior. When the nurse treats the patient as a customer, then she uses expressions indicating more "distance." This is demonstrated as follows:

Doctor to Nurse:	Yamaguchi *kun*; (Hirota san no netsu o) *hakatte*.
Patient to Doctor:	*Sen'sei*; Doomo arigatoo *gozaimashita*.
Doctor to Patient:	Yaa, Hirota *san*.
Nurse to Patient:	Tsugi no *kata*.

3.4.5   *Doo shita n desu ka?* is an expression used to ask "What's the matter with you?" "What's wrong with you?" or "What happened?"

3.4.6   *Osoku made* means "till late." The KU form of some Adjectives may be followed by a certain Relational which causes the KU form to behave like a Noun. These cases might be called the Noun-use of the KU form. Since these Adjectives are limited in use, memorize them as they appear. Here are some of them:

osoku made	"till late"
hayaku kara	"since early (morning)"
tooku made	"to the remote place"
chikaku ni	"in the vicinity"
ooku no hito	"many people"

Asa hayaku kara yoru osoku made yoku hatarakimasu nee.	"How hard you work from early morning till late at night!"
Boku wa kono chikaku ni sun'de iru n desu.	"I am living in this vicinity."
Abunai kara, tooku made ikanaide ne.	"Don't go far, since it's dangerous."

3.4.7 *Hatarakisugi* means "overworking." The Stem form of some Verbs is often used like a Noun, and may be called the Noun-use of the Stem form of a Verb. Some of them in frequent use have been and will be classified as Nouns: *yasumi* "vacation," *oyogi* "swimming," and so on.

nomisugi	"overdrinking"		iki	"(on) one's way to ~"
nusumi	"stealing"		tsukare	"fatigue"
norikae	"transferring trains"		kan'gae	"thought"
kaeri	"(on) one's way back"			

Nusumi wa warui koto desu yo.	"Stealing is a wrong thing."
Tsugi no eki de kyuukoo ni norikae desu yo.	"[We] have to transfer to an express at the next station."
Iki ni Yamada san ni atta.	"I met Mr. Yamada on my way (to ~)."

3.4.8 *Zaazaa*, when describing rain, means a pouring (rain). There are quite a few Japanese words of this type (onomatopoeic words) which are either imitations of natural sounds or voices, or are graphic expressions of actions, motions, or states. Here are some of them for passive understanding:

ame ga	zaazaa (to)	furu	"pouring" "heavily"
	potsupotsu (to)		"in small drops"
	shitoshito (to)		"quietly"
yuki ga	shin'shin to	furu	"rapidly"
	chirachira (to)		"lightly"
kaze ga	byuubyuu (to)	fuku	"with whistling sounds"
	soyosoyo (to)		"breezing gently"
hana ga	harahara (to)	chiru	"fall by ones and twos"
	chirachira (to)		"lightly"
akachan ga ogyaaogyaa to naku			"mewl"
kodomo ga waawaa (to) naku			"wail" "cry loudly"
inu ga wan'wan (to) naku			"bow-wow"
neko ga nyaanyaa (to) naku			"mew-mew"
doa o ton'ton (to) nokku suru			"knocking on the door lightly"
don'don hashiru			"runs rapidly"
dan'dan ame ga yamu			"the rain stops gradually"
iraira suru			"get irritated"
baribari hataraku			"work with great vigor"

3.4.9 *San'juu shichido nibu* means 37.2 degrees centigrade. The Japanese do not use Fahrenheit to measure temperature. To convert to Fahrenheit multiply centigrade by 1.8 and add 32. Subtract 32 from Fahrenheit and divide by 1.8 in order to convert from Fahrenheit into centigrade.

3.4.10 *Kon'do koso* means "this time for sure." *Koso* is a Relational used to put emphasis on the preceding word. *Koso* may replace the Relationals *ga* and *wa* after the subject or the topic and will follow other Relationals such as *ni*, *de*, and *kara*. But words that may precede *koso* are rather limited.

Kon'do koso yoku ben'kyoo shite okimasu.	"I will have it studied thoroughly this time for sure."
Gomen nasai. Ie, kochira koso (gomen nasai).	"I am sorry." "Not at all. It's I who should apologize."
Kore koso hon'too no Nihon desu.	"This is the true Japan."

3.4.11 *Yukkuri neru koto ni shimasu* means "I will make up my mind to be in bed as long as I can." As already introduced in Note 12.4.14, Volume II, "one decides on something" may be expressed by the pattern ~ *ni suru*: *Bifuteki ni shimasu* "I will (decide to) have a beefsteak." When one makes a decision to do something, *(suru) koto ni suru* can be used to express the idea.

plain imperfect tense form of Verb + *koto ni suru*

The difference between ~ *koto ni suru* and ~ *koto ni naru* (see Note 2.4.13) is that ~ *koto ni suru* connotes the actor's decision of his doing something while ~ *koto ni naru* connotes normally someone else's decision of the actor's doing something.

Kon'do no ryokoo wa ikanai koto ni shimashita.	"I decided not to take this (coming) trip."
Tsugi no kai wa mikka ni hiraku koto ni shimasu.	"We will hold the next meeting on the third."
Onaka ga itsumo itai node, sen'mon no isha no tokoro ni iku koto ni shimashita.	"Since I am suffering from a stomachache all the time, I decided to go to see a medical specialist."

As indicated in Note 2.4.13, ~ *ni shimasu* requires a decision-maker, while ~ *ni narimasu* does not. This fits with the Japanese tendency to try to avoid showing others that the speaker is assertive.

3.4.12 *Odaiji ni* is an expression meaning "Take care of yourself (or the hearer's family member)" and is most frequently used to a sick person. *Daiji* is an adjectival Noun meaning "important," "valuable," and so on. The full-length expression is *Odaiji ni shite kudasai*. Do not use this expression when taking leave of someone who is in normal health. In such a case *Ki-o-tsukete!* is used.

3.5　VOCABULARY

Presentation

医学	igaku	......	N	medical science
はったつして	hattatsu shite	......	V	TE form of *hattatsu suru* – develop; progress (intransitive Verb)
はったつ	hattatsu	......	N	development
（知ら）れて	(shira)-rete	......	Dv	TE form of the passive Derivative *-reru* (see 3.4.2)
かんご婦	kan'gofu	......	N	nurse
たり（ない）	tari(nai)	......	V	Pre-Nai form of *tariru* – is enough; is sufficient (intransitive Verb)
病人	byoonin	......	N	sick person; a patient
治す	naosu	......	V	cure; heal
保障	hoshoo	......	N	security
制度	seido	......	N	system
完全	kan'zen	......	Na	complete; perfect

Dialog

斉藤	Saitoo	......	N	family name
医院	iin	......	N	medical office
広田	Hirota	......	N	family name
かぜ	kaze	......	N	(a) cold
ひいた	hiita	......	V	TA form of *hiku* – draw; pull (*Kaze o hiku* is an idiomatic expression meaning "catch a cold.")
つかれて	tsukarete	......	V	TE form of *tsukareru* – get tired
に	ni	......	R	by (someone) (see 3.4.2)
おそく	osoku	......	A	KU form of *osoi* – is late (Noun-use of KU form) (see 3.4.6)
残業した	zan'gyoo shita	......	V	TA form of *zan'gyoo suru* – do overtime work
残業	zan'gyoo	......	N	overtime work
その　うえ	sono ue	......	SI	in addition to it; what is more
帰り	kaeri	......	N	(on one's) way back (opp. *iki* "(on one's) way (to)") (see 3.4.7)
すっかり	sukkari	......	Adv.	completely; thoroughly
ぬれて	nurete	......	V	TE form of *nureru* – get wet

おやおや	oyaoya	......	SI	my goodness
夕べ	yuube	......	N	last night; evening
ザーザー	zaazaa	......	Adv.	onomatopoeia for heavy rainfall (see 3.4.8)
山口	Yamaguchi	......	N	family name
熱	netsu	......	N	temperature; fever (~ *ga aru* or *nai;* ~ *ga takai* or *hikui*)
はかって	hakatte	......	V	TE form of *hakaru* – measure
度	-do	......	Nd	counter for degree (To tell one's temperature *san'juu* in *san'juu shichido*, for example, is often omitted.) (see 3.4.9)
分	-bu	......	Nd	counter for one-tenth of a degree (see 3.4.9)
注射	chuusha	......	N	shot; injection
注射する	chuusha suru	......	V	give a shot
回	-kai	......	Nd	time(s)
働きすぎ	hatarakisugi	......	N	overworking (see 3.4.7)
こそ	koso	......	R	used to emphasize the preceding word (see 3.4.10)
お大事に。	Odaiji ni.	......	(exp.)	Please take good care of yourself. (said to a sick person) (see 3.4.12)

Notes

られる	-rareru	......	Dv	passive Derivative (see 3.4.2)
ぶつ	butsu	......	V	beat
ぬすむ	nusumu	......	V	steal; rob
かわいそう	kawaisoo	......	Na	pitiful; poor
あぶない	abunai	......	A	is dangerous
おなか	onaka	......	N	stomach; belly
大事	daiji	......	Na	important; valuable
ワンワン	wan'wan	......	Adv.	bow-wow
ニャーニャー	nyaanyaa	......	Adv.	mew-mew

Drills

どろぼう	doroboo	......	N	thief
となり	tonari	......	N	next (to someone or something); next door
口	kuchi	......	N	mouth
はな	hana	......	N	nose
耳	mimi	......	N	ear

3.6　KAN'JI

3.6.1 病　(1)　BYOO　(2)　sick; illness　(3)　classifier 疒 [illness]

(4)　` 亠 广 疒 疒 病 病　(5)　病気、病院、病人、病室

3.6.2 医　(1)　I　(2)　medical　(3)　classifier 匚　(4)　一 ア 三 矢 医

(5)　医学、医院、医学部 [medical department]

3.6.3 数　(1)　*kazu*　(2)　number　(3)　classifier 攵　(4)　半 娄 敉 数

(5)　車の数がふえました

12.6.11, Vol. III

3.6.a 安　(1)　AN　(2)　safe; secure　(5)　安心、安藤、安全 [safe]

(6)　homonym 按、鞍

3.6.4 心　(1)　SHIN　(2)　heart; spirit　(3)　forms the classifier 心

(4)　丶 心 心 心　(5)　安心、心配、心理学 [psychology]、中心 [center]

3.6.5 治　(1)　*nao(su)*　(2)　heal; cure　(3)　classifier 氵　(4)　氵 氿 治

(5)　病気を治す

3.6.6 次　(1)　*tsugi*　(2)　next　(3)　classifier 冫 （欠）

(4)　冫 冫 冫 冹 次　(5)　次の方、次の駅はどこですか

3.6.7 者　(1)　SHA　(2)　person　(3)　classifier 耂　(4)　土 耂 者

(5)　医者、学者 [scholar]、芸者　(6)　homonym 煮

3.6.8 頭　(1)　*atama*　(2)　head　(3)　classifier 豆 （頁）[head]

(4)　一 豆 豆 豆 豇 頭 頭　(5)　頭がいい、頭がいたい

(6)　homonym TOO 豆

3.6.9 夜　(1)　*yoru*　(2)　night　(3)　classifier 亠（夕 [crescent moon]）

(4)　亠 亠 夜 夜　(5)　夜も昼も働く、夜おそく寝る

3.6.10 低　(1)　*hiku(i)*　(2)　low　(3)　classifier 亻

(4)　亻 亻 仟 仟 低 低　(5)　せいが低い、熱が低い

(6)　homonym TEI 底、抵、邸

3.6.11 薬　(1)　*kusuri*　(2)　medicine　(3)　classifier 艹 [grass]

(4)　艹 首 萡 薄 薬　(5)　薬屋、薬を飲む

3.6.12 回　(1)　KAI　(2)　time(s); turn　(3)　classifier 囗 [enclosure]

(4)　冂 回 回　(5)　一日一回　(6)　homonym 廻

3.6.13 寝 　(1)　*ne(ru)*　　(2)　sleep; go to bed　　(3)　classifier 宀 [roof]

(4) 　宀　宀　宀　宀　宀　寝　　(5)　十時に寝た、昼寝、早寝早起き

3.7　DRILLS

3.7.1　Transformation Drill (direct passive)

1. まどガラスを　こわしました。　⟶　まどガラスが　こわされました。

2. 新しい　学生を　しょうかいしました。　⟶　新しい　学生が　しょうかいされました。

3. あした　会を　ひらきます。　⟶　あした　会が　ひらかれます。

4. 医者を　すぐ　呼びました。　⟶　医者が　すぐ　呼ばれました。

5. 新聞に　日本の　ことを　書きました。　⟶　新聞に　日本の　ことが　書かれました。

6. 二年前に　この　絵を　かきました。　⟶　二年前に　この　絵が　かかれました。

7. お金を　ぬすみました。　⟶　お金が　ぬすまれました。

8. アメリカでは　英語を　話しています。　⟶　アメリカでは　英語が　話されています。

9. 大学で　この　本を　使っています。　⟶　大学で　この　本が　使われています。

3.7.2　Transformation Drill (direct passive)

1. あの　男が　かばんを　取りました。　⟶　かばんは　あの　男に　取られました。

2. 鈴木さんは　医者を　呼びました。　⟶　医者は　鈴木さんに　呼ばれました。

3. 父が　いもうとを　病院へ　つれて　　行きました。　⟶　いもうとは　父に　病院へ　つれて　行かれました。

4. あにが　おとうとを　ぶちました。　⟶　おとうとは　あにに　ぶたれました。

5. どろぼうが　新しい　車を　ぬすんだ　そうです。　⟶　新しい　車は　どろぼうに　ぬすまれた　そうです。

6. アメリカ人は　この　店を　よく　知っていますか。　⟶　この　店は　アメリカ人に　よく　知られていますか。

3.7.3　Transformation Drill (indirect passive)

A. 1. 先生が　用を　頼みました。　わたしは　⟶　わたしは　先生に　用を　頼まれました。

2. きょ年　父が　死にました。　わたしは　⟶　わたしは　きょ年　父に　死なれました。

3. かんご婦が　注射しました。　病人は　⟶　病人は　かんご婦に　注射されました。

4. 夜　おそく　客が　来ました。　母は　⟶　母は　夜　おそく　客に　来られました。

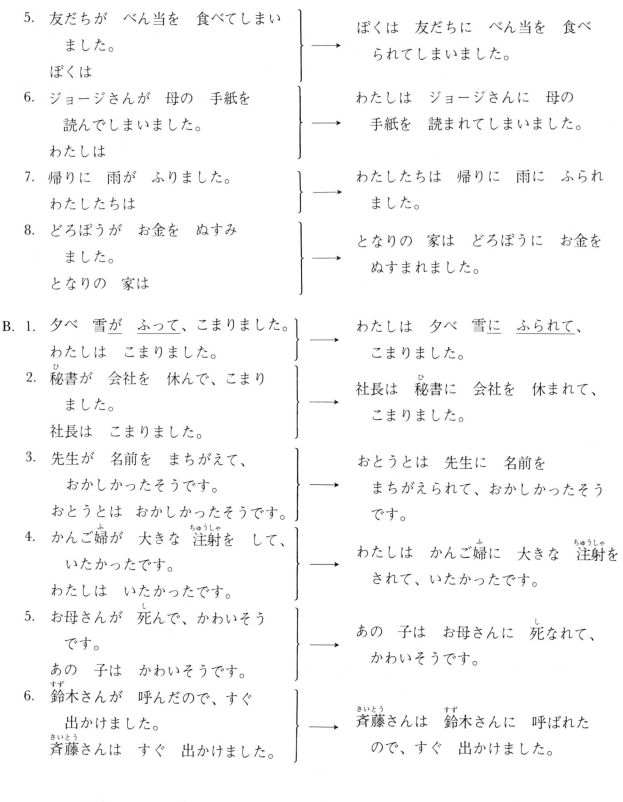

5. 友だちが　べん当を　食べてしまい
　　ました。
　　ぼくは
→ ぼくは　友だちに　べん当を　食べ
　　られてしまいました。

6. ジョージさんが　母の　手紙を
　　読んでしまいました。
　　わたしは
→ わたしは　ジョージさんに　母の
　　手紙を　読まれてしまいました。

7. 帰りに　雨が　ふりました。
　　わたしたちは
→ わたしたちは　帰りに　雨に　ふられ
　　ました。

8. どろぼうが　お金を　ぬすみ
　　ました。
　　となりの　家は
→ となりの　家は　どろぼうに　お金を
　　ぬすまれました。

B. 1. 夕べ　雪が　ふって、こまりました。
　　　わたしは　こまりました。
→ わたしは　夕べ　雪に　ふられて、
　　こまりました。

2. 秘書が　会社を　休んで、こまり
　　ました。
　　社長は　こまりました。
→ 社長は　秘書に　会社を　休まれて、
　　こまりました。

3. 先生が　名前を　まちがえて、
　　おかしかったそうです。
　　おとうとは　おかしかったそうです。
→ おとうとは　先生に　名前を
　　まちがえられて、おかしかったそう
　　です。

4. かんご婦が　大きな　注射を　して、
　　いたかったです。
　　わたしは　いたかったです。
→ わたしは　かんご婦に　大きな　注射を
　　されて、いたかったです。

5. お母さんが　死んで、かわいそう
　　です。
　　あの　子は　かわいそうです。
→ あの　子は　お母さんに　死なれて、
　　かわいそうです。

6. 鈴木さんが　呼んだので、すぐ
　　出かけました。
　　斉藤さんは　すぐ　出かけました。
→ 斉藤さんは　鈴木さんに　呼ばれた
　　ので、すぐ　出かけました。

3.7.4　Transformation Drill

1. 山口さんが　もっと　勉強しろと
　　言いました。
→ 山口さんに　もっと　勉強しろと
　　言われました。

2. 父が　銀行へ　行ってくれと　言い
　　ました。
　　　　　　　　⟶　父に　銀行へ　行ってくれと　言われ
　　　　　　　　　　ました。

3. 広田さんが　この　いみは　何です
　　かと　質問しました。
　　　　　　　　⟶　広田さんに　この　いみは　何ですか
　　　　　　　　　　と　質問されました。

4. 社長が　大阪へ　出張しろと　命令
　　しました。
　　　　　　　　⟶　社長に　大阪へ　出張しろと　命令
　　　　　　　　　　されました。

5. 斉藤部長が　手紙を　出してくれと
　　頼みました。
　　　　　　　　⟶　斉藤部長に　手紙を　出してくれと
　　　　　　　　　　頼まれました。

6. 医者が　心配は　ないと　言い
　　ました。
　　　　　　　　⟶　医者に　心配は　ないと　言われ
　　　　　　　　　　ました。

7. かないが　いつも　働きすぎだと
　　言っています。
　　　　　　　　⟶　かないに　いつも　働きすぎだと
　　　　　　　　　　言われています。

8. 課長が　新しい　仕事を　やって
　　もらいたいと　言いました。
　　　　　　　　⟶　課長に　新しい　仕事を　やって
　　　　　　　　　　もらいたいと　言われました。

3.7.5　Expansion Drill

1. ぬすまれました。
　　　　　　　　……　ぬすまれました。
　　高い　着物を
　　　　　　　　……　高い　着物を　ぬすまれました。
　　どろぼうに
　　　　　　　　……　どろぼうに　高い　着物を　ぬすまれました。
　　わたしは
　　　　　　　　……　わたしは　どろぼうに　高い　着物を
　　　　　　　　　　ぬすまれました。

2. ぬれてしまいました。
　　　　　　　　……　ぬれてしまいました。
　　すっかり
　　　　　　　　……　すっかり　ぬれてしまいました。
　　雨に　ふられて
　　　　　　　　……　雨に　ふられて、すっかり　ぬれてしまい
　　　　　　　　　　ました。
　　ザーザー
　　　　　　　　……　ザーザー　雨に　ふられて、すっかり
　　　　　　　　　　ぬれてしまいました。

3. 言われました。
　　　　　　　　……　言われました。
　　「早く　起きなさい」と
　　　　　　　　……　「早く　起きなさい」と　言われました。
　　かないに
　　　　　　　　……　かないに　「早く　起きなさい」と　言われ
　　　　　　　　　　ました。
　　むすめは
　　　　　　　　……　むすめは　かないに　「早く　起きなさい」と
　　　　　　　　　　言われました。

4. 聞かれました。   ……   聞かれました。

 「かぜを　ひいたんですか」と   …… 「かぜを　ひいたんですか」と　聞かれました。

 池田さんに   ……   池田さんに　「かぜを　ひいたんですか」と
             聞かれました。

 ぼくは   ……   ぼくは　池田さんに　「かぜを　ひいたん
             ですか」と　聞かれました。

5. こまりました。   ……   こまりました。

 来られて   ……   来られて、こまりました。

 友だちに   ……   友だちに　来られて、こまりました。

 朝　早くから   ……   朝　早くから　友だちに　来られて、こまり
             ました。

 急いでいるのに   ……   急いでいるのに、朝　早くから　友だちに
             来られて、こまりました。

6. かわいそうです。   ……   かわいそうです。

 死なれて   ……   死なれて、かわいそうです。

 りょうしんに   ……   りょうしんに　死なれて、かわいそうです。

 この　小さい　子どもたちは   ……   この　小さい　子どもたちは　りょうしんに
             死なれて、かわいそうです。

3.7.6   Substitution Drill

A.   <u>朝　早くから</u>　勉強しました。

  1. けさ　早くから   ……   けさ　早くから　勉強しました。

  2. 夜　おそくまで   ……   夜　おそくまで　勉強しました。

  3. 夕べ　おそくまで   ……   夕べ　おそくまで　勉強しました。

  4. おそくまで   ……   おそくまで　勉強しました。

  5. 寝ていました   ……   おそくまで　寝ていました。

  6. 早くから   ……   早くから　寝ていました。

  7. 起きていますね   ……   早くから　起きていますね。

B.   <u>東京に</u>　<u>住んでいます</u>。

  1. 近くに   ……   近くに　住んでいます。

  2. となりに   ……   となりに　住んでいます。

  3. とおくに   ……   とおくに　住んでいます。

  4. とおくの　町に   ……   とおくの　町に　住んでいます。

5. 買い物に　行きました　　　……　とおくの　町に　買い物に　行きました。

6. 近くへ　　　　　　　　　　……　近くへ　買い物に　行きました。

7. となりの　町まで　　　　　……　となりの　町まで　買い物に　行きました。

3.7.7　Transformation Drill

1. つかれた、寝る　　　　　　……　つかれた<u>ので</u>、寝る<u>ことに</u>　<u>しました</u>。

2. たのしかった、もう一度　行ってみる　……　たのしかったので、もう一度　行って
　　　　　　　　　　　　　　　　　みることに　しました。

3. 仕事が　終わらない、残業する　……　仕事が　終わらないので、残業する
　　　　　　　　　　　　　　　　　ことに　しました。

4. のどが　いたい、この　薬を　飲む　……　のどが　いたいので、この　薬を　飲む
　　　　　　　　　　　　　　　　　ことに　しました。

5. よく　わからない、斉藤先生に　聞く　……　よく　わからないので、斉藤先生に
　　　　　　　　　　　　　　　　　聞くことに　しました。

6. 熱が　ある、注射してもらう　……　熱が　あるので、注射してもらうことに
　　　　　　　　　　　　　　　　　しました。

7. 勉強が　忙しい、アルバイトを　やめる　……　勉強が　忙しいので、アルバイトを
　　　　　　　　　　　　　　　　　やめることに　しました。

8. 雨が　ふった、行かない　　　……　雨が　ふったので、行かないことに
　　　　　　　　　　　　　　　　　しました。

9. かぜを　ひいた、きょうは　出かけない　……　かぜを　ひいたので、きょうは　出かけ
　　　　　　　　　　　　　　　　　ないことに　しました。

10. 雨に　ふられた、洋服に　着かえる　……　雨に　ふられたので、洋服に　着かえる
　　　　　　　　　　　　　　　　　ことに　しました。

3.7.8　E-J Substitution Drill

社会制度について　<u>学生に</u>　<u>質問されました</u>。

1. by Mr. Brown　　　　　……　社会制度について　ブラウンさんに　質問されました。

2. by Prof. Hirota　　　　　……　社会制度について　広田先生に　質問されました。

3. was taught　　　　　　　……　社会制度について　広田先生に　教えられました。

4. was told so　　　　　　　……　社会制度について　広田先生に　そう　言われました。

5. was asked　　　　　　　……　社会制度について　広田先生に　聞かれました。

6. by a foreigner　　　　　……　社会制度について　外国人に　聞かれました。

3.7.9   E-J Expansion Drill

1. 取ります。

was taken	⋯⋯	取られました。
ten thousand yen	⋯⋯	一万円　取られました。
by a thief	⋯⋯	どろぼうに　一万円　取られました。
last night	⋯⋯	夕べ　どろぼうに　一万円　取られました。

2. 知っています。

is known	⋯⋯	知られています。
well	⋯⋯	よく　知られています。
by foreigners	⋯⋯	外国人に　よく　知られています。
Mt. Fuji	⋯⋯	富士山は　外国人に　よく　知られています。

3. 読んでいます。

(people) read	⋯⋯	読まれています。
a lot	⋯⋯	たくさん　読まれています。
in Japan	⋯⋯	日本で　たくさん　読まれています。
American literature	⋯⋯	アメリカ文学は　日本で　たくさん　読まれています

4. 書いています。

is written	⋯⋯	書かれています。
in *hiragana* and *kan'ji*	⋯⋯	ひらがなと　漢字で　書かれています。
the textbook	⋯⋯	教科書は　ひらがなと　漢字で　書かれています。

5. 頼みますか。

was asked	⋯⋯	頼まれましたか。
about what	⋯⋯	何について　頼まれましたか。
by Mr. Koyama	⋯⋯	小山さんに　何について　頼まれましたか。

3.7.10   E-J Response Drill

1. どう　したんですか。

I have a toothache	⋯⋯	はが　いたいんです。

2. なぜ　薬を　飲んだんですか。

because I have a stomachache	⋯⋯	おなかが　いたいので、薬を　飲んだんです。

3. どうして　医者へ　行ったんですか。

because I have a high fever	⋯⋯	熱が　高いので、医者へ　行ったんです。

4. どこが　いたいんですか。

my throat is 　　　　　　……　のどが　いたいんです。

5. どうして　学校を　休んだんですか。

because I had a headache 　　……　頭が　いたかったので、学校を　休んだんです。

6. なぜ　注射してもらったんですか。

because I caught a cold 　　……　かぜを　ひいたので、注射してもらったんです。

7. どう　したんですか。

I feel sick and I have a fever 　……　気分が　悪くて、熱が　あるんです。

3.8　EXERCISES

3.8.1　Insert an appropriate Relational into each of the following blanks and give the English equivalent for each sentence.

1. どろぼう＿＿　ぼくの　お金＿＿　ぬすんだんです。
2. 夕べ　どろぼう＿＿　ぼくの　お金＿＿　ぬすまれました。
3. ぼく＿＿　どろぼう＿＿　お金＿＿　ぬすまれたんです。
4. 広田さんは　山口さん＿＿　名前＿＿　所＿＿　聞かれたそうです。
5. 朝　早く　わたしは　社長＿＿　大事な　用＿＿　頼まれたので、出かけました。
6. 病人＿＿　大きな　注射を　されて、いたいと　言いました。
7. 病気の　子ども＿＿　夜　おそく　病院＿＿　つれて行かれました。
8. 今度　いっしょうけんめい　やります。
9. 朝　早く＿＿　夜　おそく＿＿　働くのは　よくないですよ。

3.8.2　日本語で　言いなさい。

1. Professor Hirota is well known by the students.
2. I was taught simple matters by the children.
3. My husband was told so by a man next door.
4. Last night my younger sister got sick, so I was told by my father to call a doctor.
5. The meeting was held at the dean's office.
6. I got tired, so I'll go to bed earlier.

3.8.3　Combine each of the A-group words with an appropriate B-group word and insert an appropriate Relational in the blank.

Example:　雨（が）—ふる

	A							**B**
1.	かぜ	(		)				はかる
2.	薬	(		)				呼ぶ
3.	病人	(		)				ひく
4.	どろぼう	(		)				いたい
5.	熱（ねっ）	(		)				ぬすまれる
6.	頭	(		)				安心する
7.	医者	(		)				飲む
8.	洋服（ふく）	(		)				ぬれる
								寝る
								治す

3.8.4 Change the given sentence into the passive clause and complete the sentence as shown in the example.

Example: 父が　言った。 ⟶　父に　言われて、手紙を　出しに　行きました。

1. 雨が　ふった。 ⟶

2. 母が　頼んだ。 ⟶

3. どろぼうが　カメラを　ぬすんだ。 ⟶

3.8.5 Answer the following questions based on the Dialog.

1. 広田さんは　どうして　医者に　行くことに　したんですか。

2. 広田さんは　医者に　どんな　病気だと　言われましたか。

3. 広田さんは　きのう　なぜ　ぬれてしまったんですか。

4. 広田さんは　注射（ちゅうしゃ）を　されましたか。

5. きょう　広田さんは　会社に　行くでしょうか。

3.8.6 ひらがなを　漢字に　変えなさい。

1. びょうにんの　かずに　くらべて、いしゃが　たりない。

2. あたまが　いたかったので、よる　くすりを　にかい　のんで　ねました。

3. おかねが　あれば、あんしんして　びょうきを　なおすことが　できますか。

4. わたしの　つぎの　ひとは　せいが　ひくい。

3.8.7 次の　漢字を　読みなさい。

1. 回、医

2. 帰、寝

3. 薬、花、茶

4. 治、次

5. 寝、安

6. 広、病

3.8.8   Explain the difference between the following.

1. Yuki ga furimashita.
2. Yuki ni furaremashita.

3.8.9   Explain the difference between the following.

1. Inu ga tabete shimaimashita.
2. Inu ni taberarete shimaimashita.

3.8.10   Describe the situations under which each of the given greeting expressions could be used.

1. Jaa, ogen'ki de.
2. Sayoonara.
3. Dewa, odaiji ni.
4. Ki-o-tsukete ne.

3.8.11   Give English equivalents for each of the following.

1. Shachoo wa dekakeraremashita.
2. Shachoo ni dekakeraremashita.
3. Watashi wa ame ni furareta.
4. Goshujin wa moo kaeraremashita yo.
5. Watashi wa oben'too o neko ni taberareta.
6. Yoru osoku kyaku ni korareta.
7. Yoru osoku buchoo ga korareta.
8. Kinoo sen'sei ni yobareta.

3.8.12   Which of the following conversations are made between a doctor and a nurse; a nurse and a patient; a doctor and a patient?

1.   A: Kyoo wa daibu ii desu nee.
     B: Okagesama de. Totemo yoku narimashita.
2.   A: Kyoo wa daibu yoku narimashita.
     B: Sore wa yokatta desu nee.
3.   A: Netsu o ohakari shimasu.
     B: Tabun moo daijoobu da to omoimasu.
4.   A: Kyoo wa daibu ii desu.
     B: Sore wa yokatta.
5.   A: Netsu wa doo?
     B: Amari takaku arimasen. 36°5′ desu.

3.8.13   List the words and expressions used by each party in the dialog that indicate the relative social status of doctor, nurse, and patient. How would you describe this relationship? How does it differ from American assumptions?

3.9   SITUATIONAL AND APPLICATION CONVERSATION

3.9.1   A husband asks his wife what's the matter with her.

The wife answers she has a headache.

The husband says that she might have caught a cold since she sat up until late last night.

The wife agrees, and she says she has a high fever.

The husband asks her if she also has a sore throat.

The wife says to him that she has a sore throat and she took some medicine in the morning.

The husband advises her to go to see Dr. Saitō.

3.9.2　At Mr. Yamaguchi's home.

Mr. Yamaguchi says to Mr. Saitō that Mr. Yamaguchi's car was stolen.

Mr. Saitō is surprised and asks Mr. Yamaguchi when it was stolen.

Mr. Yamaguchi explains to Mr. Saitō that it was taken away in the afternoon of the previous day while he was out of his home.

Mr. Saitō asks if there was anything important in the car.

Mr. Yamaguchi answers that the dictionary he borrowed from Mr. Hirota was also taken away with the car.

Mr. Saitō asks if Mr. Yamaguchi informed Mr. Hirota of the fact.

Mr. Yamaguchi says he hasn't.

3.9.3　Doctor:　Doo shimashita ka?

　　　　Patient:　Doomo kibun ga warukute …

　　　　Doctor:　Sore wa komarimashita ne. Sekiguchi kun, kono kata no netsu o ohakari shite.

　　　　Nurse:　Hai.

3.9.4　Mother:　Hiroshi, doo shita no, kibun ga warui no?

　　　　Hiroshi:　Un, chotto atama ga itai no. Tabun, ame ni furarete, kaze o hiita n da to omou.

　　　　Mother:　Sore wa komatta wa ne. Jaa, oishasan e itte, mite moraimashoo ka?

　　　　Hiroshi:　Daijoobu da yo. Sore ni, chuusha o sareru kara, iya da yo.

3.9.5　Suzuki:　Ano hito wa okane o torarete komatte iru n da soo da.

　　　　Hayata:　Soo. Sore wa kawaisoo ne. Watashi mo mae den'sha no naka de kaban o machigaerarete, komatta koto ga aru wa.

3.9.6　Daughter:　Okinawa wa mata taifuu de komatte iru soo yo.

　　　　Father:　Taihen daroo ne.

　　　　Daughter:　Atashi mo kinoo ame ni furarete komatta wa.

　　　　Father:　Ki-o-tsukete kure yo. Ima wa okaasan ni byooki de nerarete iru noni, mata Keiko ni kaze o hikaretara, komatte shimau kara ne.

　　　　Daughter:　Daijoobu yo, otoosan, atashi wa.

3.10   READING COMPREHENSION

3.10.1

先週　私は　五日も　大学を　休んだ。大学に　入ってから、病気に　なって　休んだのは　はじめてだった。薬屋で　薬を　買って、うちで　寝ていたが、熱が　高くて　気分も　よくならないので、近くの　医者に　行った。私は　ふつうの　かぜだろうと　思って　いたが、医者は　インフルエンザ(influenza)だろうと　言った。きらいな　注射を　されたが、後で　ずっと　気分が　よくなった。医者に　あたたかくして　二、三日　寝ていなさいと　言われた。

3.10.2

A　「どうしたの?」

B　「夕べ　るすの　間に　どろぼうに　入られて…」

A　「え! 本当? 何を　取られたの?」

B　「二万円ぐらい　お金を　取られたんだ。」

A　「まあ! それで、物は　ぬすまれなかったの?」

B　「うん、どうも　物は　持って行かれなかったらしい。」

A　「そう、お金だけだったの? よかったわね。それで、どこから　入ったの、どろぼうは?」

B　「台所の　まどの　かぎ(key)が　こわれていたんだよ。あぶないから、新しく　かぎを　つける(fix)ことに　したよ。」

A　「そうね。そうすれば　安心ね。」

LESSON 4
日本の　自然[1]

4.1　　PRESENTATION

　日本は　山が　多くて、　田や　畑が　少ない　島国である。　石炭や　石油など　資源も　けっして　ゆたかだとは　言えない[2]。　しかも、　火山が　多くて、　地震が　しばしば　起こる。　夏から　秋にかけて[3]は　よく　台風に　おそわれる。

　日本人の　性格[1]は　こういう　自然と　ふかい　関係が　ある[1]かもしれない[4]。

4.2　　DIALOG

―― 汽車の　中で ――

小川　　　　「ハンフリーさん、　こっちの　窓から[5]　ちょっと　ごらんなさい[6]。
　　　　　　だんだん畑が　見えて[2]、　いい　けしき[7]ですよ。」

ハンフリー　「ああ、　この　辺は　ずっと　みかんの　畑ばかり[8]　つづいているんですね。
　　　　　　黄色くなった　みかんが　きれいですねえ。」

小川　　　　「新聞によると、　春と　夏の　天気が　悪かったので、　いつもの　ように
　　　　　　たくさん　取れる[2]か　どうか[9]　わからないそうですよ。」

ハンフリー　「そうは　思えませんけどねえ[10]…」

小川　　　　「秋に　なってから　天気が　つづいたから、　思ったより　いいかも
　　　　　　しれませんね[4]。」

ハンフリー　「ところで、　もう　台風は　来ないでしょうね。　この　夏は
　　　　　　台風ばかりで、　本当に　いやに　なりました。」

小川　　　　「もう　だいじょうぶでしょう。　でも、　一度　台風に　おそわれれば、
　　　　　　農業は　大きな　ひがいを　うけますからね。　お米でも[11]　みかんでも
　　　　　　取り入れるまで[12]は　心配です。」

ハンフリー　「ぼくも　この　夏　はじめて　台風の　こわさ[13]を　知りました。」

島国	石炭	石油	秋	汽車	窓	この　辺
黄色	春	悪かった	お米	心配		

4.3 PATTERN SENTENCES

4.3.1

N	R
Nihon'go	GA[2]

→

V + Dv
hanasERU[2].

4.3.2

V + Dv	R	N	(C)	R
Toreru	KA[9]	DOO[9]	(da)	KA[9]

→

V	Nd	C
wakaranai	soo	desu.

4.3.3

A	N	R
Fukai	kan'kei	ga

→

V	R		E
aru	KA[4]	MO[4]	SHIREMASEN[4].

4.4 NOTES

4.4.1 Japanese personality *(seikaku)* definitely has a deep relationship *(Noun plus to kan'kei ga aru)* with nature *(shizen).*

Japan is a long, narrow collection of islands which runs north to south for approximately the same distance and latitude as the eastern coast of the United States. The country covers, then, semiarctic, temperate, and semitropical climatic zones, and experiences the change of four distinct seasons. The Japanese enjoy the rich and variegated scenery which such an environment provides, and have come to be especially aware of nature's serenity, beauty, and benevolence. In the spring they eagerly await the appearance of various flowers, and talk of the "flower front" as it moves north from Okinawa. At the same time, however, approximately 80 percent of the Japanese land area is volcanic mountain, and earthquakes *(jishin)* are rather common. Japan also experiences the regular occurance of typhoons *(taifuu)* in summer.

This combination of nature's benevolence and ferocity has undoubtedly affected the Japanese attitude toward nature as well as toward the relationship between human beings and nature, and these attitudes, in turn, are reflected in language. For instance, the Japanese view themselves as being "in nature" rather than "opposed to nature." They see humanity as part of nature, living in harmony with it. As such, they view as inappropriate the attempt to control or compete with their natural environment.

This traditional attitude was more prevalent when Japanese society was based on agriculture. Today, in a highly industrialized Japan where human livelihood no longer depends upon the temperament of nature, new trends are emerging. Nevertheless, language expressions and habits normally change in the wake of social change, and in some cases language expressions persist long after such social change occurs. Even today, then, when the Japanese population is only about 20 percent agricultural, these traditional attitudes toward nature in the form of "man-in-nature" persist, especially in language expressions. The traditional Japanese view toward beauty has been especially affected by this attitude.

Furthermore, the Japanese view nature as it is. What is, simply is. They do not attempt to interpret nature in a generalized way. They regard the context of nature to be concrete. The phenomenal appearances of nature are multiple; nature, therefore, manifests itself in a variety of forms and modes of being, without a necessary underlying unity or generality. All these phenomenal appearances in nature are, then, realities by themselves, and each object of nature carries its own soul and its own god. As such the Japanese are less inclined toward monotheism and more inclined toward pantheism. We could even say that the Japanese tend to pay less attention to things supernatural and more attention to secular matters. It is understandable that once you consider "man-in-nature" and regard humanity as a part of nature, nature could supersede the supernatural.

These tendencies have also influenced the Japanese approach to things natural and human. For instance, traditionally the Japanese have viewed the world as transitory and have emphasized the perishability of beauty. Therefore, they developed—influenced in this by Buddhist thinking—fatalistic inclinations. During the feudal period they even treated human relationships in this light. Furthermore, since all natural phenomena coexist, they developed an attitude of eclecticism. Foreign cultures were introduced, some portion of them digested, and each element of the imported culture was given its proper position in Japanese society, coexisting with what was already present in Japan. This leads to the cultural pluralism previously discussed.

Since they do not establish generalities in their understanding of nature, traditionally the Japanese have not tended to see logical and cause-effect relationships behind nature, and hence appear to be alogical, even intuitive. Therefore, when we review the Japanese attitude toward nature, we could say that they view nature on the basis of phenomenalism, transitoriness, intuition, and secularism, with eclectic selection, and according to the principle of "man-in-nature," whereby human beings are treated as a part of nature. Above all, the sum total of these attitudes and predispositions resulted in three fundamental postures of the Japanese in the face of benevolent-and-cruel nature: acceptance of nature, receptivity toward nature, and submission to nature.

These traditional approaches toward things supernatural, toward nature, and toward the "man-and-nature" relationship stem from the human experience peculiar to Japan, and to a certain degree to Japan's natural environment. At the same time, one cannot, and should not, ignore the influence of the Chinese, Indian, and Korean cultures on Japan's attitude formation, especially in terms of Buddhism and Confucianism.

In summary then, the benevolent, yet at the same time violent, features of nature as the Japanese experienced it, played an important part in the Japanese traditional society until the modernization and industrialization became dominant. As has been stated, however, language expressions—in order to become the accepted and dominant usage of a language community—need more time than does social reform or social revolution. Consequently, present-day Japanese language expressions still maintain the traits of the traditional mind to a rather surprising degree.

4.4.2 *Kesshite yutaka da to wa ienai* means "We can never say that [coal and oil] are abundant." *Ienai* is the negative form of the potential *ieru* "can say." The potential forms of Verbs are formulated as follows:

1. Vowel Verb ..... Stem form plus -*rareru**1

taberu	⟶	taberareru	"can eat"
iru	⟶	irareru	"can stay"
miru	⟶	mirareru; mieru*2	"can see"
kiru	⟶	kirareru	"can wear"
okiru	⟶	okirareru	"can get up"

2. Consonant Verb ..... Base form plus -*eru*

iku	⟶	ikeru; ikareru*3	"can go"
toru	⟶	toreru	"can get"
yasumu	⟶	yasumeru	"can rest"
hanasu	⟶	hanaseru	"can speak"
shinu	⟶	shineru	"can die"
motsu	⟶	moteru	"can have"
omou	⟶	omoeru	"can think"
harau "pay"	⟶	haraeru	"can pay"
yobu	⟶	yoberu	"can call"
oyogu	⟶	oyogeru	"can swim"
kiku	⟶	kikeru; kikoeru*4	"can hear"

3. Irregular Verb

| suru | ⟶ | dekiru*5 | "can do" |
| kuru | ⟶ | korareru | "can come" |

*1 Stem form of a Vowel Verb plus -*reru*—for example, *tabereru, mireru*—is often heard among young Japanese, but it is not yet regarded as a proper form.

*2 The potential form of the Verb *miru* is *mirareru*. There is another Verb, *mieru*, to indicate a potential meaning. *Mieru* is normally used in the meaning of "can be seen spontaneously" or "is visible."

*3 The Verb *iku* "go" has two potential equivalents: *ikeru* and *ikareru*. The use of these is a matter of preference. The Pre-Nai form of a Verb plus -*reru* is an outdated potential form. Only *ikareru* is still widely used.

*4 The Verb *kiku* "hear; listen" has the potential form *kikeru*. There is another Verb, *kikoeru*, to indicate a potential meaning. In most cases *kikoeru* is used to mean "can be heard spontaneously." Only *kikoeru* is dealt with in this lesson.

*5 The potential equivalent of *suru* is *dekiru*. Therefore, such Verbs as a Noun plus *suru* are also changed to a Noun plus *dekiru*: *ohanashi suru* "talk" → *ohanashi dekiru* "can talk," *kekkon suru* "get married" → *kekkon dekiru* "can marry." *Dekiru* can be regarded as a potential Verb.

The potential may be used in the meaning of "be possible to" or "be able to" depending upon the context. The potential Derivatives -*rareru* and -*eru* have a function to change Verbs followed by them into intransitive Verbs. Therefore, when a transitive Verb is transformed into its corresponding potential form, the object of the transitive Verb, the word followed by *o*, if expressed, is followed by *ga* or *wa* as the subject of the potential sentence. Recently people have a tendency to use *o* instead of *ga* or *wa* in the potential. However this text drills the use of *ga* or *wa*.

Noun + *o* + transitive Verb ⟶ Noun + { *ga* / *wa* } + Verb(-*rareru* or -*eru*)

(Predicate Modifier) + intransitive Verb ⟶ (Predicate Modifier) + Verb(-*rareru* or -*eru*)

Watashi wa eigo no hon *o yomimasu.*　　⟶　　Watashi wa eigo no hon *ga yomemasu.*
　"I read an English book."　　　　　　　　"I can read an English book."

Kisha kara Fujisan *o mimashita* ka?　　⟶　　Kisha kara Fujisan *ga miemashita* ka?
　"Did you see Mt. Fuji from the train?"　　"Could you see Mt. Fuji from the train?"

Aite no koe *o kikimasen deshita.*　　⟶　　Aite no koe *ga kikoemasen deshita.*
　"I didn't hear the other party's voice."　　"I couldn't hear the other party's voice."

Dono gurai *oyogimasu* ka?　　⟶　　Dono gurai *oyogemasu* ka?
　"How far do you swim?"　　　　　　　"How far can you swim?"

Ichinen ni nan'kai ryokoo *shimasu* ka?　　⟶　　Ichinen ni nan'kai ryokoo *dekimasu* ka?
　"How often do you go on a trip a　　　　"How often can you go on a trip a year?"
　　year?"

Kon'do no kai ni deraremasu ka?　　　　　"Can you attend this (coming) meeting?"

Un'ten dekinai n desu ka?　　　　　　　　"Can't you drive?"

Tsukarete, moo arukenai.　　　　　　　　"I'm so tired that I can't walk any longer."

Itsu goro haraemasu ka?　　　　　　　　"When can you pay?"

Kyuukoo ni norenakereba, takushii de　　　"If I cannot take an express, I will decide to
　iku koto ni shimasu.　　　　　　　　　　go by taxi."

4.4.3 *Natsu kara aki ni kakete wa* … means "from summer to autumn," "extending over summer and autumn."

$$\left.\begin{array}{l}\textbf{time Noun}\\\textbf{place Noun}\end{array}\right\} + \textit{kara} + \left.\begin{array}{l}\textbf{time Noun}\\\textbf{place Noun}\end{array}\right\} + \textit{ni kakete}$$

Watashi wa Amerika kara Yooroppa ni kakete　　"I traveled through America and Europe."
　ryokoo shimashita.

Niji kara san'ji ni kakete ame ga zaazaa　　　"It rained heavily between two and three
　furimashita.　　　　　　　　　　　　　　　o'clock."

4.4.4 *Fukai kan'kei ga aru ka mo shirenai* means "There may be a deep relationship." *Ka mo shirenai* means "may" or "might" and is preceded by plain forms of a Verb and an Adjective, by a Noun, or a Noun plus *datta, ja nai, de wa nakatta,* and the like, except *da. Da* is always deleted before *ka mo shirenai. Shirenai* is the negative of the potential *shireru.*

$$\left.\begin{array}{l}\textbf{Verb (plain form)}\\\textbf{Adjective (plain form)}\\\textbf{Noun (\textit{da} deleted)}\\\textbf{Noun + Copula (plain form, except \textit{da})}\end{array}\right\} + \textit{ka mo} + \textit{shirenai}$$

$$\left.\begin{array}{l}\text{kome ga toreru}\\\text{kome ga torenai}\\\text{kome ga toreta}\\\text{kome ga torenakatta}\end{array}\right\} \text{ka mo shirenai}$$

"rice may be yielded"
"rice may not be yielded"
"rice might have been yielded"
"rice might not have been yielded"

amai		"it may be sweet"
amaku nai		"it may not be sweet"
amakatta		"it might have been sweet"
amaku nakatta		"it might not have been sweet"
------------------	} ka mo shirenai	-------------------------------
sekiyu (*da* deleted)		"it may be oil"
sekiyu ja nai		
or ~ de wa nai		"it may not be oil"
sekiyu datta		"it might have been oil"
sekiyu ja nakatta		
or ~ de wa nakatta		"it might not have been oil"

Ashita wa ame ka mo shiremasen yo.	"It may rain tomorrow."
Kono karee wa kodomo ni wa karasugiru ka mo shirenai.	"This curry may be too hot (spicy) for children."
Ame ni furareta node, kaze o hiita ka mo shiremasen.	"I might have caught a cold since it rained (I got wet in the rain)."
Kotoshi wa jishin ga ooi ka mo shirenai to rajio ga iimashita.	"The radio said that we may have frequent earthquakes this year."
Kon'ban taifuu ga kuru ka mo shirenai desu yo.	"The typhoon may come tonight."
Pooru kun wa san'nen'sei ja nai ka mo shiremasen.	"Paul may not be a junior."
Sumisu san wa Igirisujin datta ka mo shiremasen.	"Mr. Smith might have been an Englishman."

4.4.5 *Mado kara goran nasai* means "Look through the window." *Kara* in such a case as this does not mean "from" but "through" or "via."

Kisha no mado kara kazan ga yoku miemashita yo.	"I could see a volcano well through the window of the train."
San Furan'shisuko yuki no hikooki ga Hon'kon kara Tookyoo ni tsukimashita.	"The airplane bound for San Francisco arrived at Tōkyō via Hong Kong."
Boku no heya no mado kara ii keshiki ga miraremasu.	"You can see good scenery through the window of my room."

4.4.6 *Goran nasai* means "Look" or "See," and is a polite equivalent of *Minasai*.

Han'furii san, goran nasai. Yuki ga futte imasu yo.	"Look, Mr. Humphrey! It's snowing!"
Atchi o goran nasai.	"Look over there."

4.4.7 Ogawa's immediate admiration for the beauty of the scene reflects the more traditional Japanese attitude. Beauty, in traditional Japanese eyes, is not defined in terms of any structural symmetry or rigidity; it is not reasoned, but rather felt and intuited. In their minds, beauty is revealed more through suggestion than through any descriptive analysis. It is irregular, ambiguous, spontaneous, implicative, austere, and perhaps even haphazard. The Japanese aesthetic sensibility avoids symmetry and prefers the incomplete. By leaving something to be done, the viewer can participate in completing the beauty. The Japanese also prefer simplicity, allowing intuitive perception of what is suggested. Simplicity gives elegance and depth. Traditionally, Japan also has preferred a sense of uncertainty and impermanence, and has thus had a special appreciation for perishability and mortality—beauty is vulnerable and finite. Accompanying this sense of beauty are terms such as *yuugen* (subtle profundity), *aware* (the pathos of nature), *wabi* (the taste for the simple and quiet), and *sabi* (tranquility). It is important to remember, however, that this traditional view of aesthetics is undergoing changes in present-day Japan.

4.4.8 *Mikan no hatake bakari tsuzuite iru* means "Nothing but tangerine fields are spread (there)." *Bakari* here is a Relational meaning "nothing but," "only," or "just," and is similar to *dake*. (See Note 9.4.9, Vol. II.) Like *dake*, *bakari* may take the place of such Relationals as *ga*, *o*, or *wa*, or it may occur between a Noun and *ga*, *o*, or *wa*. With other Relationals such as *ni*, *de*, *e*, *kara*, *to*, and so on, the Relational *bakari* may precede or follow another Relational.

Kome bakari tabete wa ikemasen yo.	"You shouldn't eat only rice."
Kono hen wa hatake bakari na n desu ne.	"I see nothing but cultivated fields in this area."
Kinoo wa uchi ni bakari imashita.	"I did nothing but stay home yesterday."

4.4.9 *Takusan toreru ka doo ka wakaranai* means "I can't tell whether a lot (of tangerines) can be produced or not." The pattern ~ *ka doo ka* is equivalent to "whether ~ or not." The forms that may occur before *ka doo ka* are the same as those which occur before *ka mo shirenai*: plain forms of a Verb and an Adjective, a Noun, or a Noun plus plain forms of the Copula except *da*. (See Note 4.4.4.)

Verb (plain form)
Adjective (plain form)
Noun (*da* deleted)
Noun + Copula (plain form, except *da*) $\Big\}$ + *ka* + *doo* + *ka* ...

When there is a subject in the ~ *ka doo ka* clause, it is followed by *ga*. *Wa* does not occur. Instead of *doo* a Predicate or a sentence may occur to give more concrete choices:

Verb 1
Adjective 1
Noun 1 (*da* deleted)
Noun 1 + Copula (plain form, except *da*) $\Big\}$ + *ka* + $\Big\{$ **Verb 2** / **Adjective 2** / **Noun 2 (")** / **Noun 2 + Copula (")** $\Big\}$ + *ka* ...

In the above pattern, Verb 1, Adjective 1, and Noun 1 may be different words from Verb 2, Adjective 2, and Noun 2. Or, they may be the same words, only with the difference of affirmative forms or negative forms. Some of the Predicates that are commonly used after ~ *ka doo ka* or ~ *ka* ~ *ka* are shown below:

~ ka doo ka ~ ka ~ ka	shin'pai da shitte iru wakaranai kiite kudasai kan'gaeta shiraberu	"[I] am worried "[I] know "[I] don't know "please ask "[I] considered "[I] will check	whether ... or not" whether ... or ..."

Raishuu shiken o suru ka doo ka sen'sei ni kikimashita ka?

"Did you ask the teacher whether we will have an exam next week or not?"

Korareru ka doo ka shin'pai shite imasu.

"I am worried if I can come or not."

Watashi ga iku ka musuko ga iku ka mada wakarimasen.

"I don't know whether I am going or my son is going."

Kono okashi, oishii ka doo ka hitotsu tabete mite kudasai.

"Please try one piece of this candy to see if it is good or not."

Mado o shimeta ka shimenakatta ka wasuremashita.

"I forgot whether I had closed the window or not."

Kono kotae ga ii ka warui ka mite kudasai.

"Please check whether this answer is good or bad."

Yamaguchi san ga buchoo datta ka kachoo datta ka oboete imasu ka?

"Do you remember whether Mr. Yamaguchi was a department chief or a section chief?"

4.4.10 Uncertainty and ambiguity are conveyed by expressions such as *Soo wa omoemasen kedo nee ...* and *Ii ka mo shiremasen*. Such expressions indicate non-definite statements. *Omoemasen kedo nee ...*, for instance, does not mean "I don't think so," but rather the more vague "I don't think there is a possibility for me to think that way." To leave the responsibility for determining something to "natural conditions" rather than to the speaker himself has been one important cultural trait in Japan. *Omoeru, ieru*, and the like have been used for this purpose. Expressions such as *omowaremasu* stem from the same pattern. When you say *omoimasu*, your responsibility would be greater than *omoemasu* or *omowaremasu*. This suggests the heteronomous tendency in the Japanese way of speaking.

4.4.11 *Okome demo mikan demo* means "whether it is rice or an orange, both are ... as well." *Demo* after a Noun means "even," "as well," "also," "though," and "even if."

Kodomo demo otona demo gohyakuen harawanakereba nararai.

"Whether one is a child or an adult, he or she must pay five hundred yen."

4.4.12 *Toriirete shimau made wa shin'pai desu* means "We are not free from anxiety until they finish the harvest." The Relational *made* "until" may follow directly a Verb, meaning "until one does such and such." Regardless of the tense of the final Predicate the Verb that occurs before *made* is always in the Dictionary form.

(Predicate Modifier) + Dictionary form of Verb + *made* ...

Anata kara kiku made, shiken no koto o shirimasen deshita.

"I didn't know about the exam until I was told by you."

Hito wa, shinu made isshooken'mei hatarakanakereba narimasen.	"Men have to work hard until they die."
Akachan ga neru made shizuka ni shite kudasai.	"Please be quiet until the baby falls asleep."

4.4.13 *Kowasa* means "fear." The suffix *-sa* turns an Adjective, such as *kowai*, into a Noun when it is attached to the Base form of the Adjective. Here are some examples:

samusa	"coldness"	itasa	"pain; painfulness"
kibishisa	"strictness"	muzukashisa	"difficulty"
nagasa	"length"	takasa	"height"

Taifuu no kowasa is "fear of typhoons" and is transformed from *Taifuu wa* (or *ga*) *kowai*. When the Adjective *kowai* changes into a Noun followed by *-sa*, the Predicate Modifier of the original sentence, *Taifuu wa* (or *ga*), changes into the Noun Modifier of the Noun *kowasa*. Thus the Relational *wa* or *ga* changes into *no: Taifuu no kowasa*.

Kono kawa no nagasa wa sekai de ichiban da soo desu.	"I understand that this river is the longest in the world."
Kono keshiki no utsukushisa wa hyoogen dekinai.	"I can't express the beauty of this scenery."

4.5 VOCABULARY

Presentation

自然	shizen	......	N	nature
田	ta	......	N	rice paddy; irrigated rice field
畑	hatake	......	N	farm; cultivated field
島国	shimaguni	......	N	island country
石炭	sekitan	......	N	coal
石油	sekiyu	......	N	petroleum
資源	shigen	......	N	resources
けっして	kesshite	......	Adv.	(not) by any means; never (always used in negation)
言え（ない）	ie(nai)	......	V + Dv	Pre-Nai form of *ieru* – can say (see 4.4.2)
火山	kazan	......	N	volcano
地震	jishin	......	N	earthquake
しばしば	shibashiba	......	Adv.	often; frequently (formal equivalent of *yoku*)
にかけて	ni kakete	......	R + V	through ~ (see 4.4.3)
台風	taifuu	......	N	typhoon

おそわれる	osowareru	......	V + Dv	is attacked; is visited (passive of *osou* – attack)
性格	seikaku	......	N	character; personality
こういう	kooiu	......	PN	this kind of~
ふかい	fukai	......	A	is deep
関係	kan'kei	......	N	relation; connection
（かも）しれない	(ka mo) shirenai	......	E	may; might (see 4.4.4)

Dialog

小川	Ogawa	......	N	family name
ハンフリー	Han'furii	......	N	Humphrey
から	kara	......	R	through; via (see 4.4.5)
ごらんなさい	goran nasai	......	N + V	look; see (see 4.4.6)
だんだん畑	dan'dan'batake	......	N	terraced fields
見えて	miete	......	V	TE form of *mieru* – can·see (see 4.4.2)
ずっと	zutto	......	Adv.	consecutively; throughout; all during
みかん	mikan	......	N	tangerine; mandarin orange
ばかり	bakari	......	R	only; just; nothing but (see 4.4.8)
つづいて	tsuzuite	......	V	TE form of *tsuzuku* – continue; follow (intransitive Verb)
によると	ni yoru to	......	R + V + R	according to~
いつもの ように	itsumo no yoo ni	......	(PM)	as usual
取れる	toreru	......	V + Dv	can take; can be yielded (see 4.4.2)
思えません	omoemasen	......	V + Dv	cannot think (see 4.4.2)
農業	noogyoo	......	N	agriculture
ひがい	higai	......	N	damage; harm
うけます	ukemasu	......	V	receive; get; is given (normal form of *ukeru*)
（お）米	(o)kome	......	N	rice
でも	demo	......	R	even (see 4.4.11)
取り入れる	toriireru	......	V	crop; gather in; take in; harvest
まで	made	......	R	until (see 4.4.12)
こわさ	kowasa	......	N	fear (see 4.4.13)

Notes

られる	-rareru	......	Dv	potential Derivative (see 4.4.2)	
える	-eru	......	Dv	potential Derivative (see 4.4.2)	
はらう	harau	......	V	pay	
聞こえる	kikoeru	......	V	can be heard (see 4.4.2)	
こえ	koe	......	N	voice	
さ	-sa	......	(suffix)	turns the preceding Adjective into a Noun (see 4.4.13)	
ほんこん	Hon'kon	......	N	Hong Kong	
食料 (りょう)	shokuryoo	......	N	food; materials to eat	
やさい	yasai	......	N	vegetables	
こわい	kowai	......	A	is fearful	

Drills

スーパー	suupaa	......	N	supermarket

4.6   KAN'JI

4.6.1 島 (1) *shima* (2) island (3) classifier 鳥（山）

(4) ⼁ ⼃ ⼝ ⼾ ⼾ 烏 島 (5) 島国、島田さん、広島

3.6.9, Vol. III

4.6.a 石 (1) SEKI (2) stone (5) 石炭、石油、宝石 [jewel]

4.6.2 秋 (1) *aki* (2) autumn (3) classifier 禾 [a plant with an ear of corn hanging to one side] (4) ⼃ 禾 秋 (5) 秋山、秋田

(6) homonym SHUU 愁

4.6.3 汽 (1) KI (2) steam; vapor (3) classifier 氵 [water]

(4) 氵 汽 (5) 汽車、汽船 [steam boat] (6) homonym KI 気

4.6.4 窓 (1) *mado* (2) window (3) classifier 宀 [roof]

(4) 宀 穴 空 窓 (5) 窓口

4.6.5 辺 (1) HEN (2) area (3) classifier 辶 [walk] (4) フ 力 辺

(5) この辺、駅の辺

4.6.6 黄 (1) KI (2) yellow (3) classifier 艹（黄）

(4) 一 艹 芏 苩 苗 黄 (5) 黄色 (いろ)

4.6.7 色 (1) *iro* (2) color (3) classifier 勹（色）

(4) ⼃ 勹 夂 多 色 (5) 白い色、赤色、青色、黒い色、みどり色

4.6.8 春 (1) *haru* (2) spring (3) classifier 夫（日）

(4) ［三］［丰］［夫］［春］ (5) 春子、春と秋、春休み

4.6.9 悪 (1) *waru(i)* (2) bad (3) classifier 心 [heart]

(4) ［一］［二］［西］［亜］［悪］ (5) 悪い

6.6.2, Vol. III

4.6.b 米 (1) *kome* (2) rice (5) 米を食べる、米を作る

4.6.10 配 (1) HAI [-PAI] (2) deliver; distribute (3) classifier 酉

[represents an ancient jar for preserving fermented liquor]

(4) ［丙］［酉］［酉］［酊］［酊］［配］ (5) 心配、配達 [deliver]

4.6.11 音* (1) ON (2) sound (3) classifier 立（音）

(4) ［亠］［立］［立］［音］ (5) 発音 [pronunciation]、音楽

4.6.12 楽* (1) GAKU (2) music (3) classifier 木 (4) ［自］［泊］［泊］［楽］

(5) 音楽、楽器 [musical instrument]

4.7 DRILLS

4.7.1 Transformation Drill

A. 1. 自分で 着物を 着ますか。 ⟶ 自分で 着物が 着られますか。

2. あなたは 英語を 教えるんですか。⟶ あなたは 英語が 教えられるんですか。

3. はしで カレーライスを
食べますか。 ⟶ はしで カレーライスが 食べられ
ますか。

4. 毎日 新しい 漢字を 覚えます。 ⟶ 毎日 新しい 漢字が 覚えられます。

5. 今 外へ 出かけません。 ⟶ 今 外へ 出かけられません。

6. 会社の 図書室では 調べないん
です。 ⟶ 会社の 図書室では 調べられないん
です。

7. けさ 四時に 起きましたか。 ⟶ けさ 四時に 起きられましたか。

8. しけんを うけませんでした。 ⟶ しけんが うけられませんでした。

B. 1. 米を たくさん 取りました。 ⟶ 米が たくさん 取れました。

2. スーパーで 食料を 安く
買います。 ⟶ スーパーで 食料が 安く 買えます。

3. あなたは 日本語を 話すんですか。⟶ あなたは 日本語が 話せるんですか。

4. わたしは お金を はらいません
でした。 ⟶ わたしは お金が はらえませんでした。

5. 台風で　パーティーを　ひらき　　　⟶　台風で　パーティーが　ひらけません。
　　ません。

6. ここから　駅まで　はしりましたか。⟶　ここから　駅まで　はしれましたか。

7. ぼくは　東京へ　行きませんでした。⟶　ぼくは　東京へ　行けませんでした。

8. いなかには　住みませんでした。　　⟶　いなかには　住めませんでした。

C. 1. 窓から　うみを　見ます。　　　　　⟶　窓から　うみが　見えます。

2. 音楽を　聞きません。　　　　　　　⟶　音楽が　聞こえません。

3. 日曜日に　うちへ　来ますか。　　　⟶　日曜日に　うちへ　来られますか。

4. どんな　スポーツを　しますか。　　⟶　どんな　スポーツが　できますか。

5. 早く　出発しますか。　　　　　　　⟶　早く　出発できますか。

6. 日本語で　説明しました。　　　　　⟶　日本語で　説明できました。

7. 日光は　一日で　けんぶつ　　　　　⟶　日光は　一日で　けんぶつできたんです。
　　したんです。

8. もっと　やさしく　表現しません　　⟶　もっと　やさしく　表現できません
　　でしたか。　　　　　　　　　　　　　　でしたか。

4.7.2　Transformation Drill

1. にわで　とりの　こえが　聞こえます。⟶　にわで　とりの　こえが　聞こえるかも
　　　　　　　　　　　　　　　　　　　　　　しれません。

2. いい　天気は　つづきません。　　　⟶　いい　天気は　つづかないかも
　　　　　　　　　　　　　　　　　　　　　　しれません。

3. 石油が　取れません。　　　　　　　⟶　石油が　取れないかもしれません。

4. しけんの　時、辞書が　いります。　⟶　しけんの　時、辞書が　いるかも
　　　　　　　　　　　　　　　　　　　　　　しれません。

5. 地震が　起こります。　　　　　　　⟶　地震が　起こるかもしれません。

6. お母さんが　心配なさいます。　　　⟶　お母さんが　心配なさるかもしれません。

7. 三千円では　たりませんでした。　　⟶　三千円では　たりなかったかも
　　　　　　　　　　　　　　　　　　　　　　しれません。

8. ハンフリーさんは　つかれました。　⟶　ハンフリーさんは　つかれたかも
　　　　　　　　　　　　　　　　　　　　　　しれません。

4.7.3　Transformation Drill

1. あしたは　天気が　悪いです。　　　⟶　あしたは　天気が　悪いかもしれません。

2. あの　道^{みち}は　あぶないです。　　　　　——→　あの　道^{みち}は　あぶないかもしれません。

3. あしたは　つごうが　よくありません。　——→　あしたは　つごうが　よくないかも
　　　　　　　　　　　　　　　　　　　　　　　　　　しれません。

4. 地震^{じ しん}は　多くありません。　　　　——→　地震^{じ しん}は　多くないかもしれません。

5. ひがいは　大きくありませんでした。　——→　ひがいは　大きくなかったかも
　　　　　　　　　　　　　　　　　　　　　　　　　　しれません。

6. 病気は　気候^{こう}と　関係^{かんけい}が　ふかいです。——→　病気は　気候^{こう}と　関係^{かんけい}が　ふかい
　　　　　　　　　　　　　　　　　　　　　　　　　　かもしれません。

7. 料理^{りょうり}は　ちょっと　からかったです。——→　料理^{りょうり}は　ちょっと　からかったかも
　　　　　　　　　　　　　　　　　　　　　　　　　　しれません。

8. 熱^{ねっ}は　低かったです。　　　　　　——→　熱^{ねっ}は　低かったかもしれません。

4.7.4　Transformation Drill

1. この　山は　火山^{ざん}です。　　　　　——→　この　山は　火山^{ざん}かもしれません。

2. これは　カリフォルニアの　お米です。——→　これは　カリフォルニアの
　　　　　　　　　　　　　　　　　　　　　　　　　　お米かもしれません。

3. 急な　用ではありません。　　　　　　——→　急な　用ではないかもしれません。

4. かず子さんは　病気でした。　　　　　——→　かず子さんは　病気だったかも
　　　　　　　　　　　　　　　　　　　　　　　　　　しれません。

5. あの　人は　音楽が　きらいです。　　——→　あの　人は　音楽が　きらいかも
　　　　　　　　　　　　　　　　　　　　　　　　　　しれません。

6. ぬすまれた　お金は　一万円では　　　——→　ぬすまれた　お金は　一万円では
　　ありませんでした。　　　　　　　　　　　　なかったかもしれません。

7. あれは　広田さんの　こえじゃ　　　　——→　あれは　広田さんの　こえじゃないかも
　　ありません。　　　　　　　　　　　　　　　しれません。

8. それは　日本語の　表現^{ひょうげん}でした。　　——→　それは　日本語の　表現^{ひょうげん}だったかも
　　　　　　　　　　　　　　　　　　　　　　　　　　しれません。

4.7.5　Transformation Drill

1. その　火山^{ざん}は　あぶないです。　　　——→　その　火山^{ざん}が　あぶないか　どうか
　　友だちに　聞かれました。　　　　　　　　　友だちに　聞かれました。

2. やさいが　取れます　　　　　　　　　——→　やさいが　取れるか　どうか　心配です。
　　心配です。

3. あの　方が　医者です。 }⟶ あの　方が　医者か　どうか　知って
　　知っていますか。 いますか。

4. 食料が　たります。 }⟶ 食料が　たりるか　どうか　まだ
　　まだ　わかりません。 わかりません。

5. 手紙が　つきました。 }⟶ 手紙が　ついたか　どうか　気に
　　気に　しています。 しています。

6. 今度の　出張は　長いです。 }⟶ 今度の　出張が　長いか　どうか
　　教えてください。 教えてください。

7. 大きな　地震でした。 }⟶ 大きな　地震だったか　どうか
　　ラジオで　言いましたか。 ラジオで　言いましたか。

8. しけんは　むずかしかったです。 }⟶ しけんが　むずかしかったか　どうか
　　聞いてみてください。 聞いてみてください。

4.7.6　Substitution Drill

行くか　行かないか　わからないそうです。

1. 電車が　こむ、こまない　　……　電車が　こむか　こまないか　わからない
　　　　　　　　　　　　　　　　　　　　そうです。

2. 熱が　高い、低い　　……　熱が　高いか　低いか　わからないそうです。

3. けい子さんが　病気、　　……　けい子さんが　病気か　病気じゃないか
　　病気じゃない　　　　　　　　　　わからないそうです。

4. 地震が　起こる、台風が　来る　……　地震が　起こるか　台風が　来るか　わからない
　　　　　　　　　　　　　　　　　　　　そうです。

5. 知りません　　……　地震が　起こるか　台風が　来るか　知りません。

6. この　おかしが　あまい、　　……　この　おかしが　あまいか　あまくないか
　　あまくない　　　　　　　　　　　　知りません。

7. 問題が　かんたん、ふくざつ　　……　問題が　かんたんか　ふくざつか　知りません。

8. 大きな　ひがいを　うけた、　　……　大きな　ひがいを　うけたか　うけなかったか
　　うけなかった　　　　　　　　　　　知りません。

9. いつもの　ように　お米が　　……　いつもの　ように　お米が　取れるか
　　取れる、取れない　　　　　　　　　取れないか　知りません。

4.7.7　Substitution Drill

1. 自然は　すばらしい　　……　自然の　すばらしさは　おどろくほどです。
2. 地震は　こわい　　……　地震の　こわさは　おどろくほどです。

3. 日本の 台風は すごい ...... 日本の 台風の すごさは おどろくほどです。

4. この 辺は さむい ...... この 辺の さむさは おどろくほどです。

5. 大仏は 大きい ...... 大仏の 大きさは おどろくほどです。

6. ぼくの 仕事は 忙しい ...... ぼくの 仕事の 忙しさは おどろくほどです。

7. 関係が ふかい ...... 関係の ふかさは おどろくほどです。

8. けしきが 美しい ...... けしきの 美しさは おどろくほどです。

4.7.8　Substitution Drill

取り入れてしまうまでは　心配です。

1. 台風が 行ってしまう ...... 台風が 行ってしまうまでは 心配です。

2. しけんが 終わる ...... しけんが 終わるまでは 心配です。

3. 注射を してもらう ...... 注射を してもらうまでは 心配です。

4. 家に つく ...... 家に つくまでは 心配です。

5. 気を つけなさい ...... 家に つくまでは 気を つけなさい。

6. あぶないです ...... 家に つくまでは あぶないです。

7. 運転を 覚える ...... 運転を 覚えるまでは あぶないです。

8. 台風が 行ってしまう ...... 台風が 行ってしまうまでは あぶないです。

4.7.9　Transformation Drill

1. 田や 畑だけ つづいています。 ⟶ 田や 畑ばかり つづいています。

2. 小川さんの こえだけ 聞こえます。 ⟶ 小川さんの こえばかり 聞こえます。

3. 飲み物だけ 飲んでいるんですね。 ⟶ 飲み物ばかり 飲んでいるんですね。

4. 石炭と 石油だけ 取れるそうです。 ⟶ 石炭と 石油ばかり 取れるそうです。

5. ここからは 島だけ 見えますね。 ⟶ ここからは 島ばかり 見えますね。

6. この 辺は みかんの 畑だけです。 ⟶ この 辺は みかんの 畑ばかりです。

7. 広田君とだけ 話しました。 ⟶ 広田君とばかり 話しました。

8. ハワイへだけ あそびに 行くんですね。⟶ ハワイへばかり あそびに
　　　　　　　　　　　　　　　　　　　　　　行くんですね。

4.7.10　E-J Transformation Drill

1. 米が 取れます。

　　may ...... 米が 取れるかもしれません。

　　may not ...... 米が 取れないかもしれません。

　　don't know whether ~ or not ...... 米が 取れるか どうか 知りません。

2. 大きな　ひがいを　うけます。

may	……	大きな　ひがいを　うけるかもしれません。
may not	……	大きな　ひがいを　うけないかもしれません。
don't know whether ~ or not	……	大きな　ひがいを　うけるか　どうか　知りません。

3. ハンフリーさんも　日本語が　話せます。

may	……	ハンフリーさんも　日本語が　話せるかもしれません。
may not	……	ハンフリーさんも　日本語が　話せないかも 　　　　　しれません。
don't know whether ~ or not	……	ハンフリーさんも　日本語が　話せるか　どうか 　　　　　知りません。

4. この　窓から　お寺が　見えます。

may	……	この　窓から　お寺が　見えるかもしれません。
may not	……	この　窓から　お寺が　見えないかもしれません。
don't know whether ~ or not	……	この　窓から　お寺が　見えるか　どうか 　　　　　知りません。

5. 三月に　さくらが　さきます。

may	……	三月に　さくらが　さくかもしれません。
may not	……	三月に　さくらが　さかないかもしれません。
don't know whether ~ or not	……	三月に　さくらが　さくか　どうか　知りません。

6. 主人は　あした　出張_{しゅっちょう}します。

may	……	主人は　あした　出張_{しゅっちょう}するかもしれません。
may not	……	主人は　あした　出張_{しゅっちょう}しないかもしれません。
don't know whether ~ or not	……	主人は　あした　出張_{しゅっちょう}するか　どうか　知りません。

4.7.11 Response Drill

1. 今晩　雨ですよ。　　　　　　……　今晩　雨だとは　思えませんけどねえ。

2. この　窓から　富士山_{ふじさん}が　　……　富士山_{ふじさん}が　見えるとは
　　見えるかもしれません。　　　　　思えませんけどねえ。

3. この　辺でも　みかんが　　　……　みかんが　取れるとは
　　取れるそうですよ。　　　　　　思えませんけどねえ。

4. しけんは　ちょっと　　　　　……　むずかしすぎたとは
　　むずかしすぎました。　　　　　思えませんけどねえ。

5. ハワイの　夏は　むしあついです。　……　むしあついとは　思えませんけどねえ。

6. ジョーンズさんは　フランス語が　　　……　フランス語が　じょうずに
　　じょうずに　話せますよ。　　　　　　　　話せるとは　思えませんけどねえ。

4.8　EXERCISES

4.8.1　Change the final Predicate to the potential form and give the English equivalent.

1. むすこは　三つに　なったので、ひとりで　くつを　はきます。
2. これは　日本語で　何と　表現しますか。
3. 一日に　いくつぐらい　漢字を　覚えますか。
4. おととい　雪が　ふったので、バスが　とまって、学校へ　来ませんでした。
5. 土曜日も　日曜日も　東京へ　行きますか。
6. ポール君は　日本語を　自由に　話しましたか。
7. 三度も　呼んだのに、聞きませんでしたか。

4.8.2　（　）に　てき当な　ひらがなを　入れなさい。

1. 君の　せい（　）高（　）は　どのぐらいですか。
2. ロバーツさんが　ずっと　日本（　）住むつもり（　）どうか
　　知っていますか。
3. 日本は　古くから　中国（　）ふかい　関係（　）ある。
4. きょうの　午後　友だちが　家へ　来る（　）（　）しれないんです。
5. 山の　上（　）うみ（　）見えるでしょう。
6. 仕事が　終わる（　）、待っていてください。すぐ　終わりますから。
7. あの　えいがが　いい（　）悪い（　）言っていましたか。
8. 秋（　）春（　）かけて　天気（　）つづきましたね。

4.8.3　日本語で　言いなさい。

1. According to Mr. Ishii, I understand that there will be a big test before the summer vacation.
2. Do you know if Mr. Itō has a red car?
3. I don't remember whether Yoshiko's birthday was the fifth or the sixth.
4. Please ask the nurse if [my] fever is high or low.
5. I'm worried whether [my] new room is quiet or noisy.
6. Mr. Humphrey may have read the magazine I lent him.
7. According to the TV [program], it is said that Okinawa through Kyūshū may be attacked by a strong [big] typhoon tomorrow morning. We had better be careful.

4.8.4 こたえなさい。

1. 日本には　どうして　だんだん畑が　たくさん　あるのですか。

2. アメリカでは　何が　よく　取れますか。

3. 日本は　よく　台風に　おそわれますが、アメリカは　どうですか。

4. あなたの　所でも　よく　地震が　起こりますか。

5. アメリカの　おもな　資源として　どんな　物が　ありますか。

6. アメリカと　日本の　歴史的、経済的な　関係について　知っていますか。

4.8.5 漢字に　変えなさい。

1. <u>にほん</u>は　<u>せまい</u>　<u>しまぐに</u>で、<u>せき</u>油や　<u>せき</u>炭は　あまり　ない。

2. <u>はる</u>に　<u>さく</u>　<u>きいろい</u>　<u>はな</u>は　なんですか。

3. <u>あき</u>に　なれば、この　<u>へん</u>は　<u>こめ</u>を　<u>とりいれる</u>のに　<u>いそがしい</u>です。

4. この　<u>まど</u>から　<u>きしゃ</u>が　<u>みえます</u>よ。

5. <u>てんき</u>が　<u>わるい</u>かもしれないので、<u>しんぱい</u>です。

6. <u>おんがく</u>ばかり　<u>きいている</u>んですね。

4.8.6 読みなさい。

1. 近、辺	4. 楽、薬	7. 急、色
2. 心、悪、窓	5. 音、春	8. 山、島
3. 米、来	6. 洗、汽	9. 火、秋

4.8.7　What differences are there between Japanese and American views toward nature?

4.8.8　What kinds of expressions showing the ''man-and-nature'' relationship would the Japanese prefer in general as compared to Americans?

4.8.9　Change the following expressions into more traditional indirect Japanese expressions.

1. Watashi no kan'gae wa chigaimasu.
2. A:　Ocha ga hoshii desu ka?
   B:　Hai, hoshii desu.

4.8.10　Which of the following sentences are passive, potential, or polite expressions?

1. Kinoo wa yoku neraremashita.
2. Kinoo wa hayaku kaeraremashita.
3. Kinoo wa kodomo ni oshieraremashita.
4. Ashita Oosaka e ikaremasu.
5. Kinoo no yoru osoku buchoo ga koraremashita.
6. Watashi wa kaban o nusumarete shimatta n desu.

4.9 SITUATIONAL AND APPLICATION CONVERSATION

4.9.1 At the school gate.

Paul asks George if Susie came to school that day or not.

George says to Paul that she didn't and she might have caught a cold, as she told George the previous day that she had a headache.

Paul says to George that the date of the exam is the next day. He is worried whether she can come to school the next day or not.

George asks Paul if Susie knows about the exam.

Paul answers that he doesn't know if she knows about it.

George says that he will make a phone call to her house to inquire if she knows about the exam or not.

Paul asks him to do so.

4.9.2 Viewing cherry blossoms.

Mr. Humphrey says to Mr. Ikeda that there is nothing but cherry blossoms around there.

Mr. Ikeda answers that the beauty of the scenery of that area in the spring is the best.

Mr. Humphrey says that he would like to come and see the cherry blossoms again in the evening and asks Mr. Ikeda if he can come with him.

Mr. Ikeda answers that he doesn't know whether he can come or not. He continues that, however, he may know around four o'clock whether he can join Mr. Humphrey or not.

Mr. Humphrey says that he hopes Mr. Ikeda can go with him.

4.9.3 Talk about the harvest of crops, fruit, and the like in your district.

4.9.4   Sagawa: Itsu mite mo midori no yama wa ii nee. Boku mo wakakatta toki wa yoku yama e itta yo.

         Kishi: Shin'bun ni yoru to, kono yama ni mo jidoosha no rippa na michi ga tsukurareru soo da yo.

      Sagawa: E! Hon'too kai? Kooiu shizen no naka ni jidoosha ga hairu to, shizen ga dame ni naru to omou yo.

         Kishi: Demo nee, kono hen ni sun'de iru hito wa motto ben'ri ni naru to ii to omotteru ka mo shirenai yo.

      Sagawa: Min'na ga soo omotteru to wa ienai to omou kedo naa.

4.10 READING COMPREHENSION

4.10.1

日本には　古くから　「地震、雷 (thunder)、火事 (fire)、おやじ (father)」
という　ことばが　あるが、これは　「こわいもの」を　じゅんに (in order) 言った

おもしろい　ことばである。この　うち、「おやじ」は　もう　こわい　ものとは
言えないだろう！　日本で　本当に　こわいのは　地震と　台風である。地震は　急に
起こるので、一番　こわいと　言えるだろう。

　　地震の　次に　こわいのは　台風である。ひがいが　あまり　ない　年も　あるが、
年によっては　三度も　四度も　台風に　おそわれて、家や　人、農業、交通などが
大きな　ひがいを　うける。今の　日本で　こわい　ものから　じゅんに　言えば、
「地震、台風」の　次に　何と　何が　来るだろうか。

4.10.2

吉田　　「スミスさん、今度の　旅行　来られますか。」

スミス　「ええ、行けることに　なりました。」

吉田　　「それは　よかった。この　前　会った　時、行けるか　どうか　わからないと
　　　　　言っていたでしょう？　気に　していたんです。」

スミス　「どうも。仕事が　忙しければ　出かけられないかもしれないと
　　　　　思っていたんですけど、休みが　取れることに　なったんです。」

吉田　　「そうですか。北海道は　はじめてでしたね。」

スミス　「ええ、今まで　南の　方へばかり　行って、北へは　行ったことが
　　　　　ないんです。」

吉田　　「北海道の　自然は　東北 (the north-eastern Japan) とも　ずいぶん
　　　　　ちがうんですよ。」

スミス　「さむい　所でしょう？　何が　取れるんですか。」

吉田　　「お米も　取れるけど、じゃがいも (potatoes) や　だいず (soy beans)、
　　　　　とうもろこし (corn) なんかが　取れます。それに、牛 (cow) が
　　　　　たくさん　いて、牛乳も　おいしいですよ。」

スミス　「ちょっと　アメリカみたい (like〜) ですね。」

吉田　　「そう　言えるかもしれませんね。」

LESSON 5
REVIEW AND APPLICATION

5.1   PATTERNS

5.1.1 Passive

a.   Forms

Vowel Verb and irregular Verb *kuru* group

取り入れる	取り入れ	
入れる	入れ	
変える	変え	
調べる	調べ	られます／られる
見せる	見せ	られません／られない
わすれる ⟶	わすれ	られました／られた
閉める	閉め	られませんでした／られなかった
見る	見	られて
出る	出	
来る／つれて来る	来_こ／つれて来_こ	

Consonant Verb and irregular Verb *suru* group

はかる／すわる／ふる	はから／すわら／ふら	
はらう／言う／使う／おそう	はらわ／言わ／使わ／ おそわ	
ぶつ／持つ	ぶた／持た	れます／れる
聞く／みがく／ひらく	聞か／みがか／ひらか	れません／れない
かえす／わたす／治す ⟶	かえさ／わたさ／治さ	れました／れた
ぬすむ／休む／飲む	ぬすま／休ま／飲ま	れませんでした／ れなかった
呼ぶ	呼ば	れて
死_しぬ	死_しな	
する／注射_{ちゅうしゃ}する／命令_{めいれい}する／ 表現_{ひょうげん}する	さ／注射_{ちゅうしゃ}さ／命令_{めいれい}さ／ 表現_{ひょうげん}さ	

b.　Direct passive sentence

どろぼう		かばん		ぬすみました	
おとうと		ぼくの　おかし		食べた	
友だち		この　手紙		読む	
秘書(ひ)	が	よやく	を	取りけしました	
お父さん		子ども		ぶっています	
あね		わたしの　くつ		はきました	
先生		学生		呼びました	

かばん		どろぼう		ぬすまれました	
ぼくの　おかし		おとうと		食べられた	
この　手紙		友だち		読まれる	
→　よやく	は	秘書(ひ)	に	取りけされました	
子ども	が	お父さん		ぶたれています	
わたしの　くつ		あね		はかれました	
学生		先生		呼ばれました	

c.　Indirect passive sentence

どろぼう		（私の）かばんを　ぬすみました
小川さん(おがわ)		（ぼくの）車の　中を　調べました
先生		（わたしを）わすれました
佐々木君(さ さ)	が	（山田さんに）そう　言った
かんご婦(ふ)	は	新聞に　書きました
りょうしん		死にました(し)
医者		（わたしに）注射しました(ちゅうしゃ)
雪		ふって、こまった

→ (私は) (ぼくは) (わたしは) (山田さんは)	どろぼう		かばんを ぬすまれました
	小川さん		車の 中を 調べられました
	先生		わすれられました
	佐々木君	に	そう 言われた
	かんご婦		新聞に 書かれました
	りょうしん		死なれました
	医者		注射されました
	雪		ふられて、こまった

5.1.2 Potential

a. Forms

Vowel Verb

うける	うけ	
取り入れる	取り入れ	
出る	出	られます／られる
食べる	食べ	られません／られない
いる →	い	られました／られた
覚える	覚え	られませんでした／られなかった
起きる	起き	られて
寝る	寝	
知らせる	知らせ	
たてる	たて	

Consonant Verb

はかる／帰る／なる	はかれ／帰れ／なれ	
はらう／言う／思う	はらえ／言え／思え	
ぶつ／待つ／持つ	ぶて／待て／持て	ます／る
ひらく／書く	ひらけ／書け	ません／ない
話す／治す／出す →	話せ／治せ／出せ	ました／た
ぬすむ／飲む／頼む	ぬすめ／飲め／頼め	ませんでした／なかった
呼ぶ／あそぶ	呼べ／あそべ	て
急ぐ／ぬぐ／およぐ	急げ／ぬげ／およげ	
死ぬ	死ね	

Others

する／安心する／用意する	でき／安心でき／用意でき	ます／る
来る	来られ	ません／ない
見る　　　⟶	見え　or　見られ	ました／た
聞く	聞こえ　or　聞け	ませんでした／なかった
行く	行け　or　行かれ	て

b.　Potential sentence

日本語	教えます	日本語	教えられます
カレーライス	作りますか	カレーライス	作れますか
お金	はらいません	お金	はらえません
おみやげ	買いませんでした	おみやげ	買えませんでした
ピアノ	ひきます	ピアノ	ひけます
パンク	なおしました	パンク	なおせました
ビール	飲みません	ビール	飲めません
医者	呼びませんでした	医者	呼べませんでした
くつ	ぬぎません	くつ	ぬげません
着がえ	用意しました	着がえ	用意できました
これ	見ませんか	これ	見えませんか
こえ	聞きました	こえ	聞こえました

（を　⟶　が）

とおくへ　行きません	とおくへ　行かれません
大学へ　つれて来ます	大学へ　つれて来られます
夕べは　寝ませんでした　⟶	夕べは　寝られませんでした
鈴木先生には　会いません	鈴木先生には　会えません

5.1.3 Uncertainty

a. "may"

残業すれば　つかれる

ハンフリーさんは　ほんこんへ　出張しない

夕べは　勉強しすぎた

病人は　薬を　飲まなかった

この　川は　ふかい

新しい　先生は　こわい

あの　みちなら、あぶなくない

この　すきやきは　ちょっと　からかった　　かも　｜　しれません

どろぼうは　あまり　大きくなかった　　　　　　　　｜　しれない

急な　用

この　子の　ほうが　かわいそう

ジョーンズさんは　事務員

あれは　ハンフリーさんの　こえじゃない

あの　レポートは　だめだった

あの　制度は　完全じゃなかった

b. *ka doo ka*　"whether or not"

米が　取れる

社長室で　会を　ひらく

地震が　起こる

医学が　はったつしている

母が　安心した　　　　　　　　　　　　　　　わかりません

大きな　ひがいを　うけた　　　　　　　　　　　聞いてください

お金が　たりた　　　　　　　か　｜　どうか　　心配です

すごく　つかれた　　　　　　　　　　　　　　　知っていますか

畑が　つづいていた　　　　　　　　　　　　　　覚えていません

　　　　　　　　　　　　　　　　　　　　　　　教えてください

頭が　いたい

京都は　雪が　多い

せいが　低かった

つごうが　悪かった

料理が　からかった

山口さんの　英語が　じょうず			わかりません
土曜日は　ひま			聞いてください
こたえが　てき当	か	どうか	心配です
ミラーさんが　病気だった			知っていますか
てんぷらが　きらいだった			覚えていません
			教えてください

c.　~ *ka* ~ *ka*　"whether ~ or ~"

うちへ　来られる		来られない			
車が　ある		ない			
うちに　いる		外へ　出かける			
東京に　住んでいた		住んでいなかった			
かぜを　ひいた		ひかなかった			
これは　あまい		からい		わかりません
色は　赤い		赤くない		知らないんです
へやが　広い	か	せまい	か	わすれました
かばんが　新しかった		古かった		教えてください
えいがが　おもしろかった		おもしろくなかった		
制度が　完全		完全じゃない		
大きなの		小さいの		
交通が　ふべんだった		べんりだった		
安藤さんが　あの　時 　　部長だった		課長だった		

5.1.4　Decision

a.　Speaker's decision

わたしは　会社を　やめる			しますか
ぼくが　大阪へ　出張する			
友だちに　ラジオを　なおしてもらう			します
よし子さんの　りょうしんに　会う	こと	に	しました
日曜日に　動物園へ　行く			しましょう
いい　天気なら、テニスを　する			
しけんを　うける			

b. Other's decision

| .... | こと | に | なるでしょう |
| .... | | | なりました |

5.1.5 Imperative expressions

a. "do" "don't"

Vowel Verb

窓を　開ける	窓を　開けろ	窓を　開けるな
おそく　寝る	おそく　寝ろ	おそく　寝るな
着物を　着る	着物を　着ろ	着物を　着るな
早く　起きる	早く　起きろ	早く　起きるな
会に　出る	会に　出ろ	会に　出るな
気を　つける	気を　つけろ	——

Consonant Verb

うちへ　帰る	うちへ　帰れ	うちへ　帰るな
お金を　はらう	お金を　はらえ	お金を　はらうな
ここで　待つ	ここで　待て	ここで　待つな
会を　ひらく	会を　ひらけ	会を　ひらくな
ゆっくり　話す	ゆっくり　話せ	ゆっくり　話すな
課長に　頼む	課長に　頼め	課長に　頼むな
みちで　あそぶ	みちで　あそべ	みちで　あそぶな
くつを　ぬぐ	くつを　ぬげ	くつを　ぬぐな
死ぬ	死ね	死ぬな

Irregular Verb

あした　来る	あした　来い	あした　来るな
出発する	出発しろ	出発するな
安心する	安心しろ	安心するな
命令する	命令しろ	命令するな

b. "please do" "please don't"

となりの　人に　知らせて	くださいませ
しばふに　入って	ください
教室では　日本語を　使って	くれ
へやの　前で　待っていて	——

あさって　大阪へ　行って
家に　入る　時、くつを　ぬいで
あの　かんご婦に　頼んで
ほんこんへ　出張して
朝　早く　来て

くださいませ
ください
くれ
——

となりの　人に　知らせ
しばふに　入ら
教室では　日本語を　使わ
へやの　前で　待ってい
あさって　大阪へ　行か
家に　入る　時、くつを　ぬが
あの　かんご婦に　頼ま
ほんこんへ　出張し
朝　早く　来

ないで

くださいませ
ください
くれ
——

c. "please do"

お｜待ち／あがり／休み／すわり／たち／取り｜ください(ませ)

5.1.6 Honorific copular expression (promotion level)

私は	銀行員	
いもうとは	秘書	
父は	サラリーマン	です
主人も	元気	でございます
これは	わたしの　かばん 社長の　命令 おせいぼ	

山口さんは	ロバーツさんの　友だち	
こちらは	お医者さん	です
おく様は	日本語が　じょうず	でいらっしゃいます
こちらは	原さんの　おじさん	

5.1.7　Honorific verbal expression

校長先生 社長さん あの　方	は が	昼ご飯を　食べます 仕事を　やめます 手紙を　書きません 病気に　なりました わたしの　うちに　とまりました そう　言いませんでした 学生に　話しました 三時に　つきます みんなに　説明します 安心しました

校長先生 ⟶　社長さん あの　方	は が	昼ご飯を　食べられます 仕事を　やめられます 手紙を　書かれません 病気に　なられました わたしの　うちに　とまられました そう　言われませんでした 学生に　話されました 三時に　つかれます みんなに　説明されます 安心されました

5.1.8　Honorific and humble verbal expressions

a.　"do"

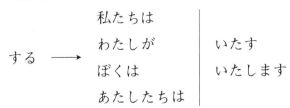

する ⟶	あなたは 先生が ご主人は お客様が	なさる なさいました

b. "be"

いる ⟶	私たちは わたしが ぼくは あたしたちは	（おる） おります

いる ⟶	あなたは 先生が ご主人は お客様が	いらっしゃる いらっしゃいます

5.2　OTHERS

5.2.1　*bakari* "only"

あの　人は　自分の　こと		話していたんです
この　辺は　田や　畑		つづいていますね
どろぼうに　お金		ぬすまれたらしいです
どうして　山田さん		出張するんですか
にく	ばかり	食べないで、やさいも　食べなさい
月曜日		忙しくて、ほかの　日は　ひまです
ひらがなで		書かないでください
家に		いないで、外で　あそびなさい

5.2.2　*made* "until one does such and such"

米を　取り入れる しけんが　終わる 病人が　元気に　なる	まで(は)	心配です 心配でした わかりません わかりませんでした

本当の　ことを　知る			心配です
先生に　言われる		まで(は)	心配でした
新聞を　読む			わかりません
台風に　おそわれる			わかりませんでした

5.2.3　"according to ～"

新聞		
ラジオ		医者の　数は　たりているらしい
テレビ	によると	今度の　台風の　ひがいは　大きかったそうです
広田さん		
父		

5.2.4　"～ through ～"

夏	秋			雨ばかり　ふりました
朝	昼	から	にかけて	ずっと　音楽を　聞いていました
この　辺	駅			みちが　こんでいます
北海道	関東			いい　天気でしょう

5.3　REVIEW DRILLS

5.3.1　Relational Checking Drill (が or を)

1. かばん、いりますか　　　　　　…… かばんが　いりますか
2. 病気、治す　　　　　　　　　　…… 病気を　治す
3. くつ、ぬれてしまいました　　　…… くつが　ぬれてしまいました
4. 畑、つづいていますね　　　　　…… 畑が　つづいていますね
5. 火山、見えますか　　　　　　　…… 火山が　見えますか
6. 台風、おそうかもしれない　　　…… 台風が　おそうかもしれない
7. ひがい、うけた　　　　　　　　…… ひがいを　うけた
8. せい、はかってください　　　　…… せいを　はかってください
9. 飛行機、出発する　　　　　　　…… 飛行機が　出発する
10. かぜ、ひいてしまいました　　　…… かぜを　ひいてしまいました
11. ラジオ、聞こえない　　　　　　…… ラジオが　聞こえない
12. お金、たりないんでしょう　　　…… お金が　たりないんでしょう

13. お金、はらってください　　　　……　お金を　はらってください
14. 地震、起こった　　　　　　　　……　地震が　起こった
15. 農業、はったつしている　　　　　……　農業が　はったつしている

5.3.2　Transformation Drill

行く　⟶　⎰ 行くかもしれません
　　　　　　行かないかもしれません
　　　　　　行くか　行かないか　わかりません
　　　　　　行くか　どうか　わかりません

1. きっぷが　いる　　　　2. つかれている　　　　3. 音楽が　聞こえる
4. 死んだ　　　　　　　　5. ほかの　会に　出られる　　6. 地震が　起こった
7. 安く　買える

5.3.3　Substitution and Transformation Drill

1. A: どう　したんですか。

   B: ぶたれたんです。

   A: だれに　ぶたれたんですか。

   B: あにに　ぶたれたんです。

   1. お金を　ぬすまれる、男　　　2. とけいを　こわされる、おとうと
   3. しゃしんを　とられる、知らない　人　　4. おべん当を　食べられる、あにか
   　　　　　　　　　　　　　　　　　　　　　　　おとうと

2. A: あした　パーティーに　出られますか。

   B: ええ、出られます。たのしみに　しているんです。

   A: そうですか。田中さんは　どうでしょう？

   B: さあ、出られるか　どうか　知りません。

   A: 聞いてみましょうか。

   B: ええ。でも、今　いないかもしれませんよ。

   1. 旅行に　行ける　　　　　　2. いっしょに　出発できる
   3. 食事に　出かけられる　　　4. あそびに　来られる
   5. 会に　出られる

3. A: どう　したんですか。

   B: 雨に　ふられてしまったんです。

   A: それは　大変でしたね。

1. どろぼうが　入る
2. 課長が　残業を　頼む
3. どろぼうが　お金を　ぬすむ
4. 雪が　ふる
5. もっと　働けと　言う

4. A: もしもし、森さんの　おたくでいらっしゃいますか。

B: はい、森でございます。

A: よし子さん　いらっしゃいますか。

B: はい、おります。どちら様でいらっしゃいますか。

A: あ、しつれいいたしました。山田でございます。

B: 山田さんでいらっしゃいますね。しょうしょう　お待ちくださいませ。

1. スミスさん、ご主人
2. 安藤さん、部長
3. 鈴木、おく様
4. 広田先生、先生

5. A: いつまで　ここに　いますか。

B: 仕事が　終わるまで　いるつもりですけど。

A: いつごろに　なりますか。

B: 九月ごろに　なるかもしれません。

1. 病気が　治る、十二月
2. 富士山が　見える、昼
3. 台風が　行ってしまう、あさって
4. 米を　取り入れる、夕方
5. 先生が　いらっしゃる、二時

5.4　REVIEW EXERCISES

5.4.1　一つの　＿＿に　一つの　ひらがなを　入れなさい。

1. 日本の　大き＿＿は　カリフォルニア＿＿＿　同じぐらいです。
2. 着がえ＿＿＿　いるので、用意しておいてくれませんか。
3. あしたの　会＿＿＿　出られますか。
4. 東京＿＿＿＿＿　この　辺＿＿＿かけて　家＿＿＿　つづいています。
5. 出発する＿＿＿＿＿は　ここで　待っていてください。
6. 雪＿＿＿　ふられて、すっかり　ぬれてしまった。
7. 新聞＿＿＿よると、このごろ　富士山＿＿＿　よく　見えるらしい。
8. コーヒー＿＿＿＿＿＿＿＿　飲まないでください。
9. 今度＿＿＿＿＿＿　がんばります。
10. 一週間＿＿＿　二回　病院に　かよっているんです。

5.4.2 Tell whether the underlined Verb shows potential (po), passive (pa), or honorific (h).

1.　先生は　きっぷを　買われましたか。

2.　いい　物が　買えましたか。

3.　山田さんは　アメリカに　来られて　うれしいと　言った。

4.　夜　おそく　友だちに　来られて、こまってしまいました。

5.　お父様は　いつ　来られましたか。

6.　大きい　さかなは　ねこに　食べられてしまいました。

7.　先生は　もう　ご飯を　食べられましたか。

8.　この　さかなは　見たことが　ないけど、食べられるの？

9.　この　問題は　長い　間　研究(けんきゅう)されている。

10.　しつれいですが、何を　研究(けんきゅう)されましたか。

5.4.3 Select the appropriate word for each of the blanks.

1.　先生は　（　　　　　　　）か。

　　〈います、おります、いらっしゃいます〉

2.　「あの　方は？」「父（　　　　　　　）。」

　　〈でございます、でいらっしゃいます〉

3.　「かずおちゃんは　よく　勉強しますね。」「ええ、勉強（　　　　　　　）

　　して、あまり　あそばないんです。」

　　〈だけ、ばかり〉

4.　今度　会社の　命令(めいれい)で　オーストラリアへ　出張(しゅっちょう)する（　　　　　　　）。

　　出張(しゅっちょう)が　かなり　長いので、家族も　つれて行く（　　　　　　　）。

　　〈ことに　した、ことに　なった〉

5.　おく様は　どんな　物を　用意(い)（　　　　　　　）か。

　　〈なさいました、いたしました、しました〉

6.　「夕べ　十二時まで　起きていました。」「（　　　　　　　）ですねえ。

　　いつも　そんなに　（　　　　　　　）まで　起きているんですか。」

　　「いつもは　もっと　（　　　　　　　）んですよ。父に　いつも

　　（　　　　　　　）寝ろと　言われていますから。」

　　〈はやく、はやい、おそく、おそい〉

7.　えいがは　何時から　（　　　　　　　）か。

　　〈見えます、見られます〉

8. ことしは　みかんや　やさいが　たくさん（　　　　　　　　）、

　　うれしいですね。

　　　〈取って、取られて、取れて〉

5.4.4 Combine each pair of sentences given below as shown in the example.

　　Example: どろぼうが　入りました、大変でした。　──→　どろぼうに　入られて、

　　　　　　　　　　　　　　　　　　　　　　　　　　　　　　大変でした。

　　1. 雨が　ザーザー　ふりました、大変でした。

　　2. 秘書が　休みました、こまりました。

　　3. 社長が　新しい　仕事を　命令しました、忙しくなりました。

　　4. へたな　かんご婦が　注射を　しました、いたかったです。

　　5. りょうしんが　死にました、かわいそうでした。

　　6. 大きな　いぬが　おそいました、あぶなかったです。

　　7. どろぼうが　おさいふを　持って行きました、こまりました。

　　8. 夜　急に　友だちが　来ました、勉強が　できなかったんです。

5.4.5 ことに　しましたか　ことに　なりましたを　入れて、いみを　言いなさい。

　　1. 勉強が　忙しいので、アルバイトを　やめる＿＿＿＿＿＿＿＿＿＿＿＿＿。

　　2. 今度　会社の　命令で、イギリスへ　出張する＿＿＿＿＿＿＿＿＿＿＿＿。

　　3. この　家は　古くて　あぶないので、新しく　たてる＿＿＿＿＿＿＿＿＿

　　　　＿＿＿＿＿。

　　4. きのう　休んだので、きょう　しけんを　うける＿＿＿＿＿＿＿＿＿＿＿。

　　5. わたしは　つかれすぎだと　思ったので、二、三日　うちに　いる＿＿＿＿＿

　　　　＿＿＿＿＿＿＿。

5.4.6 Humble か honorific の　表現に　しなさい。

　　1. 私は　学生です。

　　2. あの　方は　社長です。

　　3. 「電話を　しましたか。」「いいえ、しませんでした。」

　　4. 「おく様は　いますか。」「はい、います。お待ちください。」

　　5. 「しつれいですが、広田さんですね。」「はい、広田ですが…」

5.4.7 読みなさい。

　　おとといから　頭が　いたいので、けさ　うちの　近くの　広田医院へ　行き
ました。かんご婦に　熱を　はかってもらいましたが、八度一分も　ありました。

広田先生は　たぶん　かぜを　ひいたんだろうと　言われました。そして、注射して
くださいました。広田先生は　わたしに　すぐ　家へ　帰って　寝なさいと　言って、
薬を　くださいました。このごろ　仕事が　忙しくて、あまり　寝ていないので、
きょうは　一日　ゆっくり　寝ることに　しました。熱は　低くなるかも
しれませんが、会社に　出られるか　どうか　心配です。　もっと
自分の　ことに　気を　つけなければならないと　思いました。

5.5　MIKE HARRISON SERIES (4)
——マイク・ハリソン、取引先へ　行く——

5.5.1　——朝九時すぎ、会社で——

部長　　　「ハリソンさん、ちょっと。」

ハリソン　「はい、何でしょうか。」

部長　　　「君も　だいぶ　仕事に　なれたと　思うので、きょうは　大石君と　いっしょに
　　　　　　取引先を　まわってみませんか。」

ハリソン　「はい。」

部長　　　「書類は　大石君が　持って行くことに　なっているんだけど、行く　前に
　　　　　　いろいろ　打ち合わせてください。」

ハリソン　「はい、そう　します。」

5.5.2　——ハリソン、大石の　所へ　行く——

ハリソン　「大石さん、部長に　取引先へ　つれて行ってもらえと　言われました。よろしく
　　　　　　おねがいします。」

大石　　　「いや、こちらこそ。部長から　わたされたのは　カタログと　資料なんだけど、
　　　　　　見てから　行きますか。」

ハリソン　「読めれば　読んでおきたいです。出かけるまで　時間が　ありますか。」

大石　　　「一時ごろ　出かけることに　しましょう。その　前に　やっておきたい　ことが
　　　　　　あるので。そうそう、いっしょに　昼ご飯を　食べながら　打ち合わせませんか。
　　　　　　わからない　ところが　あれば、その　時　聞いてください。」

ハリソン　「ええ、どうも。じゃあ、後で。」

5.5.3　——取引先の　会社の　受付で——

大石　　　「(名刺を　出しながら)　あの、こういう　ものですが、営業の　青木さんと
　　　　　　一時半に　お会いする　やくそくが　あるのですが…」

受付　　　「東京工業の　大石様でいらっしゃいますね。しょうしょう　お待ちくださいませ。
　　　　　　…（電話で）営業の　青木さん　おねがいします。…こちら　一階の
　　　　　　受付ですが、東京工業の　大石様が　いらっしゃってます。…はい、わかりました。
　　　　　　…お待たせいたしました。そちらの　エレベーターで　五階まで　お上がり
　　　　　　ください。」

5.5.4　　——5階で——

青木　　　「やあ、先日は　どうも。こちらへ　どうぞ。」
大石　　　「しつれいします。青木さん、こちらは　今　アメリカの　方から　研修に
　　　　　　来ている　マイク・ハリソンさんです。きょうは　いっしょに
　　　　　　来てもらいました。」
ハリソン　「はじめまして。ハリソンと　もうします。」
青木　　　「やあ、どうも。どうぞ　おかけください。」
大石　　　「では。…　あつくなりましたね。」
青木　　　「夏は　いやですね。お忙しいですか。」
大石　　　「忙しいばかりで、どうも。おたくは？」
青木　　　「まあまあですね。しかし、おたくの　物　きょ年よりは　よく　売れていますよ。」
大石　　　「きょうは　もっと　くわしい　資料を　お持ちしました。
　　　　　　どうぞ　ごらんください。それから、新しい　カタログも　持ってまいり
　　　　　　ましたので、後で　ご説明いたします。」

5.5.5　　——会社に　もどって——

ハリソン　「部長、行ってまいりました。」
部長　　　「ごくろうさん。どうでしたか。　後で　大石君から　報告を　うけると
　　　　　　思うけど。」
ハリソン　「むこうの　会社の　ようすが　わかって、いい　勉強に　なりました。」
部長　　　「そうですか。」
ハリソン　「それに、日本の　商談の　やり方も…　」
部長　　　「勉強に　なった？」
ハリソン　「ええ。」
部長　　　「じゃあ、また　機会が　あったら、大石君と　いっしょに　行ってください。
　　　　　　今度は　出張も　頼もうか。」
ハリソン　「はい、ぜひ。」

5.5.6 New Vocabulary (for passive learning)

1. 〜に なれる   ni nareru   ......   get accustomed to

　　取引先   torihikisaki   ......   customer; client

　　まわる   mawaru   ......   visit several places

　　書類   shorui   ......   documents; papers

　　打ち合わせる   uchiawaseru   ......   talk and arrange previously

2. わたす   watasu   ......   hand

　　カタログ   katarogu   ......   catalog

　　資料   shiryoo   ......   materials; data

3. 受付   uketsuke   ......   receptionist

　　名刺   meishi   ......   visiting card; namecard

　　もの   -mono   ......   person

　　営業   eigyoo   ......   business (section); trade (section)

　　やくそく   yakusoku   ......   appointment

　　工業   koogyoo   ......   industry

　　エレベーター   erebeetaa   ......   elevator

　　上がる   agaru   ......   go up

4. 先日   sen'jitsu   ......   the other day

　　研修   ken'shuu   ......   training

　　〜と もうします   to mooshimasu   ......   is named; is called (humble)

　　かける   kakeru   ......   take a seat; sit down on a chair

　　おたく   otaku   ......   your company

　　まあまあ   maamaa   ......   so-so

　　売れる   ureru   ......   sell (intransitive Verb)

　　ごらんください   goran kudasai   ......   please look at it (honorific)

5. もどる   modoru   ......   turn back; return

　　報告   hookoku   ......   report

　　ようす   yoosu   ......   look; air; what is going on

　　商談   shoodan   ......   business talk

　　機会   kikai   ......   chance

　　今度   kon'do   ......   this time; next time

LESSON 6
祭り[1]

6.1 PRESENTATION

　日本人の　宗教には　仏教と　神道が　ある。　そして、　これら[2]は　日本人の　生活と　かなり　深い　関係を　持っており[3]、　今でも　いろいろな　行事として　のこっている。　特に、　神道の　祭りは　楽しく[4]、　子どもの　ころの　なつかしい　思い出の　一つである。

6.2 DIALOG

―― 道で ――

ジョーンズ 「さっきから　にぎやかな　音楽や　声が　聞こえるし[5]、　人が　おおぜい　行ったり[6]　来たり[6]　しているし[5]、　何が　あるのかしら[7]。」

島田　　　「お祭りですよ。　急がないから、　ちょっと　行ってみましょうか。」

ジョーンズ 「お祭りですか。　おもしろそう[8]ですね。…あ、　あれは？」

島田　　　「おみこしです。　こっちへ　来そう[8]だから、　この　辺で　待ってましょう。　…あ、　来た、　来た[9]。」

ジョーンズ 「かざりが　いっぱい　ついていて、　重そう[8]ですね。　重さは　どのくらい　あるのかしら。」

島田　　　「よく　知らないけど、　千キロ[10]ぐらいかな[7]。」

ジョーンズ 「みんな　同じ　着物を　着てるんですね。」

島田　　　「ああ、　はっぴですね。　最近は　そろいの　はっぴを　着たり、　りっぱな　おみこしを　作ったりして、　ずいぶん　さかんに　なりましたね。」

ジョーンズ 「前は　ちがったんですか。」

島田　　　「ええ、　交通の　じゃまに　なると　言って、　おみこしも　ないし、　さびしい　お祭りを　した　時も　あったんですよ。」

仏教	神道	生活	深い	特に	楽しく
道	声	重そう	重さ	同じ	最近
交通					

6.3   PATTERN SENTENCES

6.3.1

N	R
Korera	wa

→

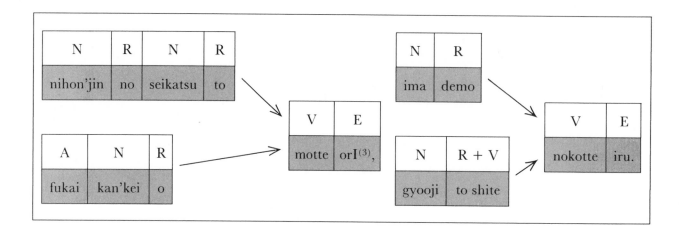

N	R	N	R
nihon'jin	no	seikatsu	to

A	N	R
fukai	kan'kei	o

V	E
motte	orI[3],

N	R
ima	demo

N	R + V
gyooji	to shite

V	E
nokotte	iru.

6.3.2

N	R
Matsuri	wa

→

A
tanoshiKU[4],

A	N	R	N	C + E
natsukashii	omoide	no	hitotsu	de aru.

6.3.3

NM	N	R
Nigiyaka na	koe	ga

→

V	Rc
kikoeru	SHI[5],

N	R
hito	ga

Adv.
oozei

V
iru.

6.3.4

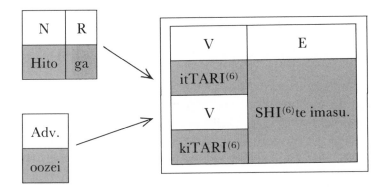

N	R
Hito	ga

Adv.
oozei

V	E
itTARI[6]	
V	SHI[6]te imasu.
kiTARI[6]	

6.3.5

A	Nd	C	SP
Omoshiro	SOO[8]	DESU[8]	ne.

6.4 NOTES

6.4.1 Many popular festivals (*matsuri*) originated with the rise of the *choonin*, or townspeople, during the Tokugawa era. Festivals and rites that originally were only found in the imperial court and that only the nobles and warriors were able to observe began to spread among and be modified to suit the tastes of the commoners and townspeople.

In recent years, beginning with the Meiji era, many traditional Japanese events have become less popular. Although Western countries have contributed celebrations such as Christmas and birthdays that have been widely adopted in Japan, *matsuri* are still quite popular. *Matsuri* provide pleasure and amusement as well as recreation, distraction, and entertainment.

In their attitudes toward pleasure, there are striking differences between the older and younger generations in Japan and clear contrasts between traditional Japanese and American cultures. According to the American Puritan ethic, pleasurable things—especially sex—are regarded as sinful. This sin-oriented morality has caused the development of a strong guilt consciousness in America. The Japanese, however, are more concerned with shame than with sin, in the sense that the social code and social conduct are scrutinized to a greater degree by the group rather than by a god or the individual's conscience. Furthermore, the Japanese people are generally less concerned with things supernatural and focus more on secular matters. They have always considered sex, for instance, to be a natural function, without any association with moral guilt. One manifestation of this attitude is mixed bathing, which was freely practiced in Japan until relatively recently.

A sense of shame, rather than one of guilt stemming from personal sin, comes into play when the conduct of a Japanese violates the best interests of the group to which he or she belongs. If such interests are not violated then there are no inhibitions checking the individual's behavior. In general, then, we may say that the Japanese view toward nature is one of naturalness: their approach to the world is largely secular, and their sense of morality is more one of shame than of sin.

The differences between Japanese and American moralities may be partially explained by the concepts "group heritage" and "group agreement," two methods whereby morality comes to be internalized by the members of a society. In the traditional Japanese context, "group heritage" is the dominant factor. It means that a tradition has been given and is accepted as such, that it is socially inherited. Participation in the celebration of *matsuri* is one of the "group heritage" activities. In such a society the individual ego is not fully developed. Rather, the ego is merely part of the greater societal chain, of the established tradition. Since the self is not emancipated but only passively receives what is handed down, the attempt to change what is established is difficult.

"Group agreement," on the other hand, is analogous to the social contract, and comes about through the decisions of the individual members of a society to participate in what is being established. Since such agreement is based on the ego it implies that the self is emancipated and, at least originally, that individuals chose the standards according to which they would live, that the individuals agreed to surrender part of their freedom for the sake of a majority behavior. Consequently, attempts to change what has been established in such a way would be much easier.

The traditional Japanese still lack individualism and the emancipation of the self, which would appear to be prerequisite to changing the established moral order. The Japanese youth, however, tend to be more individualistic while, at the present time, Americans display a marked lack of agreement, and the contemporary American situation may be interpreted as the search for a new consensus, for new standards upon which the majority can agree.

6.4.2 *Korera* means "these." *Korera, sorera,* and *arera* are the plural forms of the words *kore, sore,* and *are* with the plural suffix *-ra* attached to them. *Korera, sorera,* and *arera* are generally used for inanimate objects. *Arera* is seldom used however. "They" that refers to people is *karera,* which is the plural form of *kare* "he." The plural forms occur more frequently in formal speech or in writing than in conversation.

kore	"this thing"	⟶	korera	"these things"
sore	"that thing"	⟶	sorera	"those things"
are	"that thing"	⟶	arera	"those things"
kare	"he"	⟶	karera	"they" (generally male)

When it is necessary to use "these" and "those" adjectivally, *korera, sorera,* and *arera* may be followed by the Relational *no.*

Korera no mon'dai ni tsuite hanashite kudasai.	"Please talk about these problems."
Karera wa nihon'jin ja nai ka mo shiremasen ne.	"They may not be Japanese, don't you think?"
Karera no kan'gaekata wa chotto okashii to omoimasu.	"I think that their way of thinking is a little strange."

6.4.3 *Ori(masu)* or *oru* after the TE form of a Verb is an Extender. The Extender *oru* is used as a formal and humble equivalent of *iru.* *Oru* after the TE form of a Verb may be used to refer to the speaker's or writer's (or his in-group's) action or state. *Oru* is seldom used to refer to someone else's action or state. *Irassharu* is used instead.

TE form of Verb + *iru* ⟶ TE form of Verb + *oru*

Hitobito no seikatsu to fukai kan'kei o motte *imasu.*
⟶ Hitobito no seikatsu to fukai kan'kei o motte *orimasu.*
"It has a deep relationship with the people's life."

Compare:

Moshi moshi, Yoshiko san irasshaimasu ka?	"Hello, is Yoshiko there?" (Yoshiko is not part of the speaker's in-group.)
Moshi moshi, Yoshiko orimasu ka?	"Hello, is Yoshiko there?" (Yoshiko is a member of the speaker's family.)
Anata wa ima dono daigaku e itte irasshaimasu ka?	"Which university are you attending now?"
Oregon Daigaku ni itte orimasu.	"I am attending the University of Oregon."

Fukai kan'kei o motte ori means "(something or someone) has a deep relationship with ..." A nonfinal Predicate may be ended in the Stem form of a Verb or an Extender that is originated from a Verb. The function of this clause is the same as that of the nonfinal Predicate ending in the TE form—sequential, parallel, or causal functions. (See Note 8.4.3, Vol. III.) The use of the Stem form is more common in general statements, or in the audience type of style, while the use of the TE form is more common in colloquial spoken Japanese. (See Note 1.3.1B, Vol. III.)

(Predicate Modifier) + Stem form of $\begin{cases} \textbf{Verb, ...} \\ \textbf{verbal Extender, ...} \end{cases}$

Hito ga fue, kuruma mo fueta.	"The population has increased and automobiles have too."
Nihon'jin no shuukyoo wa fukuzatsu de ari, nakanaka kan'tan ni hanasenai.	"The Japanese people's religion is complicated, and it is hard to talk about it briefly."
Chichi wa ima kaisha no juuyaku o shite ori, mainichi isogashii.	"My father is now a top executive of a company, and is busy every day."

6.4.4   *Shin'too no matsuri wa tanoshiku,...* means "a Shinto festival is joyful, and ..." The KU form of the Adjective may be used as a nonfinal Predicate in the same functions as those of the TE form of an Adjective before a pause—parallel or causal. (See Note 8.4.11, Vol. III.) The use of the KU form of an Adjective before a pause is more common in general statements or in the audience type of style, while the TE form of an Adjective is commonly used in colloquial spoken Japanese.

(Predicate Modifier) + KU form of Adjective,...

Hon'kon wa semaku, jin'koo ga ooi.	"Hong Kong is small and has a large population."
Kono kawa wa fukaku, abunai.	"This river is deep and dangerous."
Kare wa wakaku, watashi wa wakakunai.	"He is young and I am not."
Kono shima wa yama ga ooku, hatake ga sukunai node, kome ya yasai ga amari torenai.	"Since this island is mountainous and has few cultivated fields, rice and vegetables are not produced much."

6.4.5 *Nigiyaka na on'gaku ya koe ga kikoeru shi, hito ga* ... means "I can hear lively music and voices; what's more, people are ..." The *shi* after a nonfinal Predicate is a clause Relational and may be used to emphasize parallel descriptions "one does (or is) such and such; what's more, one does (or is) such and such," "something is (or does) such and such. In addition to it, something else is (or does) such and such," and so on. Sometimes the nonfinal clause followed by *shi* is a reason or a cause of the following final clause. Like Relationals such as *kara* "because," *keredomo* "although," either normal forms or plain forms of a Verb, an Adjective, and the Copula may precede *shi*. The nonfinal clause ~ *shi* may occur more than once: ~ *shi* ~ *shi*.

Predicate Modifier + Predicate + *shi*,...

Kono mado kara wa umi mo mieru shi, yama mo miemasu.	"You can see the ocean as well as mountains through this window."
Yamaguchi san wa atama ga ii shi, un'doo mo yoku dekimasu.	"Mr. Yamaguchi is smart and can play sports well."
Hikooki no kippu mo katta shi, kaban mo motta shi, sugu dekakeraremasu yo.	"I have bought a flight ticket and I have a bag with me; I can leave right away."
Okane wa nai shi, ame wa furu shi, asobi ni iku no o yamemashita.	"I gave up going out to have a good time as I had no money, and, what's more, it was raining."
Kono hen wa shizuka da shi, kootsuu ga ben'ri da shi, sumu no ni choodo ii tokoro desu ne.	"This area is quiet and, what's more, transportation is convenient; this is just the right place to live."

6.4.6 *Hito ga oozei ittari kitari shite imasu* means "Many people are coming and going." *Ittari* and *kitari* are the TARI forms of *iku* "go" and *kuru* "come" respectively. The TARI forms of a Verb, an Adjective, and the Copula are formulated like the TA forms of them except for replacing *-ta* by *-tari*. (See Note 8.4.4 of Vol. II as to the formulation of the TA form of a Verb.)

Verb

1.   Vowel Verb ..... add *-ri* to the TA form

taberu	⟶	tabeta	⟶	tabetari
miru	⟶	mita	⟶	mitari
deru	⟶	deta	⟶	detari
dekiru	⟶	dekita	⟶	dekitari
ireru	⟶	ireta	⟶	iretari

2.   Consonant Verb ..... add *-ri* to the TA form

utau "sing"	⟶	utatta	⟶	utattari
kaku	⟶	kaita	⟶	kaitari
tanoshimu "enjoy"	⟶	tanoshin'da	⟶	tanoshin'dari
butsu	⟶	butta	⟶	buttari
kowasu	⟶	kowashita	⟶	kowashitari
toru	⟶	totta	⟶	tottari
yobu	⟶	yon'da	⟶	yon'dari
isogu	⟶	isoida	⟶	isoidari
shinu	⟶	shin'da	⟶	shin'dari

3.   Irregular Verb ..... add *-ri* to the TA form

suru   ⟶   shita   ⟶   shitari
kuru   ⟶   kita   ⟶   kitari

Adjective ..... add *-ri* to the TA form

sabishii "is lonely"	&longrightarrow;	sabishikatta	&longrightarrow;	sabishikattari
atsui	&longrightarrow;	atsukatta	&longrightarrow;	atsukattari
fukai "is deep"	&longrightarrow;	fukakatta	&longrightarrow;	fukakattari
yoi	&longrightarrow;	yokatta	&longrightarrow;	yokattari
omoi "is heavy"	&longrightarrow;	omokatta	&longrightarrow;	omokattari
karui "is light"	&longrightarrow;	karukatta	&longrightarrow;	karukattari

Copula ..... add *-ri* to the TA form

da   ⟶   datta   ⟶   dattari

The TARI form occurs most commonly in pairs, followed by the Extender *suru* "do," namely, ~ *-tari* ~ *-tari suru*. However, only one TARI form may occur before *suru* (or *dekiru*), or ~ *-tari* ~ *-tari* may be followed by *desu* instead of *suru*.

TARI form + (TARI form) + (TARI form) + $\begin{cases} \textbf{\textit{suru}} \\ \textbf{\textit{dekiru}} \textbf{ (the potential of \textit{suru})} \\ \textbf{\textit{da}} \end{cases}$

The above combinations have the following connotations:

1.   Typical actions; the speaker picks up only some facts from among many other things: "one does such things as A and B."

Nichiyoo ni watakushi wa hon o yon'dari, terebi o mitari, hirune o shitari shimasu.	"On Sundays I read books, watch television, take a nap, and the like."
Paatii de utattari odottari shita n desu ka?	"Did you do such things as singing and dancing at the party?"

2.   Repeated or alternating actions or states: "one keeps doing or being A and B" or "one does or is sometimes A and sometimes B."

Kare wa koohii o non'dari pan o tabetari shite imasu.	"He has been drinking coffee or eating bread."
Shiken wa muzukashikattari yasashikattari desu.	"Examinations are sometimes difficult and sometimes easy."
Kono mise no pan wa hachijuuen dattari hyakuen dattari shimasu.	"This store sells bread sometimes at the price of eighty yen and sometimes one hundred yen."

3.   Different actions performed or states experienced by members of a group: "some people do or are A while others do or are B."

Tomodachi no naka ni wa, byooki ni nattari, shin'dari shita hito ga imasu.	"Among friends of mine, there are some who got sick and some who died."
Hitobito ga ittari kitari shite imasu.	"There are some people going and some coming."

Mainichi kaisha de tegami o kaitari, den'wa o kaketari, kai ni detari, hito ni attari, iroiro na koto o shite imasu.	"I am doing various things at the company every day: writing letters, making phone calls, attending meetings, meeting people, and the like."
Kinoo wa ichinichijuu netari okitari deshita.	"He was in and out of bed all day yesterday."
Anata wa sake o non'dari shimasu ka?	"Do you do such things as drinking *sake?*"

Predicate Modifiers such as *toki ni yotte* "depending upon the time," *basho ni yotte* "depending upon the place," *hito ni yotte* "depending upon the person," and the like may occur in the ~ *-tari* ~ *-tari* sentence.

Boku no kaban wa hi ni yotte omokattari karukattari shimasu.	"My bag is heavy or light depending upon the day."
Hito ni yotte happi o kitari yukata o kitari shite imasu.	"Some people wear a happy coat and some wear summer kimono."

6.4.7 *Nani ga aru no kashira?* means "I wonder what is (going on) there" and *(Omosa wa) sen'kiro gurai kana?*, "I wonder if it weighs roughly one thousand kilograms." *Kashira* and *kana* at the end of a sentence are Sentence Particles used when one is asking oneself a question. These Sentence Particles normally occur after the Predicate of plain forms, except *da*, which is always deleted.

Kono heya no hirosa wa dono gurai kana?	"I wonder how large this room is."
Nakajima san kuru kana?	"I wonder if Miss Nakajima is coming."
Ano hen wa michi ga motto kon'de iru kana?	"I wonder if streets are much more crowded in that area."

6.4.8 *Omoshirosoo desu ne* means "It looks interesting" or "It appears to be interesting." *Omoshirosoo* is the combination of *omoshiro*, the Base form of the Adjective *omoshiroi* "is interesting" and the adjectival dependent Noun *-soo*. When *-soo* follows the Base form of an Adjective or an adjectival Noun or Stem form of a Verb, it means 'it looks as if something is going to happen." Both *-rashii* (see Note 6.4.7, Vol. III) and *-soo* carry the connotation "guess," but *-rashii* is used for the guess made by rather objective observation or information while *-soo* is based upon the appearance of a thing or an action. Note also, that the *soo* "hearsay" after the plain forms should not be confused with the *-soo* "look." (See Note 2.4.14, Vol. III.) Since *-soo* is an adjectival Noun, it behaves as other adjectival Nouns do: it is followed by *da, datta, de wa nai, na, ni,* and so on.

Stem form of Verb **Base form of Adjective*** } + *-soo* +	*da; datta* *desu; deshita* *na* + **Noun** *ni* + **Predicate**
adjectival Noun	

*The only exception is *yosasoo* for the Adjective *yoi* or *ii*.

ame ga furisoo da	"it looks as if it's going to rain"
kare wa kisoo desu	"he seems to be coming"
sabishisoo desu nee	"you look lonely"
oishisoo na niku	"meat that looks good"

ten'ki ga yosasoo da	"the weather seems nice"
himasoo desu nee	"you look as if you are not busy at all"
shin'setsusoo na hito	"a man who looks kind"

Ureshisoo desu nee. Doo shita n desu ka?	"You look happy. What happened?"
Ashita wa atatakaku narisoo desu yo.	"It appears to be getting warm tomorrow."
Zuibun isogashisoo ni hataraite imasu ne.	"How busily they are working!"

6.4.9 *A, kita, kita!* means "Ah! It came!" Although *A, kimashita!* can be used, the plain form *kita* is more appropriate for an exclamatory utterance. This brief form better conveys the speaker's feeling.

| Basu osoi desu ne! A, kita! | "The bus has not come yet. Ah! it came!" |
| A, wakatta! | "Ah! Now I know!" |

6.4.10 The *-kiro* is a shortened form of *-kiroguramu* "kilogram" in this case. It may be *-kiromeetoru* "kilometer" depending upon the context. The Japanese measuring system is different from the American's. Study the following:

	Nihon			Amerika		
nagasa	-kiro(meetoru)	"kilometer"		-mairu	"mile"	
	-meetoru	"meter"		-fiito	"feet"	(Even "one foot" is said
	-sen'chi	"centimeter"		-in'chi	"inch"	*ichifiito*.)
omosa	-kiro(guramu)	"kilogram"		-pon'do	"pound"	
	-guramu	"gram"				

| Anata wa nan'pon'do arimasu ka? | "How many pounds do you weigh?" |
| Boku (no sei) wa hyaku hachijissen'chi desu. | "I am a hundred and eighty centimeters in height." |

1 mile = 1.6093 kilometers   1 foot = 0.305 meters

1 pound = 0.453 kilograms   1 inch = 2.54 centimeters

6.5 VOCABULARY

Presentation

祭り	matsuri	......	N	festival
宗教	shuukyoo	......	N	religion
仏教	bukkyoo	......	N	Buddhism
神道	shin'too	......	N	Shinto
これら	korera	......	N	these (see 6.4.2)
おり	ori	......	E	Stem form of *orimasu → oru* (see 6.4.3)
行事	gyooji	......	N	event

ころ	-koro	......	Nd	(approximate) time
なつかしい	natsukashii	......	A	is dear (loving recollection or memory)
思い出	omoide	......	N	memory

Dialog

し	shi	......	Rc	what's more; in addition (see 6.4.5)
行ったり	ittari	......	V	TARI form of *iku* – go (see 6.4.6)
来たり	kitari	......	V	TARI form of *kuru* – come
して	shite	......	E	used after the TARI form (see 6.4.6)
かしら	kashira	......	SP	I wonder (if) ... (see 6.4.7)
島田	Shimada	......	N	family name
おもしろ	omoshiro	......	A	Base form of *omoshiroi* – is interesting
そう	-soo	......	Nd	look (like); appear; sound (see 6.4.8)
おみこし	omikoshi	......	N	portable shrine
かざり	kazari	......	N	decoration
いっぱい	ippai	......	Adv.	a lot; full
ついて	tsuite	......	V	TE form of *tsuku* – is attached
重	omo	......	A	Base form of *omoi* – is heavy; is serious
重さ	omosa	......	N	weight
キロ（グラム）	kiro(guramu)	......	Nd	kilogram (see 6.4.10)
かな	kana	......	SP	I wonder (if) ... (see 6.4.7)
はっぴ	happi	......	N	"happy" coat
そろい	soroi	......	N	the same; uniform
着たり	kitari	......	V	TARI form of *kiru* – wear
作ったり	tsukuttari	......	V	TARI form of *tsukuru* – make
さびしい	sabishii	......	A	is lonely; is lonesome; is deserted; is sad

Notes

それら	sorera	......	N	those things (see 6.4.2)
あれら	arera	......	N	those things
かれら	karera	......	N	they (people) (usually male)
かれ	kare	......	N	he
であり	de ari	......	C + E	Stem form of *de aru* (see 6.4.3)
楽しむ	tanoshimu	......	V	enjoy

かるい	karui	......	A	is light
だったり	dattari	......	C	TARI form of *da* (see 6.4.6)
うたう	utau	......	V	sing
おどる	odoru	......	V	dance
フィート	-fiito	......	Nd	feet; foot (see 6.4.10)
インチ	-in'chi	......	Nd	inch
グラム	-guramu	......	Nd	gram
ポンド	-pon'do	......	Nd	pound

Drills

キリスト教	kirisutokyoo	......	N	Christianity
教会	kyookai	......	N	church

6.6　KAN'JI

6.6.1 仏　(1) BUTSU [BUT-]　(2) Buddha　(3) classifier 亻

(4) [亻][化][仏]　(5) 大仏、仏教

6.6.2 神　(1) SHIN [-JIN]　(2) god　(3) classifier 礻 [divinity]

(4) [丶][ラ][ネ][ネ][神][神]　(5) 神社<ruby>神社<rt>じんじゃ</rt></ruby>、神話 [myth]、神道<ruby>道<rt>とう</rt></ruby> [Shinto]

(6) homonym 申、紳

6.6.3 活　(1) KATSU　(2) live　(3) classifier 氵　(4) [氵][汧][活]

(5) 生活、活動 [activity]

6.6.4 深　(1) *fuka(i)*　(2) deep　(3) classifier 氵　(4) [氵][氵][氵][深]

(5) 深い、深<ruby>川<rt>がわ</rt></ruby>川

6.6.5 特　(1) TOKU [TOK-]　(2) special　(3) classifier 牜 [a picture

of a head of an ox seen from the rear]

(4) [ト][牜][牜][特]　(5) 特に、特<ruby>急<rt>とっ</rt></ruby>急

6.6.a ^{4.6.12} 楽　(1) *tano(shii)*　(2) pleasant

(5) 楽しかった、楽しむ、楽しみにしています

6.6.6 道　(1) *michi*　(2) road　(3) classifier 辶

(4) [丷][丷][丷][首][首][渞][道]　(5) 近道 [short cut]、<ruby>道<rt>ちか</rt></ruby>道が悪い

6.6.7 声 (1) *koe* (2) voice (3) classifier 士 (4) 士 吉 吉 吉 声

(5) とりの声、犬の声、人の声

6.6.8 重 (1) *omo(i)* (2) heavy (3) classifier ノ（里）

(4) ノ 二 斤 旨 重 重 (5) 重いかばん、重さ

6.6.9 同 (1) *ona(ji)* (2) same (3) classifier 冂（口）

(4) 丨 冂 冋 同 (5) 同じ考え、これと同じのをください

(6) homonym DOO 洞、胴、銅

6.6.10 最 (1) SAI (2) the most (3) classifier 日

(4) 日 旦 早 最 最 最 (5) 最後、最大、最低[てい]、最高、最長

6.6.b 近 (1) KIN   2.6.6, Vol. III   (5) 最近、近所[じょ][neighborhood]、近年[recent years]

6.6.11 交 (1) KOO (2) mix; cross; association (3) classifier 亠

(4) 亠 交 (5) 交通、交番[police box]、交際[さい][association]

(6) homonym 交、郊、校、効

6.6.12 通 (1) TSUU (2) way; like; pass; street (3) classifier 辶

(4) フ マ 丮 丮 甬 涌 通 通 (5) 普[ふ]通、交通

6.6.13 元* (1) GEN (2) origin (3) classifier 二（ノL[legs of a man]）

(4) 二 テ 元 (5) 元気

6.7   DRILLS

6.7.1   Transformation Drill

1. にぎやかな 音楽が 聞こえます。   } ⟶   にぎやかな 音楽が 聞こえるし、人が
   人が おおぜい あるいています。   おおぜい あるいています。

2. おみこしも ないです。   } ⟶   おみこしも ないし、はっぴも
   はっぴも 着ません。   着ません。

3. 大川さんは 英語が 話せます。   } ⟶   大川さんは 英語が 話せるし、
   ドイツ語も じょうずです。   ドイツ語も じょうずです。

4. きのうの しけんは 長かったです。   } ⟶   きのうの しけんは 長かったし、
   きのうの しけんは むずかしかった   むずかしかったです。
   です。

5. 村の　道は　さびしいです。
   村の　道は　くらいです。　　　　→　村の　道は　さびしいし、くらいし、
   夜は　あぶないそうです。　　　　　　　　夜は　あぶないそうです。

6. かれの　家は　ここから　とおいです。　　かれの　家は　ここから　とおいし、
   タクシーも　ありません。　　　　→　　タクシーも　ないし、行きたくない
   行きたくないです。　　　　　　　　　　です。

7. あの　旅館は　しずかです。　　　　　あの　旅館は　しずかだし、
   あの　旅館は　日本的です。　　→　　日本的だし、とても　いいです。
   とても　いいです。

8. カリフォルニアは　食料が
   ゆたかです。　　　　　　　　　カリフォルニアは　食料が　ゆたかだし、
   冬も　あたたかいです。　　　→　　冬も　あたたかいし、住みやすいです。
   住みやすいです。

9. この　かばんは　重いです。
   この　かばんは　大きいです。　→　この　かばんは　重いし、大きいし、
   持ちにくいです。　　　　　　　　　　持ちにくいです。

10. 日本人の　宗教には　仏教が
    あります。　　　　　　　　　　日本人の　宗教には　仏教が　あるし、
    神道も　あります。　　　　→　　神道も　あるし、ふくざつです。
    ふくざつです。

6.7.2　Transformation Drill

1. ポール君が　見た　えいがは　　　→　ポール君が　見た　えいがは
   <u>おもしろいです</u>。　　　　　　　　　<u>おもしろそうです</u>。

2. 最近の　ジョーンズさんは　とても　→　最近の　ジョーンズさんは　とても
   さびしいです。　　　　　　　　　　　さびしそうです。

3. お祭りに　来た　人は　楽しいです。　→　お祭りに　来た　人は　楽しそうです。

4. この　くつは　新しくて、きついです。　→　この　くつは　新しくて、きつそうです。

5. おそくまで　勉強したので、ねむい　→　おそくまで　勉強したので、ねむそう
   です。　　　　　　　　　　　　　　　です。

6. この　川は　深いです。　　　　　→　この　川は　深そうです。

7. あの　おみこしは　とても　重いです。　→　あの　おみこしは　とても　重そうです。

8. この　道は　あぶないです。　　　　⟶　この　道は　あぶなそうです。

9. あしたの　天気は　よいです。　　　　⟶　あしたの　天気は　よさそうです。

6.7.3　Response Drill

1. おみこしは　こっちに　<u>来ます</u>か。　⟶　<u>ええ</u>、おみこしは　こっちに
　　　　　　　　　　　　　　　　　　　　　　　　　<u>来そうです</u>。

2. きょうは　雨が　ふるでしょうか。　⟶　ええ、きょうは　雨が　ふりそうです。

3. ここから　おみこしが　見られますか。　⟶　ええ、ここから　おみこしが
　　　　　　　　　　　　　　　　　　　　　　　　見られそうです。

4. あの　新しい　社員は　いっしょう　⟶　ええ、あの　新しい　社員は　いっしょう
　　けんめい　働くでしょうか。　　　　　　けんめい　働きそうです。

5. ここの　花は　すぐ　ぬすまれる　⟶　ええ、ここの　花は　すぐ　ぬすまれそう
　　でしょうか。　　　　　　　　　　　　です。

6. これらの　木は　交通の　じゃまに　⟶　ええ、これらの　木は　交通の
　　なりますか。　　　　　　　　　　　　じゃまに　なりそうです。

7. ご飯は　すぐ　できますか。　　　　⟶　ええ、ご飯は　すぐ　できそうです。

8. あしたも　ここへ　来られますか。　⟶　ええ、あしたも　ここへ　来られそう
　　　　　　　　　　　　　　　　　　　　　です。

6.7.4　Substitution Drill

あの　人は　<u>忙し</u>そうな　人ですね。

1. しんせつ　　　　　　　……　あの　人は　しんせつそうな　人ですね。

2. きびしい　　　　　　　……　あの　人は　きびしそうな　人ですね。

3. スポーツが　じょうず　……　あの　人は　スポーツが　じょうずそうな
　　　　　　　　　　　　　　　　人ですね。

4. やさしい　　　　　　　……　あの　人は　やさしそうな　人ですね。

5. よく　勉強する　　　　……　あの　人は　よく　勉強しそうな　人ですね。

6. お金を　持っている　　　　あの　人は　お金を　持っていそうな
　　　　　　　　　　　……　人ですね。

7. 楽しい　　　　　　　　……　あの　人は　楽しそうな　人ですね。

8. 元気　　　　　　　　　……　あの　人は　元気そうな　人ですね。

9. さびしい　　　　　　　……　あの　人は　さびしそうな　人ですね。

10. 頭が　いい　　　　　　……　あの　人は　頭が　よさそうな　人ですね。

6.7.5　Transformation Drill

1.　人が　おおぜい　<u>行きます</u>。
　　人が　おおぜい　<u>来ます</u>。　⎫⟶　人が　おおぜい　<u>行ったり</u>
　　　　　　　　　　　　　　　　　　　　　<u>来たりします</u>。

2.　ぼくは　コーヒーを　飲みます。
　　ぼくは　コーヒーを　飲みません。　⎫⟶　ぼくは　コーヒーを　飲んだり
　　　　　　　　　　　　　　　　　　　　　飲まなかったりします。

3.　夜も　残業しました。
　　夜も　会を　ひらきました。　⎫⟶　夜も　残業したり　会を　ひらいたり
　　　　　　　　　　　　　　　　　　しました。

4.　かれらは　家族の　ことを
　　　　話しています。
　　かれらは　国の　ことを　考えて　⟶　かれらは　家族の　ことを　話したり
　　　　いています。　　　　　　　　　　国の　ことを　考えたりしています。

5.　日曜日は　教会へ　行きます。
　　日曜日は　テニスを　します。　⟶　日曜日は　教会へ　行ったり　テニスを
　　日曜日は　音楽を　楽しみます。　　　したり　音楽を　楽しんだりします。

6.　それらは　大きすぎました。
　　それらは　小さすぎました。　⎫⟶　それらは　大きすぎたり　小さすぎたり
　　　　　　　　　　　　　　　　　　しました。

7.　この　辺では　米が　取れます。
　　この　辺では　やさいが　取れます。　⎫⟶　この　辺では　米が　取れたり
　　　　　　　　　　　　　　　　　　　　　やさいが　取れたりします。

8.　かれらは　毎晩　おどりました。
　　かれらは　毎晩　うたいました。　⎫⟶　かれらは　毎晩　おどったり
　　　　　　　　　　　　　　　　　　　うたったりしました。

6.7.6　Transformation Drill

1.　みち子さんの　声は　<u>高かったです</u>。
　　みち子さんの　声は　<u>低かったです</u>。　⎫⟶　みち子さんの　声は　<u>高かったり</u>
　　　　　　　　　　　　　　　　　　　　　　<u>低かったりしました</u>。

2.　いもうとの　作る　料理は　あま
　　　　かったです。
　　いもうとの　作る　料理は　　⟶　いもうとの　作る　料理は
　　　　からかったです。　　　　　　あまかったり　からかったりしました。

3.　高校の　生活は　楽しかったです。
　　高校の　生活は　きびしかったです。　⎫⟶　高校の　生活は　楽しかったり
　　　　　　　　　　　　　　　　　　　　きびしかったりしました。

4.　先週は　さむかったです。
　　先週は　あつかったです。　⎫⟶　先週は　さむかったり
　　　　　　　　　　　　　　　　あつかったりしました。

5. テーラーさんが　来る　時間は
　　おそかったです。
　　テーラーさんが　来る　時間は
　　早かったです。
　　→　テーラーさんが　来る　時間は
　　おそかったり　早かったりしました。

6. 病気は　重かったです。
　　病気は　かるかったです。
　　→　病気は　重かったり　かるかったり
　　しました。

6.7.7　Transformation Drill

1. 着ている　物は　<u>はっぴです。</u>
　　着ている　物は　<u>ゆかたです。</u>
　　→　着ている　物は　<u>はっぴだったり</u>
　　<u>ゆかただったりします。</u>

2. この　村の　家は　日本風です。
　　この　村の　家は　洋風です。
　　→　この　村の　家は　日本風だったり
　　洋風だったりします。

3. ぼくの　きょうだいは　さかなが
　　好きです。
　　ぼくの　きょうだいは　さかなが
　　好きじゃないです。
　　→　ぼくの　きょうだいは　さかなが
　　好きだったり　好きじゃなかったり
　　します。

4. 土曜日は　しずかです。
　　土曜日は　人が　来て　にぎやかです。
　　→　土曜日は　しずかだったり　人が　来て
　　にぎやかだったりします。

5. 最近の　朝ご飯は　ご飯と
　　おみおつけです。
　　最近の　朝ご飯は　パンと　コーヒー
　　です。
　　→　最近の　朝ご飯は　ご飯と　おみおつけ
　　だったり　パンと　コーヒーだったり
　　します。

6. 日本人の　宗教は　仏教です。
　　日本人の　宗教は　神道です。
　　日本人の　宗教は　キリスト教です。
　　→　日本人の　宗教は　仏教だったり
　　神道だったり　キリスト教だったり
　　します。

6.7.8　Substitution Drill

<u>日によって</u>　あの　道は　<u>さびしかったり</u>　<u>にぎやかだったり</u>します。

1. こむ、こまない　……　日によって　あの　道は　こんだり
　　こまなかったりします。

2. 時間によって　……　時間によって　あの　道は　こんだり
　　こまなかったりします。

3. きれいだ、きたない　　　……　時間によって　あの　道は　きれいだったり
　　　　　　　　　　　　　　　　　　きたなかったりします。

4. 天気によって　　　　　　　……　天気によって　あの　道は　きれいだったり
　　　　　　　　　　　　　　　　　　きたなかったりします。

5. 人が　多い、少ない　　　　……　天気によって　あの　道は　人が　多かったり
　　　　　　　　　　　　　　　　　　少なかったりします。

6. きせつによって　　　　　　……　きせつによって　あの　道は　人が
　　　　　　　　　　　　　　　　　　多かったり　少なかったりします。

6.7.9　Transformation Drill

1. にぎやかな　声が　聞こえて、みんな　　　　→　にぎやかな　声が　聞こえ、みんな
　　楽しそうです。　　　　　　　　　　　　　　　　楽しそうです。

2. あした　十時に　会って、話し合い　　　　　→　あした　十時に　会い、話し合い
　　ましょう。　　　　　　　　　　　　　　　　　　ましょう。

3. お金を　はらって、中に　入った。　　　　　→　お金を　はらい、中に　入った。

4. それらの　重さを　はかって、くらべて　　　→　それらの　重さを　はかり、くらべて
　　みてください。　　　　　　　　　　　　　　　　みてください。

5. 子どもの　時、母に　死なれて、　　　　　　→　子どもの　時、母に　死なれ、こまり
　　こまりました。　　　　　　　　　　　　　　　　ました。

6. はじめに　むすめが　生まれて、次に　　　　→　はじめに　むすめが　生まれ、次に
　　むすこが　生まれた。　　　　　　　　　　　　　むすこが　生まれた。

7. 雨が　つづいて、やさいが　取れなく　　　　→　雨が　つづき、やさいが　取れなく
　　なったそうです。　　　　　　　　　　　　　　　なったそうです。

6.7.10　Transformation Drill

1. この　川は　かなり　深くて、あぶない　　　→　この　川は　かなり　深く、あぶない
　　そうです。　　　　　　　　　　　　　　　　　　そうです。

2. うちへ　帰る　道は　さびしくて、　　　　　→　うちへ　帰る　道は　さびしく、
　　こわいです。　　　　　　　　　　　　　　　　　こわいです。

3. この　かばんは　かるくて、べんり　　　　　→　この　かばんは　かるく、べんりである。
　　である。

4. おみこしは　かざりが　多くて、　　　　　　→　おみこしは　かざりが　多く、
　　重いらしい。　　　　　　　　　　　　　　　　　重いらしい。

5. わたしの　へやは　あかるくて、　　　　　⟶　わたしの　へやは　あかるく、気持ちが
　　気持ちが　いいです。　　　　　　　　　　　　いいです。

6. その　えいがは　おもしろくて、　　　　　⟶　その　えいがは　おもしろく、子どもの
　　子どもの　ために　いいと　思います。　　　　ために　いいと　思います。

7. ジョーンズさんは　若くて、りっぱな　　　⟶　ジョーンズさんは　若く、りっぱな
　　課長さんです。　　　　　　　　　　　　　　課長さんです。

6.7.11 Expansion Drill

1. わすれられません。　　　　　　　……　わすれられません。

　　楽しく　　　　　　　　　　　　　……　楽しく、わすれられません。

　　村の　祭りは　　　　　　　　　　……　村の　祭りは　楽しく、わすれられません。

　　子どもの　ころの　　　　　　　　……　子どもの　ころの　村の　祭りは　楽しく、
　　　　　　　　　　　　　　　　　　　　　わすれられません。

2. 関係を　持っています。　　　　　　……　関係を　持っています。

　　長く　深い　　　　　　　　　　　……　長く　深い　関係を　持っています。

　　中国文化と　　　　　　　　　　　……　中国文化と　長く　深い　関係を　持っています。

　　日本文化は　　　　　　　　　　　……　日本文化は　中国文化と　長く　深い　関係を
　　　　　　　　　　　　　　　　　　　　　持っています。

3. 人が　死んだりしました。　　　　　……　人が　死んだりしました。

　　家が　こわれたり　　　　　　　　……　家が　こわれたり　人が　死んだりしました。

　　大きな　地震で　　　　　　　　　……　大きな　地震で　家が　こわれたり　人が
　　　　　　　　　　　　　　　　　　　　　死んだりしました。

4. いろいろです。　　　　　　　　　　……　いろいろです。

　　アルバイトを　したり　　　　　　……　アルバイトを　したり　いろいろです。

　　国へ　帰ったり　　　　　　　　　……　国へ　帰ったり　アルバイトを　したり
　　　　　　　　　　　　　　　　　　　　　いろいろです。

　　夏休みに　　　　　　　　　　　　……　夏休みに　国へ　帰ったり　アルバイトを
　　　　　　　　　　　　　　　　　　　　　したり　いろいろです。

　　学生たちは　　　　　　　　　　　……　学生たちは　夏休みに　国へ　帰ったり
　　　　　　　　　　　　　　　　　　　　　アルバイトを　したり　いろいろです。

5. 秋だったりするそうです。　　　　　……　秋だったりするそうです。

　　夏だったり　　　　　　　　　　　……　夏だったり　秋だったりするそうです。

村によって　　　　　　　　　……　村によって　夏だったり　秋だったりする
　　　　　　　　　　　　　　　　　　そうです。

祭りは　　　　　　　　　　　……　祭りは　村によって　夏だったり　秋だったり
　　　　　　　　　　　　　　　　　　するそうです。

6.7.12　E-J Response Drill

1. きのうは　うちへ　帰ってから、何を　しましたか。
   watched TV, read a newspaper, and the　……　テレビを　見たり　新聞を　読んだり
   like　　　　　　　　　　　　　　　　　　しました。

2. 日本語の　クラスでは　どんな　ことを　しますか。
   learn new *kan'ji*, practice conversation, and　……　新しい　漢字を　習ったり　会話を
   the like　　　　　　　　　　　　　　　　　　れんしゅうしたりします。

3. この　大学の　卒業生は　何を　していますか。
   some of them are teaching at school and　……　学校で　教えたり　会社で　働いたり
   some of them are working at business　　　　　しています。
   firms, and the like

4. 休みに　どんな　ことを　したいですか。
   swimming, taking a nap, and some other　……　およいだり　昼寝したりしたいです。
   things

5. 土曜日は　いつも　忙しいんですか。
   no, sometimes I am busy and sometimes I　……　忙しかったり　ひまだったりします。
   am free

6. あしたは　どうするつもりですか。
   go shopping, meet a friend of mine, and the　……　買い物に　行ったり　友だちに　会ったり
   like　　　　　　　　　　　　　　　　　　するつもりです。

7. 友だちの　自動車は　みんな　新しいですか。
   no, some are new and some are old　……　いいえ、新しかったり　古かったり
   　　　　　　　　　　　　　　　　　　します。

6.7.13　Response Drill

1. どこに　住んでいますか。
   大学の　そば　　　　　　　　……　大学の　そばに　住んでおります。

2. 神道について　よく　知っていますか。

　　はい　　　　　　　　　　　　　　…… はい、よく　知っております。

3. お父様は　どこに　勤めていらっしゃいますか。

　　銀行　　　　　　　　　　　　　　…… 銀行に　勤めております。

4. どこの　とけいを　使っているんですか。

　　日本製の　　　　　　　　　　　　…… 日本製のを　使っております。

5. さっき　おみこしを　見ていらっしゃいましたね。

　　いいえ　　　　　　　　　　　　　…… いいえ、見ておりませんでした。

6. 会社へは　何で　かよっていますか。

　　地下鉄　　　　　　　　　　　　　…… 地下鉄で　かよっております。

6.8　EXERCISES

6.8.1　Insert appropriate words into the blanks, according to the English equivalents given.

1. おとといは　一日じゅう　家に　いて、音楽を _____ 本を _____
テレビを _____しました。

   I stayed at home all day the day before yesterday and did things like listening to music, reading books, and watching television.

2. 最近　わたしは _____ _____します。

   Recently I have been busy sometimes and free sometimes.

3. この　学校の　学生は _____ _____ _____ いろいろな　人が
います。

   There are various students in this school: American, German, or Japanese.

4. _____だから、早く　うちへ　帰ろう。

   It looks as if it's going to rain, so I'll go home soon.

5. 手が _____ですね。どう　したんですか。

   It looks as if your hand hurts. What's the matter with you?

6. _____ くだ物ですね。いくら_____？

   They are delicious-looking fruits. I wonder how much?

6.8.2　Combine the following sentences into one, according to the instruction given, and provide the English equivalent for each sentence.

1. おみこしが　ありません。
店が　少ないです。
さびしい　お祭りです。　　　⟶　（〜し、〜し、…）

2. 月曜日に　新しい　クラスが　はじまります。
　　来週から　たぶん　忙しくなるでしょう。　　　⎫→　（～し、…）

3. 京都は　思ったより　すずしかったです。
　　しずかでした。　　　　　　　　　　　　　　　⎫→　（～し、～し、…）
　　住みやすかったです。

6.8.3　いい　ほうに　○を　つけなさい。

1. 島田さんは　あの　えいがを　見て、おもしろいと　言っていました。

　　→　あの　えいがは　⎧ おもしろそう ⎫ です。
　　　　　　　　　　　　⎩ おもしろいそう ⎭

2. あの　レストランは　おさらも　テーブルも　りっぱです。たぶん
　　高いでしょうね。

　　→　あの　レストランは　⎧ 高そう ⎫ ですね。
　　　　　　　　　　　　　　⎩ 高いそう ⎭

3. 外が　くらくなりましたね。雨が　ふるかもしれませんね。

　　→　雨が　⎧ ふりそう ⎫ ですね。
　　　　　　　⎩ ふるそう ⎭

6.8.4　The following are in written style. Rewrite them in normal polite spoken style:

Example: あしたは　忙しく、来られないと　思う。

　　　　→　あしたは　忙しくて、来られないと　思います。

1. おみこしは　かざりが　多く　ついており、なかなか　重そうである。
　　千キロぐらい　あるかもしれない。

2. 子どもの　ころ、よく　父や　母に　つれられ、お祭りに　行き、おみこしを
　　見たり　わたがし(cotton candy)を　買ってもらったりしたが、それは　今も
　　楽しく、なつかしい　思い出として　のこっている。

6.8.5　漢字に　変えなさい。

1. ぶっきょうは　にほんじんの　せいかつに　ふかい　関係を　もっている。
2. この　じんじゃの　おみこしは　とくに　おもいそうです。
3. さいきん　この　みちで　こうつうじ故が　よく　おこります。
4. たのしそうな　こえや　おんがくが　きこえますね。
5. 鎌倉と　奈良の　だいぶつは　おなじ　おおきさじゃありません。
6. げんきそうな　こどもたちですね。

6.8.6 次の　漢字を　読みなさい。

1. 交、校	5. 声、色	9. 深、活
2. 動、重	6. 持、特、時	10. 神、社
3. 取、最	7. 同、回	11. 仕、仏、低
4. 通、道	8. 私、仏	12. 天気、元気

6.8.7 This dialog presents Mr. Shimada's attitude concerning the revival of traditional Japanese festivals. Based upon this information:

1. Is it true that festivals are reviving?
2. What has been the traditional function of festivals in the mind and life of the Japanese people?
3. If it is true that festivals are now reviving, is it due to the reduced traffic, or to the improved financial conditions of the Japanese people?
4. Do you share Shimada's sentimental attachment to the traditional Japanese festivals?
5. It is suggested in the dialog that *omatsuri* once were disappearing because of the increasing traffic. Since Americans often stop traffic for parades, it would seem that the Japanese could do the same. What other reasons might help account for the ups and downs of the *omatsuri*?

6.8.8 Which of the following measures are used in Japan?

meter	gram	kilogram
yard	ounce	cubic feet
inch	kilometer	square meter
feet	pound	acre

6.8.9 The following expressions (with their English equivalents) all concern one's feelings or mood. Use each expression and formulate a short dialog.

1. "I'm glad" —ureshii desu
2. "I'm sad" —kanashii desu
3. "I'm lonely" —sabishii desu
4. "I'm envious" —urayamashii desu
5. "I'm scared" —kowai desu
6. "I want to go" —ikitai desu
7. "I want it" —hoshii desu

6.9 SITUATIONAL AND APPLICATION CONVERSATION

6.9.1 Mr. Morgan says to his friend Mr. Humphrey that he was busy the day before because his parents left home for New York at six o'clock in the morning, he took his younger brother to a hospital in the afternoon, and his friend Mr. Miller came to his home in the evening.

Mr. Humphrey asks Mr. Morgan what's the matter with Mr. Morgan's brother.

Mr. Morgan says that his younger brother seems to have caught a cold. The brother had a high fever the day before, but he looks fine by now.

Mr. Humphrey is glad to hear that, and he says that he went to church the day before in the morning and he stayed at home all day long, reading books, listening to the radio, writing letters, and the like.

6.9.2   About the festival.

Keiko asks Susie if there are village festivals in the United States.

Susie says that there are many festivals in the United States too.

Keiko asks Susie what the people do at the festivals.

Susie answers that both children and adults enjoy themselves riding various rides (*norimono*), eating, drinking, watching parades (*pareedo*), listening to lively music, and the like.

6.9.3   Mrs. Katō: Kyoo, okosan wa doo shita n desu ka?

        Mrs. Satō: Hitori de uchi ni imasu wa.

        Mrs. Katō: Daijoobu?

        Mrs. Satō: Daijoobu yo. Hiruma nara, sabishii to iwanai shi, mijikai jikan da kara.

6.9.4   Student A: Kyoo eiga o mi ni ikanai?

        Student B: Soo da nee. Kyoo wa shukudai ga aru n da kedo ... Mi ni ikoo kana.

        Student A: Yoshio san mo iku kashira?

        Student B: Saa, doo kana.

6.9.5   Student A: Nihon'go no kurasu wa totemo omoshiroi rashii ne.

        Student B: Jaa, rainen totte miyoo kana?

6.10   READING COMPREHENSION

6.10.1

　先週　国へ　帰ったが、ついた　次の　日は　ちょうど　夏祭りの　日であった。町の
中は　ひじょうに　こんでおり、はっぴを　着たり　ゆかたを　着たりした　人が　おおぜい
いた。　見物に　来た　外国人や　日本人の　観光客(tourists)も　多く、うれしそうに
見物したり　あるいたりしていた。おおぜいの　古い　友だちに　会え、なつかしかった。
いっしょに　飲んだり　歌ったり　おどったり　話したりして　楽しんだ。

6.10.2

吉田　「きのうは　出かけましたか。」

山下　「きのうは　昼寝を　したり、テレビを　見たり、買い物に　行ったりしました。
　　　　吉田さんは？」

吉田　「浅草の　お祭りが　あると　聞いたので、カメラを　持って　見に
　　　　行ったんです。」

山下　「人が　すごかったでしょう?」

吉田　「ええ、こんでいて　おどろきました。でも、おみこしは　見られたし、
　　　　にぎやかで　楽しかったです。」

山下　「いい　しゃしんが　とれたでしょう?」

吉田　「さあ、いいのが　とれたか　どうか　わかりません。しゃしんを
　　　　とっていた　時、前を　人が　行ったり　来たりしていて、とりにくかったし。」

LESSON 7
日本の　工業₁

7.1　　PRESENTATION

　日本では　近代的な　工業は　明治時代に　なって　発達しはじめた。　明治の
終わりごろから、　数度の　戦争によって　さらに　発達したが、　第二次世界大戦で
日本の　工業は　ひどい　損害を　受けた。　しかし、　戦争が　すむと₂、　急速に
発達し、　戦前以上₃の　工業国に　なった。

7.2　　DIALOG

—— 電車の　中で ——

モーガン　「込みますね。」

野村　　　「ちょうど　仕事が　終わって、　工員たちが　帰るところ₄でしょう。」

モーガン　「この　辺まで　来ると₂、　ほとんど　工場ばかりですね。」

野村　　　「ええ、　この　辺は　日本の　工業の　中心の　一つですから。」

モーガン　「工業と　言えば₅、　日本には　いい　電気製品が　多いですね。　じつは、
　　　　　　安くて　いい　ラジカセが　あったら₆、　二台₇　買おうと　思っている
　　　　　　んです。　国の　おとうとも　ほしがって₈いるし。」

野村　　　「そうだ₉！　友だちが　電気製品の　会社に　勤めています。　よかったら₆
　　　　　　安く　買えるか　どうか　聞いてあげましょう。」

モーガン　「おねがいします。　ぼくの　国も　日本から　ラジカセや　ビデオなど₁₀
　　　　　　輸入しているけど、　むこうで　買うと　高いんですよ。」

野村　　　「そうですか。　じゃあ、　きょう　帰ったら₆さっそく　電話で　れんらく
　　　　　　してみますよ。　いくらぐらいだったら₆　いいん₁₁ですか。」

モーガン　「ねだんは　野村さんに　まかせます。　野村さんが　安いと　思ったら₆、
　　　　　　それで　いいです。」

工業 (こうぎょう)	近代的 (きんだいてき)	明治時代 (めいじじだい)	発達 (はったつ)	数度 (すうど)
戦争 (せんそう)	受けた (うけた)	戦前以上 (せんぜんいじょう)	込みます (こみます)	工員 (こういん)
工場 (こうじょう)	製品 (せいひん)	二台 (だい)	勤めている (つとめている)	輸入 (ゆにゅう)

7.3 PATTERN SENTENCES

7.3.1

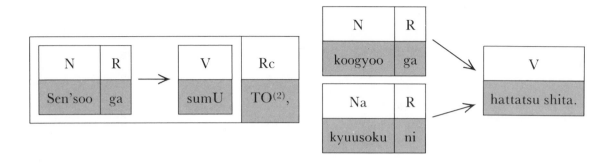

7.3.2

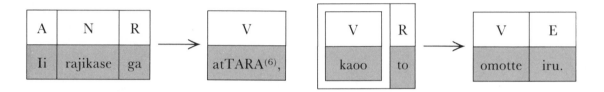

7.3.3

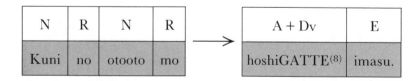

7.3.4

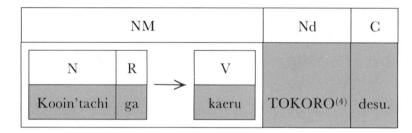

7.4 NOTES

7.4.1 Manufacturing developed in Japan long before the Meiji era (1868–1912), and the seeds of large-scale industry had been sown during the Tokugawa period. However, it was not until after the establishment of the Meiji government in 1868 that modern industry truly developed in Japan. Interestingly enough there has been in Japan's past a close correlation between the growth of the industrial sector and war. Japanese industry grew faster in both size and strength after each military involvement. For instance, the Sino-Japanese War (1894–1895), the Russo-Japanese War (1904–1905), World War I (1914–1918), and the war with China that led to the Pacific War (1931–1945) all acted as important stimuli to the development of certain areas of industry. Even the Korean War (1950–1953), in which Japan did not participate, proved highly beneficial to industry as a result of procurements and other contingencies of that conflict. There were many other, possibly more important, factors in Japan's industrial growth, but the net result is that today Japan ranks third among the industrial powers of the world, led only by the United States and the USSR.

Japan lacks an abundance of raw materials. In order to counteract this shortcoming in the past, Japan depended upon cheap labor and the diligence of the people to produce needed materials, including those for export. Today the cost of labor has spiraled upward, yet the pattern of importing raw materials and exporting manufactured products is maintained. Japan depends heavily on trade for its survival.

The ability to engage in trade and production without the drain of heavy defense spending (the present constitution, including its Preamble and Article Nine, prohibits war) has enhanced Japan's prosperity. Obviously this is not the sole reason for the economic success that Japan is now experiencing. There are a myriad of factors involved.

7.4.2 *Sen'soo ga sumu to, kyuusoku ni hattatsu shita* means "When the war was over, rapid progress was made." The *to* in the above sentence is a clause Relational that combines two sentences and turns the first sentence into a nonfinal clause meaning "whenever ...," "when ...," or "if ..." *To* may be preceded by the plain imperfect tense forms of a Verb, an Adjective, or the Copula, regardless of the tense of the final Predicate.

Verb (plain imperfect tense form)
Adjective (plain imperfect tense form) } **+ to, ...**
Noun + Copula (plain imperfect tense form)

The *to* clause has the following meanings:

1.   Habitual or spontaneous correlation with the clause following: "whenever something happens something else happens" or "when one does something such and such always happens."

Boku wa nomu to, nemuku naru n desu.	"Whenever I drink, I get sleepy."
Aki ni naru to, kome ga toreru.	"When autumn comes, rice can be harvested."
Mushiatsui to, tsukareyasui desu.	"When it's hot and humid, one easily gets tired."
Tsugi no hi shiken da to, itsumo yoru osoku made ben'kyoo shimasu.	"When I have an exam the following day, I always study till late at night."

2.   Inevitable or obvious result or consequence: "if one does such and such, something happens as an obvious result."

Kono hon o miru to, soo kaite arimasu.	"If you look at this book, (you'll see) it is written so."
Kono hen made kuru to, koojoo bakari desu nee.	"Coming to this area, you find nothing but factories."

3.   Immediate action to follow: "something happens and immediately after that something else happens."

Sen'soo ga sumu to, kyuusoku ni hattatsu shita.	"When the war ended, there was rapid progress."
Uchi e kaeru to, sugu shukudai o yarimashita.	"I did my homework right away when I went home."
Kono kodomo wa samui to, yoku kaze o hikimasu.	"This child catches a cold often when it is cold."
Ano kado o migi ni magaru to, sugu hidari ni miemasu.	"If you turn right at that corner, you can see it on your left-hand side."
Keisatsu e iku to, oshiete kuremasu yo.	"If you go to the police, they will tell you."
Kome ga tarinai to, yunyuu suru n desu.	"Whenever we are short of rice, we import it."

7.4.3 *Sen'zen ijoo* means "more than it was before the war," "above the prewar level," and so on. There are several Nouns that show something is above or below standard, beyond or within a boundary, and so on, and they may be called *i-* words.
Here are some of them:

~ ijoo	"more than ~" "above ~"
~ ika	"less than ~" "below ~"
~ inai	"within ~"
~ igai	"except ~" "other than ~"

Hyakunin ijoo no hito ga kai ni deta soo desu.	"I understand that more than a hundred people attended the meeting."
Netsu wa (san'juu) shichido ika da kara, shin'pai arimasen.	"My temperature is below (thirty-)seven degrees, so there is nothing to worry about."
Jippun inai de ikimasu kara, matte ite kudasai.	"Please be waiting for me, since I will be there within ten minutes."
Yamaguchi san igai no gakusei ga min'na kimashita.	"All the students except Mr. Yamaguchi came."

7.4.4 *Choode shigoto ga owatte, kooin'tachi ga kaeru tokoro deshoo* means "Factory workers seem to have just finished their work and to be on their way home." *-Tokoro* in this instance is a dependent Noun meaning "occasion" or "moment." *-Tokoro* is always preceded by a Noun Modifier: the Dictionary form or the TA form of a Verb or an Adjective, a Noun plus *no, na,* or *datta,* or a Pre-Noun. When *-tokoro* is preceded by the TA form of a Verb, the combination means "an action has just been done (a little while before)" and the combinaton of the Dictionary form of a Verb plus *-tokoro* means "someone is about to do such and such." Otherwise, *-tokoro* will correspond to "is in the midst of . . ."

$$\left.\begin{array}{l}\textbf{Dictionary form} \\ \textbf{TA form}\end{array}\right\} \textbf{of} \left\{\begin{array}{l}\textbf{Verb} \\ \textbf{Adjective}\end{array}\right.$$
$$\left.\begin{array}{l}\textbf{adjectival Noun} + \textit{na} \\ \textbf{Noun} + \textit{no} \\ \textbf{Noun} + \textit{datta} \\ \textbf{Pre-Noun}\end{array}\right\} + \textbf{\textit{tokoro}} + \textbf{\textit{da}}$$

In order to emphasize the meaning of "an action has just done" or "is about to do," *choodo* and/or *ima*, *sakki* "a while ago," *kore kara* "from now," and the like may be used in the above sentences.

Ima kaeru tokoro desu.	"I am on my way home." "I am about to go home."
Choodo soo omotte ita tokoro desu.	"I was just thinking so."
Ima eiga wa ichiban omoshiroi tokoro na n desu.	"It's the most interesting part (moment) of the movie right now."
Chichi wa ima dekaketa tokoro desu.	"Father has just left (home)."

The dependent Noun *-tokoro* may be followed not only by the Copula *da* but by Relationals such as *e*, *o*, or it may be used without any word following. Although *-tokoro* refers to "the moment something happens or has happened," the place where something happens or has happened is more or less considered.

$$... \textit{tokoro} + \begin{cases} \textit{e} \\ \textit{o} \end{cases}$$

Den'wa shiyoo to shita tokoro e kare ga kimashita.	"At the moment when I was about to make a phone call to him, he appeared."
Isogashii tokoro (o) ojama shite, sumimasen.	"I am sorry to bother you while you are busy."
Watashi wa doroboo ga tonari no ie ni hairu tokoro o mite, keisatsu ni shirasemashita.	"I saw a thief at the moment he was about to break into the next-door house, and I reported it to the police."
Kono tokoro zutto kibun ga yoku nai n desu.	"I haven't been feeling well these days."

7.4.5 *Koogyoo to ieba* means "speaking of industry." When the speaker wants to take up a topic, this usage, namely, a word, a phrase, or a sentence plus *to ieba*, is sometimes used.

Kome to ieba, Kariforunia no ga oishii soo desu yo.	"Speaking of rice, I understand that California rice is tasty."

7.4.6 *Rajikase ga attara* means "if there should be a radio cassette,..." *Attara* is the TARA form or the conditional form of the Verb *aru* "there is" and means "if there should be ..."

The TARA forms of a Verb, an Adjective and the Copula are formulated by adding *-ra* to the TA form:

Verb ..... add *-ra* to the TA form

yameru	$\longrightarrow$	yameta	$\longrightarrow$	yametara
miru	$\longrightarrow$	mita	$\longrightarrow$	mitara
yogoreru	$\longrightarrow$	yogoreta	$\longrightarrow$	yogoretara
kasu	$\longrightarrow$	kashita	$\longrightarrow$	kashitara
kau	$\longrightarrow$	katta	$\longrightarrow$	kattara
motsu	$\longrightarrow$	motta	$\longrightarrow$	mottara
kaku	$\longrightarrow$	kaita	$\longrightarrow$	kaitara
toru	$\longrightarrow$	totta	$\longrightarrow$	tottara

isogu	→	isoida	→	isoidara
yobu	→	yon'da	→	yon'dara
tanoshimu	→	tanoshin'da	→	tanoshin'dara
suru	→	shita	→	shitara
kuru	→	kita	→	kitara

Adjective ..... add *-ra* to the TA form

hidoi "is cruel"	→	hidokatta	→	hidokattara
sabishii	→	sabishikatta	→	sabishikattara
yoi	→	yokatta	→	yokattara

Copula ..... add *-ra* to the TA form

da → datta → dattara

The TARA form is used at the end of a nonfinal clause and is tenseless. Therefore, the tense of the final clause determines that of the whole sentence.

Verb(-*tara*),...
Adjective(-*tara*),...
Noun + Copula(-*tara*),...

The TARA forms are used in the following environments:

1.   An action shown in the *-tara* clause always precedes another action expressed in the final clause. The final Predicate is always in the perfect tense. "After something happened, something else happened" or "when one did such and such, then something happened subsequently."

Soto e detara, ame ga futte imashita.	"When I went out, I found it was raining."
Shiken o ukeru made wa shin'pai deshita ga, uketara, yasashikatta desu.	"I was worried about the exam until I took it, but I found it easy after having taken it."
Kusuri o non'dara, yoku narimashita.	"After taking medicine, I recovered well."

2.   The *-tara* clause formulates a conditional clause. The final Predicate is always in the imperfect tense. This use of the TARA form may be replaced by the BA form. "If one should do such and such, something would happen" or "if something is such and such, something else will happen."

Yasukute ii rajio ga attara, ichidai hoshii n desu.	"If there should be a good and cheap radio, I would like to have one."
Taifuu ga ookikattara, doo shimasu ka?	"What should we do if the typhoon should be a big one?"
Yasumi no hi dattara, koraremasu.	"I'll be able to come if it is a holiday."

In this case the Adverb *moshi* may be used in the *-tara* clause, if it is necessary to emphasize the conditional meaning of the clause.

3.   The final Predicate is limited to request, command, intention, decision, invitation, such as (*ki*)*te kudasai*, (*ki*)*nasai*, (*kuru*) *tsumori da*, (*kuru*) *koto ni suru*, (*ki*)*mashoo*, (*ki*)*masen ka?*, and so on.

Tomodachi ni attara, tanon'de okimashoo.	"I'll ask my friend when I meet him."

Sen'soo ga sun'dara, daigaku ni hairu tsumori desu.	"When the war ends, I am planning to enter college."
Ame ga futtara, yameru koto ni shimasu.	"Should it rain, we shall cancel it."
Yokattara, kiite agemashoo.	"I'll ask about it, if it's all right with you."

It therefore can be said that:

1. When the final clause is in the perfect tense, the nonfinal clause must be the *-tara* clause rather than the *-ba* clause. The sentence simply indicates the seqence of events in the past.

2. When the final clause is in any other tense than the perfect tense, the nonfinal clause could be either the *-tara* clause or the *-ba* clause. People tend to use the *-tara* clause if they are more concerned with the sequence events, while the *-ba* clause indicates more a concern with conditions. See the following charts:

-tara A occurs, then B occurs

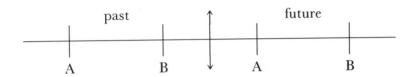

-ba B occurs only if A occurs

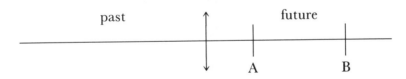

A = first event
B = second event

↑↓ present

In this connection, some differences between *toki* and *to* might now be considered. *Toki* indicates the "time reference," while *to* emphasizes the "event reference" implying immediate, inevitable, or habitual actions.

Gakkoo e iku to, sen'sei ni aimasu.	"Whenever I go to school, I meet with teachers."
Gakkoo e iku toki, hon o kaeshimashoo.	"When I am going to school, I shall return your books."

7.4.7 The *-dai* in *nidai* is a counter for radios, television sets, typewriters, cameras, automobiles, pianos, and so on. "How many" is *nan'dai*.

Kono koojoo ni wa kikai ga nan'dai gurai arimasu ka?	"How many machines are there in this factory?"
Michi ni kuruma ga godai tomatte imasu.	"Five automobiles are parked on the street."

7.4.8   *Otooto mo hoshigatte iru* means "My younger brother is also anxious to have it." The verbal Derivative *-garu* is attached to the Base form of certain Adjectives or the Base form of a compound Adjective such as *ikitai*. The subject of this expression usually is the third person indicating his/her feelings or inclinations.

third person + *wa* +	(object + *o*) + **Base form of Adjective** **Verb** + **Base form of** *-tai*	+	*-gatte iru* *-garu*

Watashi ga ii rajikase o moratta node, kare wa urayamashigatte imashita.	"Since I was given a good radio cassette, he was envious."
Gakusei wa bideo o mitagarimasu.	"Students want to watch a video."
Yamada kun wa Kyooto e ikitagatte imasu.	"Mr. Yamada is anxious to go to Kyōto."
Ishii san wa jishin o kowagatte imasu.	"Mr. Ishii is afraid of earthquakes."
Min'na maikon o hoshigatte imasu.	"Everyone is interested in having a personal computer."

7.4.9   *Soo da!* means "That's it!" Usually *soo* means "so," "like that," or "that way." But this expression can also be used in an exclamatory way such as *A, soo da!* As explained in Note 6.4.9, for an exclamatory utterance usually the plain form is used.

A, wakatta!	"Now I see!"
Yokatta!	"I'm relieved!"
Moo dame da!	"I gave up!"

7.4.10   *Rajikase ya bideo nan'ka yunyuu shite iru* means "[My country] has been importing Japanese goods such as radio cassettes and video machines and the like." When *-nan'ka* comes after a Noun usually that Noun is singled out as a sample or example. *-Nan'ka* is a more colloquial equivalent of *-nado*.

Nihon wa jishin ya taifuu nan'ka ookute, taihen desu ne.	"Japan has many problems such as earthquakes and typhoons."

7.4.11   *Ikura gurai dattara ii n desu ka?* means "What price would be acceptable to you?" As already introduced in Notes 7.4.2 and 7.4.6, the *to* clause and the *-tara* clause are similar to the *-ba* clause in some usages. The expression ... *-ba ii* "I wish ..." or "I hope ..." (see Note 11.4.9, Vol. III) may also be similar to ... *to ii* and ... *-tara ii*. Therefore, the above Japanese sentence *Ikura gurai dattara ii* may be expressed using *nara(ba)* or *da to* instead of *dattara*.

(Predicate Modifier) +	**BA form Predicate** **Predicate** + *to* **TARA form Predicate**	+	*ii* *ii n desu ga* *ii noni* *ii kedo*

Motto joozu ni nihon'go ga { hanasereba / hanaseru to / hanasetara } ii n desu ga.	"I wish I could speak Japanese better."

$$\text{Shiken ga } \begin{Bmatrix} \text{nakereba} \\ \text{nai to} \\ \text{nakattara} \end{Bmatrix} \text{ ii.}$$ "I hope there will be no exam."

$$\text{Kyoo ga doyoobi } \begin{Bmatrix} \text{nara} \\ \text{da to} \\ \text{dattara} \end{Bmatrix} \text{ ii noni.}$$ "I wish today were Saturday."

7.5   VOCABULARY

Presentation

工業	koogyoo	......	N	manufacturing industry
近代的	kin'daiteki	......	Na	modern
明治	Meiji	......	N	Meiji (name of the emperor who reigned from 1868 through 1912)
時代	jidai	......	N	era; time; age
終わり	owari	......	N	end
数度	suudo	......	N	several times (*Suu-* means "several" before a counter.)
さらに	sara ni	......	Adv.	more and more; furthermore
第二次世界大戦	dainiji sekai taisen	......	N	the Second World War
ひどい	hidoi	......	A	is cruel; is serious; is harsh; is hard
損害	son'gai	......	N	loss; damage; harm
すむ	sumu	......	V	end; is over (intransitive Verb)
と	to	......	Rc	when; if; whenever (see 7.4.2)
急速	kyuusoku	......	Na	rapid
戦前	sen'zen	......	N	prewar
以上	ijoo	......	N	above; more than (see 7.4.3)

Dialog

モーガン	Moogan	......	N	Morgan
野村	Nomura	......	N	family name
ところ	tokoro	......	Nd	moment; occasion (see 7.4.4)
ほとんど	hoton'do	......	Adv.	almost
工場	koojoo	......	N	factory (工場 may also be read *kooba*.)
中心	chuushin	......	N	center; core

電気	den'ki	......	N	electricity
製品	seihin	......	N	manufactured goods
ラジカセ	rajikase	......	N	radio cassette tape recorder
あったら	attara	......	V	if there were one (TARA form of *aru*) (see 7.4.6)
台	-dai	......	Nd	counter for TV sets, automobiles, machines, pianos, etc. (see 7.4.7)
（ほし）がって	(hoshi)-gatte	......	Dv	(see 7.4.8)
よかったら	yokattara	......	A	TARA form of *yoi* – is good (see 7.4.6)
ビデオ	bideo	......	N	video tape recorder
なんか	-nan'ka	......	Nd	colloquial equivalent of *-nado* – and the like (see 7.4.10)
輸入して	yunyuu shite	......	V	TE form of *yunyuu suru* – import
輸入	yunyuu	......	N	import
帰ったら	kaettara	......	V	TARA form of *kaeru* – go home
さっそく	sassoku	......	Adv.	instantly; quickly
れんらくして	ren'raku shite	......	V	TE form of *ren'raku suru* – contact
れんらく	ren'raku	......	N	contact
だったら	dattara	......	C	if it were such and such (TARA form of *da*) (see 7.4.6)
ねだん	nedan	......	N	price
まかせます	makasemasu	......	V	normal form of *makaseru* – leave (it to someone)
思ったら	omottara	......	V	TARA form of *omou* – think

Notes

以下	ika	......	N	below; less than (see 7.4.3)
以内	inai	......	N	within
以外	igai	......	N	except; other than
機械	kikai	......	N	machine
マイコン	maikon	......	N	microcomputer; personal computer
輸出する	yushutsu suru	......	V	export
輸出	yushutsu	......	N	export

7.6   KAN'JI

7.6.1 工   (1) KOO   (2) manufacture; mechanic; construction

(3) forms the classifier 工   (4) | 一 | 工 | 工 |

(5) 工場、工員、工事中[under construction]、しゅうり工

[repairman]、工業_{ぎょう}   (6) homonym 巧、功、江、攻、紅、項

7.6.2 業   (1) GYOO   (2) business; studies   (3) classifier 丷（木）

(4) | リ | 丷 | 业 | 业 | 业 | 業 | (5) 工業、職業_{しょく}[occupation]、卒業_{そつ}、農業_{のう}

7.6.3 代   (1) DAI   (2) generation   (3) classifier 亻

(4) | 亻 | 亻 | 代 | 代 | (5) 十代[teenage]、時代、一九四〇年代、

現代_{げん}[present time]、近代[modern time]

7.6.a ^{3.6.5} 治   (1) JI   (2) govern   (5) 明治、政治_{せい}[politics]

7.6.4 発   (1) HATSU [HAT-] [-PATSU]   (2) shoot; expose; open; departure

(3) classifier 癶   (4) | 丿 | 丿 | 癶 | 癶 | 癶 | 登 | 発 |

(5) 発達_{たつ}、発音[pronunciation]、出発_{しゅっ}、発明[invention]

7.6.5 達   (1) TATSU   (2) arrive; reach; achieve   (3) classifier 辶

(4) | 土 | 寺 | 幸 | 達 | (5) 発達、配達_{はい}[delivery]、速達_{そく}[special delivery]

7.6.b ^{3.6.3} 数   (1) SUU   (5) 数度、数回、数人、数学[mathematics]、数字[number]

7.6.6 戦   (1) SEN   (2) fight; war   (3) classifier 戈 [weapon]

(4) | 丷 | 当 | 単 | 単 | 単 | 戦 | 戦 | 戦 |

(5) 戦争_{そう}、第二次_{だい　じ}世界大戦_{たい}[the Second World War]、リーグ戦

[league game]

7.6.7 争   (1) SOO   (2) struggle   (3) classifier 宀

(4) | 丿 | 勹 | 勹 | 刍 | 刍 | 争 |

(5) 戦争、競争_{きょう}[competition]、論争_{ろん}[debate]

7.6.8 受   (1) u(keru)   (2) receive   (3) classifier 爫（又 hand])

(4) | 丿 | 夕 | 爫 | 受 | (5) しけんを受ける、被害_{ひ　がい}を受けた

7.6.c ^{8.6.5, Vol. II} 前   (1) ZEN   (5) 午前、戦前、食前、前大統領_{だいとうりょう}[former president]

7.6.d 上 ^(9.6.4, Vol. II) (1) JOO (5) 上等、上品[elegance]、以上

7.6.9 込 (1) *ko(mu)* (2) get into; get crowded (3) classifier 辶

(4) ［ノ］［入］［込］ (5) 道が込んでいる (6) This *kanji* was made in Japan. The classifier 辶 means "go" and 入 means "enter."

7.6.e 場 ^(9.6.9, Vol. III) (1) JOO (5) ゴルフ場、工場、会場[place of a meeting]、サッカー場

7.6.10 製 (1) SEI (2) manufacture; made (3) classifier 亠 (衣 [represents upper garment with sleeves at top, and robe waving and dangling at the bottom])

(4) ［亠］［台］［制］［制］［制］［製］［製］

(5) 日本製のテレビ、銀製品、外国製

(6) classifier can be written 衤; homonym 制

7.6.11 品 (1) HIN (2) goods; elegance (3) classifier 口

(4) ［口］［品］［品］ (5) 製品、外国品、上品な [elegant]

7.6.12 台 (1) DAI [TAI] (2) stand (3) classifier 厶

(4) ［亠］［厶］［台］ (5) 二台、台所[kitchen]、台風

(6) homonym 台、胎、怠

7.6.13 勤 (1) *tsuto(meru)* (2) duty; service (3) classifier 艹 (力 [power; force]) (4) ［艹］［艹］［艹］［堇］［勤］

(5) 銀行に勤める (6) homonym KIN 謹、僅

7.6.f 入 ^(13.6.8, Vol. II) (1) NYUU (2) enter (5) 輸入、入社、入学 [entering school]

7.7 DRILLS

7.7.1 Transformation Drill

1. 朝ご飯が <u>すみます</u>。
   いつも コーヒーを 二はい 飲みます。 ⟶ 朝ご飯が <u>すむと</u>、いつも コーヒーを 二はい 飲みます。

2. <u>さむいです</u>。
   かぜを ひきやすいです。 ⟶ <u>さむいと</u>、かぜを ひきやすいです。

3. アメリカ製の　機械<ruby>械<rt>かい</rt></ruby>です。
   もっと　大きいはずです。　　　 ⟶　　アメリカ製の　機<ruby>械<rt>かい</rt></ruby>だと、もっと
   　　　　　　　　　　　　　　　　　　　　大きいはずです。

4. ことわざを　たくさん　覚えておき
   ます。
   とても　べんりですよ。　　　 ⟶　　ことわざを　たくさん　覚えておくと、
   　　　　　　　　　　　　　　　　　　　とても　べんりですよ。

5. 学生が　十五人以<ruby>内<rt>ない</rt></ruby>です。
   つごうが　いいです。　　　 ⟶　　学生が　十五人以<ruby>内<rt>ない</rt></ruby>だと、つごうが
   　　　　　　　　　　　　　　　　　　　いいです。

6. 台所は　広くて　あかるいです。
   働きやすいです。　　　 ⟶　　台所は　広くて　あかるいと、
   　　　　　　　　　　　　　　　　　　　働きやすいです。

7. むすこが　ラジカセを　もらい
   ました。
   むすめも　ほしいと　言いました。　　　 ⟶　　むすこが　ラジカセを　もらうと、
   　　　　　　　　　　　　　　　　　　　むすめも　ほしいと　言いました。

8. 電話するのが　あしたです。
   おそすぎますよ。　　　 ⟶　　電話するのが　あしただと、　おそ
   　　　　　　　　　　　　　　　　　　　すぎますよ。

9. 文が　長いです。
   いみが　むずかしくなります。　　　 ⟶　　文が　長いと、いみが　むずかしく
   　　　　　　　　　　　　　　　　　　　なります。

10. 外国製です。
    ねだんは　高いでしょう？　　　 ⟶　　外国製だと、ねだんは　高いでしょう？

11. ミラーさんが　日本語を　習いはじめ
    ました。
    すぐ　モーガンさんも　習いはじめ
    ました。　　　 ⟶　　ミラーさんが　日本語を　習いはじめる
    　　　　　　　　　　　　　　　　　　と、すぐ　モーガンさんも　習い
    　　　　　　　　　　　　　　　　　　はじめました。

12. かばんが　かるいです。
    らくなんですけど。　　　 ⟶　　かばんが　かるいと、らくなんです
    　　　　　　　　　　　　　　　　　　　けど。

7.7.2　Transformation Drill

1. 工業が　発達しました。
   生活が　ゆたかに　なりました。　　　 ⟶　　工業が　発達したら、生活が　ゆたかに
   　　　　　　　　　　　　　　　　　　　なりました。

2. あっちへ　行きました。
   工場ばかり　見えました。　　　 ⟶　　あっちへ　行ったら、工場ばかり　見え
   　　　　　　　　　　　　　　　　　　　ました。

3. 子どもが　生まれます。
   もっと　広い　家に　住みたいです。　　　 ⟶　　子どもが　生まれたら、もっと　広い
   　　　　　　　　　　　　　　　　　　　家に　住みたいです。

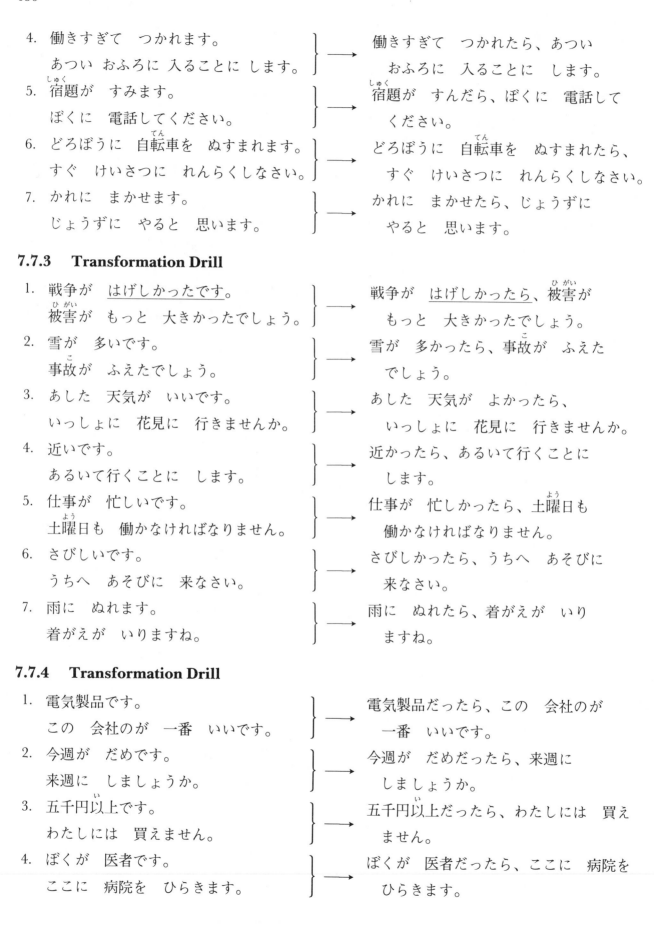

4. 働きすぎて つかれます。 }→ 働きすぎて つかれたら、あつい
   あつい おふろに 入ることに します。　　　おふろに 入ることに します。

5. 宿題が すみます。 }→ 宿題が すんだら、ぼくに 電話して
   ぼくに 電話してください。　　　ください。

6. どろぼうに 自転車を ぬすまれます。 }→ どろぼうに 自転車を ぬすまれたら、
   すぐ けいさつに れんらくしなさい。　　　すぐ けいさつに れんらくしなさい。

7. かれに まかせます。 }→ かれに まかせたら、じょうずに
   じょうずに やると 思います。　　　やると 思います。

7.7.3　Transformation Drill

1. 戦争が <u>はげしかったです</u>。 }→ 戦争が <u>はげしかったら</u>、被害が
   被害が もっと 大きかったでしょう。　　　もっと 大きかったでしょう。

2. 雪が 多いです。 }→ 雪が 多かったら、事故が ふえた
   事故が ふえたでしょう。　　　でしょう。

3. あした 天気が いいです。 }→ あした 天気が よかったら、
   いっしょに 花見に 行きませんか。　　　いっしょに 花見に 行きませんか。

4. 近いです。 }→ 近かったら、あるいて行くことに
   あるいて行くことに します。　　　します。

5. 仕事が 忙しいです。 }→ 仕事が 忙しかったら、土曜日も
   土曜日も 働かなければなりません。　　　働かなければなりません。

6. さびしいです。 }→ さびしかったら、うちへ あそびに
   うちへ あそびに 来なさい。　　　来なさい。

7. 雨に ぬれます。 }→ 雨に ぬれたら、着がえが いり
   着がえが いりますね。　　　ますね。

7.7.4　Transformation Drill

1. 電気製品です。 }→ 電気製品だったら、この 会社のが
   この 会社のが 一番 いいです。　　　一番 いいです。

2. 今週が だめです。 }→ 今週が だめだったら、来週に
   来週に しましょうか。　　　しましょうか。

3. 五千円以上です。 }→ 五千円以上だったら、わたしには 買え
   わたしには 買えません。　　　ません。

4. ぼくが 医者です。 }→ ぼくが <u>医者だったら</u>、ここに 病院を
   ここに 病院を ひらきます。　　　ひらきます。

5. 経済の　ことです。　　　　　　　　→　経済の　ことだったら、島田先生に
　　島田先生に　聞いてください。　　　　　　聞いてください。

6. 心配です。　　　　　　　　　　　　→　心配だったら、もう一度　調べた
　　もう一度　調べた　ほうが　いい　　　　ほうが　いいでしょう。
　　　でしょう。

7. 明治時代です。　　　　　　　　　　→　明治時代だったら、農業の　ほうが
　　農業の　ほうが　さかんでした。　　　　さかんでした。

7.7.5　Transformation Drill

1. いい　ラジカセが　<u>あります</u>。　→　いい　ラジカセが　<u>あったら</u>、一台
　　一台　<u>買います</u>。　　　　　　　　　<u>買おう</u>と　思っています。

2. 雨が　ひどいです。　　　　　　　　→　雨が　ひどかったら、出かけるのを
　　出かけるのを　やめます。　　　　　　　やめようと　思っています。

3. 国へ　帰ります。　　　　　　　　　→　国へ　帰ったら、さっそく　友だちに
　　さっそく　友だちに　会います。　　　　会おうと　思っています。

4. 安い　ビデオです。　　　　　　　　→　安い　ビデオだったら、買って
　　買ってもらいます。　　　　　　　　　　もらおうと　思っています。

5. 道が　込んでいます。　　　　　　　→　道が　込んでいたら、地下鉄に
　　地下鉄に　乗ります。　　　　　　　　　乗ろうと　思っています。

6. 残業が　ないです。　　　　　　　　→　残業が　なかったら、すぐ　帰ろうと
　　すぐ　帰ります。　　　　　　　　　　　思っています。

7.7.6　Transformation Drill

1. 卒業<u>すると</u>、鈴木さんは　すぐ　　→　卒業<u>したら</u>、鈴木さんは　すぐ
　　けっこんします。　　　　　　　　　　　けっこんします。

2. おととい　吉田さんの　うちへ　行くと、→　おととい　吉田さんの　うちへ　行ったら、
　　野村先生が　いらっしゃいました。　　　野村先生が　いらっしゃいました。

3. アルバイトが　ないと、勉強が　つづけ　→　アルバイトが　なかったら、勉強が
　　られません。　　　　　　　　　　　　　つづけられません。

4. 友だちに　頼むと、かんたんに　やって　→　友だちに　頼んだら、かんたんに
　　くれました。　　　　　　　　　　　　　やってくれました。

5. おびが　きついと、気分が　悪くなり　　→　おびが　きつかったら、気分が　悪く
　　ますよ。　　　　　　　　　　　　　　　なりますよ。

6. それが　本当だと、うれしいですね。　　——→　それが　本当だったら、うれしいですね。

7. 戦前だと、テレビは　なかったはず　　——→　戦前だったら、テレビは　なかったはず
　　です。　　　　　　　　　　　　　　　　　　　　　　です。

7.7.7　Response Drill

1. いつ　野村さんに　会いに　行きますか。
　　これから　　　　　　……　これから　野村さんに　会いに　行くところです。

2. いつ　工場を　出ますか。
　　ちょうど　今　　　　　……　ちょうど　今　工場を　出るところです。

3. しけんを　いつ　受けましたか。
　　さっき　　　　　　　　……　さっき　しけんを　受けたところです。

4. いつ　お米を　取り入れますか。
　　今から　　　　　　　　……　今から　お米を　取り入れるところです。

5. いつ　モーガンさんに　手紙を　書きますか。
　　今　　　　　　　　　　……　今　モーガンさんに　手紙を　書くところです。

6. 残業は　何時ごろ　終わりましたか。
　　ちょうど　今　　　　　……　残業は　ちょうど　今　終わったところです。

7. いつ　工員たちが　工場に　つきましたか。
　　さっき　　　　　　　　……　さっき　工員たちが　工場に　ついたところです。

8. いつごろ　雨が　ふりはじめましたか。
　　今　　　　　　　　　　……　今　雨が　ふりはじめたところです。

7.7.8　Transformation Drill

1. みんなで　話しています。　　　　　——→　みんなで　話しているところに、大川
　　大川さんが　来ました。　　　　　　　　　　さんが　来ました。

2. 夕べ　ご飯を　食べていました。　——→　夕べ　ご飯を　食べていたところに、
　　地震が　起こりました。　　　　　　　　　　地震が　起こりました。

3. ぼくが　るすでした。　　　　　　　　　　　ぼくが　るすだったところに、
　　伊藤さんから　電話が　あったそう　——→　伊藤さんから　電話が　あったそうです。
　　　です。

4. 心配しています。　　　　　　　　　——→　心配しているところに、いい　手紙が
　　いい　手紙が　来ました。　　　　　　　　　来ました。

5. 本を さがしています。
   図書館員が 来てくれました。 } → 本を さがしているところに、
   　　　図書館員が 来てくれました。

6. 忙しく 働いています。
   友だちから れんらくが ありました。 } → 忙しく 働いているところに、友だち
   　　　から れんらくが ありました。

7. テレビを 楽しんでいました。
   客に 来られました。 } → テレビを 楽しんでいたところに、
   　　　客に 来られました。

7.7.9　Transformation Drill

1. わたしは ラジカセが ほしいんです。
   おとうとも　　　　……　おとうとも ラジカセを ほしがっています。

2. ぼくは 最近 とても さびしいんです。
   あねも　　　　……　あねも 最近 とても さびしがっています。

3. わたしは パーティーを ひらきたいんです。
   いもうとも　　　　……　いもうとも パーティーを ひらきたがっています。

4. わたしは できるだけ 早く 日本へ 行きたいんです。
   かないも　　　　……　かないも できるだけ 早く 日本へ 行きたがっています。

5. わたしは 地震が 一番 こわいんです。
   家族も　　　　……　家族も 地震を 一番 こわがっています。

6. 私の 国は 牛肉を 輸出したいんです。
   オーストラリアも　……　オーストラリアも 牛肉を 輸出したがっています。

7. ぼくは 新しい 自転車が 一台 ほしいんです。
   友だちも　　　　……　友だちも 新しい 自転車を 一台 ほしがっています。

7.7.10　Substitution Drill

A. 日本に 石油が あると いいんですが。

1. 早く 戦争が 終わります　　……　早く 戦争が 終わると いいんですが。
2. ラジオを 一台 買います　　……　ラジオを 一台 買うと いいんですが。
3. あした 野村さんに 会えます　……　あした 野村さんに 会えると
   　　　いいんですが。
4. 病気が ひどくないです　　……　病気が ひどくないと いいんですが。
5. 近代的な 建物です　　……　近代的な 建物だと いいんですが。
6. もっと 安いです　　……　もっと 安いと いいんですが。

B.　これが　一万円以下だったら　いいんですが。

　　1.　早く　夏に　なります　　　　　…… 早く　夏に　なったら　いいんですが。

　　2.　天気が　悪くないです　　　　　…… 天気が　悪くなかったら　いいんですが。

　　3.　ひどい　そん害を　受けません　…… ひどい　そん害を　受けなかったら
　　　　　　　　　　　　　　　　　　　　　　いいんですが。

　　4.　仕事の　時間が　自由です　　　…… 仕事の　時間が　自由だったら
　　　　　　　　　　　　　　　　　　　　　　いいんですが。

　　5.　はじまる　時間が　おそいです　…… はじまる　時間が　おそかったら
　　　　　　　　　　　　　　　　　　　　　　いいんですが。

　　6.　ぼくが　君です　　　　　　　　…… ぼくが　君だったら　いいんですが。

7.8　EXERCISES

7.8.1　Clause Relational *to* を　使って、次の　文を　日本語で　言いなさい。

　　1.　I hope to be able to buy an inexpensive radio cassette tape recorder.

　　2.　If it rains, Mr. Morgan may not come.

　　3.　If this one is below two thousand yen, how much will that one be?

　　4.　When the weather is nice, we can see the mountains through this window.

7.8.2　TARA form を　使って、次の　文を　日本語で　言いなさい。

　　1.　If it should rain this afternoon, I will stay home and read a book.

　　2.　If you should have a million yen, what would you do with it?

　　3.　If I were you, I wouldn't worry about it.

　　4.　If the weather is bad, I intend not to climb Mt. Fuji.

　　5.　When I went to my friend's house last night, he wasn't home.

7.8.3　Choose one of the three words given in the parentheses to make a complete sentence.

　　1.　べんりな　機械を　輸入し {と、/たら、/れば、} 仕事が　ずっと　かんたんに
　　　　なるでしょう。

　　2.　つかれた　時に　あつい　おふろに　入る {たら、/れば、/と、} 気分が
　　　　よくなりますよ。

3. もっと　いろいろな　物が　ある { と / ば / たら } いいんですが。

4. この　工場では　電気製品 { 以内(いない) / 以外(いがい) / 以上(いじょう) } に　何を　作っているんですか。

5. 山下さんは　輸入(ゆ)した　物 { を　ほしいです。 / が　ほしいです。 / を　ほしがっています。 / が　ほしがっています。 }

6. 「もう　お米は　取り入れ終わりましたか。」「いいえ、これから　取り入れる { とき / ところ } です。」

7. あなたから　れんらくが { ないと、 / ないところに、 / なかったら、 } 電話しようと　思っていました。

7.8.4　＿＿＿に　ことばを　入れなさい。

1. かれは　カメラ＿＿＿　テープレコーダー＿＿＿　買いたがっています＿＿＿、
   安いの＿＿＿　あったら、教えてあげてください。
2. この　仕事＿＿＿　わたし＿＿＿　まかせてください。
3. ぼうえき＿＿＿　言えば、あの　国は　何＿＿＿　輸出(ゆしゅつ)したがっているんですか。
4. ここ＿＿＿　買う＿＿＿　安い＿＿＿、むこう＿＿＿は　とても　高いんですよ。
5. 大阪(さか)は　日本＿＿＿　工業＿＿＿　中心＿＿＿　一つです。
6. 出かけようと　していたところ＿＿＿　友だちが　来ました。

7.8.5　英語で　言いなさい。

1. 今　ちょうど　新宿(じゅく)へ　買い物に　出かけるところなんです。
2. カメラや　ラジオを　買いたかったら、あの　店へ　行きなさい。安くて
   いいのが　ありますよ。
3. 戦争が　はじまると、ぼくの　家族は　いなかへ　行って、住んだ。
4. 日本語と　中国語以外(い)に　どんな　外国語を　習ったんですか。
5. 私のと　同じ　セーターが　ほしかったら、あの　店に　あると　思いますよ。

6. 友だちが　十人以上　来たら、お皿や　フォークが　たりません。　どう
　　したら　いいかしら。

7. むこうに　ついたら、電話を　ください。

8. 「マイコンを　ほしがっているのは　あなたですか。」「わたしは　マイコン
　　なんか　ほしくないですよ。きょうみが　ありませんから。」

7.8.6　漢字に　変えなさい。

1. こうぎょうが　はったつしたのは　めいじじだい以ごです。

2. せんぜん　ドイツへ　いき、いい　ドイツせいの　カメラを　かいました。

3. あの　こうじょうは　ゆうめいで、こういんが　せんごひゃくにん以じょうも
　　いるそうです。

4. すうどの　たいふうで　ひどい　被害を　うけた。

5. 授ぎょうの　ない　とき、図しょかんは　こんでいません。

6. でんきせいひんを　すうまんだい　輪にゅうした。

7. せんそうご　ゴルフじょうに　つとめたことが　あります。

7.8.7　読みなさい。

1. 台、治、活
2. 働、動、勤
3. 入、込

4. 込、達、道、通、辺
5. 楽、業
6. 土、工

7. 代、化、低
8. 口、品

7.8.8　Discuss the reasons why the Japanese standard of living ranks lower in the world than does their GNP.

7.8.9　It has been said that Japan has been sacrificing its people's health and its natural beauty in order to produce more industrial products and export more goods abroad. Is it true? What could be the reason?

7.8.10　What foreign influence can you detect on language expressions? Give some examples of how the expansion of trade has affected Japanese language usage.

7.8.11　Explain the functions of *tokoro* in the following sentences.

1. Asoko wa watashi ga iku tokoro desu.
2. Watashi wa soko e iku tokoro desu.
3. Ima watashi wa den'wa o shita tokoro desu.
4. Soko wa watashi ga den'wa o shita tokoro desu.

7.8.12 The *to* carries the meaning "whenever ...," "when ...," or "if ..." Describe which of the three meanings *to* carries in each of the following.

1. Boku wa ben'kyoo suru to, atama ga itaku naru n desu.
2. Kono san'koosho o yomu to, sugu wakarimasu.
3. Natsu ni naru to, min'na umi e itta.
4. Nihon no kamera da to, takai desu.
5. Jugyoo ga hajimaru to, nemuku narimashita.
6. Fuyu ni naru to, Tookyoo kara Fujisan ga miemasu.

7.9 SITUATIONAL AND APPLICATION CONVERSATION

7.9.1 On the train.

Looking through the window, a foreigner says to his Japanese friend that there is nothing but factories around there.

The Japanese says to his friend that this place is one of the important industrial centers in Japan.

A foreigner asks what Japan imports.

The Japanese answers that Japan mainly imports iron, petroleum, and the like. He says he wishes Japan could have abundant iron, petroleum, and the like.

The foreigner asks what Japan exports besides automobiles.

The Japanese answers that his country exports electronic products, and the like.

7.9.2 On the street.

Paul sees Susie and calls her. Paul says to her that he was about to make a telephone call to her.

Susie asks why he wants to talk with her.

Paul says that should the weather be nice on Saturday he wants to go to Kamakura with her.

Susie says she would like to, but her mother is eager to go shopping on that day. And if her mother is going shopping she may not be able to go. She has to take care of her younger sisters.

Paul asks Susie to let him know by Friday evening whether she can go.

Susie answers that she will inform him of it by Friday evening.

7.9.3 Yamada: Hayaku haru ni naru to ii nee.

Suzuki: Atatakaku naru shi, sakura wa saku shi ...

Yamada: Hanami ni ikoo ka?

Suzuki: Ii ne. Sakura ga saitara, den'wa suru yo.

7.9.4 Yoshiko: Moshi moshi, Michiko san?

Michiko: Soo. A, Yoshiko san.

Yoshiko: Ima nani shiteru no?

Michiko: Choodo uchi ni tsuita tokoro na no.

Yoshiko: Soo. Kon'ban kore kara uchi e konai?

Michiko: Ashita shiken ga aru node, kore kara ben'kyoo suru tokoro na no yo.

Yoshiko: Jaa, kon'do ne.

Michiko: Gomen nasai ne.

7.10   READING COMPREHENSION

7.10.1

日本は　100年ほど前は　まだ　農業国であったが、今では　世界でも　ゆうめいな
大工業国に　なった。しかし、資源が　少ないので、これらを　ほとんど　輸入しなければ
ならない。輸入した　原料(raw material)を　使って　製品を　作り、輸出するのが
日本の　貿易の　形である。

7.10.2

スミス　「かないが　ビデオを　ほしがっているんですけど、どこへ　買いに　行ったら
　　　　いいですか。」

山下　　「秋葉原へ　行ったら　どうですか。秋葉原だったら、電気製品の　店が　数十けん
　　　　(tens of shops)も　ありますよ。」

スミス　「秋葉原ですか。」

山下　　「ええ。ねだんが　安いし、しゅるいが　多いから、えらびやすい (easy to choose)
　　　　んです。わたしなんか　とおいけど　いつも　秋葉原まで　足を　のばすんです。」

スミス　「そうですか。どう　行ったら　いいんですか。」

山下　　「山手線か　京浜東北線で　行けば　東京駅から　二つ目ですよ。」

スミス　「駅から　近いんですか。」

山下　　「ええ。駅の　すぐ　前から　ずっと　電気屋ばかりなんですよ。スミスさんは、
　　　　それで、いつ　行こうと　思っているんですか。」

スミス　「できたら、これから　行こうと　思っているんです。」

山下　　「そうだ。ぼくも　見たい　物が　あるから、いっしょに　行ってあげましょうか。」

スミス　「いっしょに　行ってくれるんですか。悪いですね。」

山下　　「こうしょう(bargaining)によっては、ねだんを　どんどん　安くすることが
　　　　できますから、ぼくに　まかせてください。」

スミス　「それは　たすかります。(That would be a great help.)」

LESSON 8
日本人の　食生活₁

8.1　PRESENTATION

　海の　産物の　ゆたかな　日本では、　昔から　魚や　貝を　おもに　食べ、　明治に
なって、　やっと　牛肉や　ぶた肉が　日本人の　食生活に　取り入れられた。

　昔に　くらべると、　日本人の　食生活は　ずいぶん　変わり、　種類が　ふえた。
現代の　日本ほど₂　いろいろな　料理が　食べられる　国は　めずらしいに　ちがいない₃。

8.2　DIALOG

石田　「おなかが　すき₄ましたね。　食事でも₅　しましょうか。」

山崎　「いいですね。　どこに　入りますか。」

石田　「いい　所に　案内しますよ。　きょうは　ぼくが　ごちそうします。」

山崎　「いや、　それは　いけません。　わりかん₆に　しましょう。」

石田　「まあ、　そう　言わないで₇　きょうは　ぼくに　おごらせて₈ください。」

山崎　「そうですか。　じゃあ、　えんりょ₉しないで、　ごちそうに　なります₁₀。」

．．．

給仕₁₁　「いらっしゃいませ。　今　すぐ　メニューを　お持ちします₁₂。…
　　　　お待たせしました₁₂。　何に　なさいますか₁₃。」

石田　「山崎さん、　好きな　物を　注文してください。　ビフテキでも　どうですか。
　　　　ここの　ビフテキは　ひょうばんが　いいんですよ。」

山崎　「ビフテキだと　ちょっと　多すぎるので、　えびフライに₁₄　スープを
　　　　いただきます。　それと　パンに　します₁₃。」

石田　「ぼくは　ビフテキ。　急がせて　悪いけど₁₅、　早くしてくれませんか。」

給仕　「はい、　なるべく　早くいたします。　ライスと　パンと、　どちらを
　　　　お持ちしましょうか。」

石田　「パンと　ライスを　一つ₁₆ずつ。」

給仕　「かしこまりました。」

．．．

山崎　「石田さん、　塩　取ってください。」

石田　「あれ、　ないですね。　給仕に　持って来させ₈ましょう。　（給仕に）塩が

　　　　ないんだけど…」

給仕　「どうも　もうしわけ　ございません。　すぐ　持ってまいります₁₇。」

8.3　PATTERN SENTENCES

8.3.1

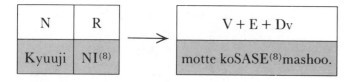

N	R		V + E + Dv
Kyuuji	NI[8]	→	motte koSASE[8]mashoo.

8.3.2

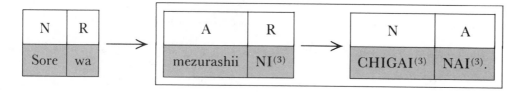

N	R		A	R		N	A
Sore	wa	→	mezurashii	NI[3]	→	CHIGAI[3]	NAI[3].

8.3.3

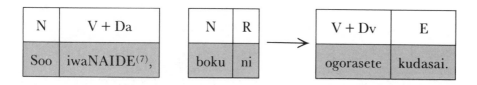

N	V + Da		N	R		V + Dv	E
Soo	iwaNAIDE[7],		boku	ni	→	ogorasete	kudasai.

8.4　NOTES

8.4.1　The traditional staples of the Japanese diet are seafood, vegetables, and rice. At one time rice was regarded as the main dish (*shushoku*), with all others serving as side dishes (*fukushoku*). Beef, pork, and chicken became an important part of the Japanese diet only during the last century. The Japanese people have also gradually shifted from rice consumption to a variety of starch sources such as bread. This is another example of eclecticism leading to pluralism in culture. As in clothing, the Japanese enjoy a wide range of dishes today—Western (French, Italian, and American), Chinese, Japanese, even hot dogs and hamburgers.

For centuries the sea has been a major source of food in Japan, providing most of the protein consumed. As a result, the Japanese language contains far greater numbers of frequently used vocabulary relating to fish. Some of the most typical Japanese seafood dishes include *ten'pura* (deep-fried food), many kinds of *sushi* (flavored rice balls with raw fish and other materials), and *sashimi* (raw fish).

8.4.2   *Nihon hodo ... kuni wa mezurashii* means "There is no country ... like Japan." The *hodo* is a Relational and carries the meaning of comparison. When it is followed by a Predicate with negative connotation, it implies that the comparison is negative. *Mezurashii* carries the negative meaning "rare."

8.4.3   *Mezurashii ni chigai nai* means "It must be rare." *~ni chigai nai* is used idiomatically to indicate that "It must be so" or "It cannot be wrong." This expression may be preceded by a Noun, an adjectival Noun, the plain forms of a Verb, or the plain forms of an Adjective, and the plain forms (except *da*) of the Copula after a Noun or an adjectival Noun.

Verb (plain form)	
Noun or adjectival Noun	$+ \textit{ni} + \textit{chigai} + \begin{cases} \textbf{\textit{nai}} \\ \textbf{\textit{arimasen}} \end{cases}$
Noun or adjectival Noun + Copula (except *da*)	
Adjective (plain form)	

Ano otoko wa doroboo ni chigai nai.	"That man must be a thief."
Ten'ki ga warukute mo, kuru ni chigai nai.	"Even though the weather might be bad, he/she will definitely come."
Ano resutoran wa amari yasuku nai ni chigai arimasen.	"That restaurant must not be very inexpensive."

8.4.4   *Onaka ga sukimashita*, as already introduced in Lesson 7, Volume I, is an expression equivalent to "I've gotten hungry" or "I am hungry." This is literally "my stomach has become almost empty." The intransitive Verb *suku* may be used not only in this particular expression but in such cases as *den'sha ga sukimashita* "the train has become almost empty or has become less crowded." Likewise "I've gotten thirsty" or "I am thirsty" is expressed by *nodo ga kawakimashita*, whose literal translation is "my throat has become dry." *Kawaku* is an intransitive Verb meaning "get dry." To express "I am hungry," and "I am thirsty," *onaka ga suite iru* and *nodo ga kawaite iru* are used. These Verbs will be treated again in Note 12.4.5.

Nodo mo kawaita shi, onaka mo sukimashita.	"I'm thirsty; what's more, I'm hungry."
Yoofuku wa, sakki aratta node, mada kawakimasen.	"As the clothes were washed only a while ago, they are not dry yet."
Onaka wa suite imasen ga, nodo ga kawaite imasu.	"I'm not hungry but thirsty."

8.4.5   *Shokuji demo shimashoo ka?* means "Shall we have dinner or something?" *Demo* in this case is a Relational used to indicate that the preceding word or phrase is only a sample suggested by the speaker at random. It denotes the meaning "~ or something," "~ or someone," "~ or somewhere," and the like, depending upon the preceding word or phrase. This Relational replaces *ga* and *o*, but it may be added to other Relationals such as *ni, de, kara*.

$$\text{Noun} + \begin{Bmatrix} ga \\ o \end{Bmatrix} + \text{Predicate} \longrightarrow \text{Noun} + demo + \text{Predicate}$$

$$\text{Noun} + \begin{Bmatrix} ni \\ de \\ kara \\ .. \\ .. \\ to \end{Bmatrix} + \text{Predicate} \longrightarrow \text{Noun} + \begin{Bmatrix} ni \\ de \\ kara \\ .. \\ .. \\ to \end{Bmatrix} + demo + \text{Predicate}$$

Eiga demo mimashoo ka?	"Shall we see a movie or something?"
Nodo ga kawaita kara, koohii demo nomitai desu nee.	"I am thirsty; I would like to drink coffee or something."
Bifuteki demo doo desu ka?	"How about beefsteak or something?"
Anata wa Amerika kara demo irasshatta n desu ka?	"Did you come from the United States or somewhere?"

8.4.6 In this Dialog Yamazaki suggests going dutch (*warikan*). In Japan such a suggestion cannot be made either to a superior or an inferior. In general, it is suggested only among equals. The one who suggests a dutch treat shows consideration toward his partner by doing so.

The Japanese word *ogorimasu* means "treat someone to food," or "one pays for another's food, drink, movie, and the like." However, this term is not necessarily the equivalent of the American "it's on me" or "my treat," since *ogorimasu* indicates that one is not only offering to pay for the bill, but also offering good food and drink. Although this connotation is disappearing rapidly, the offer implies that the host is taking his guest to the best restaurant within his means. The guest, of course, will display his courtesy by trying to order an inexpensive meal.

8.4.7 *Maa, soo iwanaide* means "Don't insist on it!" or "Don't say so!" The negative TE form of a Verb, *-naide*, may be used as a nonfinal clause in the meaning of "without doing such and such" or "instead of doing such and such." The *-naide* form of a Verb is formulated by the combination of the Pre-Nai form of a Verb plus *-naide*.

(Predicate Modifier) + Pre-Nai form of Verb + -naide,...

Yoku ben'kyoo shinaide, shiken o uketa n desu ka?	"Did you take the exam without studying enough?"
Watashi ga ikanaide, kodomo o ikasemashita.	"Instead of going myself, I had my child go."
Kyoo wa asagohan o tabenaide, gakkoo e kimashita.	"I came to school today without having breakfast."
Kamera o kaoo to omotte imashita ga, kamera wa kawanaide, bideo o kaimashita.	"I had been thinking of buying a camera, but I bought a video tape recorder instead of a camera."

8.4.8 *Boku ni ogorasete kudasai* means "Please let me treat you." *Ogoraseru* is the combination of *ogora*, the Pre-Nai form of *ogoru* "treat," and the causative Derivative *-seru*. The causative expression with *-seru* or *-saseru* is used in the meaning of (a) "make someone do such and such," "have someone do such and such," or (b) "let someone do such and such." In other words -*saseru* and -*seru* are used as (a) causative or (b) permissive. Usually the context indicates which meaning is called for.

Depending upon the type of the Verb, -*seru* or -*saseru* is used.

Both -*seru* and -*saseru* conjugate as Vowel Verbs do:

-seru	-seta	-sete	-setari	-semasu	etc.
-saseru	-saseta	-sasete	-sasetari	-sasemasu	etc.

The causative is formulated as follows:

1. Vowel Verb ..... Stem form plus -*saseru*

taberu	⟶	tabesaseru	"make someone eat"
iru	⟶	isaseru	"make someone stay"
kan'gaeru	⟶	kan'gaesaseru	"make someone think"
ukeru	⟶	ukesaseru	"make someone receive"

2. Consonant Verb ..... Pre-Nai form plus -*seru*

iku	⟶	ika(nai)	⟶	ikaseru	"make someone go"
kau	⟶	kawa(nai)	⟶	kawaseru	"make someone buy"
ogoru "treat"	⟶	ogora(nai)	⟶	ogoraseru	"make someone treat"
watasu	⟶	watasa(nai)	⟶	watasaseru	"make someone hand"
matsu	⟶	mata(nai)	⟶	mataseru	"make someone wait"
isogu	⟶	isoga(nai)	⟶	isogaseru	"make someone hurry"
tanoshimu	⟶	tanoshima(nai)	⟶	tanoshimaseru	"let someone enjoy"
yobu	⟶	yoba(nai)	⟶	yobaseru	"make someone call"

3. Irregular Verb

chuumon suru "order"	⟶	chuumon saseru	"make someone order"
kuru	⟶	kosaseru	"make someone come"

There are two types of causative sentences depending upon the type of the original Verb—(1) transitive Verb and (2) intransitive Verb.

1. When the original Verb is a transitive Verb, the actor (the subject) of the original sentence is followed by the Relational *ni* in the causative. That is, the person who is made to do such and such is followed by the Relational *ni*.

person $\left\{ \begin{array}{c} ga \\ wa \end{array} \right\}$ + (Noun + o) + transitive Verb

⟶ **person *ni* + (Noun + o) + Verb(-*seru* or -*saseru*)**

Kyuuji *ga* satoo o *motte kuru.*   ⟶ Kyuuji *ni* satoo o *motte kosaseru.*
  "The waiter brings sugar with him."   "One makes the waiter bring sugar."

Gakusei *ga* repooto o *kakimashita.*   ⟶ Sen'sei wa gakusei *ni* repooto o
  "The students wrote reports."   *kakasemashita.*
                                             "The teacher made the students write
                                                reports."

Kare *ga* kono shigoto o *yarimasu.*   ⟶ Kare *ni* kono shigoto o *yarasemasu.*
  "He'll do this work."   "I'll have him do this work."

144

2. When the original Verb is an intransitive Verb the actor (the subject) of the original sentence is followed by the Relationals *ni* or *o* in the causative. That is, the person who is made to do such and such is followed by the Relationals *o* or *ni*. But the use of *o* is more common than *ni*.

$$\text{person } \textit{ga} + \text{intransitive Verb} \longrightarrow \text{person} \left\{ \begin{matrix} \textbf{\textit{o}} \\ \textbf{or} \\ \textbf{\textit{ni}} \end{matrix} \right\} + \textbf{Verb}(\textit{-seru} \text{ or } \textit{-saseru})$$

Musume *ga ikimashita.* $\longrightarrow$ Musume *o ikasemashita.*
  "My daughter went."   "I let my daughter go."

Ten'in *ga isogimashita.* $\longrightarrow$ Ten'in *o isogasemashita.*
  "The salesclerk hurried."   "I made the salesclerk hurry."

Since the causative is a strong command, the person who is made to do such and such is normally someone inferior to the speaker or to the person who makes or lets him do it, such as children, servants, younger people, and so forth. When the use of *-saseru* or *-seru* is not adequate, ~ *ni* … *-te morau* may be used instead.

Compare:

Ojisan ni tori ni itte moraimashita.   "I asked my uncle go to pick it up, and he did."

Otooto ni (*or* o) tori ni ikasemashita.   "I made my younger brother go to pick it up."

Ookawa san kara den'wa nara, watashi ni mo hanasasete kudasai.   "If it is a telephone call from Mr. Ōkawa, please let me talk with him too."

Kodomo wa kaze o hiita rashii node, gakkoo o yasumasemashita.   "Since the child seemed to have caught a cold, I made him stay home from school."

Atarashii koto o iroiro kikasete kudasai.   "Please let me hear what is new."

Dare ni harawaseru tsumori desu ka?   "Whom are you going to make pay?"

Kyuuji ni matchi o motte kosasetara, doo desu ka?   "Why don't you make the waiter bring a match for you?"

8.4.9 *En'ryo suru* means "hesitate," "have a reserved attitude." It is quite revealing as a concept in understanding Japanese groupism. Within an intimate group such as the family, it is not necessary for family members to exercise *en'ryo*. This amounts to "being at home" in America, or to "feeling free." Outside the family, yet still within one's in-group, it is most important to have *en'ryo*. Outside the in-group, when one is with total strangers, *en'ryo* is again less necessary. Therefore *en'ryo* can be used to distinguish between the intimate group, the formal in-group, and the out-group, or strangers.

This concept explains the traditional Japanese behavior toward intimate group's in-group members, formal group's in-group members, and strangers. Many Japanese behave with less reserve when traveling, since among total strangers their conduct will not be seen as a shameful reflection on the group. Once they have returned to the confines of the in-group, however, their behavior will be entirely different since unorthodox and unacceptable behavior would bring shame to the family or the group. Bringing shame to one's group is the source of Japanese guilt; where no shame results, there is consequently no guilt. As previously discussed, in Japan it is group conscience not individual conscience which governs one's behavior. Feelings of personal shame arise when the group is hurt or betrayed by the individual's conduct. This groupism, therefore, affects behavior such as *en'ryo* and feelings of shame or guilt, which in turn affect language expressions. For example:

Doozo goen'ryo naku.	"Please feel free."
Futari wa en'ryo no nai aidagara da.	"Two are good friends."
Kimi to boku no aida de en'ryo wa iranai yo.	"We are good friends. (We can be frank with each other.)"
Yamada san wa en'ryo bukai.	"Mr. Yamada is a man of restraint."
Goen'ryo itashimasu.	"I should decline it."

8.4.10 The first part of the dialog reveals the traditional Japanese reserve with respect to gifts or offers of favors. There is an attempt not to show ready acceptance of another's beneficence. Japanese prefer, and are expected, to turn down such an offer at least once. The offer of course will be made again, and pressed by the giver of the favor as a part of this ritual. Mr. Ishida suggests, "Let me treat you." Mr. Yamazaki promptly and properly refuses. Ishida then insists, and Yamazaki finally accepts.

This Japanese trait is illustrated by Takeo Doi in his book *The Structure of Amae* (*amae* means "depending on" or "taking things for granted"). According to Doi, while visiting an American family he was offered some ice cream. Although he wanted it, he properly said "No, please don't bother." The result was that he did not get any ice cream—the Americans had taken him at his word.

In America, the general attitude is not to force others to have that which they expressly state they do not want. In Japan, however, even when someone refuses something you must continue to press it upon him or her knowing that the first rejection may be only an expression of proper Japanese etiquette and not a factual statement. In Kyōto, for instance, this rejection ritual may go to extremes. A guest might be expected to turn down an offer of refreshments, for example, and even when repeatedly urged to have some, he is not supposed to touch it. Generally speaking, in Japan one is not supposed to demonstrate any greediness, aggressiveness, or directness. For younger people in Japan, however, a frank attitude is desirable among peers, but a reserved attitude is suggested when dealing with elders or superiors.

8.4.11 This dialog demonstrates the relationship between a waiter and a customer. The waiter is the inferior and the customer is the superior. This is demonstrated in the language used by the waiter. The waiter uses, for example, the *-mase* ending, and the polite form of placing *o-* before a Verb, as well as *nasaimasu*, the polite version of *shimasu*, and *itashimasu* instead of *shimasu*. The waiter also uses in extremely polite form in apologizing—*mooshiwake gozaimasen*, the polite version for *mooshiwake arimasen*, which in turn is more polite than *sumimasen*. His use of *motte mairimasu*, the first-person polite version of *motte ikimasu* or *motte kimasu*, also indicates his inferior status.

8.4.12 *Sugu menyuu o omochi shimasu* means "I will bring a menu right away." The polite prefix *o-* plus the Stem form of a Verb plus *suru* carries the connotation "the speaker or his in-group member will do such and such resulting in the listener's or the third party's receiving a certain service." This pattern makes a contrast with the *o-...ni naru* pattern which refers to someone else's doing. (See Note 13.4.12, Vol. III.)

o- + Stem form of Verb + $\left\{\begin{array}{l} \textit{\textbf{suru}} \\ \textit{\textbf{itasu}} \textbf{ (polite equivalent of } \textit{suru}\textbf{)} \end{array}\right.$

Here are several common examples of this combination:

omochi suru	"I'll bring it to you"
okiki shimasu	"I'll ask someone about it"
omachi shimashita	"I waited for someone"
oyobi shimashoo	"I will call someone in"
oshirase shimashita	"I informed someone of it"
omatase shimashita	"I kept you waiting"

Watakushi ga otetsudai shimashoo.	"I will help you do it."
Shujin ga hon'too no koto o ohanashi suru soo desu.	"My husband says he will tell you the truth."
Oyu mo omochi shimashoo ka?	"Shall I bring you hot water too?"
Omatase itashimashita.	"I'm sorry to have kept you waiting."

8.4.13 *Nan ni nasaimasu ka?* means "What have you decided to order?" *Nasaimasu* is a polite version of *shimasu*. Only the waiter or clerk uses *nasaimasu* in asking for the customer's decision. When the customer decides to order (certain dishes) or to purchase something, he/she may not use ~*ni nasaimasu*; ~*ni shimasu* must be used.

Irasshaimase. Nan ni nasaimasu ka?	"Welcome. What would you order?"
Eeto, koohii to keeki o kudasai.	"Well, give me coffee and cake."
Yappari kore ni shimasu. Kore o kudasai.	"I have decided to have this one (as I thought so before). Please give this to me."

8.4.14 *Ni* in this case is a Relational used when adding items.

Sugoi gochisoo desu nee. Sakana ni gyuuniku ni ebi mo arimasu ne.	"Gee, this is a real feast. There are fish, beef, and, what's more, even prawns."
Kono teeburu ni wa shio ni satoo, sore ni koshoo mo arimasen yo.	"There is no salt, no sugar, nor even pepper on this table."

8.4.15 *Warui kedo* and *Sumanai kedo* are usually used toward an informal equal or an inferior, and *Sumimasen kedo* and *Mooshiwake arimasen kedo* are used toward a formal equal or superior. *Warui kedo* is used more frequently than *Sumanai kedo* in recent times.

Chotto warui n da kedo ...	"I hesitate (to say this), but ..."
Nani?	"What is it?"

8.4.16 When people count they use different counters, such as *-satsu*, *-mai*, *-hai*, and so forth, to formulate numbers. *Issatsu*, *san'mai*, and *gohai* are examples. However, when people order something in a restaurant, *hitotsu*, *futatsu*, *mittsu*, *too*, and the like are used.

Sumimasen. Koohii o hitotsu kudasai.	"One coffee please."
Anoo, juusu hitotsu.	"Well, one juice please."
Gochuumon wa?	"What would you order?"
Eeto, koohii hitotsu to keeki futatsu.	"Let me see … one coffee and two cakes please."

8.4.17 *Motte mairimasu* here means "I'll bring it here." This expression is a humble equivalent of *Motte kimasu*. Actually *mairimasu* could mean either *ikimasu* or *kimasu*. The honorific equivalent of *ikimasu* or *kimasu* is *irasshaimasu*. (See Note 4.4.5, Vol. III.)

Sorosoro mairimashoo ka?	"Shall we go now?"
Hitori de irasshaimashita ka?	"Did you go (or come) there (or here) alone?"
Hai, hitori de mairimashita.	"Yes, I did go (or come) there (or here) alone."
Otooto o tsurete mairitai no desu ga …	"I would like to bring my younger brother with me …"
Doozo, tsurete irasshatte kudasai.	"Please take him/her with you."

8.5   VOCABULARY

Presentation

食生活	shokuseikatsu	……	N	eating habits; dietary life
産物	san'butsu	……	N	product of a district
貝	kai	……	N	shellfish; sea shell
やっと	yatto	……	Adv.	at last; finally
牛肉	gyuuniku	……	N	beef
ぶた肉	butaniku	……	N	pork
種類	shurui	……	N	kinds
現代	gen'dai	……	N	present age
めずらしい	mezurashii	……	A	is rare
（に）ちがいない	(ni) chigai nai	……	V + E	must (be) (see 8.4.3)

Dialog

石田	Ishida	……	N	family name
でも	demo	……	R	or something; or somewhere; or someone; etc. (see 8.4.5)
山崎	Yamazaki	……	N	family name
案内します	an'nai shimasu	……	V	take someone to a place; guide

案内<ruby>あん</ruby>	an'nai	......	N	guide
わりかん	warikan	......	N	dutch treat; each person pays for his own food, drinks, movies, etc.
まあ	maa	......	SI	used to stop someone
（言わ）ないで	(iwa)naide	......	Da	without (saying); instead of (saying) (see 8.4.7)
に	ni	......	R	used after a person who is made to do (see 8.4.8)
おごら（せて）	ogora(sete)	......	V	Pre-Nai form of *ogoru* – treat someone to food; one pays for someone else's food, drinks, movies, etc.
せて	-sete	......	Dv	TE form of the causative Derivative *-seru* – make someone do such and such (see 8.4.8)
えんりょし （ないで）	en'ryo shi(naide)	......	V	Pre-Nai form of *en'ryo suru* – have reservations; hesitate
えんりょ	en'ryo	......	N	reserve; hesitation
給仕<ruby>きゅうじ</ruby>	kyuuji	......	N	waiter
メニュー	menyuu	......	N	menu
注文して<ruby>ちゅうもん</ruby>	chuumon shite	......	V	TE form of *chuumon suru* – order
注文<ruby>ちゅうもん</ruby>	chuumon	......	N	order
ひょうばん	hyooban	......	N	reputation
えび	ebi	......	N	prawn; lobster; shrimp
フライ	furai	......	N	fried food
に	ni	......	R	and; in addition (see 8.4.14)
スープ	suupu	......	N	soup
なるべく	narubeku	......	Adv.	if possible
ライス	raisu	......	N	rice
塩	shio	......	N	salt
あれ	are	......	SI	oh?
させましょう	-sasemashoo	......	Dv	OO form of the causative Derivative *-saseru* (see 8.4.8)
もうしわけ ございません。	Mooshiwake gozaimasen.	......	(exp.)	I am sorry. (lit. There is no excuse.)
まいります	mairimasu	......	E	polite equivalent of *kimasu* and *ikimasu* (see 8.4.17)

Notes

さとう	satoo	......	N	sugar
を	o	......	R	used after a person who is made to do (see 8.4.8)
マッチ	matchi	......	N	a match
こしょう	koshoo	......	N	pepper
まいる	mairu	......	V	polite equivalent of *kuru* and *iku* (see 8.4.17)
ひとりで	hitori de	......	Adv.	alone; by oneself

Drills

日本料理店	Nihon ryooriten	......	N	Japanese restaurant

8.6   KAN'JI

8.6.1 海 (1) *umi* (2) sea; ocean (3) classifier 氵
(4) 氵 汁 泣 泃 海 海 (5) 海と山 (6) homonym KAI 悔 [regret]

8.6.a 物 (1) BUTSU (5) 産物、動物園、見物   [12.6.8, Vol. II]

8.6.2 昔 (1) *mukashi* (2) ancient times; old days (3) classifier 日
(4) 一 サ 昔 昔 (5) 昔々、ある所に… [once upon a time, there was …]

8.6.3 魚 (1) *sakana* (2) fish (3) forms the classifier 魚
(4) ク 勹 甶 魚 (5) 魚や貝、魚屋、魚料理
(6) the shape of fish

8.6.4 貝 (1) *kai* (2) shellfish; shell (3) forms the classifier 貝
(4) 目 貝 (5) 貝料理 (6) the shape of shell

8.6.5 肉 (1) NIKU (2) meat; flesh (3) classifier 冂（肉）
(4) 冂 内 肉 (5) 牛肉のすきやき、肉屋 [butcher]、牛肉、鳥肉、肉料理

8.6.6 料 (1) RYOO (2) materials; charge (3) classifier 米（斗）
(4) 米 米 料 料 (5) 食料、給料 [salary]、料金 [fare]、料理、サービス料

8.6.7 理　(1)　RI　(2)　reason; logic　(3)　classifier 王

(4)　王　珇　理　理　(5)　料理、日本料理店、理由 [reason]、物理

[physics]、地理 [geography]、心理学 [psychology]　(6)　homonym

里、狸

8.6.8 内　(1)　NAI　(2)　inside　(3)　classifier 冂 [enclosure]

(4)　丨　冂　内　内　(5)　案内、家内、内戦 [civil war]、国内

[inland]、内外のニュース [domestic and foreign news]、以内

(6)　originally this *kan'ji* was written 內 which means to enter the enclosure,

therefore ''inside.''

8.6.9 塩　(1)　*shio*　(2)　salt　(3)　classifier 土 [soil]

(4)　扌　扩　垆　塩　塩　塩　(5)　塩水、塩味 [salty taste]、塩からい

[salty]

8.6.10 払*　(1)　*hara(u)*　(2)　pay　(3)　classifier 扌 [hand]　(4)　扌　扗　払

(5)　お金を払う、払いもどし [refund]

8.6.11 鳥*　(1)　*tori*　(2)　bird; chicken　(3)　forms the classifier 鳥

[shape of a bird]　(4)　亻　户　鸟　鳥　鳥

(5)　鳥の声、鳥肉、鳥料理、小鳥 [small bird]

8.6.12 皿*　(1)　*sara*　(2)　plate; dish　(3)　forms the classifier 皿

(4)　冂　四　皿　(5)　皿を洗う、灰皿 [ashtray]、皿洗い機 [dishwasher]

8.6.13 歩*　(1)　*aru(ku)*　(2)　walk　(3)　classifier 止 [represents a foot,

hence to march or stop]　(4)　丨　卜　止　止　歨　歩

(5)　歩く、山歩き

8.7　DRILLS

8.7.1　Transformation Drill

1.　子どもが　ご飯を　食べます。　　　⟶　　子どもに　ご飯を　食べさせます。

2.　二年生が　しけんを　受けました。　⟶　　二年生に　しけんを　受けさせました。

3.　むすめが　ピアノを　ひきます。　　⟶　　むすめに　ピアノを　ひかせます。

4.　小川さんが　お金を　払います。　　⟶　　小川さんに　お金を　払わせます。

5.　あの　子が　窓を　開けました。　　⟶　　あの　子に　窓を　開けさせました。

6.　工員が　機械を　調べます。　　　　⟶　　工員に　機械を　調べさせます。

7. 社員が　銀行へ　電話を　かけました。   ⟶   社員に　銀行へ　電話を　かけさせ
                                ました。

8. 給仕が　塩を　持って来ます。   ⟶   給仕に　塩を　持って来させます。

9. 友だちが　えびフライを　おごり   ⟶   友だちに　えびフライを　おごらせ
  ました。   ました。

10. 家内が　客を　案内します。   ⟶   家内に　客を　案内させます。

11. 山崎さんが　いぬを　つれて来ます。   ⟶   山崎さんに　いぬを　つれて
                                来させます。

12. 学生が　会話を　れんしゅうします。   ⟶   学生に　会話を　れんしゅうさせます。

13. 子どもが　新聞を　読みました。   ⟶   子どもに　新聞を　読ませました。

14. みんなが　日本語を　話します。   ⟶   みんなに　日本語を　話させます。

15. むすこが　かばんを　持ちました。   ⟶   むすこに　かばんを　持たせました。

8.7.2 Transformation Drill

1. 家内が　うちに　います。   ⟶   家内を　うちに　いさせます。

2. 子どもが　うちへ　帰りました。   ⟶   子どもを　うちへ　帰らせました。

3. むすこが　公園で　あそんでいます。   ⟶   むすこを　公園で　あそばせています。

4. かれが　二かいへ　あがりました。   ⟶   かれを　二かいへ　あがらせました。

5. 秘書が　買いに　行きました。   ⟶   秘書を　買いに　行かせました。

6. 社員が　土曜日も　働くんです。   ⟶   社員を　土曜日も　働かせるんです。

7. 事務員が　課長の　所へ　来ます。   ⟶   事務員を　課長の　所へ　来させます。

8. 子どもが　おふろに　入りました。   ⟶   子どもを　おふろに　入らせました。

8.7.3 Substitution Drill

医者は　かんご婦を　行かせました。

1. 来る   ……   医者は　かんご婦を　来させました。

2. ぼくを   ……   医者は　ぼくを　来させました。

3. 社長は   ……   社長は　ぼくを　来させました。

4. やめる   ……   社長は　ぼくを　やめさせました。

5. いすに　すわる   ……   社長は　ぼくを　いすに　すわらせました。

6. 出張する   ……   社長は　ぼくを　出張させました。

7. 斉藤さんを   ……   社長は　斉藤さんを　出張させました。

8. 野村部長は   ……   野村部長は　斉藤さんを　出張させました。

9. おどろく　　　　　……　野村部長は　斉藤さんを　おどろかせました。
10. 急ぐ　　　　　　　……　野村部長は　斉藤さんを　急がせました。

8.7.4　Response Drill

1. だれに　この　仕事を　してもらいましょうか。
   わたし　　　　　　　……　わたしに　させてください。
2. だれに　手つだってもらいましょうか。
   わたしたち　　　　　……　わたしたちに　手つだわせてください。
3. だれに　銀座へ　案内してもらいましょうか。
   わたし　　　　　　　……　わたしに　案内させてください。
4. だれに　料理を　作ってもらいましょうか。
   わたしと　いもうと　……　わたしと　いもうとに　作らせてください。
5. だれに　しゃしんを　とってもらいましょうか。
   ぼく　　　　　　　　……　ぼくに　とらせてください。
6. どなたに　行っていただきましょうか。
   わたし　　　　　　　……　わたしに　行かせてください。
7. どなたに　日本人の　食生活について　調べてもらいましょうか。
   わたしたち　　　　　……　わたしたちに　調べさせてください。
8. だれに　プレゼントを　開けてもらいましょうか。
   ぼく　　　　　　　　……　ぼくに　開けさせてください。

8.7.5　Substitution Drill

えんりょしないで、来てください。

1. 食事を　しません　　　　……　食事を　しないで、来てください。
2. 心配しません　　　　　　……　心配しないで、来てください。
3. 牛肉を　買いません　　　……　牛肉を　買わないで、来てください。
4. 時間を　まちがえません　……　時間を　まちがえないで、来てください。
5. おくれません　　　　　　……　おくれないで、来てください。
6. 気に　しません　　　　　……　気に　しないで、来てください。
7. クラスを　休みません　　……　クラスを　休まないで、来てください。
8. モーガンさんを　待ちません　……　モーガンさんを　待たないで、来てください。

8.7.6　Transformation Drill

1. 勉強<u>しませんでした</u>。
   昼寝しました。　　　　　　　　　　　　⟶　勉強<u>しないで</u>、昼寝しました。

2. そこで　まがらないでください。
   まっすぐ　行ってください。　　　　　　⟶　そこで　まがらないで、まっすぐ
   　　　　　　　　　　　　　　　　　　　　　　行ってください。

3. わりかんに　しません。
   わたしが　おごるつもりです。　　　　　⟶　わりかんに　しないで、わたしが
   　　　　　　　　　　　　　　　　　　　　　　おごるつもりです。

4. 車は　ふえませんでした。
   自転車が　ふえました。　　　　　　　　⟶　車は　ふえないで、自転車が　ふえ
   　　　　　　　　　　　　　　　　　　　　　　ました。

5. あしたは　あそびません。
   一日じゅう　仕事を　しなければ　　　　⟶　あしたは　あそばないで、一日じゅう
   なりません。　　　　　　　　　　　　　　　仕事を　しなければなりません。

6. かれは　たばこを　すいません。
   おさけを　よく　飲みます。　　　　　　⟶　かれは　たばこを　すわないで、
   　　　　　　　　　　　　　　　　　　　　　　おさけを　よく　飲みます。

8.7.7　Substitution Drill

なるべく　早く　<u>お持ちします</u>。

1. 知らせる　　　　　……　なるべく　早く　お知らせします。
2. 聞く　　　　　　　……　なるべく　早く　お聞きします。
3. 呼ぶ　　　　　　　……　なるべく　早く　お呼びします。
4. 取りけす　　　　　……　なるべく　早く　お取りけしします。
5. むかえる　　　　　……　なるべく　早く　おむかえします。
6. 払う　　　　　　　……　なるべく　早く　お払いします。
7. 頼む　　　　　　　……　なるべく　早く　お頼みします。
8. 作る　　　　　　　……　なるべく　早く　お作りします。

8.7.8　Response Drill

1. さっき　魚屋へ　行きましたか。　　　　　……　はい、まいりました。
2. 今晩　うちへ　いらっしゃいませんか。　　　……　はい、まいります。
3. うちの　辺まで　歩いて　来ますか。　　　　……　はい、歩いてまいります。
4. お弁当を　持って　来ましたか。　　　　　　……　はい、持ってまいりました。
5. タクシーに　乗って行きましょうか。　　　　……　はい、乗ってまいりましょう。
6. おとうとさんを　つれていらっしゃいましたか。……　はい、つれてまいりました。
7. 旅行の　飲み物を　持っていらっしゃいますか。……　はい、持ってまいります。

8.7.9　Transformation Drill

A. 1. あの　店で　食事を　しましょうか。　　⟶　　あの　店で　食事でも　しましょうか。

2. のどが　かわいたから、スープを　　　⟶　　のどが　かわいたから、スープでも
　　　注文しましょう。　　　　　　　　　　　　　注文しましょう。

3. 鳥肉と　やさいを　料理　　　　　　　⟶　　鳥肉と　やさいでも　料理
　　　しましょうか。　　　　　　　　　　　　　しましょうか。

4. 貝の　フライを　おごらせて　　　　　⟶　　貝の　フライでも　おごらせて
　　　ください。　　　　　　　　　　　　　　　ください。

5. 頭が　いたいんですか。　　　　　　　⟶　　頭でも　いたいんですか。

6. 水か　お湯が　ほしいんですか。　　　⟶　　水か　お湯でも　ほしいんですか。

7. さんぽを　しましょうか。　　　　　　⟶　　さんぽでも　しましょうか。

B. 1. 野村さんに　話してみましょう。　　　⟶　　野村さんにでも　話してみましょう。

2. 十時から　はじめませんか。　　　　　⟶　　十時からでも　はじめませんか。

3. 海へ　いっしょに　まいりましょう。　⟶　　海へでも　いっしょに　まいりましょう。

4. この　いすに　すわっていて　　　　　⟶　　この　いすにでも　すわっていて
　　　ください。　　　　　　　　　　　　⟶　　　　ください。

5. 駅の　前で　会いましょうか。　　　　⟶　　駅の　前ででも　会いましょうか。

6. 日本料理店に　案内いたし　　　　　　⟶　　日本料理店にでも　案内いたし
　　　ましょうか。　　　　　　　　　　　　　　ましょうか。

8.7.10　Expansion Drill

1. 注文させました。　　　　　　　　　……　注文させました。

　　新しい　電気製品を　　　　　　　　……　新しい　電気製品を　注文させました。

　　社員に　　　　　　　　　　　　　……　社員に　新しい　電気製品を　注文させました。

　　社長が　　　　　　　　　　　　　……　社長が　社員に　新しい　電気製品を
　　　　　　　　　　　　　　　　　　　　　注文させました。

2. 案内させようと　思っています。　……　案内させようと　思っています。

　　めずらしい　所へ　　　　　　　　……　めずらしい　所へ　案内させようと　思って
　　　　　　　　　　　　　　　　　　　　　います。

　　山崎さんを　　　　　　　　　　　……　山崎さんを　めずらしい　所へ　案内
　　　　　　　　　　　　　　　　　　　　　させようと　思っています。

　　石田さんに　　　　　　　　　　　……　石田さんに　山崎さんを　めずらしい　所へ
　　　　　　　　　　　　　　　　　　　　　案内させようと　思っています。

3. おごらせてください。 ...... おごらせてください。

　西洋料理でも ...... 西洋料理でも　おごらせてください。

　ぼくに ...... ぼくに　西洋料理でも　おごらせてください。

　きょうは ...... きょうは　ぼくに　西洋料理でも　おごらせて
　　　　　　　　　　　　　　ください。

4. 持って来させましょう。 ...... 持って来させましょう。

　給仕に ...... 給仕に　持って来させましょう。

　塩と　こしょうが　ないので ...... 塩と　こしょうが　ないので、給仕に　持って
　　　　　　　　　　　　　　来させましょう。

5. 払わせるんです。 ...... 払わせるんです。

　千円ずつ ...... 千円ずつ　払わせるんです。

　みんなに ...... みんなに　千円ずつ　払わせるんです。

　わりかんに　したから ...... わりかんに　したから、みんなに　千円ずつ
　　　　　　　　　　　　　　払わせるんです。

6. 書かせてください。 ...... 書かせてください。

　名前と　所を ...... 名前と　所を　書かせてください。

　この　紙に ...... この　紙に　名前と　所を　書かせて
　　　　　　　　　　　　　　ください。

　わすれないで ...... わすれないで、この　紙に　名前と　所を
　　　　　　　　　　　　　　書かせてください。

8.7.11　E-J Expansion Drill

1. 赤ちゃんが　飲みました。

　made the baby drink ...... 赤ちゃんに　飲ませました。

　cow's milk ...... 牛乳を　赤ちゃんに　飲ませました。

　I ...... わたしは　牛乳を　赤ちゃんに　飲ませ
　　　　　　　　　　　　　　ました。

2. 学生が　考えました。

　had the students think ...... 学生に　考えさせました。

　difficult problems ...... むずかしい　問題を　学生に　考えさせ
　　　　　　　　　　　　　　ました。

　Professor Suzuki ...... 鈴木先生は　むずかしい　問題を　学生に
　　　　　　　　　　　　　　考えさせました。

3. むすめが　皿を　洗います。

have my daughter wash	……	むすめに　皿を　洗わせます。
every day	……	毎日　むすめに　皿を　洗わせます。
my wife	……	家内は　毎日　むすめに　皿を　洗わせます。

4. 小学生が　帰りました。

let the elementary-school boys go home	……	小学生を　帰らせました。
the teacher	……	先生は　小学生を　帰らせました。
since a typhoon came	……	台風が　来たので、先生は　小学生を　帰らせました。

5. 店員が　来ます。

please let the clerk come	……	店員を　来させてください。
to the office	……	事務所へ　店員を　来させてください。
at two o'clock	……	二時に　事務所へ　店員を　来させてください。

8.8　EXERCISES

8.8.1　Transform the following sentences so that they will mean "I will make or I made (a person) do so."

れい：友だちが　おごります。 → 友だちに　おごらせます。

1. 井上君は　仕事を　手つだいます。
2. 木下さんは　事務所で　三十分も　待ちました。
3. めずらしい　鳥肉の　料理を　家内が　作りました。えんりょしないで、食べてください。
4. クラークさんは　ひとりで　病院へ　来たんですか。
5. 子どもたちは　夕ご飯を　食べなければなりません。
6. 社員が　紙を　用意した。

8.8.2　What would you say when:

1. you tell someone that you are planning to let the secretary go home at three o'clock?
2. you want to ask someone to let you explain about Japanese products?
3. you tell someone that you made the children play in the garden?
4. you tell someone that Mr. Morgan made his brother go to the repair shop to get Mr. Morgan's car?
5. you tell someone to come to your house without hesitation?
6. you apologize to someone politely?
7. you tell someone politely that you are sorry for having kept him waiting?
8. you tell someone politely that you are going to bring coffee and sugar right away?

8.8.3 次の _____に てき当な ひらがなを 入れなさい。

1. 医者は かんご婦_____ 病人_____ 熱_____ はからせました。

2. わりかん_____ しましょう。

3. 昼ご飯は 何_____ なさいますか。

4. ビフテキ_____ スープを 注文しましょう。

5. のど_____ かわいた_____、きっさ店_____ つめたい 物_____
   飲みましょうか。

6. かれ_____ しんせつな 人は めずらしい_____ ちがいない。

8.8.4 次の _____に てき当な ひらがなを 入れなさい。

1. お皿を 洗_____て ごめんなさい。

2. あしたは わすれ_____、電話してください。

3. 部長は 修理屋に 車を なお_____そうです。

4. 急_____て 悪い_____、すぐ 注文した 物を 持って来てね。

5. 課長に わたしたい レポートが ありますから、秘書に 取りに 来_____
   ください。

6. どうぞ えんりょ_____、好き_____ 物を 注文してください。

8.8.5 Change the underlined part into a more polite expression.

1. 悪いけど、お塩を 取ってください。

2. おそくなって すみませんでした。

3. メニュー 持って来ましょうか。

4. カレーライスでも どうですか。

5. えびフライは きょう ありません。

6. 「つめたい 飲み物を 頼みます。」「わかりました。すぐ 作ります。」

7. お皿を 洗わせてもらえませんか。

8. 急いでいますか。もし そうなら、タクシーを 呼びますけど。

8.8.6 次の ていねいな 文を 普通の 文に 変えなさい。

1. けっして きたなくいたしません。

2. すぐ お茶を 持ってまいりますから、お待ちくださいませ。

3. お金は けい子さんに お払いしました。

4. 山口先生は あさっての 午後 研究室で お仕事を なさいますか。

5. 家族を つれてまいりましょうか。

6. あした　おたくへ　うかがうことに　なっておりますが、何時ごろ　まいり
　ましょうか。ごつごうを　お聞かせください。

7. みな様の　おしゃしんを　おとりしましょうか。

8.8.7　漢字に　変えなさい。

1. にほんでは　むかしから、かいや　さかななど　うみの　産ぶつを　たべ、
　めいじに　なるまでは、ぎゅうにくや　ぶたにくを　たべなかった。

2. ぼくに　ゆうべの　とりりょうりの　おかねを　はらわせてください。

3. さとう、しお、こしょう、さらなどが　テーブルの　うえに　あります。

4. あるいたら、りょうりてんまで　にじっぷんは　かかるでしょう。

5. いい　みせに　案ないさせましょう。

8.8.8　読みなさい。

1. 貝、買
2. 土、塩、場
3. 者、昔、黄
4. 料、米
5. 少、歩
6. 内、肉
7. 鳥、島
8. 払、仏、私
9. 皿、四
10. 毎、海
11. 魚、黒

8.8.9　For what purpose would you say *Shokuji demo shimashoo ka?* instead of *Shokuji o shimashoo ka?*

8.8.10　Classify each of the following sentences as either that of "promotion of others" or "demotion of the speaker."

1. Menyuu o omochi ni narimashita.
2. Menyuu o omochi shimasu.
3. Suki na hoo o chuumon itashimashita.
4. Suki na hoo ni nasatta n deshoo.
5. Chiisai ko o tsurete mairimashita.
6. Chiisai ko o tsurete irasshaimashita.

8.8.11　In what cases would you say *Goen'ryo naku?*

8.8.12　Rank the following expressions of apology from formal to less formal.

1. Doomo mooshiwake arimasen.
2. Mooshiwake gozaimasen.
3. Warui desu ne.
4. Sumimasen.
5. Gomen ne.

8.8.13 In what case would you say the following?

    1. Otori shimashita.

    2. Otori ni narimashita.

8.8.14 Fill in an appropriate subject-person in the blank.

    1. ——————— wa hashitte mairimashita.

    2. ——————— wa hashitte irasshaimashita.

    3. ——————— wa hashitte kimashita.

8.8.15 Fill in an appropriate subject-person in the blank.

    1. ——————— wa moo chuumon nasaimashita.

    2. ——————— wa moo chuumon itashimashita.

    3. ——————— wa moo chuumon shimashita.

8.8.16 When you tell someone that you'll send your younger brother to the post office, which expression would you use?

    1. Yuubin'kyoku e otooto o ikaseru yo.

    2. Yuubin'kyoku e otooto ni itte morau yo.

8.9   SITUATIONAL AND APPLICATION CONVERSATION

8.9.1 At Mr. Yamaguchi's home.

Mr. Saitō says to Mr. Yamaguchi that it's about dinner time and he is leaving.

Mr. Yamaguchi tells Mr. Saitō that he has already had his wife prepare dinner for Mr. Saitō. Mr. Yamaguchi asks Mr. Saitō to have dinner with them if he is not in a hurry.

Mr. Saitō appreciates it.

Mr. Yamaguchi says to Mr. Saitō that they are going to have fried prawns. He explains to Mr. Saitō that his younger brother went to their hometown last week and Mr. Yamaguchi had his brother buy prawns. Prawns are famous products of their hometown.

Mr. Saitō says that he will accept dinner with pleasure.

8.9.2 Going to a coffee shop.

Mr. Ishii asks Mr. Yamazaki if he is thirsty.

Mr. Yamazaki says yes and adds that he wants to have some coffee or something.

Mr. Ishii suggests going to a coffee shop nearby.

They enter the coffee shop and make their order: Mr. Yamazaki orders a cup of coffee from the waiter and Mr. Ishii orders a cold Coke.

After drinking a cup of coffee, Mr. Yamazaki says that he is so thirsty that he will have the waiter bring a glass of water.

Leaving the table, Mr. Ishii asks Mr. Yamazaki to let Mr. Ishii pay for Mr. Yamazaki's drink. Mr. Yamazaki wants to go dutch.

8.9.3   Create a conversation between a customer and a waiter at a restaurant, a coffee shop, a Japanese restaurant, and the like.

8.9.4

Salesclerk:	Irasshaimase. Nani o sashiagemashoo ka?
Customer:	Tan'joobi no purezen'to o sagashite iru n da kedo.
Salesclerk:	Otomodachi no desu ka?
Customer:	Ee, on'na no tomodachi no.
Salesclerk:	Sore deshitara, kore nado wa ikaga deshoo ka? Ima wakai on'na no kata ni wa totemo yorokobarete orimasu ga.
Customer:	Soo da naa. Jaa, sore ni shiyoo.
Salesclerk:	Arigatoo gozaimasu. Sugu otsutsumi itashimasu. Shooshoo omachi kudasaimase.

8.9.5

Suzuki:	Nodo ga kawaita!
Yoshida:	Moo sukoshi mate yo. Moo sugu Keiko san no uchi da kara, mizu demo moraoo ka?
Mrs. Katō:	Ara, Suzuki san to Yoshida san, chotto uchi e irasshaimasen ka? Keiko mo orimasu kara.
Suzuki:	Iie, kyoo wa ... Mata kono tsugi ojama shimasu.
Mrs. Katō:	Maa, son'na koto ossharanaide. Doozo goen'ryo naku. Kyoo wa totemo atsui kara nani ka tsumetai mono demo, doozo.
Yoshida:	Jaa, Suzuki kun chotto ojama shiyoo ka?
Suzuki:	Jaa, chotto dake ojama shimasu.

8.9.6

Shachō:	Ocha ga hoshii ne.
Buchō:	Yokota kun ni motte kosasemashoo.
	....
Buchō:	Yokota kun, shachoo ni ocha o sashiagete.
Yokota:	Hai, sugu motte mairimasu.

8.9.7

Ōmori:	Murata kun, warui kedo, tabako (o) katte kite kureru?
Murata:	Hai.

8.9.8

Asai:	Shimizu san, sumimasen kedo, kore (o) chotto mite itadakenai deshoo ka?
Shimizu:	Ii yo, dore?

8.10   READING COMPREHENSION

8.10.1

　普通の　日本人が　牛肉を　食べ始めたのは　明治時代に　なってからである。それまでの
日本人は　牛肉や　ぶた肉を　食べないで、魚ばかり　食べていた。「けもの(beasts)を
食べると、けものに　なる」と　思っていた　人が　多く　いたそうである。

　明治の　はじめごろ　牛なべ屋（すきやき屋）で　牛なべを　食べさせ、新しい　物の
好きな　若い　人たちの　間で　ひょうばんに　なった。その　後、肉を　食べる　人が
だんだん　ふえて、今では　若い　人たちは　魚より　牛肉や　ぶた肉の　ほうが　好きに
なった。その　若い　人たちでも　長く　外国に　住んでいたりすると、おさしみ(raw
fish)が　食べたくなるそうだ。やはり　日本人の　食生活は　魚と　深い　関係を　持って
いると　言えるに　ちがいない。

8.10.2

おくさん　　「いらっしゃいませ。」

若い　客　　「おじゃまします。」

おくさん　　「どうぞ。まあ、そんな　所に　すわらないで、こちらへ　どうぞ。」

若い　客　　「しつれいします。」

おくさん　　「飲み物は　何に　なさいますか。」

ご主人　　　「君、ウイスキーでも　どう? ビールも　あるけど。」

若い　客　　「ビールを　いただけますか。」

おくさん　　「はい、すぐ　お持ちしましょう。あなたは　何を?」

ご主人　　　「ぼくも　ビールに　しようかな。」

おくさん　　「じゃあ、すぐ　ビールを　持ってまいります。」

- -

ご主人　　　「あ、たばこ　ないかい。」

おくさん　　「ええ。かずおに　買って来させましょう。」

若い　客　　「わざわざ　買いに　行かないで、ぼくのを　すってください。」

おくさん　　「どうも　すみません。でも、ほかに　ほしい　物も　ありますから、やっぱり
　　　　　　　かずおを　行かせますわ。」

8.10.3

客　　　「メニュー　見せて。」

給仕　　「はい、どうぞ。」

客　　　「ええと、何が　いいかな。えびフライは　ないですか。」

給仕　「もうしわけございません。きょうは　かき(oyster)の　フライしか　ないの
　　　ですが、とても　いい　かきでございます。」

客　　「じゃあ、それに　しようかな。」

給仕　「ほかには？」

客　　「パンに　コーヒーを　持って来て。サラダは　ついているんですね。」

給仕　「はい、かきフライに　ついております。コーヒーは　食後に　お持ち
　　　しましょうか。」

客　　「いや、急ぐから、いっしょに　持って来てください。」

給仕　「かしこまりました。」

LESSON 9
日本の　歴史₁

9.1　PRESENTATION

　世界の　ほかの　国々と　同じ₂ように、　日本の　歴史も　外国から　強い
えいきょうを　受けた。　まず、　江戸時代までは　中国の　えいきょうが　大きかった。
　西洋との₃　交通は　十六世紀に　始まったが、　本格的に　なったのは　明治時代
である。　その　後、　わずか　百年あまり₄の　間に、　日本は　近代化を
なしとげたが、　その　速さは　世界にも　例が　ないと　言われている₅。

9.2　DIALOG

しず子₆「谷川先生₇の　歴史の　授業、　あいかわらず　おもしろいわね。」

ジョン₆「ぼくも　先生の　講義を　聞く　たびに₈、　ますます　歴史が　好きに　なるんです。」

しず子「ジョンさんは　歴史を　専攻するつもり？」

ジョン「まだ　決めた₉わけ₁₀ではないです。　先生に　そうだんしてから、　決めようと
　　　　思って₁₁。」

しず子「今度の　歴史の　レポート、　どういう₁₂　ことについて　書くか₁₃　決めたの？」

ジョン「明治以後₁₄の　日本について　書こうと　思っているんです。　日本の　ように、
　　　　古い　文化が　残っていて、　近代産業の　発達している　国に　興味が　あるので。」

しず子「資料は　あるの？　書くより　資料を　あつめるほうが　大変でしょう？」

ジョン「ほとんど　図書館に　あるよう₂です。　それで、　ないのだけ　谷川先生から
　　　　借りようと　思っているんですけど。」

しず子「先生、　貸してくださるかしら？」

ジョン「長い　間、　借りるわけ₁₀には　いかないだろうけど、　四、五日なら
　　　　貸してもらえると　思います。」

しず子「そうね。　谷川先生、　今　ろう下に　いらっしゃるようだから、　頼んで
　　　　みたら₁₅？」

西洋	始まった	速さ	授業	専攻
以後	残っていて	産業	興味	借りよう
貸して				

9.3   PATTERN SENTENCES

9.3.1

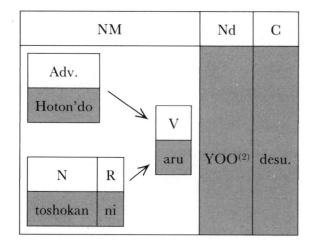

9.3.2

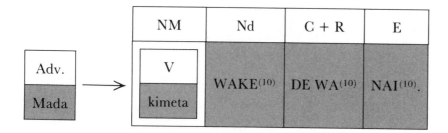

9.3.3

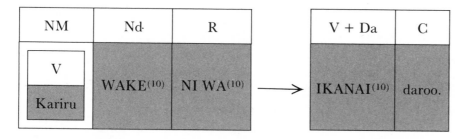

9.4   NOTES

9.4.1   An important factor in the shaping of Japanese history is the separation of Japan from the Asian mainland by the sea. Cultural eclecticism has played a significant role in overcoming Japan's geographic isolation. Cultural elements were drawn into Japanese society first from China and Korea, and then from the West. As has already been pointed out, such eclecticism has resulted in the pluralism that characterizes Japanese culture. The Japanese have been very skillful in creatively adopting and adapting features of other cultures to suit their own environment and situation.

One notable topic in Japanese history is the pluralistic nature of the *samurai* regimes of the

Kamakura period. They exercised a kind of dual rule, whereby the group with actual political power ruled behind a legitimate but relatively powerless figurehead represented by the nobility.

The relationship between Japanese history and Japanese culture, as well as between Japanese history and Japanese language, is another interesting area of inquiry. The study of Japanese history was quite restricted by the government until 1945. Prior to that time the sacrosanct nature of the emperor, imperial rule, and the like made scholarly investigation of those areas of history taboo. Although far more information is available today, there are still primary source materials that are lacking. Most imperial tombs, for example, are still not open to scholarly investigation. The result is that reconstruction of important segments of history, especially premodern history, continues to be difficult.

A number of Western scholars—Sir George Sansom, John W. Hall, and Edwin O. Reischauer to name a few—have made Japanese history accessible to English-speaking readers. A great deal can be gained by studying their writings. Through them one can become familiar with historical periodization and begin to identify the forces behind the dynamics of Japanese history.

9.4.2 *Sekai no hoka no kuniguni to onaji yoo ni,...* means "In the same way as other countries in the world did,..." The *yoo* in the above sentence is a dependent Noun whose meaning cannot be easily defined. It is, generally speaking, close to "manner," "likeliness," or "resemblance," and is often translated as "like," "as," "way," "as if," "so that," and so forth. It serves the purpose of making the statement less decisive, definite, or clear-cut. The Japanese use this expression quite often. The difference between *-rashii* (Note 6.4.7, Vol. III) and *yoo* is sometimes vague. However, *-rashii* attributes the source of information mainly to other people, while *yoo* serves mainly as a softener. The dependent Noun *yoo* is always preceded by a Noun Modifier. Since *yoo* is a dependent adjectival Noun, it is, like an adjectival Noun, followed by the Copula or the Relational of manner *ni*. In the above sentence *onaji* is directly followed by *yoo* since it is a Noun that behaves differently from other Nouns. (See Note 8.4.5, Vol. II.)

$$
\left.
\begin{array}{l}
\textbf{Verb (plain form)}\\
\textbf{Adjective (plain form)}\\
\textbf{adjectival Noun} + \textit{na}\\
\textbf{Noun} + \textit{no}\\
\textbf{Noun} + \textbf{Copula (plain form, except \textit{da})}\\
\textbf{Pre-Noun}
\end{array}
\right\}
+ \textit{yoo} +
\left\{
\begin{array}{l}
\textit{da}\\
\textit{datta}\\
\textit{na} + \textbf{Noun}\\
\textit{ni} + \textbf{Predicate}
\end{array}
\right.
$$

yuki ga futte iru yoo da	"it looks as if it is snowing" "it seems to be snowing"
wakaranakatta yoo desu	"it seems [he] did not understand"
sen'sei ga osshatta yoo ni	"as the teacher said"
taifuu wa totemo ookii yoo da	"the typhoon seems very powerful"
nigiyaka na yoo da	"it seems to be bustling"
kono yoo na mon'dai	"a problem like this"
Nihon no yoo na kuni ni	"in a country like Japan"
anata no yoo na hito	"a person like you"
Amerikajin no yoo ni eigo o hanasu	"[he] speaks English as if he were an American"
min'na ga wakaru yoo ni setsumei suru	"[she] explains (well) so that everyone can understand"
kono yoo ni	"like this"

Anata ga iu yoo ni, kin'dai Nihon ni tsuite
  kakeba yokatta.

"I should have written about modern Japan
  as you said."

Ano shachoo wa izen kooin o shite ita yoo
  desu.

"It is my understanding that that company
  president used to be a factory worker."

Kore wa tekitoo de nai rei datta yoo desu ne.

"This seems to have been an inadequate
  example."

Okinawa no yoo na atatakai tokoro de wa,
  don'na kudamono ga toremasu ka?

"What kind of fruits are produced in a
  warm place like Okinawa?"

Byooki wa karui yoo desu kara, an'shin shite
  kudasai.

"His illness is not serious, so please feel free
  from anxiety."

Mon'dai ga kan'tan na yoo dattara, sukoshi
  muzukashiku shimashoo.

"If the questions are easy, I'll make them a
  little difficult."

9.4.3 *Seiyoo to no kootsuu* means "communication with Western countries." When a Noun is derived from a Verb—for example, "communication" is derived from "communicate"—a Predicate Modifier which is closely related to the original verbal expression may precede the Noun. In this case the Relational *no* has to be inserted between the Predicate Modifier and the Noun in order to transform the Predicate Modifier into a Noun Modifier.

Chuugoku kara no eikyoo

"influence from China"

boku kara no okurimono

"gift from me"

tomodachi to no ken'kyuu

"research work with my friend"

Yooroppa e no ryokoo

"traveling to Europe"

suupaa de no kaimono

"shopping at a supermarket"

Okyakusan kara no chuumon wa koko ni kaite
  arimasu.

"Orders from customers are written here."

Kare to no kekkon seikatsu wa tanoshiku
  nakatta.

"My married life with him wasn't
  pleasant."

9.4.4 *Hyakunen amari* means "one hundred or more years." *-Amari* after a Noun indicating number conveys the meaning of "over," "more than," "above," or "-odd."

gopon'do amari

"over five pounds"

juunen amari

"more than ten years"

-Amari is different from *ijoo* however. *Hyakunen ijoo*, which means "minimum of one hundred years," has no upper limit, therefore even "one hundred ninety years" can be described as *hyakunen ijoo*. *Hyakunen amari*, on the other hand, cannot be used to cover such a case. Although the upper limit is not definable, there nevertheless is a limit psychologically.

9.4.5 The Japanese, at least the older generation, tend to use indirect expressions, especially when speaking in polite language. *~ To iwarete iru* is one such case.

1. Make the end of an utterance vague and ambiguous. For example:
   Ano hito wa ii hito da kara …
   Sore wa soo deshoo ga …

2. Place an indecisive word in the sentence. For example:

   Yokohama e wa san'kai hodo ikimashita.

   Okuni wa dochira ni osumai desu ka?

   Azabu no hoo ni sun'de orimasu.

3. Attach a stylistic ending such as *no, yoo,* and *wake* to the Copula to make the utterance more indirect. For example:

   Amerika e itta no de aru.

   Ame ga futte iru yoo desu.

   Kyonen kekkon shita wake desu.

4. Use vague expressions. For example:

   sorosoro, shibaraku, shooshoo

   (nan'tonaku, sono uchi ni, and nan'daka, yet to be studied, also show vagueness)

5. Use Adverbs indicating moderate, reserved, temperate, and restrained attitudes. For example:

   Amari muzukashii hito ja nakatta.

6. Omission of subject. For example:

   Moo tabemashita.

7. Use negative expressions. For example:

   Yoji ni naranakereba kaerimasen.

   Dame ni chigai nai.

   Iya na wake dewa nai n desu.

   Soo de wa nai deshoo ka?

   Gakkoo e ikanakereba narimasen.

   Ashita gin'koo e ikanai ka mo shiremasen.

   Gohan o tabenakereba ikemasen.

   Okane o harawanai wake ni wa ikimasen.

9.4.6 John and Shizuko are classmates and know each other very well. Normally the two would use the plain informal speech styles. However, John is a foreign student and may not be familiar with the plain informal speech styles. Thus, John has used normal speech style quite often. Compare the following:

Normal	*Plain informal*
Omoshiroi desu (wa) ne.	Omoshiroi (wa) ne.
Sen'koo suru tsumori desu ka?	Sen'koo suru tsumori?
Kimeyoo to omotte iru n desu.	Kimeyoo to omotte …
Kimeta n desu ka?	Kimeta no?
Shiryoo wa aru n desu ka?	Shiryoo wa aru no?
Kashite kudasaru deshoo ka?	Kashite kudasaru kashira?
Ikanai deshoo kedo, …	Ikanai daroo kedo, …
Soo desu ne.	Soo ne.
Tanon'de mitara doo desu ka?	Tanon'de mitara?

If a Japanese male classmate of Shizuko should be talking to Shizuko, the conversation might contain more plain informal styles.

John	*Japanese male classmate*
Rekishi ga suki ni naru n desu.	Rekishi ga suki ni naru n da.
Kakoo to omotte iru n desu.	Kakoo to omotte iru n da.
Toshokan ni aru yoo desu.	Toshokan ni aru yoo da yo.
Kariyoo to omotte iru n desu kedo …	Kariyoo to omotte iru n da kedo …
Kashite moraeru to omoimasu.	Kashite moraeru to omou yo.

9.4.7 Traditionally Japanese professors are treated with dignity and authority, and students are expected to show them respect and obedience. A group with a hierarchical relationship (of teacher and student) is thus formed. The Japanese call this teacher-student relationship a "wet" relationship, and consider the American counterpart as "dry." The Japanese did not produce college graduates en masse until recently. This "wet" relationship is the result of Confucian teaching. According to Confucius, students should not even tread on the shadow of their teacher and must walk three steps behind him. Today, however, this is not the case, and radical students treat conservative professors with little respect.

Japanese professors usually purchase and keep their own books. Book owning in fact has been regarded as a symbol of scholars. Japanese professors would not use the library frequently as their American counterparts might—they have their own collections and are unwilling to loan books to students. This explains Shizuko's comment wondering if the professor would lend his books to John.

9.4.8 *Boku mo sen'sei no koogi o kiku tabi ni, masumasu . . .* means "Every time I attend the professor's lecture, more and more I . . . too." The *tabi* is a dependent Noun meaning "every time," and is always preceded by a Noun Modifier—the Dictionary form of a Verb or a Noun plus *no*. The tense of the final Predicate governs that of the whole sentence. The time Relational *ni* may follow *tabi*.

$$\left.\begin{array}{l}\textbf{Dictionary form of Verb}\\ \textbf{Noun} + \textit{\textbf{no}}\end{array}\right\} + \textit{\textbf{tabi (ni)}} \ ...$$

Shizuko san ni au tabi ni	"whenever I meet Shizuko"
tan'joobi no tabi ni	"on every birthday"
shiken no tabi ni	"every time I have an examination"
Jon san wa rekishi no shiken no tabi ni, hyakuten torimasu.	"On every history examination John gets a hundred."
Komatta koto ga okoru tabi ni, watashi wa oji no tokoro e soodan ni ikimashita.	"Whenever some trouble occurred, I went to consult my uncle."

9.4.9 *Kimeta* in *Mada kimeta wake de wa nai desu* is a transitive Verb. Quite a few Verbs have transitive and intransitive pairs. Usually the transitive Verb is preceded by a direct object with the Relational *o*. The intransitive Verb, on the other hand, is not preceded by the direct object with the Relational *o*.

The following are Verbs which have transitive and intransitive pairs and have appeared so far:

~*ga* + intransitive Verb	~*o* + transitive Verb
kimaru	kimeru "decide"
atsumaru	atsumeru "collect"
kowareru	kowasu "destroy"
naoru	naosu "repair" "heal"
hajimaru	hajimeru "begin"
kaeru	kaesu "return"

The following pairs have not appeared in any previous lesson but will be useful to learn:

agaru	ageru "raise"
aku	akeru "open"
arawareru	arawasu "indicate"[2]

ataru	ateru "hit"
fueru	fuyasu "increase"
heru	herasu "reduce"
narabu	naraberu "place in order"
noru	noseru "place on"
ochiru	otosu "drop"
sagaru	sageru "lower down"
shimaru	shimeru "close"
tsuku	tsukeru "attach"
yakeru	yaku "burn"

9.4.10 *Mada kimeta wake de wa nai* means "It is not that I have decided yet" or "I don't mean that I have already decided." *Wake* is a dependent Noun that is used in such connotations as "circumstances," "reason," "meaning," and so on, but it occurs in some limited formulations. Here are some of them:

1. "one doesn't mean that ..." "it is not that ..."

Verb (plain form)
Adjective (plain form)
adjectival Noun + *na*
Noun + *no*
Noun + Copula (normal form, except *da*)
sooiu, son'na, etc.

$\Big\}$ *+ wake* $\begin{cases} \textit{de wa nai} \\ \textit{ja arimasen} \end{cases}$

Edo jidai wa seiyoo to no kootsuu ga nakatta wake de wa arimasen.	"It is not that communication with Western countries did not exist in the Edo era."
Kirai na wake de wa nai kedo, sushi wa amari tabenai n desu.	"I don't mean that I dislike *sushi*, but I don't eat it often."
Sooiu wake ja arimasen yo.	"I don't mean that."

2. (a) "doing such and such is not permitted or adequate under this circumstance" "one cannot do such and such" "one is not supposed to do such and such"

Dictionary form of Verb
sooiu, son'na, etc.

$\Big\}$ *+ wake ni (wa)* $\begin{cases} \textit{ikanai} \\ \textit{ikimasen} \end{cases}$

Yametai kedo, yameru wake ni ikanai n desu.	"I wish I could quit, but I cannot."
Nagai aida, kariru wake ni wa ikanai daroo.	"I don't think that I can borrow it for a long time."
Hitori de kimeru wake ni wa ikimasen.	"I cannot make a decision by myself."
Kawaisoo da keredo, katte ageru wake ni wa ikanai yo.	"Sorry, but I can't buy it for you."

(b) "one has to do such and such"

plain negative imperfect tense form of Verb + *wake ni (wa)* $\begin{cases} \textit{ikanai} \\ \textit{ikimasen} \end{cases}$

Chuusha ga kirai de mo, shinai wake ni wa ikimasen yo.	"Even if you don't like shots, you have to get them."
Taifuu da kedo, dekakenai wake ni ikanai n desu.	"In spite of the typhoon I have to go out."

3. "reason why one does or doesn't do such and such"

$$\left. \begin{array}{l} \textbf{Verb (plain form)} \\ \textbf{Adjective (plain form)} \\ \textbf{adjectival Noun} + \textit{na} \\ \textbf{Noun} + \textit{no} \\ \textbf{Noun} + \textbf{Copula (plain form, except \textit{da})} \\ \textit{kooiu, sooiu, etc.} \end{array} \right\} + \textit{wake} \left\{ \begin{array}{l} \textit{ga} \ldots \\ \textit{wa} \ldots \\ \textit{o} \ldots \\ \textit{de} \ldots \\ \qquad \textbf{etc.} \end{array} \right.$$

Boku ga shitte iru wake ga nai deshoo?	"Why should I know that?"
Hanasenai wake demo aru no desu ka?	"Is there any reason why you cannot tell me?"
Kyuuji ga menyuu o wasureta wake o shitte imasu yo.	"I know the reason why the waiter forgot to bring the menu."
Dooiu wake de son'na koto o shita n desu ka?	"For what reason did you do such a thing?"
Kono kuni ga yowai wake o shitte imasu ka?	"Do you know the reason why this country is weak?"

9.4.11 *Kime yoo to omotte* is an incomplete sentence and *imasu* is omitted. Or, a clause such as *mada kimete imasen* is omitted. In many cases, an incomplete sentence ends with the TE form, particularly in stating a reason.

Dooshite sugu nomanai no?	"Why don't you drink it right away?"
Atsukute.	"It's hot."

9.4.12 *Dooiu* is a Pre-Noun meaning "what sort of?" and is used in the same manner as *don'na*. *Kooiu, sooiu,* and *aaiu* are also possible as is the case with *kon'na, son'na,* and *an'na*. *Dooiu, kooiu,* and so forth are pronounced *dooyuu, kooyuu,* and so on.

kooiu	"this sort of"	*aaiu*	"that sort of"
sooiu	"that sort of"	*dooiu*	"what sort of?"

Dooiu koojoo de hataraite iru n desu ka?	"What sort of factory is he working at?"
Kooiu baai ni wa sugu isha ni ikanakereba narimasen yo.	"You have to rush to the doctor on such occasions as this."

9.4.13 *Dooiu koto ni tsuite kaku ka kimeta no?* means "Did you decide on what subject to write?" When a question with an interrogative word is included as part of a sentence, the Predicate of the question is normally in plain form. The question without any interrogative word within a sentence has already been introduced in Note 4.4.9—*ka (doo) ka*.

interrogative word + (Relational) + Predicate + *ka*?

$$\longrightarrow \textbf{interrogative word} + \textbf{(Relational)} + \begin{array}{c} \textbf{Predicate} \\ \textbf{(plain form)} \end{array} + \textit{ka} + \left\{ \begin{array}{l} \textit{kimeru} \\ \textit{shitte iru} \\ \textit{oshieru} \\ \textit{iu} \\ \textit{kiku} \\ \qquad \textbf{etc.} \end{array} \right.$$

nani o kaku ka kimemashita	"one decided what to write"
dare ni soodan suru ka wakarimasen	"[I] don't know whom [I] will consult with"
dotchi ga ii ka shitte imasu ka?	"do you know which is better?"
itsu kaetta ka shiranai	"[I] don't know when [he] returned"
dono hon ka kiita	"[I] asked which book it would be"
don'na mono ga hoshikatta ka iimashita	"one said what sort of thing he wanted"
Doko e itta ka shirabete mimashita.	"I have checked on where it's gone."
Dore ga ichiban ii ka oshiete agemashoo.	"I'll tell you which is the best."
Dooiu hanashi o kikitai ka itte kudasai.	"Please tell me what kind of talk you want to listen to."

9.4.14 *Meiji igo* means "in and after Meiji." "In and before" may be expressed with *izen*. Both *igo* and *izen* may be grouped with the *i-* words introduced in Note 7.4.3.

9.4.15 *Tanon'de mitara?* means "How about asking him?" or "Why don't you ask him?" The complete sentence will be *Tanon'de mitara doo desu ka?* or *Tanon'de mitara ii deshoo?*, and so on. *Tanon'de mitara doo?* is also possible. As explained before, this has a softening effect in suggesting that others do something. Together with *wake de wa nai, wake ni wa ikanai, kashira, kana, ja nai n desu ka*, and many other expressions, this approach reveals the Japanese preference for suggestive rather than commanding, indirect rather than direct, vague rather than overly clear, and implicative rather than frank ways of talking.

Kibun ga warusoo ne. Kaettara?	"You look sick. Why don't you go home?"
Koo shitara doo?	"How about doing it this way?"
Sen'sei ni kashite morattara?	"Why don't you ask your teacher to loan it to you?"

9.5   VOCABULARY

Presentation

よう	yoo	......	Nd	like; as; as if; so that; way (see 9.4.2)
強い	tsuyoi	......	A	is strong
江戸	Edo	......	N	the old name of Tōkyō
世紀	-seiki	......	Nd	century
本格的	hon'kakuteki	......	Na	full-scale; real; earnest
わずか	wazuka	......	Adv.	only; barely; merely
あまり	-amari	......	Nd	a little more than ~ (see 9.4.4)
近代化	kin'daika	......	N	modernization

なしとげた	nashitogeta	......	V	achieved; completed (TA form of *nashitogeru*)
速さ	hayasa	......	N	speed
例	rei	......	N	precedent; example

Dialog

しず子	Shizuko	......	N	girl's first name
谷川	Tanikawa	......	N	family name
授業	jugyoo	......	N	class; instruction
あいかわらず	aikawarazu	......	Adv.	as usual
ジョン	Jon	......	N	John
講義	koogi	......	N	lecture
たび	tabi	......	Nd	every time (see 9.4.8)
ますます	masumasu	......	Adv.	more and more
決めた	kimeta	......	V	decided (TA form of *kimeru*) (transitive Verb) (see 9.4.9)
わけ	wake	......	Nd	reason; circumstance; meaning (see 9.4.10)
そうだんして	soodan shite	......	V	TE form of *soodan suru* – consult (~ *ni soodan suru* "consult with ~")
そうだん	soodan	......	N	consultation
どういう	dooiu	......	PN	what sort of ~? (see 9.4.12)
以後	igo	......	N	in and after (see 9.4.14)
近代	kin'dai	......	N	modern age (As far as Japan is concerned, *kin'dai* covers the period from the Meiji era to the present while *gen'dai* covers the period after the Second World War.)
産業	san'gyoo	......	N	industry
資料	shiryoo	......	N	data; research material; reference
あつめる	atsumeru	......	V	gather; collect (transitive Verb)
ろう下	rooka	......	N	narrow hall; corridor

Notes

以前	izen	......	N	before (see 9.4.14)
点	-ten	......	Nd	counter for marks; points
弱い	yowai	......	A	is weak
あつまる	atsumaru	......	V	get together; be collected (intransitive Verb)

決まる	kimaru	......	V	is determined; is decided (intransitive Verb)
ああいう	aaiu	......	PN	that sort of 〜 (see 9.4.12)
そういう	sooiu	......	PN	that sort of 〜

9.6   KAN'JI

9.6.a ^{11.6.9, Vol. II} 西 (1) SEI (5) 西洋、西洋風

9.6.1 始 (1) *haji(maru)*; *haji(meru)* (2) begin; start (3) classifier 女

(4) 女 奼 始 (5) 仕事が始まる

9.6.2 速 (1) *haya(i)* (2) speedy; quick (3) classifier 辶

(4) 束 速 (5) 速くはしる、速さ

9.6.3 授 (1) JU (2) is given; grant (3) classifier 扌 [hand]

(4) 扌 授 (5) 授業、教授[professor] (6) homonym 受

9.6.4 専 (1) SEN (2) exclusive; only (3) classifier 寸

(4) 专 専 (5) 専攻、専門

9.6.5 以 (1) I (2) with; on account of (3) classifier 人

(4) 以 (5) 以上、以下、以外、以内、以前、以後

9.6.6 残 (1) *noko(ru)* (2) remain (3) classifier 歹 [remains of a skeleton, hence death or evil] (4) 歹 死 残 残 残

(5) 残る、残り[the rest]、残り物[leftover]

9.6.7 産 (1) SAN (2) produce; fortune; give birth to (3) classifier 立 (生 [produce]) (4) 产 産

(5) 産業、産物、カリフォルニア産のオレンジ [California orange]

9.6.8 興 (1) KYOO (2) interesting (3) classifier 臼 (ハ)

(4) 興 (5) 興味 (6) raise something together 同 with many hands = rise

9.6.b ^{7.6.8, Vol. III} 味 (1) MI (2) taste (5) 興味、意味

(6) 未 [MI] represents pronunciation; homonym 未、魅

9.6.9 借 (1) *ka(riru)* (2) borrow; rent (3) classifier 亻 (4) 亻 借
(5) 借り物 [borrowed thing]

9.6.10 貸 (1) *ka(su)* (2) lend; loan (3) classifier 貝 [seashell (money)]
(4) 代 貸 (5) 貸(し)家 [house for rent]、貸(し)間 [room for rent]

9.6.11 研* (1) KEN (2) study (3) classifier 石 [stone] (4) 石 矴 研
(5) 研究

9.6.12 究* (1) KYUU (2) study (3) classifier 宀 (4) 宀 穴 究
(5) 研究、研究室、研究会[research society] (6) homonym 九

9.6.13 門* (1) MON (2) gate (3) forms the classifier 門
(4) 丨 冂 冃 門 門 門 (5) 専門、校門、門を出る
(6) homonym 問、聞

9.7 DRILLS

9.7.1 Transformation Drill

1. 京都には 古い 建物が 残っています。⟶ 京都には 古い 建物が 残っている
ようです。

2. ジョンさんは 歴史を 専攻しません。 ⟶ ジョンさんは 歴史を 専攻しないよう
です。

3. 資料は ほとんど 図書館に あります。⟶ 資料は ほとんど 図書館に あるよう
です。

4. けい子さんは 貸してくださいません。 ⟶ けい子さんは 貸してくださらないよう
です。

5. おとうとは りょうしんに そうだん ⟶ おとうとは りょうしんに そうだん
しました。 したようです。

6. 歴史の レポートの 題を 決めました。⟶ 歴史の レポートの 題を 決めたよう
です。

7. 沖縄の 文化は 中国から 強い ⟶ 沖縄の 文化は 中国から 強い
えいきょうを 受けました。 えいきょうを 受けたようです。

8. 母は 牛肉を 注文しませんでした。 ⟶ 母は 牛肉を 注文しなかったようです。

9.7.2　Transformation Drill

1. 谷川先生の　授業は　特に　おもしろい　 ⟶ 　谷川先生の　授業は　特に　おもしろい
です。　　　　　　　　　　　　　　　　　　　ようです。

2. 日本は　西洋からの　えいきょうが　 ⟶ 　日本は　西洋からの　えいきょうが
強いです。　　　　　　　　　　　　　　　　強いようです。

3. この　辺は　交通が　あまり　多くあり　 ⟶ 　この　辺は　交通が　あまり　多くない
ません。　　　　　　　　　　　　　　　　　ようです。

4. この　みやげは　めずらしくあり　 ⟶ 　この　みやげは　めずらしくないよう
ません。　　　　　　　　　　　　　　　　です。

5. しず子さんは　とても　やさしかった　 ⟶ 　しず子さんは　とても　やさしかった
です。　　　　　　　　　　　　　　　　　　ようです。

6. 哲学の　講義は　長かったです。　 ⟶ 　哲学の　講義は　長かったようです。

7. お湯は　あまり　あつくなかったです。 ⟶ 　お湯は　あまり　あつくなかったよう
です。

8. この　本は　ひょうばんが　いいです。 ⟶ 　この　本は　ひょうばんが　いいよう
です。

9.7.3　Transformation Drill

1. あの　辺は　しずかです。　　　　 ⟶ 　あの　辺は　しずかなようです。

2. あの　人は　ジョンさんです。　　 ⟶ 　あの　人は　ジョンさんのようです。

3. お祭りは　にぎやかです。　　　　 ⟶ 　お祭りは　にぎやかなようです。

4. それは　適当な　例です。　　　　 ⟶ 　それは　適当な　例のようです。

5. きのうは　しず子さんの　たんじょう日　 ⟶ 　きのうは　しず子さんの　たんじょう日
でした。　　　　　　　　　　　　　　　　　だったようです。

6. 野村さんが　たてた　家は　とても　 ⟶ 　野村さんが　たてた　家は　とても
近代的でした。　　　　　　　　　　　　　近代的だったようです。

7. ジョージさんの　しけんは　百点　 ⟶ 　ジョージさんの　しけんは　百点だった
でした。　　　　　　　　　　　　　　　　ようです。

8. ポール君のと　同じじゃありません　 ⟶ 　ポール君のと　同じじゃなかったよう
でした。　　　　　　　　　　　　　　　　です。

9.7.4　Substitution Drill

<u>あなたも　知っている</u>ように、わたしは　日本史を　研究しています。

1. ジョンさんが　言いました　　……　ジョンさんが　言ったように、わたしは
　　　　　　　　　　　　　　　　　　　　　日本史を　研究しています。

2. 前に　決めました　　　　　　……　前に　決めたように、わたしは　日本史を
　　　　　　　　　　　　　　　　　　　　　研究しています。

3. 谷川先生が　おっしゃいました　……　谷川先生が　おっしゃったように、わたしは
　　　　　　　　　　　　　　　　　　　　　日本史を　研究しています。

4. あなたと　同じです　　　　　……　あなたと　同じように、わたしは　日本史を
　　　　　　　　　　　　　　　　　　　　　研究しています。

5. ハンフリーさんです　　　　　……　ハンフリーさんのように、わたしは　日本史を
　　　　　　　　　　　　　　　　　　　　　研究しています。

6. 松本さんが　思っています　　……　松本さんが　思っているように、わたしは
　　　　　　　　　　　　　　　　　　　　　日本史を　研究しています。

7. 先生に　言われました　　　　……　先生に　言われたように、わたしは　日本史を
　　　　　　　　　　　　　　　　　　　　　研究しています。

9.7.5　Response Drill

1. それは　どういう　物ですか。

　　プラスチック　　　　　　　……　プラスチックのような　物です。

2. しず子さんは　どんな　方ですか。

　　あなた　　　　　　　　　　……　あなたのような　方です。

3. この　おかしは　どんな　味ですか。

　　コーヒー　　　　　　　　　……　コーヒーのような　味です。

4. そこは　どういう　町ですか。

　　京都や　奈良　　　　　　　……　京都や　奈良のような　町です。

5. どんな　人に　会いましたか。

　　アメリカ人　　　　　　　　……　アメリカ人のような　人に　会いました。

6. その　島は　どんな　気候ですか。

　　ハワイ　　　　　　　　　　……　ハワイの　ような　気候です。

7. どういう　物が　ほしかったんですか。

　　マイコン　　　　　　　　　……　マイコンのような　物が　ほしかったんです。

9.7.6 Substitution Drill

A. <u>興味を　持っている</u>わけではありません。

1. もう　決めました　　　　　…… もう　決めたわけではありません。

2. ひとりで　なしとげます　　…… ひとりで　なしとげるわけではあり
　　　　　　　　　　　　　　　　　　　ません。

3. わたしが　おごります　　　…… わたしが　おごるわけではありません。

4. ここから　海や　山が　見えます …… ここから　海や　山が　見えるわけでは
　　　　　　　　　　　　　　　　　　　ありません。

5. 広田君を　行かせます　　　…… 広田君を　行かせるわけではありません。

6. お金が　たりません　　　　…… お金が　たりないわけではありません。

7. あなたの　声が　聞こえません …… あなたの　声が　聞こえなかったわけ
　　　でした　　　　　　　　　　　　　ではありません。

B. <u>それが　全部　ほしい</u>わけじゃありません。

1. えいきょうが　強いです　　…… えいきょうが　強いわけじゃありません。

2. スポーツが　特に　弱いです …… スポーツが　特に　弱いわけじゃあり
　　　　　　　　　　　　　　　　　　　ません。

3. かばんが　重いです　　　　…… かばんが　重いわけじゃありません。

4. 料理が　からかったんです　…… 料理が　からかったわけじゃありません。

5. 講義が　つまらなかったです …… 講義が　つまらなかったわけじゃ
　　　　　　　　　　　　　　　　　　　ありません。

6. 母が　やさしくありません　…… 母が　やさしくないわけじゃありません。

C. <u>まだ　本格的な</u>わけではありません。

1. 牛乳が　きらいです　　　　…… 牛乳が　きらいなわけではありません。

2. めずらしい　名前です　　　…… めずらしい　名前のわけでは
　　　　　　　　　　　　　　　　　　　ありません。

3. ことしが　最後です　　　　…… ことしが　最後のわけではありません。

4. ここだけが　しずかです　　…… ここだけが　しずかなわけでは
　　　　　　　　　　　　　　　　　　　ありません。

5. 社会保障制度が　完全です　…… 社会保障制度が　完全なわけでは
　　　　　　　　　　　　　　　　　　　ありません。

6. 特に　この　授業が　好きです …… 特に　この　授業が　好きなわけでは
　　　　　　　　　　　　　　　　　　　ありません。

9.7.7　Response Drill

1. 世界に　例が　ないんですか。
   めずらしいそうです。　　　　　　　　……　世界に　例が　<u>ないわけでは</u>
   　　　　　　　　　　　　　　　　　　　　　<u>ありませんが</u>、めずらしいそうです。

2. 日本史を　専攻したいんですか。
   興味を　持っているんです。　　　　　……　日本史を　専攻したいわけでは
   　　　　　　　　　　　　　　　　　　　　　ありませんが、興味を　持っている
   　　　　　　　　　　　　　　　　　　　　　んです。

3. レポートの　題は　決めたの?
   アメリカの　産業について　書きたいと　……　レポートの　題は　決めたわけでは
   　　思っています。　　　　　　　　　　　ありませんが、アメリカの　産業に
   　　　　　　　　　　　　　　　　　　　　　ついて　書きたいと　思っています。

4. 本は　全部　図書館で　借りられるんですか。
   ほとんど　借りられるようです。　　　……　本は　全部　図書館で　借りられるわけ
   　　　　　　　　　　　　　　　　　　　　　ではありませんが、ほとんど　借り
   　　　　　　　　　　　　　　　　　　　　　られるようです。

5. レポートの　資料は　あつめ終わったんですか。
   もう　書き始めようと　思っています。　……　レポートの　資料は　あつめ終わった
   　　　　　　　　　　　　　　　　　　　　　わけではありませんが、もう　書き
   　　　　　　　　　　　　　　　　　　　　　始めようと　思っています。

6. 先生に　そうだんしたんですか。
   話してみたんです。　　　　　　　　　……　先生に　そうだんしたわけでは
   　　　　　　　　　　　　　　　　　　　　　ありませんが、話してみたんです。

9.7.8　Substitution Drill

A.　ひとりで　決めるわけには　いかないんです。

　　1. むすこを　行かせます　　　　　　……　むすこを　行かせるわけには　いかない
   　　　　　　　　　　　　　　　　　　　　　んです。

　　2. 十万円も　払います　　　　　　　……　十万円も　払うわけには　いかない
   　　　　　　　　　　　　　　　　　　　　　んです。

　　3. 谷川さんに　資料を　借ります　　……　谷川さんに　資料を　借りるわけには
   　　　　　　　　　　　　　　　　　　　　　いかないんです。

4. 説明を　かんたんに　します　　　…… 説明を　かんたんに　するわけには
　　　　　　　　　　　　　　　　　　　　　　いかないんです。

5. 先生に　そうだんします　　　　　…… 先生に　そうだんするわけには　いか
　　　　　　　　　　　　　　　　　　　　　　ないんです。

6. あさっての　会に　まいります　　…… あさっての　会に　まいるわけには
　　　　　　　　　　　　　　　　　　　　　　いかないんです。

B. 友だちに　教科書を　貸さないわけには　いかないんです。
1. 注射しません　　　　　　　　　　…… 注射しないわけには　いかないんです。
2. 山本さんに　知らせません　　　　…… 山本さんに　知らせないわけには　いか
　　　　　　　　　　　　　　　　　　　　　　ないんです。
3. 友だちに　酒を　おごりません　　…… 友だちに　酒を　おごらないわけには
　　　　　　　　　　　　　　　　　　　　　　いかないんです。
4. 石油を　輸入しません　　　　　　…… 石油を　輸入しないわけには　いかない
　　　　　　　　　　　　　　　　　　　　　　んです。
5. 古くなった　建物は　こわし　　　…… 古くなった　建物は　こわさない
　　ません　　　　　　　　　　　　　　　　わけには　いかないんです。
6. 毎日　勉強しません　　　　　　　…… 毎日　勉強しないわけには　いかないん
　　　　　　　　　　　　　　　　　　　　　　です。

9.7.9　Response Drill

1. 本を　借りたいんですか。　　　　…… 本を　借りたくても、借りる　わけには
　　　　　　　　　　　　　　　　　　　　　　いかないんです。

2. 仕事を　やめたいんですか。　　　…… 仕事を　やめたくても、やめるわけには
　　　　　　　　　　　　　　　　　　　　　　いかないんです。

3. 先生に　そうだんしたいんですか。…… 先生に　そうだんしたくても、そうだん
　　　　　　　　　　　　　　　　　　　　　　するわけには　いかないんです。

4. その　授業を　取りたいんですか。…… その　授業を　取りたくても、取るわけ
　　　　　　　　　　　　　　　　　　　　　　には　いかないんです。

5. お金を　貸したいんですか。　　　…… お金を　貸したくても、貸すわけには
　　　　　　　　　　　　　　　　　　　　　　いかないんです。

6. あの　先生の　講義を　聞きたいん…… あの　先生の　講義を　聞きたくても、
　　ですか。　　　　　　　　　　　　　　　聞くわけには　いかないんです。

7. そういう ことについて 書きたいん
   ですか。
   …… そういう ことについて 書きたくても、
       書くわけには いかないんです。

8. 子どもに その 仕事を まかせたい
   んですか。
   …… 子どもに その 仕事を まかせた
       くても、まかせるわけには いかない
       んです。

9.7.10 Substitution Drill

山田さんが 大阪へ 行かないわけを 知っていますか。

1. そう 決めました
   …… 山田さんが そう 決めたわけを 知っていますか。

2. 英語を 勉強しています
   …… 山田さんが 英語を 勉強しているわけを 知って
       いますか。

3. 頭が いたいです
   …… 山田さんが 頭が いたいわけを 知っていますか。

4. 授業に おくれました
   …… 山田さんが 授業に おくれたわけを 知って
       いますか。

5. ほしがりません
   …… 山田さんが ほしがらないわけを 知っていますか。

6. あなたに しんせつです
   …… 山田さんが あなたに しんせつなわけを 知って
       いますか。

7. とても ていねいです
   …… 山田さんが とても ていねいなわけを 知って
       いますか。

9.7.11 Transformation Drill

1. 先生の 講義を 聞きます。
   歴史を 専攻したくなります。
   ⟶ 先生の 講義を 聞く たびに、歴史を
       専攻したくなります。

2. 戦争が あります。
   産業が 発達しました。
   ⟶ 戦争が ある たびに、産業が 発達
       しました。

3. 友だちに 資料を 貸してあげます。
   かんしゃされます。
   ⟶ 友だちに 資料を 貸してあげる
       たびに、かんしゃされます。

4. 外国人の 友だちが 日本へ 来ます。
   わたしは 日光へ 案内します。
   ⟶ 外国人の 友だちが 日本へ 来る
       たびに、わたしは 日光へ 案内
       します。

5. 時代が 変わります。
   洋服の 形も 変わります。
   ⟶ 時代が 変わる たびに、洋服の
       形も 変わります。

6. 公園を　さんぽします。
　　小川さんに　会います。　　　　　}→　公園を　さんぽする　たびに、小川
　　　　　　　　　　　　　　　　　　　　さんに　会います。

9.7.12　Expansion Drill

1. 交通は　いつ　始まりましたか。
　　西洋と　　　　　　　……　西洋との　交通は　いつ　始まりましたか。
2. 手紙は　来ませんでした。
　　父から　　　　　　　……　父からの　手紙は　来ませんでした。
3. レポートは　とても　いいと　先生に　言われました。
　　江戸時代について　……　江戸時代についての　レポートは　とても　いいと　先生に
　　　　　　　　　　　　　　　　言われました。
4. きっぷは　買えなかったんです。
　　大阪まで　　　　　……　大阪までの　きっぷは　買えなかったんです。
5. 旅行は　やめることに　したんです。
　　中国へ　　　　　　　……　中国への　旅行は　やめることに　したんです。
6. 考えを　言ってみてください。
　　外国人として　　　……　外国人としての　考えを　言ってみてください。

9.7.13　Transformation Drill

1. どういう　ことについて　書きますか。　}→　どういう　ことについて　書くか
　　決めましたか。　　　　　　　　　　　　　　決めましたか。
2. 何を　専攻しますか。　　　　　　　　}→　何を　専攻するか　教えてください。
　　教えてください。
3. だれが　資料を　貸してくれますか。　}→　だれが　資料を　貸してくれるか
　　わからないんです。　　　　　　　　　　　　わからないんです。
4. どうして　近代化が　速かったのですか。}→　どうして　近代化が　速かったのか
　　説明してくださいませんか。　　　　　　　　説明してくださいませんか。
5. 何時ごろ　うかがったら　いいですか。　}→　何時ごろ　うかがったら　いいか
　　おっしゃってください。　　　　　　　　　　おっしゃってください。
6. どの　色が　一番　わたしに　にあい
　　　ますか。　　　　　　　　　　　　　}→　どの　色が　一番　わたしに　にあうか
　　知っています。　　　　　　　　　　　　　　知っています。

9.7.14 E-J Substitution Drill

<u>よく　わかるように</u>　説明してください。

1.	in the same way	······ 同じように　説明してください。
2.	as I said	······ わたしが　言ったように　説明してください。
3.	as you heard	······ あなたが　聞いたように　説明してください。
4.	in that way	······ そのように　説明してください。
5.	as you thought	······ あなたが　思ったように　説明してください。
6.	like Mr. Smith	······ スミスさんのように　説明してください。
7.	so that they understand clearly	······ はっきり　わかるように　説明してください。
8.	like yesterday	······ きのうのように　説明してください。

9.7.15 E-J Response Drill

1. アルバイトを　やめるつもりなんですか。

   I want to, but I *cannot*　　　······ やめたいけど、やめる<u>わけに　いかないんです。</u>

2. 日曜日に　ムーアさんに　会うんですか。

   I don't want to, but I have to　······ 会いたくないけど、会わないわけに　いかないんです。

3. 林さんのように　医者に　なるつもりですか。

   I want to, but I cannot　　　······ なりたいけど、なるわけに　いかないんです。

4. 日光へ　案内してくれませんか。

   I'd like to, but I cannot　　　······ 案内してあげたいけど、案内するわけに　いかないんです。

5. あさって　あなたは　しけんを　受けるんですか。

   I don't want to, but I have to　······ 受けたくないけど、受けないわけに　いかないんです。

6. みんなに　昼ご飯を　おごるんですか。

   I want to, but I cannot　　　······ おごりたいけど、おごるわけに　いかないんです。

9.8 EXERCISES

9.8.1　よい　ほうに　○を　つけなさい。

1. 資料を　あつめるのが　むずかしいので、その　問題について

書く {
　わけではありません。
　わけに　いかないんです。
}

2. どっちの　ほうが {
　重いですか
　重いか
} わかるでしょう?

3. よし子さんは、しず子さんに {
　会う
　会った
} たびに　病気が　よくなっている

　　ようなので、安心しました。

4. お金は、 {
　ぬすまれません
　ぬすまれない
} ように、おさいふに　入れておきなさい。

5. きょうは {
　春のように
　春ような
　春のような
　春ように
} 日ですね。

9.8.2　Make complete sentences using the following.

1. この　町へ　来る　たびに…

2. あなたも　知っているように…

3. なぜ…か…

4. ポールさんのような…

5. …わけではありません

6. …わけには　いかない

7. …たら　どう(ですか)?

9.8.3　Fill in the blanks with an appropriate word and give the English equivalent for each sentence.

1. あの　方は　小林一郎さん＿＿＿＿ようですね。

2. そういう　ことについて　話す＿＿＿＿には　いかないらしいです。

3. 日曜日に　天気が　よかったら、どこへ　あそびに　行く＿＿＿＿　決めましたか。

4. 友だち＿＿＿＿の　手紙ですから、見せる＿＿＿＿に　いきません。

5. お寺の　しゃしんを　見る　＿＿＿＿に、アジアへ　行ってみたいと　思います。

6. 例が　ない＿＿＿＿ではないが、ひじょうに　めずらしいと　言える。

9.8.4　日本語で　言いなさい。

1. I wish I could help you with your homework, but I can't, because I won't be at home tonight.

2. Every time I consult my uncle he gives me a good idea.

3. I don't mean that I don't like Mr. Hirota.

4. If I can't find reference books at the library, I can't write a report on Japanese culture.

5. Did you decide when you return to your hometown?

6. I wonder if the Japanese language is difficult, as you say it is.

7. Mr. Morgan speaks Japanese as if he is a Japanese.

8. It looks as if Mr. Watanabe caught a cold.

9.8.5 男の　言い方を　女のに、女の　言い方を　男のに　変えなさい。
1. 先生に　そうだんしてから　決めるつもりなんだ。
2. この　説明で　よく　わかったでしょう?
3. 子どもたち　もう　寝たかしら。
4. レポートは　もう　書いてしまったよ。
5. 仕事が　あって、早く　帰るわけには　いかないのよ。

9.8.6 Make a sentence using each of the following.
1. あいかわらず　 2. わずか　 3. ほとんど　 4. 〜あまり　 5. ますます

9.8.7 漢字に　変えて、英語で　文の　いみを　言いなさい。
1. じゅぎょうは　きのうと　おなじ　じかんに　はじまります。
2. めいじじだいいごに　にほんの　ぶんか、さんぎょうは　きんだいかされた。
3. せいようの　れきしを　けんきゅうし、せん攻することに　決めました。
4. やまださんから　かりなさい。いいのを　たくさん　かしてくれますよ。
5. かれの　あるく　はやさに　おどろきました。
6. なんに　きょうみが　あるんですか。
7. のこっている　資りょうを　みせてください。
8. せんもんてきな　おかんがえを　おきかせくださいませんか。

9.8.8 読みなさい。
1. 受、授
2. 生、産
3. 貝、貸
4. 昔、借
5. 借、貸
6. 速、達
7. 夕、残
8. 代、貸
9. 台、治、始
10. 九、究
11. 同、興
12. 人、以
13. 門、問、間、聞、開、閉

9.8.9   Describe the speakers (A, B, C, and D) of the following dialog.

A: Anata, kon'ban irassharu kashira?

B: Dare ga kuru no.

A: Ojisan yo.

C: Koko de terebi mitete ii?

D: Aa, ii yo. Demo, tabun konai daroo.

A: Soo kashira.

D: Kyoo kaimono ni ikanakatta no ka?

A: Ashita ikoo to omotte.

D: Boku mo ikoo ka?

B: Atashi mo issho ni tsuretette!

9.8.10   The following is a conversation between a boy and two girls. Distinguish them with an "M" for male and "F" for female.

—Kon'nichi wa.

—Ara, shibaraku nee. Ogen'ki?

—Aa, gen'ki da yo.

—Mainichi ren'shuu shite irassharu no?

—Iya, tokidoki da yo. Demo, kon'do mi ni konai kai?

—Soo ne, itte miyoo kashira.

—Matteru yo.

—Anata mo iku?

—Un, ikitai wa.

9.8.11   Write a conversation between a student and a company section chief wherein they refer to the student's own professor.

9.8.12   Formulate five sentences involving the use of *mitara*.

9.9   SITUATIONAL AND APPLICATION CONVERSATION

9.9.1   On campus.

George asks John where he is going.

John answers that he is now on his way to the library. He says that he has to write a report about the Meiji era in Japan by the sixteenth. He is going to look for reference materials.

George says that whenever he goes to the library, he sees Susie there.

John says that Susie is majoring in modern Japanese history and is studying hard. In case he cannot find any proper reference materials, he will ask Susie where he can get them, John says.

George says that is a good idea, and tells John that he must study hard, as Susie does.

9.9.2 In the hallway.

Kazuko meets Keiko near Professor Aoki's research room.

Keiko asks Kazuko where she is going.

Kazuko answers that she is about to go to talk to Dr. Aoki.

Keiko says it seems that Dr. Aoki is not in his office at that time and asks if Kazuko has decided to major in American literature.

Kazuko says that it's not that she has decided to major in it yet, but she wants to consult with Dr. Aoki about it.

9.9.3 Converse about your major, assignments, papers to be written, lectures, and the like.

9.9.4 Keiko: Kinoo, toshokan e itta?

Hiroshi: Ikanakatta yo. Keiko san wa?

Keiko: Watashi wa itta wa. Demo, an'mari nagaku wa inakatta no.

Hiroshi: Chotto sono hen de ocha demo nomanai?

Keiko: Ee, ii wa. Doko ga ii kashira.

Hiroshi: Den'en ga ii yo.

9.9.5 Younger Brother: Okaasan, moo gohan dekita?

Mother: Iie, mada desu yo.

Older Sister: Kazuo, chotto tetsudatte kurenai?

Mother: Oneesan o tetsudatte agenasai. Sugu, gohan dekiru kara. Otoosan wa osoi wa nee.

Older Sister: Basutei made itte miyoo kana.

Younger Brother: Jaa, boku ga iku yo.

9.9.6 Michiko: Hiroko san, kyoo Kan'da e iku?

Hiroko: Ee, eigo no jisho o kaoo to omou no.

Michiko: Jaa, atashi mo issho ni ikoo kashira.

Hiroko: Ee, irasshai yo.

9.9.7 Minoru: Tsutomu kun, doko iku no?

Tsutomu: Depaato. Kimi wa?

Minoru: Boku, hon'ya.

Tsutomu's Mother: Minoru san, kyoo okaasan uchi ni irassharu kashira.

Minoru: Hai, haha wa uchi ni orimasu kedo.

9.10   READING COMPREHENSION

9.10.1

　日本は　江戸時代の　1639年から　1858年まで　鎖国(national isolation)を　した。これは、220年もの　間、外国からの　えいきょうを　受けないで、日本的な　文化が　つづいたということである。もし　日本が　鎖国を　しなかったら、もっと　早く　近代化、国際化(internationalization)が　始まって、現在(the present time)のとは　ちがう　日本や　文化が　あったかもしれない。しかし、また、外国の　植民地(colony)のように　なっていたと　考えることも　できる。

　明治に　なって、外国との　交通が　自由に　なると、日本人は　ひじょうな　速さで　外国文化を　とり入れようと　した。おどろくほど　いっしょうけんめいだったと　言われている。

9.10.2

大谷　「もしもし、中村さん? 急で　すみませんけど、今晩　会う　やくそく(appointment)、あしたに　するわけには　いきませんか。」

中村　「どう　したんですか。」

大谷　「じつは、五時に　仕事が　終わるはずだったんですが、急な　仕事が　できて、何時に　帰れるか　わからないんです。」

中村　「そうですか。あいかわらず　忙しいんですね。いいですよ、あしたで。それで、あしたは　何時に　しましょうか。」

大谷　「五時半だったら　だいじょうぶだと　思いますけど。」

中村　「五時半ね、いいですよ。大谷さんのように　忙しいのも　大変ですね。」

大谷　「でも、いつも　忙しいわけではないんですよ。この　仕事が　終われば、あしたは　早く　帰れそうです。」

中村　「むりを　しないで、あしたも　おそくなるようだったら、また　電話を　ください。ぼくは　かまいませんから。」

大谷　「どうも　すみません。じゃあ、よろしく。」

LESSON 10
REVIEW AND APPLICATION

10.1　PATTERNS

10.1.1　TARI form

a.　Verb

夏休みは　国へ　帰ったり	帰らなかったり	
かれらは　お金は　払ったり	払わなかったり	
日によって　残業したり	早く　帰ったり	
時によって　自分で　決めたり	先生に　そうだんしたり	します／する
みんなは　うたったり	おどったり	しました／した
日本は　機械を　輸出したり	石油を　輸入したり	しています／
運動を　していると、のどが　かわいたり	おなかが　すいたり	している
母は　心配したり	安心したり	して、…
友だちの　間で　ごちそうを　おごったり	おごられたり	です／だ
日本は　よく　台風に　おそわれたり	地震が　起こったり	

b.　Adjective, Noun, and adjectival Noun plus Copula

あたしの　作る　すきやきは　あまかったり	からかったり	
この　辺の　道は　さびしかったり	にぎやかだったり	します／する
時間によって　交通は　多かったり	少なかったり	しました／した
日本人の　宗教は　仏教だったり	神道だったり	しています／
しけんは　長かったり	みじかかったり	している
建物は　近代的だったり	古かったり	して、… です／だ

父の　おみやげは　めずらしい 　　物だったり	つまらない　物だったり	します／する しました／した しています／ 　　している して、… です／だ
ぼくの　かばんは　授業の　ある 　　日によって　重かったり	かるかったり	
ことしの　春は　あたたかかったり	さむかったり	

10.1.2 Causative

a. Forms

Vowel Verb

調べる	調べ	
決(き)める	決(き)め	させます／させる
あつめる	あつめ	させません／させない
食べる　⟶	食べ	させました／させた
受ける	受け	させませんでした／させなかった
やめる	やめ	させて
覚える	覚え	

Consonant Verb

おごる／おどる	おごら／おどら	
習う／言う	習わ／言わ	せます／せる
待つ／たつ	待た／たた	せません／せない
働く／行く　⟶	働か／行か	せました／せた
こわす／さがす	こわさ／さがさ	せませんでした／せなかった
すむ／楽しむ	すま／楽しま	せて
あそぶ／呼ぶ	あそば／呼ば	
ぬぐ／急ぐ	ぬが／急が	

Irregular Verb

来る／持って来る	来(こ)／持って来(こ)	させます／させる
する／案内(あんない)する／注文(ちゅうもん)する　⟶	案内(あん)／注文(ちゅうもん)	させません／させない
輸入(ゆにゅう)する／輸出(ゆしゅつ)する	輸入(ゆ)／輸出(ゆしゅつ)	させました／させた
		させませんでした／ 　　させなかった
		させて

b. Transitive-Verb causative sentence

父		秘書		電話を　かけさせた
ぼく		おとうと		昼ご飯を　おごらせます
社長	は	給仕		お茶を　持って来させました
先生	が	子どもたち	に	ことばの　意味を　調べさせた
かれ		会社		お金を　払わせたそうです
だれ	が	店員		医者を　呼ばせたんですか

c. Intransitive-Verb causative sentence

ぼく		むすこ		ゆうびん局へ　行かせましょう
父		子ども		あそびに　帰らせます
部長		社員		銀行へ　行かせました
学長	は	学生	を	取りに　来させるらしいです
ミラーさん	が	あの　人	(に)	出張させるらしいです
木村さん		一郎君		けいさつへ　知らせに　行かせた
主人		おとうと		修理屋へ　行かせるそうです

d. "please let someone do"

（わたしを）外へ　行かせて	
（わたしたちに）その　仕事を　やらせて	ください
（いもうとを）もうすこし　休ませてやって	くれない？
つかれたから、すわらせて	くれませんか
おたくで　パーティーを　ひらかせて	くださいませんか

10.1.3 Verbal Derivative *-garu*

（わたしは）	電話で	れんらくしたい	んです
（わたしたちは）	同じような　物が	ほしい	
（あなたは）	どんな　電気製品が	買いたい	んですか
（君は）		ほしい	

（かれは） （吉田さんは）	もっと　最近の　えいがを	見たがっています
（かれらは） （みんなは） （子どもは）	おそろいの　はっぴを	作りたがっています ほしがります ほしがっている

10.1.4 Relational *shi* "what's more"

この　窓からは　海が　見える		山も　見えます
父も　安心しない		母も　安心しない
戦後　工業が　発達した	し、	生活が　ゆたかに　なりました
かばんを　ぬすまれた		お金も　ぬすまれたんです
仕事が　すんだ		ゆっくり　休んでください

時間が　ない		お金も　たりないんです
あの　道は　くらい		せまいから、この　道を　行きましょう
かばんは　重い	し、	とおいし、つかれてしまいました
あの　女の子は　かわいい		頭も　いいし、ひょうばんが　いいです
道は　あぶない		雨も　ひどく　ふっていました

へやは　日本風だ		サービスも　いいです
子どもが　病気だ		ほかにも　急な　用が　あるので、帰ります
病院は　近代的だ	し、	医者も　いい
そのころ　あには　大学の 　　　三年生だった		おとうとは　高校生でした
みんなは　しんせつだった		さびしくありませんでした

10.1.5 Stem form of Verb

お祭りの 時は おみこしを かつぎ、	ごちそうを 食べます
山崎さんは えびフライを 注文し、	ぼくは スープと パンを 頼んだ
りょうしんに そうだんし、	決めたんです
古い 建物を こわし、	広い にわを 作りました
一日じゅう 音楽を 楽しみ、	にぎやかな 日曜日でした
むずかしい 仕事が すみ、	やっと 安心しました

10.1.6 KU form of Adjective

米国では まだまだ 日本語を 勉強する 人が 少なく、	めずらしいそうです
お祭りが なくなるのは さびしく、	ざんねんです
中国と 日本の 関係は 深く、	長い
悪い 友だちの えいきょうが 強く、	こまっています
かれは やさしく、	しんせつな 人です
この 料理は からく、	まずい

10.1.7 Relational *to*

a. "whenever" "when" "if"

のどが かわく		たいてい 学校の 食堂で 紅茶を 飲みます
授業が 終わる		いつも 図書館へ 行きます
むすこが 生まれる	と、	すぐ 東京へ 来ました
おじさんに そうだんする		いい 考えを 出してくれました
熱を はからない		なかなか 病気が わからないですよ
早く 決めない		後で こまりますよ
問題が やさしい		時間が かかりません
川が もうすこし 深い		泳ぐことが できます
説明が 長い	と、	わかりにくいです
お金が ない		おごってあげられませんね
おかしは あまくない		おいしくありません

建物が　近代的だ	便利なんですが
道が　夜も　にぎやかだ	さびしくないんですが
かれが　医者だ　　　と、	つごうが　いいんですが
弱い　地震だ	被害が　少ないです
五千円以下じゃない	買えません

b. "I wish" "I hope"

八時までに　修理が　すむ	
母が　心配しない	いいんですが
あたしの　せいが　高い	いいのに
仕事が　忙しくない　　と	いいけど
社会保障が　完全だ	いいねえ
スミスさんが　きらいじゃない	

10.1.8 TARA form

a. "when" "if"

今　戦争が　起こったら、	どう　しますか
おなかが　いたくなったら、	この　薬を　すぐ　飲みなさい
お客様が　いらっしゃったら、	着物を　着るつもりです
駅へ　行ったら、	小山さんの　おくさんに　会いました
父に　そうだんしたら、	いいだろうと　言った

天気が　よくなかったら、	花見に　行くのを　やめましょう
気分が　悪かったら、	学校を　休んだほうが　いいですよ
この　へやが　うるさかったら、	となりの　へやに　行ってください

土曜日が　ひまだったら、	うちへ　あそびに　来ませんか
あなたのと　同じだったら、	ぼくも　ほしいんです
六千円以上の　物だったら、	たぶん　いい　物でしょう

b. "I wish" "I hope"

自動車が　二台　あったら	
友だちに　そうだんしたら	いいんですが
早く　決めたら	いいのに
道が　ひどくなかったら	いいけど
教室が　広かったら	いいねえ
わたしが　もっと　自由だったら	
先生が　ドイツ人だったら	

c. "Why don't you ～?"

すぐ　調べたら	（どうですか）
アルバイトを　やめたら	（いかがですか）
降りそうだから、うちに　いたら	

10.1.9 "without ～" "instead of ～"

えんりょしないで、	いただきます
心配しないで、	やってみましょう
残業しないで、	うちへ　帰った
お金を　借りないで、	働いて　払うことに　した
仕事に　行かないで、	あそびに　行ったんですか

10.1.10 "decide when ～" "know what ～" etc.

いつ	出発する		決めましたか
何が	昔から　ある		知っている？ ごぞんじですか
いくらぐらい	旅行に　かかる	か	教えてください
どなたが	デパートへ　案内してくださる		わからないそうです

10.1.11 *tokoro*

a. "is about to do"

（これから）	お金を　払う	ところ	です
（今）	テニスを　れんしゅうする		なんです

| （ちょうど）（今） | 買い物に　出かける
ジョンさんを　案内する
会う　場所を　決める | ところ | でした
だったんです |

b. "is now doing"

| （ちょうど）（今） | 昼ご飯を　作っている
赤ちゃんが　昼寝している
お医者さんに　そうだんしている
さくらが　さいている | ところ | です
でした
なんです
だったんです |

c. "have just done"

| （ちょうど）（今） | あなたに　電話を　かけた
宿題を　終わった
よやくを　取りけした
かんご婦に　注射された | ところ | です
でした
なんです
だったんです |

d. *tokoro* + Relational *ni* or *o*

| けい子さんと　話している
食事を　している
出発の　用意を　始めた | ところ | へ
に | 山田さんが　来ました |
| 畑で　取り入れている
ぼくが　きっさ店に　入る | | を | 見ました
見られました |

10.1.12 *wake*

a. "cannot"

| 仕事が　すんでも、すぐ　家へ　帰る
かぜを　ひいても、学校を　休む
古いけど、この　建物を　こわす
ほしいけれど、もらう | わけに(は)　いきません
わけに(は)　いかないんです |

b. "have to"

| あまり　安くなくても、買わない
日本語が　へたでも、話さない
病気だけれど、出張しない
次の　日曜日は　うちに　いない | わけに(は)　いきません
わけに(は)　いかないんです |

c. "I don't mean that"

借りた　本を　かえさない	
毎朝　電車が　込む	
日本語が　特に　むずかしい	わけではありません
かれが　やさしくない	わけではないんです
料理が　そんなに　まずかった	

d. "reason"

小川君が　勉強が　きらいな	わけを　知っていますか
山崎さんが　来なかった	わけが　わかりますか
注文が　思ったより　少なかった	わけを　聞いてみました

10.1.13 *yoo*

a. "like" "in the same way" "as"

あなたも　知っている		この　電気製品は　こわれやすいです
いもうとが　する		あなたも　してみてください
友だちが　決めた	ように	やってみましょう
かれが　言った		そこは　とても　さびしい　所でした
しず子さんから　聞いた		それは　ほとんど　本当の　ことです
スミスさんの		日本語が　じょうずに　なりたいです

b. "seem" "look"

漢字は　全部　わすれた		
課長は　もう　会に　出た		です
伊藤さんは　かぜを　ひいている	よう	でした
地震は　大きかった		だ
あの　学生は　ポール君の		だった
昼ご飯は　魚の		

c. "～ like ～"

小川君が　持っている		かばんが　ほしいんです
おととい　貸してくれた		ざっしを　また　貸してください
あの　人は　フランス人の	ような	話し方を　しますね
こういう		問題は　なかなか　むずかしいです
それは　松本さんと　同じ		考え方です

10.1.14 -soo

a. "seem as if it's going to happen"

雨が　降^ふり

さむくて、かぜを　ひき

しゃしんは　五日までに　でき　　｜　そうです

ますます　人口が　ふえ　　　　　　　そうでした

出張^{しゅっちょう}が　つづき

b. "look (like)" "seem"

山口さんは　あいかわらず　楽し

広田さんは　はが　いた

おとうとは　これと　同じような　本が　ほし　　｜　そうです

よし子さんは　とても　元気　　　　　　　　　　　　そうでした

ロバーツさんは　日本語が　じょうず

谷川^{たに}さんは 母は	楽し	そうに	テレビを　見ています
	忙し		働いています
	ご飯を　おいし		食べていました
	ねむ		話していました
	元気		なりました
	心配		言っていました

島田先生は　きびし	そうな	先生です
にぎやかで　楽し		音楽が　聞こえます
いつも　さびし		人ですね
とても　しんせつ		おばさんが　いましたよ
子どもが　好き		絵本が　ありますか

10.1.15 *tabi* "every time"

谷川^{たに}先生の　講義^{こうぎ}を　聞く	たび(に)	ますます　歴史が　おもしろく なります

新しい　仕事を　なしとげる		みんなが　おどろきます
台風が　来る		大きな　被害を　受けます
大川さんの　おたくへ　うかがう	たび(に)	ごちそうに　なりました
こたえを　まちがえる		もっと　勉強しなければ　ならないと　思います

10.2　OTHERS

10.2.1　*demo* "or some-~"

あそこで　食事		しませんか
鳥肉	でも	料理させましょう
安い　ラジカセ		おみやげに　買っておくつもりです
レコード		聞きながら、本を　読みましょう

ひまだから、東京へ		行きましょう
日本の　産業について	でも	調べてみましょう
わたしの　おじに		頼んでみましょう
ろう下で		話しましょうか

10.2.2　*ni* "addition"

牛肉		やさい	
魚		貝	の　料理でも　作りましょう
パン	に	スープ	
ご飯		おみおつけ	が　いいです
ビール		ジュース	
紅茶		おかし	を　買っておいてください

10.2.3　Multiple Relationals

中国文化	と		関係が　深い
日本	と	の	交通は　いつ　始まりましたか

アメリカ	へ		輸出は　何が　一番　多いですか
その　会社	で	の	仕事は　どうですか
ドイツ	から		えいきょうは　とても　大きかったです

10.2.4 Sentence Particle "I wonder"

ムーアさんに　この　意味が　わかる	
ひらがなと　かたかなは　覚えた	
ここから　海が　見えない	
しゃしんは　とらなかった	かな
この　えびフライは　おいしい	かしら
しけんの　点は　よかった	
モーガンさんは　しんせつな　人	
大事な　用だったの	

10.2.5 "above" "below" "within" etc.

この　おみこしは　千キロ	以上も　あるそうです
学生は　三百人	以上　いると　思います
一万円	以下の　みやげに　してください
熱は　三十七度	以下らしいです
大学まで　バスで　十分	以内です
宿題は　二十ページ	以内だそうです
日本語	以外の　外国語を　知っていますか
神道と　仏教	以外　どんな　宗教が　ありますか
江戸時代	以前には　工業が　発達していなかった
第二次大戦	以後　どこに　住んでいたんですか

10.3　REVIEW DRILLS

10.3.1　Relational Checking Drill (を or が)

1. 電気製品、輸入する　　　　　…… 電気製品を　輸入する
2. みんな、あつまる　　　　　…… みんなが　あつまる

3. 行く　場所、決める　　　　　…… 行く　場所を　決める

4. あつまる　時間、決まる　　　…… あつまる　時間が　決まる

5. お金、あつめる　　　　　　　…… お金を　あつめる

6. 計画、まかせる　　　　　　　…… 計画を　まかせる

7. 食事、すむ　　　　　　　　　…… 食事が　すむ

8. 昼ご飯、おごる　　　　　　　…… 昼ご飯を　おごる

9. コーヒーと　ケーキ、注文する　…… コーヒーと　ケーキを　注文する

10. わたし、まいる　　　　　　　…… わたしが　まいる

10.3.2 Substitution and Transformation Drill

1. A: 休みに　なると、どんな　ことを　しますか。

   B: 旅行したり　アルバイトしたりします。（スミス）さんは？

   A: わたしも　旅行したり　アルバイトしたりです。

   1. 雨が　ふる、本を　読む、手紙を　書く
   2. ひまが　ある、料理を　手つだう、洋服を　作る
   3. 天気が　いい、テニスを　する、さんぽに　行く
   4. 友だちに　会う、えいがを　見る、話す
   5. ひまに　なる、テレビを　見る、本を　読む

2. A: 石川君に　しゃしんを　とらせようと　思うんだけど、どうかな？

   B: しゃしんなら、ぜひ　わたしに　とらせてください。

   A: 君が　とってくれるんですか。じゃあ、頼みますよ。

   1. 絵を　かく
   2. 東京を　案内する
   3. 車を　運転する
   4. 英語の　手紙を　書く
   5. レポートを　作る

3. A: 外は　さむそうですね。

   B: 本当ですね。

   A: 雪は　どうかしら？

   B: 降りそうですよ。

   1. みんな　楽しい、おみこし、こっちへ　来る
   2. あの　車は　速く　はしれる、ねだん、高い
   3. 天気が　悪くなる、あした、降る
   4. あの　えいがは　おもしろい、きっぷ、まだ　ある

4. A: （スミスさんは） 旅行に 行かないんですか。

   B: ええ、行きません。

   A: 行きたくないんですか。

   B: 行きたくないわけじゃないんですけど、…

   A: どう したんですか。

   B: 仕事が あるので、行くわけに いかないんです。

   1. 毎晩 テレビを 見る、勉強が ある

   2. アルバイトを する、勉強が 忙しい

   3. 週末 あそぶ、宿題が いっぱい ある

   4. 今晩 出かける、客が 来る

5. A: 映画を 見たいと 思っています。

   B: おにいさんも 見たがっていますか。

   A: いいえ、あには 見たくないらしいです。

   1. 国へ 帰りたい、おとうとさん

   2. ゴルフを 習いたい、おにいさん

   3. 早く 出発したい、ご主人

   4. お祭りの はっぴを 着たい、お子さん

10.4　REVIEW EXERCISES

10.4.1　____に ひらがなを 一つ 入れなさい。

1. 父は おとうと____ 銀行____ 行かせました。

2. 仕事が すむ____、すぐ 帰れる____ いいんだけど。

3. いつ 先生の お宅に うかがう____ もう 決めましたか。

4. 今晩 いっしょに 食事____ ____ しませんか。

5. この 辺は 工場____ ____ ____で、けしきが よくないです。

6. はが いたい____、熱が ある____、うちに いました。

7. 雨が 降る____、たいてい 本を 読んだり 絵を かいたりします。

8. 本の 注文____ 先生____ おまかせします。

9. ぼくは ビフテキ____ ライスを もらおうかな。

10. 安藤先生は 毎日 学生____ 漢字____ れんしゅうさせます。

11. アメリカ____の ぼうえきは 何世紀____ 始まったのですか。

12. むすこは ビデオや ラジカセ____ ____ ____ ほしがっているんです。

10.4.2 Select the appropriate word for each of the blanks.

1. （　　　）休みに　なったので、（　　　）早く　国へ　帰ります。

   〈さっそく、やっと　なるべく、さらに〉

2. （　　　）忙しそうですね。

   〈ほとんど、いっぱい、あいかわらず〉

3. （　　　）使わなかったら、（　　　）わすれてしまいました。

   〈ますます、ほとんど、しばらく〉

4. 図書館に　資料が　（　　　）二つしか　なく、かれは　こまっているそうだ。

   〈ますます、わずか、なるべく〉

5. 地震が　起こり、（　　　）台風にも　おそわれた。

   〈さらに、やっと、ほとんど〉

10.4.3 文を　作りなさい。

1. ～だったら
2. ～に　ちがいない
3. ～ところだ
4. ～たり、～たり
5. ～し、～し
6. ～そうだ

10.4.4 Circle the correct one.

1. ぼくは　まだ　十七さいだから、たばこを　すう｛ わけじゃない。
   わけには　いかない。

2. 山下さんに｛ 会ったら、
   会うと、
   会えば、 ｝よろしく　言ってください。

3. わたしは　日本へ｛ 行くように、
   行く　たびに、 ｝京都旅行を　楽しみます。

4. 高い　物ばかり　注文｛ すると、
   しないで、
   して、 ｝安いのも　注文してね。

5. わたしと　島田さんは　食事に　行くと、
   ｛ おごったり　おごられたりします。
   おごるし、おごられるし、します。

6. 「もしもし、みち子さん？　今　何を　してるの？」「勉強が

$$終わったので、\begin{bmatrix}出かけそう\\出かけるよう\\出かける ところ\end{bmatrix}なんです。」$$

7. おとうとは いろいろな 国の 切手$\begin{cases}を あつめたいです。\\を あつめたがっています。\end{cases}$

10.4.5 Connect each of the A-group expressions with an appropriate B-group expressions and give the English equivalent.

A	B
わたしは ちょうど 今 あなたに 電話しようと した	させてください。
これは 子どもには むずかしすぎる	に ちがいない。
お父さんと よく そうだんしたら	そうです。
ぜひ ぼくに 説明	わけには いかないんです。
お金が いるので、アルバイトを やめる	ところです。
さむくて、かぜを ひき	どうですか。
	ようです。

10.4.6 Transform the Japanese sentences into the meanings indicated in English and then complete the sentences.

1. 友だちに 会います。

   a. If you should meet
   b. Whenever I meet
   c. Please let me meet
   d. I have just met
   e. I sometimes meet my friend and sometimes
   f. You must have met
   g. Without meeting
   h. I cannot meet

2. さびしいです。

   a. He looks lonely, so
   b. If you are lonely
   c. I'm lonely, what's more
   d. I don't mean that I am lonely, but
   e. He must be lonely as

3. しんせつです。

   a. If he looks kind,
   b. Some of the station employees are kind and some are

10.4.7 Transform the Japanese sentences into the meanings indicated in English.

    1.   Father made me

        a. たばこを　買いに　行く

        b. 手紙を　速達で　出す

        c. 車を　洗う

    2.   Please let me

        a. いすに　すわる

        b. あなたの　しゃしんを　とる

        c. 早く　帰る

10.4.8 Indicate with either 男 or 女 in the parentheses provided whether the sentence following is spoken by a man or a woman. Next, change the sentence into the *desu* or *-masu* ending.

    1. （　　）わたしは　えびフライに　ご飯を　注文しようかな。

    2. （　　）お父さんに　そうだんしてから、決めたほうが　いいんじゃないかしら。

    3. （　　）地下鉄の　事故で　電車も　バスも　込んで、乗るのに　大変だった

            だろう？

    4. （　　）資料は　いろいろ　あるの？

    5. （　　）あの　方は　野村さんのようだけれど、ちがうかしら。

    6. （　　）ぼくも　君のと　同じ　カメラを　買ったんだよ。

    7. （　　）会社まで　急いで　かばんを　持って来てくれないか。

    8. （　　）あら、もう　四時半だわ。

    9. （　　）あたし　のどが　かわいたわ。

   10. （　　）そんなに　たくさん　飲むなよ。

10.4.9　ふつうの　文に　しなさい。

    1. なるべく　早く　いたします。

    2. コーヒーは　すぐ　お持ちしましょうか。

    3. いもうとたちは　こちらへ　つれてまいりません。

    4. 何に　なさるつもりですか。

    5. 道が　わかっておりますので、ひとりで　まいりました。

10.4.10 読みなさい。

    夕べ　ご飯を　食べ終わり、特に　することも　ないし、映画でも　見に

行こうと　思っていたところに、ポール君が　来ました。ポール君は　日本史の

レポートを　書くために、ぼくに　聞きたいことが　あるようでした。それで、ぜひ　見たい　映画が　あるわけではないし、出かけるのを　やめて、かれの質問に　こたえたり、本を　しょうかいしてあげたりしました。日本語のレポートの　書き方も　教えてあげました。かれが　いい　レポートを　書けるといいと　思います。

10.5　　MIKE HARRISON SERIES (5)

——マイク・ハリソン、旅行を　計画する——

10.5.1　——会社で——

山本　　　「あら、地図。ご旅行ですか。」

ハリソン　「ええ、九州へ　前から　行きたいと　思っていたんですけど、今度　休みが取れることに　なったので、長崎や　伊万里へ　行こうと　思っているんです。」

山本　　　「いいですね。」

ハリソン　「山本さんは　旅行の　予約なんか　どこで　するんですか。」

山本　　　「そんなに　旅行するわけではないけど、行く　時は　たいてい　旅行センターに頼むんです。旅行センターなら、電車や　飛行機の　きっぷも　ホテルの予約も　一度に　できるし、便利ですよ。」

ハリソン　「どこですか、その　旅行センターというのは？」

山本　　　「東京駅にも　ありますよ。」

ハリソン　「駅の　中に？」

山本　　　「ええ。」

ハリソン　「それは　いい。昼休みに　ちょっと　行ってみましょう。どうも　いい　所を教えてくれて　ありがとう。」

山本　　　「いいえ。」

10.5.2　——旅行センターで——

ハリソン　「長崎へ　旅行したいんですが、予約を　おねがいできますか。」

男の人　　「いつの　ご予定ですか。」

ハリソン　「今月の　二十六日から　三十一日までなんですが。」

男の人　　「往復は　飛行機ですね。」

ハリソン　「やっぱり　飛行機が　いいですか。」

男の人　　「そう、新幹線だと　博多まで　七時間、飛行機だったら　羽田から　大村まで一時間四十五分で　行けますよ。」

ハリソン　「じゃあ、行きは　朝九時ごろ　出る　便で、帰りは　三十一日の　四時ごろのに
　　　　　　してください。」

男の人　　「じゃあ、まず　席が　取れるか　どうか　調べてみましょう。…お待たせしま
　　　　　　した。両方とも　だいじょうぶです。ホテルの　ご予約は？」

ハリソン　「長崎に　三泊して、あと　伊万里に　一泊、博多に　一泊しようと
　　　　　　思っているんですけど。一泊　いくらぐらいですか。」

男の人　　「いろいろ　ありますけどね。普通　二食つきだと　八千円から　一万三千円
　　　　　　ぐらい、食事が　つかないと　五千円ぐらいからが　普通ですね。ご予算は？」

ハリソン　「あまり　高くない　ところを　おまかせします。」

男の人　　「じゃあ、これから　調べてみますから、お待ちください。」

ハリソン　「どのくらい　かかりますか。」

男の人　　「十五分ぐらいは　かかると　思いますけど。」

ハリソン　「そろそろ　会社へ　もどらなくては　ならないんですけど。」

男の人　　「じゃあ、後で　ごれんらくしましょうか。」

ハリソン　「そう　お願いできますか。では、会社の　方へ　電話　お願いします。」

10.5.3　――ハリソン、会社へ　もどる――

山本　　　「ハリソンさん、ちょっと　お願いが　あるんですが。」

ハリソン　「何ですか。」

山本　　　「じつは、友だちが　アメリカ旅行に　行きたがっているんですけど、カリフォル
　　　　　　ニアの　辺の　ことを　知りたいらしいんです。ハリソンさんは　カリフォル
　　　　　　ニアでしたね。」

ハリソン　「そうです。」

山本　　　「いつか　友だちに　会ってくださいませんか。」

ハリソン　「いいですよ。さ来週は　休みを　取るけど、その　前なら、いつでも
　　　　　　いいですよ。」

山本　　　「じゃあ、一度　つれて来ますから、よろしく。」

ハリソン　「前もって　日時を　教えておいてください。カリフォルニアの　地図や
　　　　　　案内書なんか　持って来ますから。」

山本　　　「すみません、お忙しいのに。」

10.5.4 New Vocabulary (for passive learning)

1. 計画　　　　　keikaku　　　　　......　plan

　今度　　　　　kon'do　　　　　......　this time

　伊万里　　　　Imari　　　　　......　place famous for porcelain

　旅行センター　Ryokoo Sen'taa　......　Travel Service Center

2. 往復　　　　　oofuku　　　　　......　going and returning; roundtrip

　大村　　　　　Oomura　　　　　......　domestic airport near Nagasaki

　便　　　　　　bin　　　　　　......　flight

　席　　　　　　seki　　　　　　......　seat

　三泊　　　　　san'paku　　　　......　three nights' lodging

　一泊　　　　　ippaku　　　　　......　overnight stay

　二食つき　　　nishoku-tsuki　　......　with two meals

　つく　　　　　tsuku　　　　　......　is served; is attached

　予算　　　　　yosan　　　　　......　budget; estimate

　もどる　　　　modoru　　　　　......　turn back; return

3. さ来週　　　　saraishuu　　　　......　week after next (week)

　日時　　　　　nichiji　　　　　......　the date; the time

　案内書　　　　an'naisho　　　　......　guide book

LESSON 11
学生生活₁

11.1 PRESENTATION

　日本の　学生は　よく　クラス、ゼミ、　クラブの　なかまで　旅行したり、　コンパを
開いたり、　運動を　したりする。

　学生生活の　中で、　最も　楽しく、　卒業した　後も₂　思い出されるのは、　こういう
さまざまな　行事や　クラブ活動、　友だちとの　交際などであろう₃。

11.2 DIALOG

—— 二年生の　クラスで₄ ——

学生(一)　「皆さん、　帰らないで、　しばらく　教室に　残っていてください。　黒板に
　　　　　書いてある₅ように、　次の　土曜日に　クラスで　どこか₆へ　ピクニックに
　　　　　行こうという　計画が　あるんですが、　どうでしょうか。」

学生(二)　「みんなで　まだ　どこへも₇　行ったことが　ないから、　いいと　思います。」

学生(三)　「どこか₆　あまり　遠くない　所へ　行くのなら、　さんせいです。」

学生(二)　「ぼくも。　だれでも₈　さんかできるような、　近くて　便利な　所なら、
　　　　　どこでも　いいんじゃないですか₉。」

学生(三)　「できたら、　湖とか₁₀　川とか　海岸を　えらんだら　いいと　思うけど。
　　　　　みんなで　泳いだり　ゲームを　して　遊んだり、　歌を　歌ったりできて
　　　　　おもしろいんじゃないか₉かしら。」

学生(二)　「さんせい。　林先生も　さそったら　どうですか。」

学生(三)　「いいと　思います。」

学生(一)　「だれか₆　ほかの　意見の　人は　手を　上げてください。　だれも₇
　　　　　はんたいする　人は　いませんね。　では、　だいたい　決まりましたね。」

学生(二)　「きょう　来ていない₁₁　人が　いますけど。」

学生(一)　「まだ　行く　場所とか　集まる　時間が　決めてない₅ので、　あした　もう
　　　　　一度　話し合いたいと　思います。」

学生(二)　「じゃあ、　来てない　佐藤さんたちには　ぼくから　れんらくして
　　　　　おきます。」

開いたり　運動　最も　卒業した　皆さん
教室　遠くない　便利　湖　海岸
泳いだり　遊んだり　意見　決まりました
集まる　決めてない

11.3　PATTERN SENTENCES

11.3.1

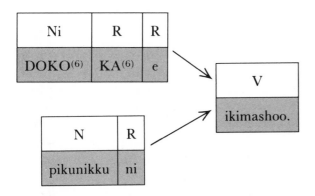

11.3.2

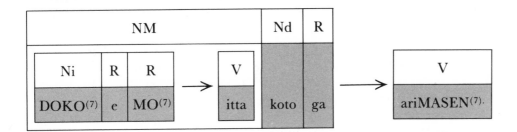

11.3.3

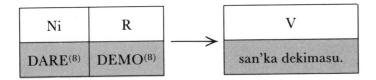

11.3.4

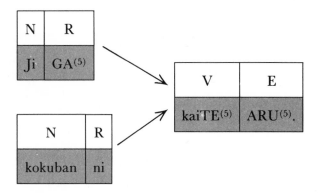

11.4 NOTES

11.4.1 Two or three years of *yoochien* (kindergarten), six years of *shoogakkoo* (elementary school), three years of *chuugakkoo* (middle school), three years of *kootoogakkoo* (high school), and two years of *tan'ki daigaku* (community college) or four years of *daigaku* (college) comprise the Japanese school system. Faculty ranks in Japanese universities or colleges are divided into full professor, assistant professor, lecturer, and assistant positions. There is no associate professor or instructor rank. Normally, there are *gakka* "departments" (such as *gen'gogakka* "language or linguistics department," *eigogakka* "English department"). *Gakka* come under the broader division of *gakubu* "colleges or schools" (such as *keizaigakubu* "college of economics," *bun'gakubu* "college of literature"). If *gakka* can be equated with departments, *shunin kyooju* might be called the chairman of a department. *Gakubuchoo* could then be equated with the dean of a college or school, except that this position in Japan is more academic and less administrative in nature than its American counterpart. *Soochoo* or *gakuchoo* is president and *daigakuin* is the equivalent of graduate school.

As has been stated previously, Japanese university students usually do not spend as much time in class as do American students. Japanese students also have a great deal of leisure time outside class. In the afternoon, coffee shops (*kissaten*) are favorite gathering places, while window shopping, and sports are popular activities. In the evening there are movie theaters, beer halls, discoteques, snack bars, *kissaten*, and so forth. Students often form clubs called *dookookai* (hobby clubs for tennis, skiing, and so forth) and pursue group activities. Japanese students usually frequent such places with members of the same sex. It has been mentioned that traditionally the Japanese date less frequently than do Americans. In addition, if Japanese wish to go somewhere with a member of the opposite sex, they sometimes go with a group, although one-to-one dating has become more and more popular.

11.4.2 *Sotsugyoo shita ato mo omoidasareru* means "one can recall it even after he's graduated." *Ato* is a Noun meaning "after," while *mae* means "before," and may be preceded by a Noun Modifier—normally the TA form of a Verb, a Noun plus *no*, and *kono, sono, ano,* and the like. The Relational *de* may occur after *ato*. After the TA form of a Verb, *ato* is similar to the *-te kara* clause in its meaning (see Note 7.4.8, Vol. III), and there is no restriction as to the tense of the final clause.

> **Verb (TA form)**
> **Noun + *no*** } + *ato (de),...*
> ***kono, sono, ano***

San'ka shita ato de, watakushi wa kan'gae o kaemashita.	"After having participated in it, I changed my mind."
Ken'gaku ni itta ato, repooto o dasanakereba narimasen.	"We have to submit a report after a field trip."
Jugyoo no ato, mina de pikunikku ni iku keikaku ni tsuite hanashita n desu.	"After class we all talked about a plan of going on a picnic."
Kono ato, watakushi ga sen'sei ni ren'raku itashimasu.	"After this (meeting) I'll contact the teacher."

11.4.3 *De aroo* is the OO form of the copular expression *de aru* and means "it will probably be such and such." Both *de aroo* and *daroo* are the suppositional, presumptive, uncertain, and less confirmative forms of the Copula. The only difference is that *de aroo* is mainly used in writing.

Daigaku seikatsu de mottomo in'shooteki na koto wa nan de aroo ka?	"What should be the most impressive happening throughout one's college life?"
Kono mon'dai ni tsuite wa iroiro na iken ga aru de aroo.	"It is understandable that there will be many opinions on this issue."

11.4.4 This dialog demonstrates the manner in which a class meeting or a consultation might be conducted. Actually, this is a postwar situation, since a relatively democratic procedure is employed in the decision-making process. Prior to the Second World War, decisions in such gatherings were made by consensus rather than by vote with the majority ruling. Even today decision by consensus is still the prevailing way of making decisions in Japan. The Japanese propensity for vagueness and indirectness is apparent in this dialog. The expressions *shibaraku*, *dekitara*, *kedo* (ending a clause), *ii n ja nai desu ka*, and *daitai* all show softening, indirectness, considerateness, and suggestive intentions.

11.4.5 *Kokuban ni kaite aru* means "It is written on the blackboard." Here ~ *te aru* after a transitive Verb implies that something has been done and is in that state.

> **Noun (object) + *o* + transitive Verb*** ⟶
> **Noun (subject) + *ga* + TE form of transitive Verb* +** { *aru* / *nai* }

*Only a limited number of transitive Verbs are used in this way.

ji o kaku	⟶	ji ga kaite aru
biiru o kau	⟶	biiru ga katte aru
ii uta o erabu	⟶	ii uta ga eran'de aru
osara o arau	⟶	osara ga aratte aru
kurabu no koto o ren'raku suru	⟶	kurabu no koto ga ren'raku shite aru
jikan o kimeru	⟶	jikan ga kimete aru

Ishii san ni den'wa shite arimasu ka?	"Have you called Mr. Ishii?"

| Iie, mada shite arimasen. | "No, I haven't called him yet." |
| Ashita shiken na noni, kono peeji no ato wa zen'zen yon'de nai n desu. | "I haven't read anything at all after this page, despite the fact that I have an exam tomorrow." |

11.4.6 *Doko ka e pikunikku ni ikoo* means "Let's go on a picnic somewhere." An interrogative Noun followed by the Relational *ka* means "some ~" in an affirmative statement and "any ~" in an affirmative or negative question. This combination is used to refer to an indefinite or uncertain place, person, thing, and the like, depending upon the interrogative Noun.

Study the following list:

interrogative Noun + *ka* + another Relational		English equivalent	
		in an affirmative statement	in an affirmative or negative question
nani ka	(ga) (o) no to kara *etc.*	"something"	"anything?"
dore ka		"some(one) / (thing)"	"any(one) / (thing)?"
dare ka donata ka		"somebody"	"anybody?"
doko ka	(ga) (o) e ni de kara no *etc.*	"somewhere"	"anywhere?"
dotchi ka dochira ka		"one or the other"	"one or the other?"
itsu ka	no	"sometime"	"anytime?"
ikura ka		"some (amount)"	"any (amount)?"
ikutsu ka		"some (items)"	"any (items)?"

As you see in the above list, if another Relational should occur with *nani ka*, *doko ka*, and so on, it always follows *nani ka*, *doko ka*, and the like. The Relational *ga* and *o* can be omitted.

$$\textbf{interrogative Noun} + \textit{\textbf{ka}} + \begin{Bmatrix} \textit{\textbf{(ga)}} \\ \textit{\textbf{(o)}} \\ \textit{\textbf{e}} \\ \textit{\textbf{ni}} \\ \textit{\textbf{to}} \\ \textbf{etc.} \end{Bmatrix} + \begin{Bmatrix} \textbf{Predicate (affirmative)} \\ \textbf{Predicate (affirmative)} + \textit{\textbf{ka}}? \\ \textbf{Predicate (negative)} + \textit{\textbf{ka}}? \end{Bmatrix}$$

Dare ka (o) sasoimashoo ka?	"Shall we invite anyone?"
Sen'sei wa rooka de dare ka to hanashite irasshaimashita.	"The teacher was talking with someone in the hall."
Doko ka e pikunikku ni ikimasen ka?	"Won't you go on a picnic anywhere?"
Itsu ka kimi no iken o kikasete kudasai.	"Please let me hear your opinion sometime."
Kono daigaku ni mo ikutsu ka no kurabu ga atte, hoton'do no gakusei ga san'ka shite imasu.	"There are some clubs and societies in this college, and most of the students have joined them."

It is also possible, in Japanese, to express ideas such as "something interesting," "some place where noisy music cannot be heard," using the interrogative Noun plus *ka*. In this case the interrogative Noun plus *ka* usually precedes the phrase or word that describes the place, time, person, and so on more specifically.

No Relational follows directly the interrogative Noun plus *ka*, but a Relational may occur after the end of a phrase following the interrogative Noun plus *ka*.

$$\textbf{interrogative Noun} + \textbf{\textit{ka}} + \textbf{(Noun Modifier)} + \textbf{Noun} + \left\{ \begin{array}{l} \textbf{\textit{ga}} \\ \textbf{\textit{o}} \\ \textbf{\textit{e}} \\ \textbf{\textit{ni}} \\ \textbf{\textit{to}} \\ \textbf{etc.} \end{array} \right\} + \textbf{Predicate}$$

nani ka omoshiroi mono	"something interesting"
doko ka urusai on'gaku ga kikoenai tokoro	"someplace where noisy music cannot be heard"
dara ka ii hito	"someone nice"
Dare ka kono keikaku ni han'tai no hito wa imasen ka?	"Isn't there anyone who is against this plan?"
Itsu ka hima na toki ni issho ni oyogi ni ikimashoo.	"Let's go swimming sometime when we are free."
Doko ka tooi tokoro ni itte mitai desu nee.	"I wish I could go to some remote place."
Dochira ka ii hoo o eran'de kudasai.	"Please choose either one that seems good to you."

11.4.7 *Doko e mo itta koto ga nai* means "We have never been anywhere." The interrogative Noun plus *mo* may be used in an affirmative sentence as well as in a negative sentence, but only the negative case will be studied in this lesson. The interrogative Noun + *mo* with negation is "not any ~" or "no ~." In this case a Relational may occur between the interrogative Noun and *mo*, but the Relational *ga* and *o* never occur with the interrogative Noun plus *mo*. Here is a list of the interrogative Noun plus *mo* combinations:

interrogative Noun + another Relational + *mo*			English equivalent	
			in a negative sentence	in an affirmative sentence
nani	kara to ni *etc.*	mo	"nothing"	"everything"
dore		mo	"none (of the things)"	"every one (of the things)"
dare donata		mo	"nobody"	"everybody"
doko	e ni de kara *etc.*	mo	"nowhere"	"everywhere"
dotchi dochira		mo	"neither one"	"either one"
itsu	—	mo	"never"	"always"
ikura	—	mo	"not much"	"some (amount)"
ikutsu	—	mo	"not many"	"some (items)"

$$\text{interrogative Noun} + \left\{ \begin{array}{l} \textit{e} \\ \textit{ni} \\ \textit{de} \\ \textit{kara} \\ \textit{etc.} \end{array} \right\} + \textit{mo} + \textbf{negative Predicate}$$

Koojoo ni wa moo dare mo imasen yo.	"There is no one in the factory."
Nani mo irimasen.	"I don't need anything."
Okane wa ikura mo nokotte imasen.	"There isn't much money left."
Dochira mo toku ni yoku arimasen deshita.	"Neither one was particularly good."
Doko kara mo uta ga kikoemasen deshita.	"The song was not heard from anywhere."
Byoonin wa ima donata ni mo aitaku nai to itte imasu.	"The patient says that he doesn't want to see anybody now."

When it is necessary to explain the person, time, thing, and so forth more specifically, a phrase describing it may follow the interrogative Noun plus *mo*. In this case a Relational should not occur between the interrogative Noun and *mo*, but it should occur at the end of the phrase.

interrogative Noun + *mo* + (Noun Modifier)

$$+ \text{ Noun } + \begin{Bmatrix} to \\ ni \\ de \\ kara \\ etc. \end{Bmatrix} + \textbf{negative Predicate}$$

Dare mo han'tai suru hito wa imasen ka?   "Isn't there anyone who objects to it?"

Saikin nani mo omoshiroi koto ga
okorimasen.   "Nothing interesting has happened recently."

11.4.8   *Dare demo san'ka dekiru* means "Anyone can participate in it." The interrogative Noun plus *demo* means "no matter (who) it may be" or "any(one) without an exception." A Relational may occur between the interrogative Noun and *demo*, but the Relational *ga* and *o* should never occur. When the interrogative Noun plus *demo* is used as the subject or the object of a sentence, it occurs without any Relational. Notice that interrogative Pre-Nouns may also occur with *demo*.
Study the following list:

interrogative word	+ another Relational	+ *demo*	English equivalent
nan		demo	"anything" "whatever it may be"
dore	to ni etc.	demo	"any one" "whichever it may be"
dare donata		demo	"anybody" "whoever it may be"
doko	e ni de kara etc.	demo	"anywhere" "wherever it may be"
dotchi dochira		demo	"either one" "whichever it may be"
itsu	kara made	demo	"anytime" "whenever it may be"
ikura		demo	"no matter how much it may be"
ikutsu		demo	"no matter how many it may be"
doo	—	demo	"no matter how it may be"
dono ~		demo	"whichever ~ it may be"
don'na ~		demo	"no matter what kind of ~ it may be"
dooiu ~		demo	"no matter what kind of ~ it may be"

$$\text{interrogative Noun} \atop \text{interrogative Pre-Noun + Noun} \Bigg\} + \begin{Bmatrix} to \\ ni \\ e \\ de \\ kara \\ \text{etc.} \end{Bmatrix} + \textit{demo} + \textbf{Predicate}$$

Nan demo omoidashite kudasai.	"Please recall anything."
Kore wa mezurashii mono de wa arimasen. Doko ni demo arimasu yo.	"This is not a rare thing. You can find it anywhere."
Itsu demo ii desu.	"Anytime will do."
Dotchi demo ii desu.	"Either way will do."
Ima dono kurasu demo shiken o yatte imasu.	"They have an exam in every class now."

When it is necessary to describe the place, person, or time more specifically, the following pattern will be used:

$$\textbf{interrogative Noun} + \textit{demo} + \textbf{(Noun Modifier)} + \textbf{Noun} + \begin{Bmatrix} to \\ ni \\ e \\ de \\ kara \\ \text{etc.} \end{Bmatrix} + \textbf{Predicate}$$

Paatii wa rokuji kara de gozaimasu kara, itsu demo osuki na toki ni irasshatte kudasaimase.	"The party is from six, so you can come any time you like."
Dore demo ii no o torinasai.	"Take whichever you think is good."
Doko demo ryoori dekiru tokoro nara ii desu.	"Any place will be all right if we can cook there."

11.4.9 *Ii n ja nai desu ka?* means "Isn't that good?" or "It's good, isn't it?" Note that this expression is different from the negative of an Adjective, *-ku nai*, which has been introduced in Volume I.

Compare:	Ii ja nai desu ka?	"Isn't it good?"
	Yoku nai desu ka?	"Is it no good?"

When a plain form of a Verb, an Adjective, or the Copula (except *da*: *na* replaces *da*) is followed by *n ja nai desu ka?*, *no de wa arimasen ka?*, *n ja nai?*, it is not a simple negative expression like *oishiku nai*, *tabenai*, and so on, but is an expression used when the speaker is urging the hearer's agreement to the statement preceding *n ja nai desu ka?*, *no de wa arimasen ka?*, and so on. The sense of this expression is close to ... *deshoo?*

$$\begin{matrix} \textbf{Verb (plain form)} \\ \textbf{Adjective (plain form)} \\ \textbf{Noun} + \textit{na} \\ \textbf{Noun} + \textbf{Copula (plain form, except } \textit{da}\textbf{)} \end{matrix} \Bigg\} + \begin{Bmatrix} \textit{no de wa arimasen ka?} \\ \textit{n ja nai desu ka?} \\ \textit{n ja nai?} \end{Bmatrix}$$

Tsukareta n ja nai desu ka?	"Aren't you tired?"
Kono kutsu wa chiisasugiru no de wa arimasen ka?	"Aren't these shoes too small?"
Byooki ga omoi n ja nai?	"Isn't he seriously ill?"
Anata wa mae nihyakupon'do gurai datta n ja arimasen ka?	"Didn't you weigh about two hundred pounds before?"

11.4.10 *Mizuumi toka kawa toka kaigan* means "a lake, or a river, or seashore." *Toka* between Nouns is a Relational that is used to list two or more items as selective samples.

| Kinoo no paatii ni wa Moogan san toka Sumisu san ga irasshaimashita. | "Mr. Morgan, Mr. Smith, and others came to the party yesterday." |
| Kare wa un'doo toka dan'su toka deeto bakari shite ite, nani mo ben'kyoo shite imasen. | "He is not studying at all, only doing such things as playing sports, dancing, dating, and the like." |

11.4.11 *Kyoo kite inai hito* means "the people who are not here today." *Kite iru* is literally "one did come and as a result is here." When the TE form of such Verbs as *kuru*, *iku*, *kaeru*, and the like is followed by the Extender *iru*, the combination does not mean "one is coming," "one is going," "one is going (coming) back," and so on, but means "one came and is here," "one went and is there," "one returned and is there," and so on.

itte	"one went there and as a result is there"
kite	"one came here and as a result is here"
kaette + iru	"one went (came) back and as a result is back"
haitte	"one entered something or somewhere and as a result is there."
dete	"one went out of something or somewhere and as a result is in it"
dekakete	"one went out and as a result is out"

A general explanation about the use of the TE form of a Verb plus *iru* as "an action and its result" has been given in Notes 2.4.2 and 13.4.3, Volume II.

Musume wa ima kaimono ni itte imasu.	"My daughter is now out shopping."
Anata ni hagaki ga kite imashita yo.	"A postcard addressed to you has come."
Jon wa ima dekakete orimasu ga, nan deshoo ka?	"John is out at the moment. May I help you?"

11.5 VOCABULARY

Presentation

ゼミ	zemi	......	N	seminar
クラブ	kurabu	......	N	club; society
なかま	nakama	......	N	associate; fellow; partner; companion
コンパ	kon'pa	......	N	party (usually students') (originated from "company")

運動	un'doo	......	N	sport
後	ato	......	N	afterward; later; after (see 11.4.2)
思い出さ	omoidasa	......	V	Pre-Nai form of *omoidasu* – recall
さまざま	samazama	......	Na	various kinds
活動	katsudoo	......	N	activity
交際 (さい)	koosai	......	N	association
であろう	de aroo	......	C + E	OO form of *de aru* (see 11.4.3)

Dialog

皆（さん）	mina(san)	......	N	everybody; (you) all (*Min'na* is used to refer to one's in-group members or in informal speech and is never followed by -*san*. *Mina* may or may not be followed by -*san*, but it should be followed by -*san* when it is addressed to a group of people.)
（書いて）ある	(kaite) aru	......	E	(see 11.4.5)
どこか	doko ka	......	Ni + R	somewhere; anywhere (see 11.4.6)
ピクニック	pikunikku	......	N	picnic
計画 (けいかく)	keikaku	......	N	plan
計画する (けいかく)	keikaku suru	......	V	plan
どこ（へ）も	doko (e) mo	......	Ni + R	(not) anywhere (see 11.4.7)
さんせい	san'sei	......	N	approval; consent; agreement
さんせいする	san'sei suru	......	V	agree; approve; consent; support
だれでも	dare demo	......	Ni + R	anybody (see 11.4.8)
さんか	san'ka	......	N	participation
さんかする	san'ka suru	......	V	participate; join (~ *ni san'ka suru*) (intransitive Verb)
どこでも	doko demo	......	Ni + R	anywhere (see 11.4.8)
湖 (みずうみ)	mizuumi	......	N	lake (lit. "freshwater sea")
とか	toka	......	R	and/or (see 11.4.10)
海岸 (がん)	kaigan	......	N	beach; seashore
えらんだら	eran'dara	......	V	TARA form of *erabu* – choose; select
ゲーム	geemu	......	N	game
歌 (うた)	uta	......	N	song
さそったら	sasottara	......	V	TARA form of *sasou* – invite someone to do
だれか	dare ka	......	Ni + R	someone (see 11.4.6)

意見	iken	......	N	opinion
上げて	agete	......	V	TE form of *ageru*–raise; hold up (transitive Verb)
だれも	dare mo	......	Ni + R	(not) anyone (see 11.4.7)
はんたいする	han'tai suru	......	V	oppose; (say) against
はんたい	han'tai	......	N	opposition; dissent; negative
佐藤	Satoo	......	N	family name

Notes

か	ka	......	R	(see 11.4.6)
何か	nani ka	......	N + R	something (see 11.4.6)
も	mo	......	R	(see 11.4.7)
何も	nani mo	......	N + R	(not) anything (see 11.4.7)
でも	demo	......	R	(see 11.4.8)
何でも	nan demo	......	N + R	anything (see 11.4.8)
見学	ken'gaku	......	N	observation study; field trip
見学する	ken'gaku suru	......	V	visit someplace for study
ダンス	dan'su	......	N	dance
デート	deeto	......	N	date

11.6 KAN'JI

11.6.a 開 ^2.6.2 (1) *hira(ku)* (2) open; hold (5) 会を開く、門を開く

11.6.1 運 (1) UN (2) carry; transport (3) classifier ⻌

(4) ⼢ 軍 運 (5) 運動、運転

11.6.b 最 ^6.6.10 (1) *motto(mo)* (5) 世界で最も高い建物はどれですか

11.6.2 卒 (1) SOTSU (2) finish (3) classifier 亠 （十）

(4) 亠 六 立 卒 (5) 卒業、卒業生、大学卒

11.6.3 皆 (1) *mina* (2) all; everyone (3) classifier 比 （白）

(4) ⺊ 比 皆 (5) 皆さん、皆様

11.6.4 室 (1) SHITSU (2) room (3) classifier 宀 [roof]

(4) 宀 宀 宀 宏 室 (5) 教室、図書室、寝室、社長室

11.6.5 遠　(1) *too(i)*　(2) far; remote　(3) classifier 辶

(4) ⬚土 ⬚吉 ⬚幸 ⬚袁 ⬚遠　(5) 遠い国、遠くに住む

11.6.6 便　(1) BEN　(2) convenient　(3) classifier 亻

(4) ⬚亻 ⬚仁 ⬚㑒 ⬚便 ⬚便　(5) 便利、不便

11.6.7 利　(1) RI　(2) advantage　(3) classifier 禾（刂 [knife]）　(4) ⬚禾 ⬚利 ⬚利

(5) 便利、有利[advantaged]　(6) homonym 痢、梨

11.6.8 湖　(1) *mizuumi*　(2) lake　(3) classifier シ

(4) ⬚氵 ⬚汁 ⬚湖 ⬚湖　(5) 海とか湖へ行く

(6) 古[KO] represents the original pronunciation. Homonym KO 古、故、個、
固、枯、胡

11.6.c 海 ^8.6.1　(1) KAI　(5) 海岸、日本海　(6) homonym 悔

11.6.9 泳　(1) *oyo(gu)*　(2) swim　(3) classifier シ

(4) ⬚氵 ⬚氵 ⬚氵 ⬚沊 ⬚泳　(5) 海で泳ぐ、泳ぎ

(6) homonym EI 永、詠、泳

11.6.10 遊　(1) *aso(bu)*　(2) enjoy oneself; play　(3) classifier 辶

(4) ⬚方 ⬚扩 ⬚斿 ⬚遊　(5) 公園で遊ぶ、遊びに行く、水遊び、遊び着、
遊び場[playground]

11.6.11 意　(1) I　(2) mind; heart; attention　(3) classifier 立（心）

(4) ⬚立 ⬚音 ⬚意　(5) 意見、意気 [spirit]、同意する[agree]、決意
[determination]、意味

11.6.d 見 ^4.6.5, Vol. II　(1) KEN　(5) 意見、見学、見物する、発見[discover]

11.6.12 決　(1) *ki(maru); ki(meru)*　(2) is decided; decide　(3) classifier シ

(4) ⬚氵 ⬚氵 ⬚江 ⬚決　(5) 時間が決まる、時間を決める

11.6.13 集　(1) *atsu(maru); atsu(meru)*　(2) gather; collect　(3) classifier 隹
[birds]　(4) ⬚亻 ⬚疒 ⬚仲 ⬚隹 ⬚隼 ⬚集　(5) 集まる、集める

(6) birds 隹 on a tree 木 = gather

11.7　DRILLS

11.7.1　Transformation Drill

1. <u>あした</u>　計画〔けいかく〕しましょう。　　　⟶　<u>いつか</u>　計画〔けいかく〕しましょう。

2. <u>湖へ</u>　行きませんか。　　　　　　　⟶　どこかへ　行きませんか。

3. <u>しず子さんを</u>　さそいたいんです。　⟶　だれか　さそいたいんです。

4. <u>見学を</u>　してください。　　　　　　⟶　何か　してください。

5. <u>島田さんに</u>　れんらくしましょう。　⟶　だれかに　れんらくしましょう。

6. <u>ろう下で</u>　会うわけに　いかないん　　　どこかで　会うわけに　いかないん
　　ですか。　　　　　　　　　　　　⟶　　ですか。

7. <u>大きい　方を</u>　もらいましょう。　　⟶　どっちか　もらいましょう。

8. <u>三千円ほど</u>　持っています。　　　　⟶　いくらか　持っています。

9. <u>二つ</u>　注文〔ちゅうもん〕しなさい。　　　⟶　いくつか　注文〔ちゅうもん〕しなさい。

10. <u>名前を</u>　思い出しましたか。　　　　⟶　何か　思い出しましたか。

11. <u>ジョンさんと</u>　いっしょに　歌〔うた〕って　⟶　だれかと　いっしょに　歌〔うた〕って
　　ください。　　　　　　　　　　　　　　ください。

12. <u>来週</u>　パーティーを　開こうと　思って　⟶　いつか　パーティーを　開こうと
　　いるんです。　　　　　　　　　　　　　思っているんです。

11.7.2　Transformation Drill

1. おいしい　<u>物</u>を　食べましょう。　　⟶　<u>何か</u>　おいしい　<u>物</u>を　食べましょう。

2. めずらしい　所へ　行きましょう。　⟶　どこか　めずらしい　所へ　行き
　　　　　　　　　　　　　　　　　　　　ましょう。

3. 日本語の　じょうずな　人を　知って　⟶　だれか　日本語の　じょうずな　人を
　　いますか。　　　　　　　　　　　　　知っていますか。

4. <u>歌〔うた〕</u>を　歌〔うた〕ってください。　　⟶　何か　歌を　歌〔うた〕ってください。

5. つごうの　いい　日に　さそいましょう。⟶　いつか　つごうの　いい　日に　さそい
　　　　　　　　　　　　　　　　　　　　ましょう。

6. 安い　方が　ほしいです。　　　　　⟶　どっちか　安い　方が　ほしいです。

7. 神社の　ある　所を　見学しましょう。⟶　どこか　神社の　ある　所を　見学
　　　　　　　　　　　　　　　　　　　　しましょう。

8. きょう　来ていない　学生が　いますか。⟶　だれか　きょう　来ていない　学生が
　　　　　　　　　　　　　　　　　　　　いますか。

11.7.3 Response Drill

1. <u>何が</u> いいですか。   …… <u>何でも</u> いいです。
2. どっちが いいですか。   …… どっちでも いいです。
3. いつが よろしいですか。   …… いつでも よろしいです。
4. いくつ 食べられますか。   …… いくつでも 食べられます。
5. いくら 払いましょうか。   …… いくらでも 払ってください。
6. だれが さんかできますか。   …… だれでも さんかできます。
7. どこを 見学したいですか。   …… どこでも 見学したいです。
8. 何が 一番 食べたいですか。   …… 何でも 食べたいです。
9. どこへ 一番 行きたいですか。   …… どこへでも 行きたいです。
10. いつが 一番 つごうが いいですか。   …… いつでも いいです。

11.7.4 Transformation Drill

1. <u>おたくへ</u> まいります。 ⟶ <u>どこへでも</u> まいります。
2. さんせいと 言ってください。 ⟶ 何とでも 言ってください。
3. あしたから 始められますか。 ⟶ いつからでも 始められますか。
4. 先生に そうだんした ほうが いい です。 ⟶ だれにでも そうだんした ほうが いいです。
5. クラブ活動に さんかするつもりです。 ⟶ 何にでも さんかするつもりです。
6. 上野(の)で さくらが 見られますか。 ⟶ どこででも さくらが 見られますか。
7. あなたと 話し合いたいです。 ⟶ だれとでも 話し合いたいです。
8. 佐藤(さとう)さんに れんらくしてあげますよ。 ⟶ だれにでも れんらくしてあげますよ。

11.7.5 Transformation Drill

1. 好きな <u>時</u>に さんかしてください。 ⟶ <u>いつでも</u> 好きな 時に さんかして ください。
2. さんせいの 人は 手を 上(あ)げなさい。 ⟶ だれでも さんせいの 人は 手を 上(あ)げなさい。
3. 海岸(かいがん)の そばなら いいでしょう。 ⟶ どこでも 海岸(かいがん)の そばなら いい でしょう。
4. おもしろそうな クラブを しょうかい してください。 ⟶ どこでも おもしろそうな クラブを しょうかいしてください。
5. この 中の 物を えらんでください。 ⟶ どれでも この 中の 物を えらんで ください。

6. 学生なら、見学することが できます。 —→ だれでも 学生なら、見学することが
　　　　　　　　　　　　　　　　　　　　　　　　できます。

7. ほしい 物を 言ってください。 —→ 何でも ほしい 物を 言ってください。

8. 好きな 人を さそったら どうですか。—→ だれでも 好きな 人 を さそったら
　　　　　　　　　　　　　　　　　　　　　　　どうですか。

11.7.6 Transformation Drill

1. 見学も 見物も しませんでした。 —→ 何も しませんでした。

2. 渡辺君は 研究室にも 教室にも —→ 渡辺君は どこにも いません。
　　　いません。

3. 京都へも 奈良へも 行きたくない —→ どこへも 行きたくないんですか。
　　　ですか。

4. かず子さんも みち子さんも デートに —→ だれも デートに さそわないんです。
　　　さそわないんです。

5. ダンスを することも 歌を 歌う —→ どっちも じょうずじゃありません。
　　　ことも じょうずじゃありません。

6. ぼくは 朝も 昼も 夜も コーヒーを —→ ぼくは いつも コーヒーを 飲ま
　　　飲まないんです。 ないんです。

7. クラブにも ゼミにも 入っていないん —→ 何にも 入っていないんです。
　　　です。

8. おとなも 子どもも 教会に —→ だれも 教会に 集まりませんでした。
　　　集まりませんでした。

11.7.7 Response Drill

1. おととい どこか おもしろい 所へ 行きましたか。
　　　no, nowhere 　　　　　…… いいえ、どこへも 行きませんでした。

2. だれかに れんらくできますか。
　　　no, nobody 　　　　　…… いいえ、だれにも れんらくできません。

3. この ゲームか その ゲームか どっちか 知っていますか。
　　　no, neither 　　　　　…… いいえ、どっちも 知りません。

4. あなたは 大学の パーティーに いつも さんかしますか。
　　　no, never 　　　　　…… いいえ、いつも さんかしません。

5. 何を　ぬすまれたか　思い出せますか。

    no, nothing　　　　　　　…… いいえ、何も　思い出せません。

6. いろいろな　計画(けいかく)は　全部(ぜん)　決まりましたか。

    no, none of them　　　　…… いいえ、どれも　決まりませんでした。

7. どなたから　れんらくしてもらうつもりなんですか。

    no, no one　　　　　　　…… いいえ、どなたからも　れんらくしてもらわないつもり
                       です。

11.7.8　Transformation Drill

1. 黒板(こくばん)に　字を　書きました。　　　　⟶　黒板(こくばん)に　字が　書いてあります。

2. 旅行の　計画(けいかく)について　話しません　⟶　旅行の　計画(けいかく)について　話して
   でした。　　　　　　　　　　　　　　ありません。

3. 佐藤(さとう)さんに　コンパの　ことを　　　⟶　佐藤(さとう)さんに　コンパの　ことが
   れんらくしました。　　　　　　　　　　れんらくしてあります。

4. お皿を　全部(ぜん)　洗いました。　　　　　⟶　お皿が　全部(ぜん)　洗ってあります。

5. ピクニックに　持って行く　物を　　　　　⟶　ピクニックに　持って行く　物が
   買いませんでした。　　　　　　　　　　買ってありません。

6. いい　歌(うた)を　えらびました。　　　　　⟶　いい　歌(うた)が　えらんであります。

7. ゼミの　なかまに　電話しました。　　　　⟶　ゼミの　なかまに　電話してあります。

8. 集まる　時間を　決めましたか。　　　　　⟶　集まる　時間が　決めてありますか。

11.7.9　Transformation Drill

1. 歌(うた)を　歌(うた)ったりできて　いいでしょう?　⟶　歌(うた)を　歌(うた)ったりできて　いいじゃない
                            ですか。

2. おもしろい　ことを　計画(けいかく)しているん　⟶　おもしろい　ことを　計画(けいかく)しているん
   でしょう?　　　　　　　　　　　　　じゃないですか。

3. ジョンさんは　とても　しんせつな　　　⟶　ジョンさんは　とても　しんせつな
   人でしょう?　　　　　　　　　　　　人じゃないですか。

4. どこかへ　見学に　行くんでしょう?　　⟶　どこかへ　見学に　行くんじゃない
                          ですか。

5. しず子さんは　ダンスが　じょうず　　　⟶　しず子さんは　ダンスが　じょうずじゃ
   でしょう?　　　　　　　　　　　　　ないですか。

6. この　意味は　ちょっと　わかり　　　　⟶　この　意味は　ちょっと　わかり
   にくいんでしょう?　　　　　　　　　にくいんじゃないですか。

ニックに 林先生も さそうん
でしょう?　→　ピクニックに 林先生も さそうんじゃ
ないですか。

ぜを ひいたんでしょう?　→　かぜを ひいたんじゃないですか。

ラブ活動は おもしろかったん
でしょう?　→　クラブ活動は おもしろかったん
じゃないですか。

Transformation Drill

ンフリーさんは きょう 学校に
来ました。　→　ハンフリーさんは きょう 学校に
来ています。

ーティーに 来なかった 人は
クラークさんだけです。　→　パーティーに 来ていない 人は
クラークさんだけです。

内は かぜで 病院へ 行きました。　→　家内は かぜで 病院へ 行っています。

どもたちは 駅へ おばさんを
むかえに 行ったはずです。　→　子どもたちは 駅へ おばさんを
むかえに 行っているはずです。

ちには いろいろな クラブに
入りました。　→　あには いろいろな クラブに 入って
います。

6. 社長は 大事な 会に 出ました。　→　社長は 大事な 会に 出ています。

7. 宿題を 持って来なかった 人は
手を 上げてください。　→　宿題を 持って来ていない 人は
手を 上げてください。

8. 父は まだ 会社から 帰りません。　→　父は まだ 会社から 帰っていません。

9. 母たちは ダンスに 出かけました。　→　母たちは ダンスに 出かけています。

11.7.11 Transformation Drill

A.　1. 授業が 終わります。
　　　教室に 残ってください。　→　授業が 終わった 後、教室に
残ってください。

　　2. 大学を 卒業しました。
　　　日本に 興味を 持ち始めました。　→　大学を 卒業した 後、日本に
興味を 持ち始めました。

　　3. みんなで 工場を 見学しました。
　　　泳ぎに 行きました。　→　みんなで 工場を 見学した 後、
泳ぎに 行きました。

　　4. 計画が 決まります。
　　　はんたいしないでください。　→　計画が 決まった 後、はんたい
しないでください。

　　5. 高木さんと 話しました。
　　　昔の ことを 思い出しました。　→　高木さんと 話した 後、昔の
ことを 思い出しました。

B.   1. <u>ピクニックでした</u>。   <u>ピクニックの</u>　後、とても

          とても　つかれました。   ⎫→   つかれました。

    2. ジョンさんの　意見でした。   ジョンさんの　意見の　後、だれも

          だれも　何も　言いませんでした。   ⎫→   何も　言いませんでした。

    3. 楽しい　ダンスパーティーでした。   楽しい　ダンスパーティーの　後、

          みんなで　お茶を　飲みました。   ⎫→   みんなで　お茶を　飲みました。

    4. 日本の　ゲームです。   日本の　ゲームの　後、アメリカの

          アメリカの　ゲームを　しましょう。 ⎫→ ゲームを　しましょう。

    5. 長い　病気でした。   長い　病気の　後、しばらく　元気が

          しばらく　元気が　なかったんです。 ⎫→ なかったんです。

11.7.12 E-J Response Drill

1. いつか　あまり　遠くない　所へ　遊びに　行きませんか。

    yes, any time will be fine   ……　はい、いつでも　いいです。

2. だれか　この　ことわざの　意味が　わかりますか。

    no, nobody   ……　いいえ、だれも　わかりません。

3. 学生時代　どんな　運動を　しましたか。

    didn't do anything   ……　何も　しませんでした。

4. どこで　歌を　歌ったり　ゲームを　したりできると　思いますか。

    we can do it at any place   ……　どこででも　できると　思います。

5. えびフライと　すきやきと、どっちが　食べたいですか。

    neither one   ……　どっちも　食べたくありません。

6. だれに　案内してもらいましょうか。

    anyone who knows the way   ……　だれでも　道を　知っている　人に　案内して

                                     もらいましょう。

7. どこかへ　お祭りを　見に　行ったことが　ありますか。

    no, nowhere   ……　いいえ、どこへも　行ったことが　ありません。

8. きょうは　あなたに　昼ご飯を　おごってあげたいんですが、何が　いいですか。

    anything will be fine   ……　何でも　いいです。

11.7.13 Transformation Drill

1. バスの　方が　便利<u>だろう</u>。   ⟶ バスの　方が　便利<u>であろう</u>。

2. 学生生活で　最も　楽しかったのは ⟶ 学生生活で　一番　楽しかったのは

    クラブ活動だった。   クラブ活動であった。

3. かれは　私の　意見に　はんたいする　　　　⟶　かれは　私の　意見に　はんたいする
　　だろう。　　　　　　　　　　　　　　　　　　　であろう。

4. そこは　不便で、行きにくい　所だ。　　　　⟶　そこは　不便であり、行きにくい　所で
　　　　　　　　　　　　　　　　　　　　　　　　ある。

5. あした　ピクニックに　行こうという　　　　⟶　あした　ピクニックに　行こうという
　　計画は　だめに　なるだろう。　　　　　　　　　計画は　だめに　なるであろう。

6. 今度のは　最も　大きな　台風だった。　　　　　今度のは　最も　大きな　台風であった。

7. 今も　思い出されるのは　子どもの　　　　　　今も　思い出されるのは　子どもの
　　ころの　祭りだ。　　　　　　　　　　　　　　　ころの　祭りである。

11.8　EXERCISES

11.8.1　What would you say when:

1. you want to suggest to your friend that he have something with you?

2. you want to tell someone anytime will be convenient to you?

3. you want to ask someone if he knows any good shop that specializes in *han'ga*?

4. you want to answer in reply to someone's question that if the weather is nice, yes, you would like to go some place?

5. you want to ask someone if you can invite anyone to the party?

6. you want to say that you don't want to participate in any (one) of the club activities?

11.8.2　適当な　Relational を　入れなさい。それから、英語で　意味を　言いなさい。

1. どこ_____　機械の　工場_____　見学に　行った　ほうが　いいんじゃない?

2. きょうは　何_____　ほしい　物_____　ないので、いつ_____　また　買いに
　　来ましょう。

3. いくら_____　残っていません。ほとんど　食べてしまいましたから。

4. この　中から　どれ_____　あなたの　好きな　歌_____　おえらびください。

5. だれ_____　何_____　知らせてくれないので、どこで　パーティーを
　　開くの_____　知らないんです。

6. 「ピクニックは　いつが　よろしいでしょうか。」「いつ_____　いいです。」

7. 学生は　勉強_____　クラブ活動_____　アルバイト_____　友だち_____の
　　交際などで、かなり　忙しい。

11.8.3 <u>いるか</u> <u>ある</u>を 使って、いい 文に しなさい。(いると あるは 適当な 形
(form)に していい) そして、意味を 言いなさい。

1. きょう 学生が 三人 来て＿＿＿＿。病気かしら。
2. 母は 出かけて＿＿＿＿が、晩ご飯が 作って＿＿＿＿ので、安心です。
3. 手紙に 書いて＿＿＿＿ 場所で 会いました。
4. おふろに 入って＿＿＿＿ 時 電話が あると、こまってしまいます。
5. お弁当は もう 買って＿＿＿＿はずですから、作らなくても いいです。

11.8.4 日本語で こたえなさい。

1. きょうは だれも 授業を 休みませんでしたか。
2. クラスで だれか 病気の 人は いませんか。
3. きょうの 授業で 何か わからないことが ありましたか。
4. きのう どこかへ 遊びに 行きましたか。
5. いつか 京都を 見物したいと 思いますか。
6. 何か 日本の 食べ物を 食べたことが ありますか。それは 何ですか。
7. 日本の 食べ物は 何でも 好きですか。
8. あなたは もう 漢字を 五百ぐらい 知っているんじゃないですか。

11.8.5 Change the style of the following passage into the formal written style.

　山下さんの 生活は ひじょうに 大変です。両親に 死なれて、弟や 妹の
ために 毎日 買物を して、食事を 作って、アルバイトと 勉強を する
生活です。

　きのう 会った かれは つかれているようでした。今の かれに 必要なのは
まず 家の 仕事を してくれる 人を 見つけることでしょう。

11.8.6 漢字に 変えなさい。

1. <u>うんどう</u>も <u>べんきょう</u>も しなければ なりません。
2. <u>およ</u>いだり <u>かい</u>岸で <u>あそ</u>んだりするのが <u>す</u>きです。
3. どこか <u>とお</u>くない <u>ところ</u>へ <u>けんがく</u>に <u>い</u>くことに <u>き</u>めました。
4. この <u>ことば</u>の <u>いみ</u>が <u>わ</u>かった <u>ひと</u>は <u>て</u>を <u>あ</u>げなさい。
5. <u>みな</u>さん、ちょっと <u>きょうしつ</u>に <u>のこ</u>ってください。そして、<u>まえ</u>の
   <u>ほう</u>に <u>あつ</u>まってください。
6. <u>そつぎょう</u>しても、クラスの パーティーを <u>ひら</u>きますから、ぜひ
   さんかしてください。
7. <u>もっとも</u> <u>こうつう</u>の <u>べんり</u>な <u>みずうみ</u>を <u>えら</u>びました。

11.8.7 読みなさい。

   1. 泳、水　　　　4. 車、運

   2. 海、湖　　　　5. 便、使

   3. 意、思　　　　6. 利、私

11.8.8 Using less vague and more direct expressions in the plain style, rewrite the conversation presented in the Dialog.

11.8.9 Reconstruct the Dialog by changing the situation to that of a meeting among close friends.

11.8.10 It is said that a Japanese person's first consideration is always "What will they think of me?" rather than "What do I think of them?" Explore the relationship between this trait in Japanese thinking and the Japanese language (in terms of softening, indirection, considerateness, suggestive expressions, etc.).

11.8.11 Describe the difference between Japanese and American educational systems and student life-styles.

11.8.12 Explain the different usages of the following expressions and list three sentences, each using these expressions.

   1. de aru
   2. de atta
   3. de wa nai
   4. de wa nakatta
   5. de ari
   6. de aroo

11.9 SITUATIONAL AND APPLICATION CONVERSATION

11.9.1 A male student tells his girl friend that if she is free next Saturday evening he wants to take her to a dance party.

The girl says that she will be glad to go with him.

The boy says he will take her to Shinjuku to have dinner before the party and asks if she knows any good restaurants in Shinjuku.

The girl hasn't been to any restaurant in Shinjuku and says any restaurant will be fine with her.

The boy asks her what time he should meet her.

The girl says any time will be all right with her if it's after six o'clock. She asks him if any other friends of the boy are also going to the party.

The boy says he didn't tell anybody about the party.

11.9.2 A senior student who is an active member of the ski club asks a freshman to join the ski club.

The freshman says that he has never skied.

The senior says that anyone can join the club because they teach how to ski.

The freshman asks where they practice skiing during winter.

The senior answers that they go to various places; they even go to Hokkaidō once a year. He emphasizes that the club members become good friends with each other during those trips, as well as becoming good at skiing.

The freshman asks what they do while there is no snow.

The senior says they do nothing during July and August; otherwise they do such things as going on picnics, playing other sports, swimming, running, etc.

The freshman says that the ski club's activities seem interesting.

11.9.3 Girl: Nee, ashita doko ka e ikanai? Nani mo suru koto ga nai no yo, ashita.

Boy: Eiga nan'ka wa?

Girl: Doko ka de omoshiroi no yatteru?

Boy: Yatte iru to omou yo. Shirabete miyoo ka?

11.9.4 Friend A: Anoo ...

Friend B: Nani ka?

Friend A: Eeto ..., hora, are totte!

Friend B: Nani mo iwanai kara, wakaranai ja nai?! Dore?

Friend A: Ano shin'bun.

Friend B: Aa, wakatta wa.

11.9.5 Suzuki: Otaku e ichido ukagaitai n desu ga ...

Honda: Aa, doozo irasshai.

Suzuki: Itsu ga gotsugoo ga ii deshoo ka?

Honda: Itsu demo ii desu yo.

Suzuki: Dewa, ashita wa ...

Honda: Ii desu yo.

Suzuki: Nan'ji goro ...?

Honda: Nan'ji demo.

Suzuki: Sochira no gotsugoo no ii jikan o kimete kudasaimasen ka?

Honda: Jaa, niji goro wa doo?

Suzuki: Hai, dewa, ashita niji goro ojama shimasu node, yoroshiku onegai shimasu.

11.10   READING COMPREHENSION

11.10.1

　日本では、高校生活は　大学の　入学試験(しけん)の　じゅんび(preparation)で　かなり　忙しい。大学に　入るのが　なかなか　むずかしいからである。そのため、大学に　入りたいと　思っている　日本の　高校生には　アメリカの　高校生の　ように　アルバイトを　したり、なかまと　いろいろな　活動を　したりする　機会(きかい)(chance)が　あまり　ない。

　それで、大学に　入ると、急に　自由(ゆう)を　感(かん)じて、何でも　したがり、遊ぶことが　多くなる。　アメリカ人の　大学生は　しばしば　日本の　大学生が　よく　遊ぶと　言うが、アメリカ人学生に　くらべれば　そうかもしれない。大学は　高校より　ずっと　学生を　自由(ゆう)に　させている。宿題(しゅく)も　少なくなる。

　しかし、日本の　学生たちも、会社に　入った　後　かなり　勉強するのではないだろうか。日本の　会社などでは、新しく　入った　社員に　社内教育(いく)を　するが、これは　なかなか　きびしく、大学時代に　なまけていた(having been lazy)　もの(person)も　いっしょうけんめい　やるようである。

11.10.2

しず子　「ねえ、休みに　なったら、みんなで　どこかへ　行かない?」

みのる　「いいね、さんせい。どこが　いいだろう?」

しず子　「あたしは　泳ぎに　行きたいわ。」

みのる　「ぼくは　キャンプ(camping)が　いいな。富士山(ふじさん)の　辺の　湖なんか　どう?　泳げるし、キャンプも　できるし　いいんじゃない?」

しず子　「わたしは　いいわ、湖でも。でも、ほかの　人は　きょう　だれも　来てないから、あした　もう一度　どこに　するか　そうだんしない?」

みのる　「そうだね。中山さんは　きょう　急ぐの?」

しず子　「ううん、べつに。何か?」

みのる　「コーヒーか　何か　飲まない?」

しず子　「ええ。行きましょう。」

みのる　「どこが　いいかな。」

しず子　「どこでも　いいわ。」

みのる　「じゃあ、いつもの　所に　行こうか。」

LESSON 12
日本人と 気候₁

12.1　PRESENTATION

　日本人によって₂ 書かれた 小説、　ずい筆、　手紙、　日記などには、　たいてい 四季の 変化や 天気の ことが 書いてあり、　俳句₃には 季節の ことばが なければならない。　また、　顔を 合わせると、「よく 降りますね」とか 「あつく なったね」とか あいさつする。

　このように、　気候の 変化や 天気の ことを いつも 話題に するのは₄ 日本人が 自然の 変化を 感じやすいから₄であろう。

12.2　DIALOG

戸田　「さっきまで 空が 明るかったのに、　曇ってきた₅ようね。」

清水　「本当だ。　風も だんだん 強くなってきたし、　雨が 降り出し₆そうだね。
　　　　あした 雨に 降られる₇と、　困るんだけどなあ₈。」

戸田　「どうして そんなに 困った₉ 顔を している₁₀の? 何か あるの、　あした₁₁?」

清水　「うん、　あしたは 大切な テニスの 試合なんだ。　雨で 試合が なく
　　　　なったら がっかりだな₁₂あ。　せっかく₁₃ 調子が 上がってきたのに…」

戸田　「〈てるてるぼうず₁₄〉を 下げて、〈てるてるぼうず〉の 歌でも 歌ったら
　　　　どう?」

清水　「じょうだんじゃないよ。　でも、　そうでも したい 気₁₅が するけど…」

戸田　「天気予報₁₆じゃ 降るって 言わなかったから、　あしたに なれば 晴れて
　　　　くるんじゃないかしら。」

清水　「そうなら いいけど。　ぬれた₉ コートじゃ やりにくいから、　とにかく
　　　　降ってほしくないなあ。」

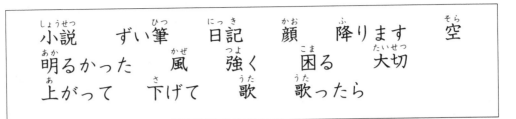

小説	ずい筆	日記	顔	降ります	空
明るかった	風	強く	困る	大切	
上がって	下げて	歌	歌ったら		

12.3 PATTERN SENTENCES

12.3.1

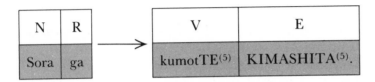

N	R
Sora	ga

→

V	E
kumotTE[5]	KIMASHITA[5].

12.3.2

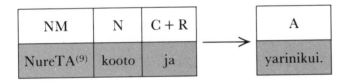

NM	N	C + R
NureTA[9]	kooto	ja

→

A
yarinikui.

12.3.3

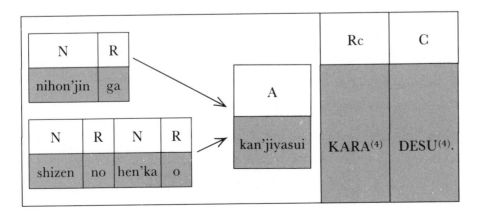

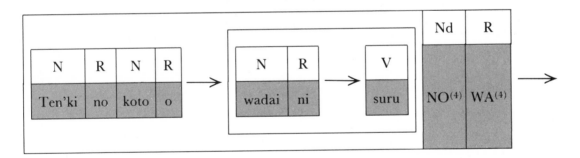

12.4   NOTES

12.4.1   As has been discussed in a previous lesson, Japanese culture has been affected by the Japanese climate. The traditional view of nature is such that the weather is an important part of daily life—the Japanese are very weather conscious and refer to the weather constantly. For instance, in letter writing, an initial mention of the weather is always made; in novels, essays, and diaries allusions to the weather are quite frequent. In fact, the weather has been described in such detail that any given season or subdivision of season could be described by reference to weather. For example, *tsuyudoki* refers to the rainy season of the month of June. *Samidare*, the spring rain, evokes a dreamlike, poetic feeling for the Japanese. The weather indeed has affected poetic mood and aesthetic sentiment as revealed in Japanese poetry and literature. Especially in *haiku*, *kigo* (words indicating seasons) are indispensable.

12.4.2   *Nihon'jin ni yotte kakareta shoosetsu* means "novels written by Japanese people." In ordinary passive sentences the actor is followed by the Relational *ni* "by." (See Note 3.4.2.) In some passive sentences, however, the actor is followed by *ni yotte* instead of *ni*. When the original active sentence has or may have *ni*, *ni yotte* must be used in its corresponding passive sentence to avoid possible confusion. In the above sentence *kaku* normally requires the indirect object Relational *ni*, so *ni yotte* is preferred after the actor *nihon'jin*.

Igirisujin ni yotte Nihon ni hajimete kisha ga   "Trains were introduced to Japan for the
   shookai saremashita.   first time by Englishmen."

Gakubuchoo wa kyoojutachi ni yotte   "The dean is elected by the professors."
   erabaremasu.

Kore wa amerikajin ni yotte kakareta.   "This was written by an American."

12.4.3   At the beginning of each volume of this series is a *haiku* by Seien, the pen name of the senior author of this textbook. The four seasons and their characteristics are reflected in these *haiku*.
   The *haiku* in Volume I is as follows:

Yuku kumo ya   Clouds drifting
   Hotaka no mine no   Over the mountains of Hotaka
Nokori yuki   Snow lingers.

"Snow lingers" refers to spring. Spring brings with it expectation, the realization of the beginning of new life, growth, and change.
   In Volume II the reference is to summer. We are moving along, our endeavors are now almost half completed. We have gained more confidence. The pond is fragrant, reflecting two lilies, two volumes, and two authors.

Shirayuri ya   The elegant reflection
   Nikei utsurite   of two white lilies;
Ike kaoru   Now the pond is fragrant.

   In Volume III we read:

Miagureba   Looking up
   Ou kage mo nashi   I see all life revealed;
Mochi no tsuki   Unshadowed full moon of autumn.

The peak approaches signaled by the satisfaction and fulfillment of autumn. We see our accomplishments as the full moon of autumn—the moon most admired.

With Volume IV the end has come. Now it is time to part, and we are left with the unknown, settling into *mu*, a Zen feeling of "nothingness."

Urayama no	Back mountain icicles
Yuuhi ni utsuru	Transcendent in the setting sun;
Tsurara kana	Splendid—ephemeral.

Generally speaking, three factors must be considered in order to understand *haiku* and its author's intentions: (1) linguistic structure; (2) semantic connotation; and (3) cultural implications. *Haiku* aims to convey maximum content with a mere seventeen syllables; therefore, unless the connotations and implications are shared by both the author and the reader, the poem will be rather difficult to understand.

12.4.4 *Itsumo wadai ni suru no wa nihon'jin ga shizen no hen'ka o kan'jiyasui kara de aroo* means "The reason why the Japanese (talk about the weather) is probably because they are sensitive to the changes of nature." This is an inverted sentence. A clause ending with *kara* showing the reason for a resulting event can be transformed into this kind of inverted sentence.

$$\ldots kara, \ldots \atop \text{(reason)(result)} \longrightarrow \text{plain form of} \left\{ {\text{Verb} \atop \text{Adjective} \atop \text{Copula} \atop \text{(except } da\text{)}} \right\} + {no\ wa \ldots kara \atop \text{(reason)}} \left\{ {da \atop desu \atop deshoo \atop daroo \atop \text{etc.}} \right\}$$

Shigoto ga atta kara, Nihon e itta. ⟶ Nihon e itta no wa shigoto ga atta kara da.

"I went to Japan because I found a job there."

"The reason why I went to Japan is because I found a job there."

Igirisu no ten'ki ga warui kara, igirisujin wa ten'ki no koto o yoku wadai ni shimasu. ⟶ Igirisujin ga ten'ki no koto o yoku wadai ni suru no wa, Igirisu no ten'ki ga warui kara desu.

"Because of the bad weather in England, the English people always talk about the weather."

"It is because the weather is bad in England that the English people always talk about the weather."

Watashi wa uta ga heta da kara, uta o utaimasen. ⟶ Watashi ga uta o utawanai no wa heta da kara desu.

"I don't sing well, so I don't sing."

"The reason why I don't sing a song is because I am not good at it."

Anata ga yoku ben'kyoo shite konakatta kara, gakkari shimashita. ⟶ Gakkari shita no wa, anata ga yoku ben'kyoo o shite konakatta kara desu.

"I was disappointed because you did not study well."

"The reason why I was disappointed is because you did not study well."

12.4.5 *Kumotte kita yoo ne* means "It seems to have become cloudy." *Kumotte kuru* means "it has been getting cloudy" or "it will be getting cloudy." There are a group of intransitive Verbs in Japanese that describe the change of a state. Here are some of them:

kumoru	"get cloudy"	futoru	"get fat"
hareru	"become fair"	yaseru	"get thin"

kawaru	"change"	komu	"get crowded"
fueru	"increase"	suku	"get less crowded"
naru	"become"	kawaku	"get dry"
tsukareru	"get tired"	nureru	"get wet"
yogoreru	"get dirty"		

When the TE form of Verbs such as those shown above is followed by the Extender *kuru* or *iku*, the *kuru* and *iku* do not mean "come" and "go" referring to a place, but rather they suggest a change of state (1) toward the future starting at a point in time, or (2) through a period up to a point in time. *Kuru* in this construction has the added connotation of a change developing toward a point in time which might be referred to as present, whereas *iku* has the added connotation of a change originating in a point in time and moving toward future (viewed from that point in time). In contrast to *-te kuru*, *-te iku* is used less frequently.

Thus:

$$\text{past} \xrightarrow{\text{-te kuru}} \text{a point in time} \xrightarrow{\text{-te iku}} \text{future}$$

TE form of Verb + $\begin{cases} \textbf{\textit{kuru}} \\ \textbf{\textit{iku}} \end{cases}$

Adverbs or phrases that emphasize the above functions of *-te kuru* or *-te iku* may be used with them: *don'don* "rapidly," *dan'dan* "gradually," *ima made ni* "by now," *kore kara* "from now," and so on.

Compare:

Jin'koo ga fuete kimashita.	"The population has been increasing (until now)."
Jin'koo ga fuete ikimashita.	"The population has been increasing (since then)."
kaze ga tsuyoku natte kita	"it has been more windy"
harete kuru deshoo	"it will become fair (by a certain time)"
kawa no mizu ga fuete kimashita	"the water of the river has been increasing"
onaka ga suite kita	"I'm getting hungry"
nodo ga kawaite kuru	"you will become thirsty"
chooshi ga agatte kita	"conditions have gone well"
takusan no hito ga shin'de iku deshoo	"many people will die (from a certain time on)"
kore kara dan'dan samuku natte ikimasu yo	"it will gradually be getting colder from now on"
Anata, kono goro futotte kimashita ne.	"You have been gaining weight recently."
Nihon'go wa dan'dan yasashiku natte kita deshoo?	"Don't you think that (the study of) Japanese has been getting easier gradually?"
Watashi wa Shimizu san ga suki ni natte kimashita.	"I've come to like Mr. Shimizu."
Natsu goro kara akachan wa gyuunyuu o nomanaide, yasete kimashita.	"Since the summer the baby hasn't been drinking milk and has become thinner."

12.4.6 *Ame ga furidashisoo da* means "It looks like it's starting to rain." When the Stem form of a Verb is followed by *dasu*, a compound component, it formulates a compound Verb carrying the meaning of "one starts doing such and such" or "some happening begins." *Dasu* as a compound component carries almost the same meaning as *hajimeru* (see Note 3.4.2, Vol. III), but *dasu* is an intransitive Verb while *hajimeru* is a transitive Verb. Likewise, *owaru* "finish" as a compound component is a transitive Verb while *yamu* "stop; cease" is an intransitive Verb. Although both *dasu* and *hajimeru* are used interchangeably, *owaru* and *yamu* clearly differ in their use: *owaru* is used to mean "one finishes doing such and such" while *yamu* is used to mean "some happening ceases" or "one's doing such and such stops." Thus, Verbs that may precede *yamu* are limited to such Verbs as "rain," "snow," "blow," "cry," and so on, while *dasu* has a wide application.

kaze ga fukidasu	"the wind starts blowing"
hon o yomidashita	"one started reading a book"
kono ko wa saikin futoridashimashita	"this child has begun getting fat recently"
ame ga furiyamu	"it stops raining"
yuki ga furiyan'da	"it stopped snowing"
akachan ga nakiyan'da	"the baby stopped crying"

When it is clear what stops or ceases, only *yamu* may occur as an independent Verb. *Dasu* is never used this way.

kaze ga yan'da	"the wind stopped"
taifuu wa sugu yamimasu	"the typhoon will stop soon"
koe ga yamu	"the voice stops"
rajio ga yamu	"the radio stops"

Shigatsu ni naru to, minami kaze ga fukidashite, atatakaku narimasu.	"When April comes, the south winds start blowing and it gets warm."
Ame ga furiyan'dara, soto de asobinasai.	"When it stops raining, play outside."
Sakura wa mikka mae ni saita noni, moo chiridashimashita.	"The cherry blossoms bloomed three days ago, but they have already begun falling."

12.4.7 The formation of the effective passive in Japanese has been discussed in Lesson 3. Shimizu's statement here should be viewed as his feeling of displeasure about the rain.

12.4.8 *Komaru n da kedo naa* means "Gee, I don't know what to do." *Naa* is a Sentence Particle used to show an exclamation like *nee*, and normally occurs after the plain-form Predicate. *Naa* is mainly used by men in a monolog while *nee* is used to get the listener's attention.

Atsui naa.	"How hot it is!"
Odoroita naa.	"I'm surprised!"
Ten'ki ga yokute ureshii naa.	"I'm glad to have a nice day (weather)!"
Kaze ga fuite, iya da naa.	"The wind blows and I don't like it!"

12.4.9 *Komatta kao* means "a face that looks troubled," and *nureta kooto* means "a wet court." *Komatta* and *nureta* are the TA forms of the Verbs *komaru* "get into trouble" and *nureru* "get wet" respectively. As already introduced in Note 12.4.5, there are a group of Verbs that describe a change of state—a state changes into another. The TE form of such Verbs as those introduced in Note 12.4.2 plus the Extender *iru* carries a connotation that a change has happened and a result of the change exists.

komatta	"got into trouble"	$\longrightarrow$	komatte iru	"is in trouble"
nureta	"got wet"	$\longrightarrow$	nurete iru	"is wet"
kawaita	"got dry"	$\longrightarrow$	kawaite iru	"is dry"
shin'da	"died"	$\longrightarrow$	shin'de iru	"is dead"
tsukareta	"got tired"	$\longrightarrow$	tsukarete iru	"is tired"
kumotta	"got cloudy"	$\longrightarrow$	kumotte iru	"is cloudy"
hareta	"got clear"	$\longrightarrow$	harete iru	"is clear"
kon'da	"got crowded"	$\longrightarrow$	kon'de iru	"is crowded"
suita	"got empty"	$\longrightarrow$	suite iru	"is not crowded"
futotta	"got fat"	$\longrightarrow$	futotte iru	"is fat"
yaseta	"got thin"	$\longrightarrow$	yasete iru	"is thin"
yogoreta	"got dirty"	$\longrightarrow$	yogorete iru	"is dirty"
odoroita	"got surprised"	$\longrightarrow$	odoroite iru	"is surprised"
gakkari shita	"got disappointed"	$\longrightarrow$	gakkari shite iru	"is disappointed"
bikkuri shita	"got surprised"	$\longrightarrow$	bikkuri shite iru	"is surprised"

Kono inu wa yasete imasu nee.	"This dog is skinny!"
Onaka ga suite imasu ka?	"Are you hungry?"
Nodo ga totemo kawaite imashita.	"I was very thirsty."
Sora wa kumotte imasen.	"The sky is not cloudy."

In addition to the TE form of a Verb of this group plus *iru*, the TA form itself can be used to describe a state, when it occurs before a Noun in a Noun Modifier. Therefore, the TA form of a Verb of this group may be used as an equivalent for *-te iru* to explain either a past happening or a present state.

$$\left.\begin{array}{l} \textbf{TA form of Verb*} \\ \textbf{TE form of Verb* + } \textit{\textbf{iru}} \end{array}\right\} \textbf{+ Noun}$$

*Verbs are limited to those introduced in this note.

tsukareta hito tsukarete iru hito	"a person who is tired"
hareta sora harete iru sora	"the fair sky"
yogoreta te yogorete iru te	"dirty hands"
futotta kodomo futotte iru kodomo	"a fat child"

Kon'da den'sha ni noru no wa iya da kara, moo ichidai machimasu.	"I hate to ride on a crowded train. I'll wait for the next train."

Koogyoo ga hattatsu shita kuni no namae o
iinasai.

"Tell the names of countries where industry
has progressed."

Yogoreta kutsu wa hayaku kirei ni shite
kudasai.

"Please clean the dirty shoes right away."

12.4.10 *Komatta kao o shite iru* means "He looks troubled," or "He has a troubled look." In this expression *kao* "face" is always preceded by a Noun Modifier and is followed by *o shite iru* and the combination means "one has such and such a face."

odoroita		"one looks surprised"
komatta		"one has a troubled face"
tsukareta		"one looks tired"
aoi		"one looks pale"
akai	kao o shite iru	"one is red in the face" "one looks flushed"
okashina		"one has a funny face"
sabishisoo na		"one looks lonely"
gakkari shita		"one looks disappointed"
dooiu		"how does one look?"

This expression may be used in the pattern introduced in Note 12.4.9.

... kao o { shita / shite iru } hito   "a person who has such and such a face"

The above pattern is also applicable to say "one has such and such eyes, legs, and so on" or "something bears such and such color, shape, and so on."

kawaii me o shite iru	"one has cute eyes"
ookina mimi o shite iru	"one has big ears"
nagai ashi o shite iru	"one has long legs"
rippa na karada o shite iru	"one has a fine body or good constitution"
ookii kuchi o shite iru	"one has a big mouth"
ii koe o shite iru	"one has good voice"
akarui iro o shite iru	"it has a light color"
hen na katachi o shite iru	"it has a strange shape"

Aoi kao o shite imasu ne. Doo shita n desu ka?

"You look pale. What's the matter with
you?"

Toda san to iu hito wa don'na kao o shita hito
desu ka?

"How does a person called Toda look?"

12.4.11 *Nani ka aru no, ashita?* means "Is there anything tomorrow?" This is an inverted sentence which is very frequently heard in plain-style conversations.

12.4.12 *Gakkari da* means "is disappointing." *Gakkari suru* means either "get discouraged" or "get tired out." This kind of onomatopoeic or mimetic word (such as *bikkuri* "surprise" for example) is usually followed by a Copula or *suru* to describe or indicate the taking of such action. The following are a few of such words for passive learning: *yukkuri* "slowly," *hakkiri* "clearly," *non'biri* "free from care," *chakkari* "cunning," and *shikkari* "sturdy."

12.4.13 *Sekkaku* means "with much trouble or effort." Usually when something happens contrary to or is not up to one's expectation, this expression is used together with *noni*, *kedo*, or *ga* at the end of a clause. When this expression is used with *kara* at the end of a clause, it indicates that the speaker would like to avoid falling short of others' expectations.

Sekkaku ben'kyoo shita noni, shiken wa nakatta.	"I studied with much effort, but the exam was not held."
Sekkaku chooshi ga agatte kita noni ...	"Things have gone well, however ..."
Sekkaku motte kite kudasatta no desu kara, ima itadakimashoo.	"Let us eat it now, since [you] have brought it here for me."

12.4.14 *Teru-teru-boozu* is a paper doll made and hung outside the window to pray for fine weather. There is also a children's song of the same name, which goes: *Teru-teru-boozu, teru-boozu, ashita ten'ki ni shite okure. Itsu ka no yume no sora no yoo ni, haretara gin no suzu ageyoo.* (*yume* = dream; *suzu* = bell). The Japanese farmer's ritualistic supplication for rain is called *amagoi*.

12.4.15 *Soo demo shitai ki ga suru* means "I feel as if I want to do that or something." *Ki* "mind" is usually preceded by a Noun Modifier and is followed by *ga suru*. The combination ... *ki ga suru* means "I feel such and such." Such expressions as *-tai*, *-soo na*, *yoo na*, and the like often occur before *ki ga suru*.

Watashi wa hitori de kaeru ki ga shinai.	"I don't feel like going home by myself."
Sooiu ki ga shimashita.	"I felt that way."
Uta demo utaitai ki ga suru wa.	"I feel as if I'd like to sing."
Ashita wa yuki ga furu yoo na ki ga shimasu.	"I feel it will snow tomorrow."

Ki is very broadly used and covers many areas including weather, feelings, sentiments, spirit, character, personality—in other words, the natural environment as well as mental phenomena. Among its various usages are the following:

ki ni naru	"worry" "mind" "care"
ki ni suru	"be bothered by"
ki ga yowai	"not bold" "be cowardly"
ki o tsukau	"pay attention to" "mind"
ki ni sawaru	"be angry" "annoy"

The Japanese most often use natural processes to describe human processes. For instance, *seisoo* (star and frost) is a counting system for years, as in *san'seisoo* (three years). "The wind and snow of human life" *jin'sei no fuusetsu* ... refers to the hardships of life.

12.4.16 *Ten'ki yohoo ja* is the contracted form of *ten'ki yohoo de wa*. The multiple Relationals *de wa* may be contracted to *ja* in plain speech, as may the Copula *de* plus *wa*. (See Notes 7.4.12, Vol. I, and 1.3.2A, Vol. III.)

Hokkaidoo ja moo yuki ga futte iru soo desu yo.	"I understand that it's already snowing in Hokkaidō."
Fune ja kimasen. Hikooki de kuru hazu desu.	"He is not coming by boat. He is expected to come by plane."

Japanese weather is rather unpredictable and therefore difficult to forecast (*ten'ki yohoo*). It is said that during the Tokugawa period the official forecaster put up exactly the same sign every day and, depending on the weather, either inserted a period, making one sentence into two, or left the sentence whole, allowing the first "sentence" to modify the noun of the second. The result was as follows:

Ashita wa ame ga furu ten'ki de wa nai.
—"Tomorrow will not be good raining weather."
Ashita wa ame ga furu. Ten'ki de wa nai.
—"Tomorrow it will rain. It will not be good weather."

12.5   VOCABULARY

Presentation

によって	ni yotte	......	R + V	by (see 12.4.2)
小説	shoosetsu	......	N	novel
ずい筆	zuihitsu	......	N	essay
日記	nikki	......	N	diary
四季	shiki	......	N	four seasons
変化	hen'ka	......	N	change; variation
俳句	haiku	......	N	*haiku*; 5-7-5-syllabled Japanese poem
顔	kao	......	N	face
合わせる	awaseru	......	V	bring together (*kao o awaseru* means "see each other")
あいさつする	aisatsu suru	......	V	greet
あいさつ	aisatsu	......	N	greeting
話題	wadai	......	N	topic
感じ	kan'ji	......	V	Stem form of *kan'jiru* – feel; be sensitive

Dialog

戸田	Toda	......	N	family name
空	sora	......	N	sky
曇って	kumotte	......	V	TE form of *kumoru* – get cloudy
きた	kita	......	E	TA form of *kuru* – has come to such and such a state (see 12.4.5)
清水	Shimizu	......	N	family name
風	kaze	......	N	wind
出す	dasu	......	V	start (doing); begin (doing) (compound component) (see 12.4.6)
なあ	naa	......	SP	exclamatory Sentence Particle (see 12.4.8)

試合	shiai	......	N	(sport) game; match
なくなる	nakunaru	......	V	disappear; run out
がっかり	gakkari	......	N	disappointment (colloquial) (see 12.4.12)
がっかりする	gakkari suru	......	V	get disappointed
せっかく	sekkaku	......	Adv.	with much trouble; specially (see 12.4.13)
調子	chooshi	......	N	condition
上がる	agaru	......	V	go up; rise
てるてるぼうず	teru-teru-boozu	......	N	(see 12.4.14)
下げて	sagete	......	V	TE form of *sageru* – hang; lower; bring down (intransitive Verb)
じょうだん	joodan	......	N	joke
気	ki	......	N	mind; spirit (see 12.4.15)
予報	yohoo	......	N	forecasting; predict
晴れて	harete	......	V	TE form of *hareru* – become fair; clear up
ぬれた	nureta	......	V	got wet (TA form of *nureru*) (see 12.4.9)
コート	kooto	......	N	(tennis) court
とにかく	tonikaku	......	Adv.	anyway

Notes

教授	kyooju	......	N	professor
ふとる	futoru	......	V	get fat
やせる	yaseru	......	V	get thin
いく	iku	......	E	(see 12.4.5)
やむ	yamu	......	V	stop; cease (intransitive Verb) (compound component) (see 12.4.6)
ふき	fuki	......	V	Stem form of *fuku* – blow (intransitive Verb)
なき	naki	......	V	Stem form of *naku* – cry; mew; twitter
ちり	chiri	......	V	Stem form of *chiru* – fall; scatter (intransitive Verb)
青い	aoi	......	A	is pale
体	karada	......	N	body; construction
雲	kumo	......	N	cloud
びっくりする	bikkuri suru	......	V	get surprised (colloquial equivalent for *odoroku*)
下がる	sagaru	......	V	hang down; go down (intransitive Verb)

12.6 KAN'JI

12.6.1 筆 (1) HITSU [-PITSU] (2) writing brush (3) classifier 竹 [bamboo] (4) ⌐ ⌐ ⌐ 竹 竺 笙 筀 筆
(5) ずい筆、えん筆

12.6.2 記 (1) KI (2) chronicle (3) classifier 言 (4) 言 訁 訂 記
(5) 日記、記者 [journalist; pressman]、記事 [article]
(6) homonym 己、記、紀

12.6.3 顔 (1) *kao* (2) face (3) classifier 頁 [head]
(4) 立 产 彦 彥 顔 顔
(5) 顔を合わせる、変な顔をする [show a suspicious face]

12.6.4 降 (1) *fu(ru)* (2) fall (3) classifier 阝 [hill]
(4) 阝 阝 阝 阝 阹 降 降 (5) 雨や雪が降る

12.6.5 空 (1) *sora* (2) sky (3) classifier 宀 (穴 [hole]) (4) 宀 穴 空
(5) 青い空、空色 [light blue]

12.6.a 明 *11.6.5, Vol. III* (1) *aka(rui)* (5) 明るいへや、明るい空、明るい性格 [seikaku]

12.6.b 風 *8.6.7, Vol. III* (1) *kaze* (5) 風がふく、北風、南風

12.6.c 強 *3.6.6, Vol. III* (1) *tsuyo(i)* (5) 強い風がふく、強そうな人、強気 [confident]

12.6.6 困 (1) *koma(ru)* (2) is troubled (3) classifier 囗 [enclosure]
(4) 冂 困 困 (5) 困った顔、困った人、困りました
(6) a tree in an enclosure → trees cannot grow freely

12.6.d 上 *9.6.4, Vol. II* (1) *a(garu); a(geru)* (2) step up; rise
(5) お上がりください、調子 [chōshi] が上がってきた、手を上げる [hold hands up]

12.6.e 下 *9.6.10, Vol. II* (1) *sa(garu); sa(geru)* (2) hang down (5) 洋服 [fuku] を下げる

12.6.7 歌 (1) *uta; uta(u)* (2) song; sing (3) classifier 欠
[a man breathing air = open mouth]
(4) 一 可 可 哥 哥 歌 歌
(5) 歌が好きです、みんなで歌いましょう、子もり歌 [a lullaby]

12.6.8 耳[*] (1) *mimi* (2) ear (3) forms the classifier 耳

(4) | 一 | 丆 | 干 | 王 | 耳 |

(5) 長い耳をしている、耳がいい [have good hearing]

12.6.9 暗[*] (1) *kura(i)* (2) dark (3) classifier 日 (4) | 日 | 晬 | 暗 |

(5) 暗いへや、暗い顔 [gloomy face]

12.6.10 体[*] (1) *karada* (2) body; health (3) classifier イ (4) | イ | 体 |

(5) 体にいい [good for health]、体が強い

12.6.11 弱[*] (1) *yowa(i)* (2) weak (3) classifier 弓 [bow]

(4) | フ | 弓 | 弓 | 弱 | 弱 | (5) 体が弱い、強さと弱さ

12.6.12 死[*] (1) SHI (2) death (3) classifier 歹

(4) | 一 | 厂 | 歹 | 歹 | 死 | (5) 死んだ人、死者 [the dead]

(6) 匕 represents the shape of a man. 歹 represents a broken bone 占. 死 means that bones of a corpse become broken, therefore death. Practically all *kan'ji* with this classifier connote the meaning of death and destruction. 殉、歿、残

12.6.13 公[*] (1) KOO (2) public (3) classifier ハ [openness]

(4) | ハ | 公 | (5) 公園、公立学校 [public school] (6) ハ signifies openness and ム signifies enclosing → public

12.6.14 園[*] (1) EN (2) garden (3) classifier 囗 [enclosure]

(4) | 冂 | 門 | 闶 | 園 | 園 | (5) 公園、動物園、ようち園 [kindergarten]

(6) homonym 遠、猿

12.7 DRILLS

12.7.1 Transformation Drill

1. 空が 曇りました。　　　　　　　　⟶　空が 曇っています。

2. いもうとは がっかりしました。　　⟶　いもうとは がっかりしています。

3. テニスコートが ぬれました。　　　⟶　テニスコートが ぬれています。

4. 強い 風が やみました。　　　　　　⟶　強い 風が やんでいます。

5. さくらの 花は もう ちりました。⟶　さくらの 花は もう ちっています。

6. 父は もう 死にました。　　　　　　⟶　父は もう 死んでいます。

7. ぼくは とても つかれました。　　⟶　ぼくは とても つかれています。

8. 戦争は もう 終わりました。　　　⟶　戦争は もう 終わっています。

9. おなかが　すきました。　　　　　⟶　おなかが　すいています。

10. 空が　晴れました。　　　　　　　⟶　空が　晴れています。

11. 君の　車が　よごれました。　　　⟶　君の　車が　よごれています。

12. へやが　きれいに　なりました。　⟶　へやが　きれいに　なっています。

13. それを　聞いて、びっくりしました。⟶　それを　聞いて、びっくりしています。

14. かれは　とても　困りました。　　⟶　かれは　とても　困っています。

15. あねは　ふとりました。　　　　　⟶　あねは　ふとっています。

12.7.2 Transformation Drill

1. <u>ふとっている</u>　人　　　　　⟶　<u>ふとった</u>　人

2. ぬれている　レインコート　　　　⟶　ぬれた　レインコート

3. 困っている　顔　　　　　　　　　⟶　困った　顔

4. つかれている　学生　　　　　　　⟶　つかれた　学生

5. こんでいる　道　　　　　　　　　⟶　こんだ　道

6. やせている　手　　　　　　　　　⟶　やせた　手

7. 晴れている　空　　　　　　　　　⟶　晴れた　空

8. よごれている　洋服　　　　　　　⟶　よごれた　洋服

9. 死んでいる　犬　　　　　　　　　⟶　死んだ　犬

10. かわいている　ハンカチ　　　　　⟶　かわいた　ハンカチ

12.7.3 Substitution Drill

A. あの　<u>ふとった</u>　子どもは　だれですか。

　　1. やせている　　　　　　　……　あの　やせている　子どもは　だれですか。

　　2. 手が　よごれている　　　……　あの　手が　よごれている　子どもは
　　　　　　　　　　　　　　　　　　だれですか。

　　3. 困った　顔を　している　……　あの　困った　顔を　している　子どもは
　　　　　　　　　　　　　　　　　　だれですか。

　　4. 教室に　残っている　　　……　あの　教室に　残っている　子どもは
　　　　　　　　　　　　　　　　　　だれですか。

　　5. 青い　顔を　した　　　　……　あの　青い　顔を　した　子どもは
　　　　　　　　　　　　　　　　　　だれですか。

　　6. かわいい　顔を　した　　……　あの　かわいい　顔を　した　子どもは
　　　　　　　　　　　　　　　　　　だれですか。

B. <u>ずいぶん　込んでいる</u>　地下鉄ですね。

  1. わりあい　すいた   …… わりあい　すいた　地下鉄ですね。

  2. とても　よごれている   …… とても　よごれている　地下鉄ですね。

  3. 新しくなった   …… 新しくなった　地下鉄ですね。

  4. きれいな　色を　した   …… きれいな　色を　した　地下鉄ですね。

  5. めずらしい　形を　している   …… めずらしい　形を　している　地下鉄ですね。

C. <u>晴れた　空が　見えますよ。</u>

  1. 曇った   …… 曇った　空が　見えますよ。

  2. よごれた   …… よごれた　空が　見えますよ。

  3. 青い   …… 青い　空が　見えますよ。

  4. 晴れた   …… 晴れた　空が　見えますよ。

  5. 明るくなった   …… 明るくなった　空が　見えますよ。

D. <u>ぬれた　ハンカチで　いいです。</u>

  1. かわいた   …… かわいた　ハンカチで　いいです。

  2. よごれた   …… よごれた　ハンカチで　いいです。

  3. 変な　色をした   …… 変な　色を　した　ハンカチで　いいです。

  4. ぬれている   …… ぬれている　ハンカチで　いいです。

  5. 黒くなっている   …… 黒くなっている　ハンカチで　いいです。

12.7.4　Transformation Drill

1. 空が　曇りました。   ⟶　空が　曇ってきました。

2. 東の　空が　晴れました。   ⟶　東の　空が　晴れてきました。

3. だんだん　つかれました。   ⟶　だんだん　つかれてきました。

4. 冬に　なって、やせました。   ⟶　冬に　なって、やせてきました。

5. けい子さんは　ふとりました。   ⟶　けい子さんは　ふとってきました。

6. さくらが　さきました。   ⟶　さくらが　さいてきました。

7. おなかが　とても　すきました。   ⟶　おなかが　とても　すいてきました。

8. あたたかくなりました。   ⟶　あたたかくなってきました。

9. 風が　強くなりました。   ⟶　風が　強くなってきました。

10. 調子が　上がりました。   ⟶　調子が　上がってきました。

12.7.5　Transformation Drill

1. これから　さむくなりますよ。   ⟶　これから　さむくなっていきますよ。

2. 計画を　一つずつ　決めます。   ⟶　計画を　一つずつ　決めていきます。

3. 漢字を　毎日　覚えましょう。　　　　⟶　漢字を　毎日　覚えていきましょう。

4. 話題が　すぐ　変わります。　　　　　⟶　話題が　すぐ　変わっていきます。

5. これから　天気が　よくなります。　　⟶　これから　天気が　よくなっていきます。

6. だんだん　テニスコートが　かわきます。⟶　だんだん　テニスコートが　かわいて
　　　　　　　　　　　　　　　　　　　　　　　いきます。

7. 空が　どんどん　暗くなりますね。　　⟶　空が　どんどん　暗くなっていきますね。

12.7.6　Response Drill

1. 空は　晴_はれていますか。
　　曇_{くも}る　　　　　　　　　　　　　……　いいえ、曇_{くも}ってきました。

2. 病気は　まだ　悪いんですか。
　　よくなる　　　　　　　　　　　　　……　いいえ、よくなってきました。

3. おなかは　まだ　いっぱいですか。
　　すく　　　　　　　　　　　　　　　……　いいえ、すいてきました。

4. くつは　ぬれているんですか。
　　かわく　　　　　　　　　　　　　　……　いいえ、かわいてきました。

5. 中村さんは　今も　ふとっていますか。
　　やせる　　　　　　　　　　　　　　……　いいえ、やせてきました。

6. まだ　雨が　降っていますか。
　　晴_はれる　　　　　　　　　　　　　……　いいえ、晴_はれてきました。

7. 外は　まだ　あたたかいですか。
　　さむくなる　　　　　　　　　　　　……　いいえ、さむくなってきました。

12.7.7　Transformation Drill

戸_と田さんは　青い　顔を　しています。

1. 足が　長い　　　　　　　　……　戸_と田さんは　長い　足を　しています。

2. 声が　いい　　　　　　　　……　戸_と田さんは　いい　声を　しています。

3. 耳が　大きい　　　　　　　……　戸_と田さんは　大きい　耳を　しています。

4. 口が　小さい　　　　　　　……　戸_と田さんは　小さい　口を　しています。

5. 目が　黒い　　　　　　　　……　戸_と田さんは　黒い　目を　しています。

6. 体が　弱い　　　　　　　　……　戸_と田さんは　弱い　体を　しています。

7. 手が　つめたい　　　　　　……　戸_と田さんは　つめたい　手を　しています。

8. 頭が いい …… 戸田さんは いい 頭を しています。

9. 顔が かわいい …… 戸田さんは かわいい 顔を しています。

10. 声が やさしい …… 戸田さんは やさしい 声を しています。

12.7.8 Substitution Drill

あしたは 天気が よくなるような 気が します。

1. じょうだんだったようです …… じょうだんだったような 気が します。

2. この 映画は おもしろいようです …… この 映画は おもしろいような 気が します。

3. よし子さんは すこし やせたようです …… よし子さんは すこし やせたような 気が します。

4. テニスの 試合を 見たいようです …… テニスの 試合を 見たいような 気が します。

5. おととしの 冬は 雪が 多かったよう です …… おととしの 冬は 雪が 多かった ような 気が します。

6. この 音楽は 聞いたことが あるよう です …… この 音楽は 聞いたことが ある ような 気が します。

7. だいぶ 調子が 上がってきたようです …… だいぶ 調子が 上がってきたような 気が します。

8. 公園は きょう 込んでいます …… 公園は きょう 込んでいるような 気が します。

12.7.9 E-J Transformation Drill

空は 晴れています。

1. the train is crowded …… 電車は 込んでいます。

2. I am fat …… わたしは ふとっています。

3. Mr. Toda is tired …… 戸田さんは つかれています。

4. Tomoko is hungry …… 友子さんは おなかが すいています。

5. flowers are in bloom …… 花は さいています。

6. my father is surprised …… 父は おどろいています。

7. the tennis court is dirty …… テニスコートは よごれています。

8. the sky is cloudy …… 空は 曇っています。

9. Mr. Shimizu is disappointed …… 清水さんは がっかりしています。

10. this raincoat is wet …… この レインコートは ぬれています。

12.7.10 Transformation Drill

1. この ずい筆は 山本さんが 書き
   ました。　　　　　　　　　　　　⟶　この ずい筆は 山本さんによって
   　　　　　　　　　　　　　　　　　　　書かれました。

2. この 小説は おおぜいの 人が
   読んでいます。　　　　　　　　　⟶　この 小説は おおぜいの 人によって
   　　　　　　　　　　　　　　　　　　　読まれています。

3. 新しい 先生は 学長が しょうかい
   します。　　　　　　　　　　　　⟶　新しい 先生は 学長によって しょう
   　　　　　　　　　　　　　　　　　　　かいされます。

4. 事故は けいさつが 父に 知らせ
   ました。　　　　　　　　　　　　⟶　事故は けいさつによって 父に
   　　　　　　　　　　　　　　　　　　　知らされました。

5. あの 人は みんなが えらびました。　⟶　あの 人は みんなによって えらばれ
   　　　　　　　　　　　　　　　　　　　ました。

6. 計画は 学生が 決めました。　　　⟶　計画は 学生によって 決められました。

7. 試合は 戸田君と 清水君が 始め
   ました。　　　　　　　　　　　　⟶　試合は 戸田君と 清水君によって
   　　　　　　　　　　　　　　　　　　　始められました。

12.7.11 Transformation Drill

1. 新聞に ずい筆を 書きました。　　⟶　新聞に ずい筆が 書いてあります。

2. 窓に てるてるぼうずを 下げました。　⟶　窓に てるてるぼうずが 下げて
   　　　　　　　　　　　　　　　　　　　あります。

3. 計画を くわしく 決めました。　　⟶　計画が くわしく 決めてあります。

4. 使い方を 説明しました。　　　　　⟶　使い方が 説明してあります。

5. 試合の ために 練習を しましたか。　⟶　試合の ために 練習が してありますか。

6. お酒を 買いましたか。　　　　　　⟶　お酒が 買ってありますか。

7. タクシーを 呼びましたか。　　　　⟶　タクシーが 呼んでありますか。

12.7.12 Substitution Drill

もうすぐ 雨が 降り出すかもしれません。

1. 風が ふき出す　　　　　……　もうすぐ 風が ふき出すかもしれません。

2. 赤ちゃんが なき出す　　　……　もうすぐ 赤ちゃんが なき出すかもしれません。

3. むすこが 歩き出す　　　　……　もうすぐ むすこが 歩き出すかもしれません。

4. さむくなり出す　　　　　　……　もうすぐ さむくなり出すかもしれません。

5. 雪が 降りやむ　　　　　　……　もうすぐ 雪が 降りやむかもしれません。

6. 風が ふきやむ　　　　　　……　もうすぐ 風が ふきやむかもしれません。

7. なきやむ　　　　　　　　　……　もうすぐ なきやむかもしれません。

12.7.13 Response Drill

1. 清水さんは　<u>どんな</u>　顔を　した　人ですか。

   とても　かわいい　　　　　…… とても　かわいい　顔を　した　人です。

   ちょっと　やせた　　　　　…… ちょっと　やせた　顔を　した　人です。

   いつも　さびしそうな　　　…… いつも　さびしそうな　顔を　した　人です。

2. <u>新しい</u>　課長さんは　どういう　方ですか。

   ふとった　　　　　　　　　…… ふとった　方です。

   目が　大きい　　　　　　　…… 目が　大きい　方です。

   頭が　いい　　　　　　　　…… 頭が　いい　方です。

3. <u>何を</u>　きれいに　してほしいんですか。

   あの　よごれた　つくえ　　…… あの　よごれた　つくえを　きれいに　してほしいんです。

   ぬれている　いす　　　　　…… ぬれている　いすを　きれいに　してほしいんです。

   古くなった　車　　　　　　…… 古くなった　車を　きれいに　してほしいんです。

4. <u>どんな</u>　電車に　乗って来たんですか。

   とても　込んだ　　　　　　…… とても　込んだ　電車に　乗って来たんです。

   かなり　すいている　　　　…… かなり　すいている　電車に　乗って来たんです。

   みどり色を　した　　　　　…… みどり色を　した　電車に　乗って来たんです。

12.7.14 Transformation Drill

1. あした　試合が　ある<u>から</u>、天気を　　　──→　天気を　心配している<u>のは</u>　あした
   心配しているんです。　　　　　　　　　　　　試合が　ある<u>から</u>です。

2. 雨が　降り出しそうだから、かれ<u>は</u>　　──→　かれが　困った　顔を　しているのは
   困った　顔を　しているんです。　　　　　　　雨が　降り出しそうだからです。

3. けさ　何も　食べなかったから、　　　　──→　おなかが　すいているのは　けさ　何も
   おなかが　すいているんです。　　　　　　　食べなかったからです。

4. 毎日　よく　練習したから、清水さんは　──→　清水さんが　英語が　じょうずなのは
   英語が　じょうずなんです。　　　　　　　　毎日　よく　練習したからです。

5. かさを　持って行くのを　わすれたから、──→　ぬれてしまったのは　かさを　持って
   ぬれてしまったんです。　　　　　　　　　　行くのを　わすれたからです。

6. お金が　なくなったから、旅行を　　　　──→　旅行を　とちゅうで　やめたのは
   とちゅうで　やめたんです。　　　　　　　　お金が　なくなったからです。

7. 皆 泳ぐほうが 好きだから、海岸を　　　⟶　　海岸を えらんだのは 皆
　　えらんだんです。　　　　　　　　　　　　　　　泳ぐほうが 好きだからです。

8. 前 おごってもらったから、きょう　　　⟶　　きょう 山口さんに ごちそうしたのは
　　山口さんに ごちそうしたんです。　　　　　　前 おごってもらったからです。

12.8　EXERCISES

12.8.1 日本語で　言いなさい。

1. Since I had a tennis tournament yesterday, I'm very tired today.

2. Even though you hurry, the movie may be over (by now).

3. When a mother comes, a baby stops crying at once.

4. What is the name of that slender person?

5. You look pale. Aren't you feeling sick?

6. The reason why I got fat is because I don't do any sport.

12.8.2　英語で　言いなさい。

1. 空が 暗くなってきたし、強い 風が ふいてきたから、今晩 雨が 降り出す
　　かもしれないなあ。

2. どうして そんなに むずかしい 顔を しているの? 何か 困った ことが
　　あるの?

3. 清水先生によって 新しい 日本語の 先生が しょうかいされました。

4. 若い 人たちが 戦争で どんどん 死んでいくことは とても ざんねんな
　　ことです。

5. かれが 試合を したがっているのは 調子が 上がってきたからである。

12.8.3　(　)に　ひらがなを　入れて、いい 文に　しなさい。

1. 歌(　) 歌いたい 気(　) するけど、ここで 歌う(　)には
　　いきませんね。

2. 日本人は 顔(　) 合わせる(　) すぐ 天気の 話を する。

3. 台風(　) 受けた 被害は 建物だけではなかった。

4. 赤ちゃんが かぜ(　) ひきやすい(　)は さむさ(　) 感じやすい(　)
　　でしょう?

12.8.4 （　　）の　中に　<u>います</u>か　<u>あります</u>か　<u>きます</u>を　入れなさい。（〜ましたでも
いい。）そして、英語で　意味を　言いなさい。

1. 今晩　お客様が　いらっしゃるので、客間は　きれいに　して（　　　　）。
2. その　ことは　もう　戸田さんに　話して（　　　　）。だから、よく　知って
いるはずですよ。
3. まさえさんは　大切な　かばんを　ぬすまれて、とても　困って（　　　　）。
4. 「あつくなって（　　　　）ね。」「本当に　毎日　あついですね。」
5. ぼくの　ほしい　物は　もう　注文して（　　　　）。
6. 熱が　低くなったから、安心して（　　　　）。
7. 西の　空が　晴れて（　　　　）ね。あしたも　たぶん　いい　天気でしょう。
8. だんだん　つかれて（　　　　）。すこし　休みましょうか。

12.8.5 次の　日記を　読んで、いくつか　質問を　作りなさい。
四月二十三日　（火曜日）曇り

　おとといから　降っていた　雨が　やっと　やんだが、きょうは　ほとんど　一日
じゅう　曇っていた。午前中　歴史と　社会学の　授業に　出て、午後は　三時間
テニスの　練習を　した。来月　試合が　あるから、毎日　練習しなければ
ならない。テニスの　後、友だちの　広田君に　会って　ちょっと　話したが、とても
青い　顔を　していた。ひどく　つかれているようだった。夕食を　してから、
けい子さんと　映画を　見に　行った。帰る　時に　なって、雨が　降り出した。
あしたも　雨だと、テニスが　できないから、がっかりだ。

12.8.6 漢字で　書きなさい。

1. <u>わたし</u>は　<u>有</u>めいな　<u>ひと</u>の　<u>しょうせつ</u>、<u>ずいひつ</u>、<u>にっき</u>などを　<u>よむ</u>のが
<u>すき</u>です。
2. <u>あかるかった</u>　<u>そら</u>が　<u>くらく</u>なってきましたね。<u>つよい</u>　<u>かぜ</u>も　<u>ふきだし</u>
ました。
3. <u>あした</u>　<u>あめ</u>が　<u>ふる</u>と　<u>こまる</u>ので、<u>こんばん</u>　てるてるぼうずを　<u>さげて</u>
おきましょう。
4. <u>こうえん</u>で　<u>しった</u>　<u>かお</u>に　<u>あい</u>ましたよ。
5. 何か　<u>うた</u>を　<u>うたって</u>ください。
6. この　犬は　<u>からだ</u>が　<u>よわく</u>、<u>みみ</u>も　<u>わるい</u>んです。<u>しんで</u>しまうかも
しれません。
7. どうぞ　お<u>あ</u>がりください。

12.8.7 読みなさい。

1.	読、話、語、記	5.	死、残	9.	室、空
2.	耳、聞	6.	困、園、国	10.	降、部
3.	休、体	7.	遠、園	11.	顔、頭
4.	弱、強	8.	暗、明	12.	何、歌

12.8.8 Use each of the following phrases to write a complete sentence.

1. ki ni suru
2. ki ga yowai
3. ki o tsukeru
4. ki ni naru
5. ~ki ga suru

12.8.9 Give the English equivalent for each of the following.

1. Kodomo ga hashitte kimasu.
2. Sora ga kumotte kimasu.
3. Ban'gohan wa tabete kimashita.
4. Chichi ga kaette kimasu.
5. Ame ga futte kimashita.
6. Kaimono ni itte kimasu.
7. Kyoo wa oben'too o motte kimashita.
8. Sukoshi tsukarete kimashita.

12.8.10 Rewrite the dialog using the affective passive form wherever possible.

Kimura: Shuumatsu wa Nikkoo e itta n desu ga, ame wa furu shi, kodomo wa kaze o hiku shi, taihen deshita yo.

Ishii: Soo desu ka? Sore wa taihen deshita nee. Uchi de mo kanai ga kaze de nete ite, watashi ga shokuji o tsukutte iru n desu yo.

Kimura: Anata mo taihen na n desu ne. Kodomo ga naku to, yoru mo neraremasen yo, hon'too ni.

12.8.11 Change Miss Toda to Mr. Toda, and Mr. Shimizu to Mrs. Shimizu, and make the appropriate changes in the forms used in the Dialog of this lesson.

12.9 SITUATIONAL AND APPLICATION CONVERSATION

12.9.1 Mr. Toda meets Mr. Shimizu in a bus.

Mr. Toda says to Mr. Shimizu that Mr. Shimizu looks as if he is troubled and asks the reason.

Mr. Shimizu says that strong winds have started to blow, so he is afraid the weather might change and become bad.

Mr. Toda asks why Mr. Shimizu worries about that.

Mr. Shimizu answers that he has a tennis tournament at college the next day. He says that he can't play on a wet tennis court. Mr. Shimizu says that he feels like crying.

Mr. Toda says that the weather forecast says the wind will stop blowing and the sky will clear gradually, so it will be fine the day after.

12.9.2 Mr. Smith says to Mr. Brown that Japanese lessons are getting difficult.

Mr. Brown says that he received a bad score on the exam the day before and is very disappointed.

Mr. Smith asks whose exam it was.

Mr. Brown answers that it was a history exam given to Professor Ueki's class.

Mr. Smith asks if Professor Ueki is a comparatively slender person.

Mr. Brown says that he is. He continues that he is very tired since he did not sleep well the night before. He says he will go home and take a nap.

12.9.3 Imagine that you are a Japanese and you meet a friend, a neighbor, an acquaintance, a colleague, and the like. Start each conversation by referring to the weather, the climate, or the season.

12.9.4 Mr. Wada: Kyoo wa nani ka ii koto ga aru yoo na ki ga shita n da kedo.

Mr. Imai: Sore de, ii koto ga atta?

Mr. Wada: Sore ga nee. Ame ni furareru shi, zan'gyoo wa shinakereba naranai shi ...

Mr. Imai: Ha-ha-ha-ha-ha!

12.9.5 Aoki: Ashita no shiken wa moo dame da!

Sasaki: Doo shite?

Aoki: Son'na ki ga suru n da yo.

Sasaki: Son'na ki no yowai koto o itte wa dame da yo!

12.10 READING COMPREHENSION
12.10.1

　日本は　四季（しき）の　くべつが　わりあい　はっきりしていて、東京の　辺では　春、夏、秋、冬が　それぞれ　3か月ずつある。日本人は　季節（きせつ）の　変化に　敏感（びんかん）(sensitive)で、着る　物も　春の　着物、夏の　着物、秋の　服（ふく）、冬の　服（ふく）と　季節によって　変える。また、いやな　むしあつさを　わすれる　ために、夏が　近くなると、すずしそうな　夏の　茶わん (tea cup)を　使ったり、カーペット (carpet)を　夏のに　変えたりする。

　季節（きせつ）によって　生活の　いろいろな　めん (aspect)を　変えるのは　大変な　ことであるが、日本人は　それを　楽しんでいると　言うことも　できる。

12.10.2

A　「おはようございます。」

B　「おはようございます。」

A　「さむくなってきましたね。」

B　「本当に　ひえます(is chilly)ね。おたく　だんぼう(heating)は?」

A　「ええ、もう　こたつ(a foot warmer with a quilt over it)を　出しました。お宅も?」

B　「うちも　石油ストーブ(stove)を　出したところなんです。石油が　高いから　がまん
　　　(patience)していたんですけど。」

A　「かぜなど　ひかないように。」

B　「ええ、どうも。」

12.10.3

サラリーマン (1)　「むします(is humid)ね。」

サラリーマン (2)　「きょうは　電車が　込んでいて、むしぶろ(steam bath)のようでしたよ。
　　　　　　　　　早く　帰って、シャワーを　あび(take a shower)たいです。」

サラリーマン (1)　「つゆ(rainy season)が　早く　終わると　いいですね。」

12.10.4

おくさんA　　「雨が　やっと　上がりました(stopped)ね。」

おくさんB　　「晴れてきて　うれしいですね。」

おくさんA　　「おふとん(quilt; mattress)　ほさなければ…(must dry)」

おくさんB　　「わたしも　きょうは　せんたく物(the washing)が　いっぱい　あって…。
　　　　　　　じゃあ、急ぎますから。」

おくさんA　　「わたしも…。じゃあ。」

LESSON 13
辞書の　引き方

13.1　PRESENTATION

　日本語を　学ぶ　場合、　初級では　辞書は　特に　必要ない。　しかし、　中級や
上級に　なると、　漢字の　辞書と　ことばの　辞書と　少なくとも₂　二種類の　辞書が
必要に　なってくる。　ほん訳の　ためには、　英和や　和英の　辞書さえ₃　ほしくなる。
　漢字の　辞書を　引く　時、「へん₄」とか　「かんむり₄」とか　「かまえ₄」などの
部首が　わかれば、　後は　わりあい　かんたんである。　この　部首が　早く
見つけられることと、　字画が　正しく　数えられることが　最も　大切なことである。

13.2　DIALOG

学生　「先生、　前　先生は　漢字の　辞書を　買うよう₅に　おっしゃいましたね。」

先生　「ええ。　買ったんですか。」

学生　「はい。　でも、　あまり₆　説明が　ふくざつで、　使い方が　全然　わからない
　　　んです。　教えていただけ₇ますか。」

先生　「辞書の　使い方は　まだ₈　練習してなかった₈ですね。　教えてあげましょう。」

学生　「たとえば、　この　字なんですけど…」

先生　「ああ、　自転車の　転ですね。　これは　左がわの　車が　〈へん〉です。　車は
　　　七画ですから、　部首の　表の　七画の　所で　車を　見つけるんです。」

学生　「あ、　ありました。」

先生　「あったでしょう？　そこに　ページ数が　書いてありますから、　その　ページを
　　　開くと、　車へんの　字が　全部　ならんでいます。　転という　字の、　〈へん〉を
　　　取った　残りの　部分(云)は　四画ですから、　四画の　所を　さがせば、　転が
　　　見つかります。　これで　だいたい　わかったろうと₉　思いますが。」

学生　「なれる₁₀まで　大変ですね。」

先生　「そう、　基本に　なる　形、　つまり　部首を　知らないと、　何から　始めたら
　　　いいのか　わからないことが　あります₁₁から、　これを　たくさん　覚えて
　　　おいたほうが　いいですね。　じゃあ、　今度は　〈酒〉という　字を　ひとりで
　　　引いてごらんなさい₁₂。」

学生　「はい、　やってみます。」

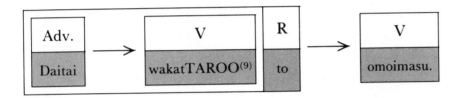

辞書　　引き方　　学ぶ　　　場合　　必要ない
ほん訳　英和　　和英　正しく　全然　　練習
自転車　全部　　形　　酒

13.3　PATTERN SENTENCES

13.3.1

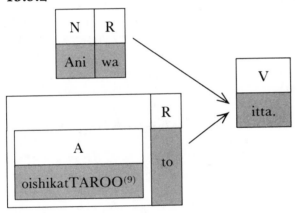

Adv. Daitai → V wakatTAROO[9] R to → V omoimasu.

13.3.2

N Ani R wa
A oishikatTAROO[9] R to → V itta.

13.3.3

Na	C
Taihen	DATTAROO[9].

13.3.4

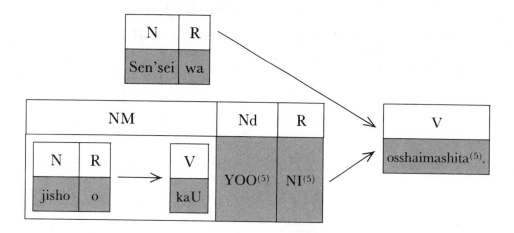

13.4 NOTES

13.4.1 Students of Japanese language need three kinds of dictionaries, namely, a *kan'ji* dictionary, a Japanese word, or vocabulary, dictionary, and an English-Japanese dictionary.

1. *Kan'ji* dictionaries: *Kan'ji Nyūmon* (five hundred basic characters) published by the Japan Foundation, *The Modern Reader's Japanese-English Character Dictionary* by Andrew Nathaniel Nelson, Charles Tuttle Company, publisher, and *A Guide to Reading and Writing Japanese*, Charles Tuttle Company, are available for beginners. As their language skills develop, it is recommended that students start using *Shin Kan'wa Jiten* (revised edition, 1968) published by Taishūkan. Centering around 3,000 *kan'ji*, this dictionary contains 8,600 *kan'ji* headings and 55,000 *kan'ji* words or compounds. For those advanced students of Japanese who are seeking the authoritative and all-inclusive dictionary, Tetsuji Morohashi's *Dai Kan'wa Jiten* is available. It contains 49,700 *kan'ji* and 520,000 *kan'ji* words and compounds.

2. Japanese word, or vocabulary, dictionaries: For beginners, Kenkyūsha's *Japanese-English Dictionary* and *Kokugo Shin'jiten* are recommended. The latter's headings are written in *rōmaji*, paraphrased in Japanese, with given English equivalents. Sanseidō's *New Concise Japanese-English Dictionary* is pocket-size and very convenient. For the more advanced student, however, it is advisable to move on to Japanese-Japanese dictionaries, such as Sanseidō's *Shin Meikai Kokugo Jiten* and *Shin Kokugo Chūjiten*. Eventually, students should consult dictionaries such as Izuru Shinmura's *Kōjien* published by Iwanami.

3. English-Japanese dictionaries: Kenkyūsha's *English-Japanese Dictionary* is useful and Sanseidō's *New Concise English-Japanese Dictionary* is handy.

Since Japan adopted simplified *kan'ji* after World War II, classification of *kan'ji* has become more difficult. For instance, most *kan'ji* dictionaries still classify 会 under 日(會); 当 under 田(當); 旧 under 臼(舊); 写 under 宀(寫); 声 under 耳(聲); and 医 under 酉(醫). Students find such a system cumbersome for locating classifiers and stroke orders. It is regrettable that no more effective system exists at this time. As long as *kan'ji* exists, there remains a need for a more efficient and effective method of classification.

13.4.2 *Sukunaku tomo* means "at least," and *ooku tomo* "at most." These are further forms of *sukunakate mo* "even if it's a little" or "even if they are few" and *ookute mo* "even if it's a lot" or "even if they are many" respectively, and are used as idiomatic phrases for "at least" and "at most."

13.4.3 *Sae* is a Relational meaning "even." It replaces the Relationals *ga* and *o*, but it may be placed after such Relationals as *ni, de, kara, to*.

$$\text{Noun} + \begin{Bmatrix} ga \\ o \end{Bmatrix} + \text{Predicate} \longrightarrow \text{Noun} + sae + \text{Predicate}$$

$$\text{Noun} + \begin{Bmatrix} ni \\ de \\ kara \\ .. \\ .. \\ to \end{Bmatrix} + \text{Predicate} \longrightarrow \text{Noun} + \begin{Bmatrix} ni \\ de \\ kara \\ .. \\ .. \\ to \end{Bmatrix} + sae + \text{Predicate}$$

We have already studied the Relational *mo* "even" (see Note 9.4.5, Vol. II). The Relational *sae* cannot replace *mo* in such patterns as the permission -*te mo ii*, the nonfinal clause "even if . . ." -*te mo*, and the like. Otherwise, that is, after a Noun or after a Noun plus a Relational, *sae* may be used instead of *mo*. *Sae* is a little more emphatic than *mo*.

Pan $\begin{Bmatrix} \text{sae} \\ \text{mo} \end{Bmatrix}$ kaenai bin'boo na hito ga imasu.

"There are poor people who cannot afford even bread."

Kono mon'dai wa shoogakusei ni $\begin{Bmatrix} \text{sae} \\ \text{mo} \end{Bmatrix}$ dekiru.

"This problem may be answered even by an elementary-school boy."

Ano gakusei wa chuukyuu no kurasu ni iru noni, mada jibun no namae sae nihon'go de kakenai n desu.

"Although that student is in the intermediate class, he cannot even write his name in Japanese."

13.4.4 *Hen*, *kan'muri*, and *kamae* are the general names of classifiers, or composite elements of Chinese characters, that are commonly seen. There are more classifiers than these three, as you have already noticed. The following list is not exhaustive, nor is it given for the purpose of memorization, but merely for reference.

Hen: the left-hand portion of a *kan'ji*

nin'ben イ	*san'zuihen* シ	*tehen* 扌	*kuchihen* 口
kihen 木	*hihen* 日	*mehen* 目	*tahen* 田
itohen 糸	*gon'ben* 言	*kurumahen* 車	*kanehen* 金
shokuhen 食	*gyoonin'ben* 彳	*shimesuhen* ネ	

Kan'muri: the upper part of a *kan'ji*

ukan'muri 宀　　*wakan'muri* 冖　　*kusakan'muri* 艹　　*amekan'muri* 雨　　*takekan'muri* 竹

Kamae: the embracing shape of a *kan'ji*

mon'gamae 門　　*kunigamae* 囗

Nyoo: the circular shape of a *kan'ji*

shin'nyoo 辶　　*en'nyoo* 廴

13.4.5 *Sen'sei wa kan'ji no jisho o kau yoo ni osshaimashita ne?* means "You told us to buy a *kan'ji* dictionary, didn't you?" *Yoo ni* followed by such Verbs as *iu* "say," *ossharu* "say," and *tanomu* "ask" is an expression similar to "tell someone to do," "ask someone to do," and so on. The person who is told or asked is followed by the Relational *ni*. The Verb before *yoo ni* is always in its imperfect tense form.

$$\text{(person) } ni + \left\{ \begin{array}{l} \textbf{Dictionary form of Verb} \\ \textbf{plain imperfect negative form of Verb} \end{array} \right\} yoo\ ni + (to) + \left\{ \begin{array}{l} \textit{iu} \\ \textit{ossharu} \\ \textit{hanasu} \\ \textit{tanomu} \\ \textit{onegai suru} \\ \textit{meirei suru} \end{array} \right.$$

$$\left. \begin{array}{l} kau \\ kawanai \end{array} \right\} yoo\ ni \left\{ \begin{array}{ll} \text{iu} & \text{``tell} \\ \text{ossharu} & \text{``tell} \\ \text{hanasu} & \text{``tell} \\ \text{tanomu} & \text{``ask} \\ \text{onegai suru} & \text{``ask} \\ \text{meirei suru} & \text{``order} \end{array} \right\} \text{someone} \left\{ \begin{array}{l} \text{to buy''} \\ \text{not to buy''} \end{array} \right.$$

Isogu yoo ni itte kudasai.	"Please tell him to hurry."
Sen'sei wa shiraberu yoo ni osshatta.	"The teacher told us to check it."
Konai yoo ni tanon'da.	"I asked him not to come."
Tanaka san ni oshiete kudasaru yoo ni onegai suru tsumori desu.	"I intend to ask Mr. Tanaka to teach me."
Buchoo ni okurenai yoo ni iwareta.	"My department head told me not to be late."

13.4.6 *Amari setsumei ga fukuzatsu de, tsukaikata ga zen'zen wakaranai n desu* means "The explanation is so complicated that I don't know how to use it [the dictionary] at all." The Adverb *amari* may be used not only with a negative Predicate but also with an affirmative Predicate, and it connotes "something is so ~ that ~." Therefore, the Adverb *amari* of this meaning normally occurs in a causal clause—a clause describing reason or cause, such as ~ *node*, ~ *kara*, ~ *te*. Colloquially *an'mari* may also be heard.

$$\left. \begin{array}{l} \textit{amari} \\ \textit{an'mari} \end{array} \right\} + \left\{ \begin{array}{l} \textbf{Predicate} + \textit{node}, \ldots \\ \textbf{Predicate} + \textit{kara}, \ldots \\ \textbf{Predicate}(\textit{-te}), \ldots \end{array} \right.$$

amari tsukareta node, neta	"[I] got so tired that [I] went to bed"
an'mari fuben da kara, sumu tokoro o kaeta	"[it] was so inconvenient that [I] changed the place [I] live"
amari ookute, oboerarenai	"[there] are so many that [I] can't remember [them]"
Anata ga amari futotta node, odorokimashita.	"I was surprised that you had gained so much weight."
Kaze ga amari tsuyoi kara, mado o shimemashoo ka?	"Shall I close the window, since it's so windy?"
Kono kan'ji ni wa an'mari yomi ga takusan aru node, kono baai dore ga ii no ka wakarimasen.	"This *kan'ji* has so many readings that I don't know which (reading) is correct in this case."
Sono tokei wa amari rippa de, watashi ni wa yosugimasu.	"That watch is so fine that it's too good for me."

13.4.7 *Oshiete itadakemasu ka?* means "Could you please teach me?" This expression is more polite than *Oshiete moraemasu ka?* If a negative form is used, the expression would become more polite.

Oshiete itadakemasu ka?	⟶	Oshiete itadakemasen ka?
Oshiete moraemasu ka?	⟶	Oshiete moraemasen ka?
Sukoshi tetsudatte moraemasen ka?	⟶	"Could you help me a little bit?"
Sumimasen ga, shashin o totte itadakemasu ka?	⟶	"Pardon me, may I ask you to take a picture for me?"
Atarashii apaato o sagashite moraemasu ka?	⟶	"Would you please search for an apartment for me?"

13.4.8 *Mada ren'shuu shite nakatta* means "You haven't practiced it yet." This expression is a contracted version of the sentence *Mada ren'shuu shite inakatta.* The TE form of a Verb plus the Extender *inai*, when used with the Adverb *mada*, has the connotation of "not yet." Likewise, the TE form of a Verb plus the Extender *iru*, when used with the Adverb *moo*, has the connotation of "already."

moo + TE form of Verb + *iru*
mada + TE form of Verb + *inai*

Watashitachi wa mada Kyooto ni itte inai n desu.	"We haven't been to Kyōto yet."
Kono hon wa moo yon'de imasu ga, sotchi wa mada yon'de imasen.	"I have already read this book, but I haven't read that one yet."
Kyooiku kan'ji wa mada zen'bu naratte inai to omoimasu.	"I don't think that we have studied all the Education Kan'ji yet."

13.4.9 *Kore de daitai wakattaroo to omoimasu* means "I think you might have gotten a rough idea with this (explanation)." *Wakattaroo* is the TAROO form of *wakaru* and this form suggests a suppositional, presumptive, or uncertain statement of a past happening. The TAROO forms of Verbs, Adjectives, and the Copula are formulated by adding *-roo* to the TA forms of them:

Verb

1. Vowel Verb

kaesu	⟶	kaeshita	⟶	kaeshitaroo
taberu	⟶	tabeta	⟶	tabetaroo
mitsukeru	⟶	mitsuketa	⟶	mitsuketaroo
kazoeru "count"	⟶	kazoeta	⟶	kazoetaroo
nareru "get accustomed"	⟶	nareta	⟶	naretaroo

2. Consonant Verb

wakaru	⟶	wakatta	⟶	wakattaroo
sasou	⟶	sasotta	⟶	sasottaroo
matsu	⟶	matta	⟶	mattaroo
kawaku	⟶	kawaita	⟶	kawaitaroo
kaesu	⟶	kaeshita	⟶	kaeshitaroo
manabu "study"	⟶	manan'da	⟶	manan'daroo

tanomu   ⟶   tanon'da   ⟶   tanon'daroo
isogu   ⟶   isoida   ⟶   isoidaroo
shinu   ⟶   shin'da   ⟶   shin'daroo

3. Irregular Verb

kuru ⟶ kita ⟶ kitaroo
suru ⟶ shita ⟶ shitaroo

Adjective
nai   ⟶   nakatta   ⟶   nakattaroo
tadashii "is right; is correct"   ⟶   tadashikatta   ⟶   tadashikattaroo

Copula
da ⟶ datta ⟶ dattaroo

Wakattaroo has the same connotation as *wakatta daroo*, the plain equivalent of *wakatta deshoo*, but the use of *wakattaroo* is more limited than that of *wakatta deshoo*. See below:

1. The TAROO form may occur at the end of a sentence said by men in plain speech.
2. The TAROO form may occur in a quotation, that is, before the quotation Relational *to*.

Even in these cases the TA form plus *daroo* is used more commonly. In other cases such as women's speech or men's normal speech the TA form plus *deshoo* is preferred. Therefore, the TAROO forms need not be studied to such an extent that the student can use them freely.

$$\left.\begin{array}{l}\textbf{Verb}(\textit{-taroo})\\\textbf{Adjective}(\textit{-taroo})\\\textbf{Noun + Copula}(\textit{-taroo})\end{array}\right\} + \textit{to} + \left\{\begin{array}{l}\textit{iu}\\\textit{omou}\\\textit{kiku}\\\qquad\textbf{etc.}\end{array}\right.$$

Kyuushuu wa taifuu ni osowaretaroo to omou.	"I presume Kyūshū was hit by the typhoon."
Jisho no hikikata wa moo narattaroo to omoimasu ga.	"I guess you have already learned how to look words up in the dictionary."
Yuube wa chotto samukattaroo?	"Wasn't it a little cold last night?" (said by men)
Chichi wa boku ni inaka no hito wa min'na shin'setsu dattaroo to iimashita.	"Father said to me that people in the countryside must all have been kind."

13.4.10 *Nareru made taihen desu* means "It is tough until we get used to it." *Nareru* follows the Relational *ni* meaning "get used to ∼."

Nihon de no atarashii seikatsu ni naremashita ka?	"Did you get accustomed to a new life in Japan?"
Eigo ni nareta hito wa eigo de hanashitagarimasu.	"The man who is used to English wants to speak in English."

13.4.11 *Wakaranai koto ga arimasu* means "There are times when you don't know (what you should start on)." When *koto ga aru* or *nai* is preceded by the plain imperfect tense form of a Verb, an Adjective or the NA form, or by the plain negative imperfect tense form of the Copula, it has the connotation "there are times when one does such and such," "something is sometimes such and such," and so on.

$$
\left.\begin{array}{l}
\text{Verb (plain imperfect tense form)} \\
\text{Adjective (plain imperfect tense form)} \\
\text{adjectival Noun} + \textit{na} \text{ or } \sim \textit{de (wa) nai} \\
\text{Noun} + \textit{no} \text{ or } \textit{de (wa) nai}
\end{array}\right\} + \textit{koto} + \left\{\begin{array}{l} \textit{ga} \\ \textit{wa} \end{array}\right\} + \left\{\begin{array}{l} \textit{aru} \\ \textit{nai} \end{array}\right\}
$$

Do not confuse the TA form of a Verb followed by *koto ga aru* "one has done such and such before," "one has an experience of doing such and such" (see Note 7.4.7, Vol. II) with the Dictionary form of a Verb followed by *koto ga aru*.

Compare:

Hayashi kyooju ni atta koto ga arimasu ka?   "Have you ever met Professor Hayashi?"
Hayashi kyooju ni au koto ga arimasu ka?   "Do you ever see Professor Hayashi?"

Kimi wa kuni e kaeru koto ga arimasu ka?   "Do you sometimes go to your hometown?"
Oshoogatsu toka natsuyasumi ni wa   "I go home on New Year's day(s) or during
  kaerimasu.   summer vacation."

Dono bubun ga kan'ji no bushu ka nakanaka   "There are times when you can't tell easily
  wakaranai koto ga arimasu yo.   which part of the *kan'ji* is the classifier."

13.4.12 *Hitori de hiite goran nasai* means "Look up (the character in) the dictionary by yourself." As already noted in Note 4.4.5, *goran nasai* may be used instead of *minasai*. This is also true when *minasai* is used as an Extender. *Goran nasai* is more polite and softer than *minasai*.

Hitori de *hiite minasai*. $\longrightarrow$ Hitori de *hiite goran nasai*.

Asoko ni iru hito ni michi o kiite goran   "Ask the man over there the way to get
  nasai.   there."

Nijuu gopeeji o akete goran nasai.   "Open the book to page twenty-five. There
  Setsumei ga kaite arimasu.   is an explanation there."

Jibun de jisho o hikinagara, yakushite   "Translate it using a dictionary by yourself.
  goran nasai. Ato de shirabete agemasu   I'll check it later."
  kara.

In informal speech *goran* without *nasai* may be heard.

Chotto kotchi e kite goran.   "Come over here."

13.5   VOCABULARY

Presentation

引き	hiki	......	V	Stem form of *hiku* – draw; pull; look up
学ぶ	manabu	......	V	study
場合	baai	......	N	case; occasion
初級	shokyuu	......	N	elementary level
中級	chuukyuu	......	N	intermediate level
上級	jookyuu	......	N	advanced level
少なくとも	sukunaku tomo	......	Adv.	at least (see 13.4.2)

種類	-shurui	......	Nd	kinds; sorts
ほん訳	hon'yaku	......	N	translation
ほん訳する	hon'yaku suru	......	V	translate
英和	eiwa	......	N	English-Japanese (dictionary)
和英	waei	......	N	Japanese-English (dictionary)
さえ	sae	......	R	even (see 13.4.3)
へん	hen	......	N	(see 13.4.4)
かんむり	kan'muri	......	N	(see 13.4.4)
かまえ	kamae	......	N	(see 13.4.4)
部首	bushu	......	N	classifier
見つけ	mitsuke	......	V	Pre-Nai form of *mitsukeru* – find; discover (transitive Verb) (cf. *mitsukaru*)
字画	jikaku	......	N	number of strokes
正しく	tadashiku	......	A	KU form of *tadashii* – is correct; is right
数え	kazoe	......	V	Stem form of *kazoeru* – count

Dialog

あまり	amari	......	Adv.	so ... that (see 13.4.6)
がわ	-gawa	......	Nd	side
画	-kaku	......	Nd	counter for strokes
表	hyoo	......	N	list; table
数	-suu	......	Nd	number
ならんで	naran'de	......	V	TE form of *narabu* – line up; is listed; is in a row (intransitive Verb)
残り	nokori	......	N	the rest; the remainder
部分	bubun	......	N	part; portion
わかったろう	wakattaroo	......	V	TAROO form of *wakaru* – understand (see 13.4.9)
なれる	nareru	......	V	get accustomed; is tame (~ *ni nareru* "get accustomed to ~) (see 13.4.10)
基本	kihon	......	N	basis
つまり	tsumari	......	SI	that is; in other words
ごらんなさい	goran nasai	......	E	equivalent for *minasai* after TE form (see 13.4.12)

Notes

多くとも	ooku tomo	......	Adv.	at most (see 13.4.2)
びんぼう	bin'boo	......	Na	poor; poverty
金持ち	kanemochi	......	N	the rich
あんまり	an'mari	......	Adv.	so ... that (see 13.4.6)
だったろう	dattaroo	......	C	TAROO form of the Copula *da* (see 13.4.9)
訳して	yakushite	......	V	TE form of *yakusu* – render; translate (The difference between *yakusu* and *hon'yaku suru* is that *yakusu* may be used for "translation" of a single sentence or for giving an equivalent to a word while *hon'yaku suru* is a word for "translation" of a book, an article, etc.)
音	on	......	N	reading based on the original Chinese sounds
訓	kun	......	N	reading based on the Japanese meaning

13.6   KAN'JI

13.6.1 辞   (1) JI   (2) word; speech   (3) classifier 舌（辛）[crime; painful]

(4) ［丶］［二］［千］［舌］［辞］［辞］   (5) 辞書、辞典 [dictionary]

13.6.2 引   (1) *hi(ku)*   (2) draw; pull; quote   (3) classifier 弓 [bow]

(4) ［フ］［コ］［弓］［引］   (5) 辞書を引きます、ことわざを引く、字引 [dictionary]

13.6.a ^{2.6.2, Vol. II} 学   (1) *mana(bu)*   (5) 日本語を学ぶ、よく学びよく遊べ [Work while you work, play while you play.]

13.6.b ^{4.6.6, Vol. III} 合   (1) *ai*   (5) 試合、場合   (6) Stem form of Verb *au* → Noun

13.6.3 必   (1) HITSU   (2) necessity; without fail   (3) classifier 心 [heart; mind]

(4) ［丶］［ノ］［必］［必］［必］   (5) 必要

13.6.4 要　(1)　YOO　(2)　necessity; main point; need　(3)　classifier 西

(4) ［西］［要］　(5)　必要、重要な [essential]

13.6.5 訳　(1)　YAKU; YAKU(*su*)　(2)　translation　(3)　classifier 言 [word]

(4) ［言］［訂］［訳］［訳］［訳］　(5)　ほん訳、英語に訳す、英訳

13.6.6 和　(1)　WA　(2)　Japan; harmony; peace　(3)　classifier 禾（口）

(4) ［禾］［和］　(5)　英和、和英、漢和辞典 [Chinese-Japanese dictionary]、平和 [peace]、和服、和室、和訳、和風

9.6.1, Vol. III
13.6.c 正　(1)　*tada(shii)*　(5)　正しいことばを使いなさい、正しく読みなさい

13.6.7 全　(1)　ZEN　(2)　whole; entire　(3)　classifier 人

(4) ［人］［人］［仝］［全］　(5)　全部、全然、完全、全国 [the entire nation]

13.6.8 然　(1)　ZEN　(2)　proper　(3)　classifier 夕（灬 [fire]）

(4) ［ク］［夕］［夕］［妖］［狱］［然］　(5)　自然、全然

13.6.9 練　(1)　REN　(2)　discipline; polish; train　(3)　classifier 糸 [thread]

(4) ［ノ］［タ］［糸］［糸］［練］　(5)　練習、訓練 [training]

9.6.5, Vol. II
13.6.d 習　(1)　SHUU　(5)　練習、習字 [penmanship]、復習 [review]、予習 [preparation]

13.6.10 転　(1)　TEN　(2)　turn around; change　(3)　classifier 車

(4) ［車］［転］［転］　(5)　運転、自転車、転校 [school transfer]

13.6.11 形　(1)　*katachi*　(2)　shape; form　(3)　classifier 开（彡 [a design]）

(4) ［二］［干］［开］［形］［形］［形］　(5)　漢字の形、形がいい車、色や形

13.6.12 酒　(1)　*sake*　(2)　rice wine; alcohol　(3)　classifier 酉 [the shape of a wine jar]　(4) ［氵］［汀］［汀］［洒］［酒］［酒］

(5)　酒を飲む、酒は米から作られている

13.6.13 両*　(1)　RYOO　(2)　two; both　(3)　classifier 一

(4) ［一］［厂］［冂］［両］［両］［両］　(5)　両親、両方 [both]、両国

(6)　a shape of a balanced steelyard 兪

13.6.14 親*　(1)　SHIN　(2)　parent　(3)　classifier 立（見）

(4) ［立］［亲］［親］［親］　(5)　両親、親切な人、親類 [relatives]

(6)　homonym 新、辛

13.7   DRILLS

13.7.1 Transformation Drill

1. これで わかったろうと 思います。　　⟶　これで わかっただろうと 思います。

2. 学生生活に すぐ なれたろうと 　　　⟶　学生生活に すぐ なれただろうと
   思います。　　　　　　　　　　　　　　 　思います。

3. 山田君は いい 辞書を 見つけた 　　⟶　山田君は いい 辞書を 見つけた
   ろうと 思います。　　　　　　　　　　　 だろうと 思います。

4. 辞書の 引き方を 学んだろうと 　　　⟶　辞書の 引き方を 学んだだろうと
   あにが 言いました。　　　　　　　　　　 あにが 言いました。

5. ぼくが 英語に ほん訳したろうと 　　⟶　ぼくが 英語に ほん訳しただろうと
   聞かれました。　　　　　　　　　　　　　 聞かれました。

6. 父は ぼくに つかれたろうと 言い 　　⟶　父は ぼくに つかれただろうと 言い
   ました。　　　　　　　　　　　　　　　　 ました。

13.7.2 Transformation Drill

1. 北海道の 冬は さむかったろうと 　　⟶　北海道の 冬は さむかっただろうと
   思います。　　　　　　　　　　　　　　　 思います。

2. あにが 自分の したことは 　　　　　⟶　あにが 自分の したことは
   正しかったろうと 言いました。　　　　　 正しかっただろうと 言いました。

3. 友だちが それを 聞いて うれし 　　⟶　友だちが それを 聞いて うれし
   かったろうと 聞きました。　　　　　　　 かっただろうと 聞きました。

4. きのうの 映画は おもしろかった 　　⟶　きのうの 映画は おもしろかった
   ろうと 聞かれました。　　　　　　　　　 だろうと 聞かれました。

5. あの 人は 体が 弱かったろうと 　　⟶　あの 人は 体が 弱かっただろうと
   両親が 言っていました。　　　　　　　　 両親が 言っていました。

6. 京都の ほうが むしあつかったろうと ⟶　京都の ほうが むしあつかった
   思いました。　　　　　　　　　　　　　　 だろうと 思いました。

13.7.3 Transformation Drill

1. 戸田さんは 銀行員だったろうと 　　　⟶　戸田さんは 銀行員だっただろうと
   思います。　　　　　　　　　　　　　　　 思います。

2. 山本さんは 前 びんぼうだったろうと ⟶　山本さんは 前 びんぼうだった
   思います。　　　　　　　　　　　　　　　 だろうと 思います。

3. あの　建物は　そのころ　近代的
　　だったろうと　聞かれました。 　　⟶　あの　建物は　そのころ　近代的
　　　　　　　　　　　　　　　　　　　　だっただろうと　聞かれました。

4. 友子さんは　親切だったろうと　母が
　　言っていました。 　　⟶　友子さんは　親切だっただろうと　母が
　　　　　　　　　　　　　　　　　　言っていました。

5. 十五日は　試合だったろうと　先生に
　　言われました。 　　⟶　十五日は　試合だっただろうと　先生に
　　　　　　　　　　　　　　　　　　言われました。

6. あの　花は　さくらだったろうと
　　ぼくは　こたえました。 　　⟶　あの　花は　さくらだっただろうと
　　　　　　　　　　　　　　　　　　ぼくは　こたえました。

13.7.4　Transformation Drill

1. 時々　よく　わかりません。 　　⟶　よく　わからないことが　あります。

2. たまに　大学で　けい子さんに
　　会います。 　　⟶　大学で　けい子さんに　会うことが
　　　　　　　　　　　　　　　　あります。

3. 時々　長い　文を　日本語に　ほん訳
　　します。 　　⟶　長い　文を　日本語に　ほん訳する
　　　　　　　　　　　　　　ことが　あります。

4. たまに　一年じゅう　国へ　帰りません。　⟶　一年じゅう　国へ　帰らないことが
　　　　　　　　　　　　　　　　　　　　あります。

5. 時々　ここから　いろいろな　鳥の　声が　⟶　ここから　いろいろな　鳥の　声が
　　聞こえます。 　　　　　　　　　　　　　　聞こえることが　あります。

6. 時々　晴れた　日には　この　窓から　⟶　晴れた　日には　この　窓から　山が
　　山が　見えます。 　　　　　　　　　　　　見えることが　あります。

7. 時々　ぼくは　昼ご飯を　食べません。　⟶　ぼくは　昼ご飯を　食べないことが
　　　　　　　　　　　　　　　　　　　　あります。

13.7.5　Transformation Drill

1. あの　人の　言うことは　時々　正しく　⟶　あの　人の　言うことは　正しくない
　　ありません。 　　　　　　　　　　　　　　ことが　あります。

2. この　辺は　たまに　風が　ひどいです。⟶　この　辺は　風が　ひどいことが
　　　　　　　　　　　　　　　　　　　　あります。

3. 東京は　時々　ひじょうに　むしあつい　⟶　東京は　ひじょうに　むしあついことが
　　です。 　　　　　　　　　　　　　　　　あります。

4. わたしは　時々　日によって　コーヒーが　⟶　わたしは　日によって　コーヒーが
　　ほしくありません。 　　　　　　　　　　ほしくないことが　あります。

5. 山田先生が　クラスに　いらっしゃる　　　　→　山田先生が　クラスに　いらっしゃる
　　　　時間は　たまに　おそいです。　　　　　　　　　時間は　おそいことが　あります。

6. ここの　品物(しな)は　時々　よくないです。　→　ここの　品物(しな)は　よくないことが
　　　　　　　　　　　　　　　　　　　　　　　　　　あります。

7. 課長の　話は　時々　わかりにくいです。→　課長の　話は　わかりにくいことが
　　　　　　　　　　　　　　　　　　　　　　　　　あります。

13.7.6 Transformation Drill

1. この　仕事は　<u>たまに　ひまです。</u>　　　→　この　仕事は　<u>ひまなことが　あります。</u>

2. わたしの　家は　時々　とても　にぎやか→　わたしの　家は　とても　にぎやかな
　　　です。　　　　　　　　　　　　　　　　　　　　ことが　あります。

3. 人によっては　時々　牛肉が　大きらい　→　人によっては　牛肉が　大きらいなことが
　　　です。　　　　　　　　　　　　　　　　　　　　あります。

4. わたしの　学生は　時々　アメリカ人だけ→　わたしの　学生は　アメリカ人だけじゃ
　　　じゃありません。　　　　　　　　　　　　　　ないことが　あります。

5. 店員の　ことばは　時々　ていねいじゃ　→　店員の　ことばは　ていねいじゃない
　　　ありません。　　　　　　　　　　　　　　　　ことが　あります。

6. 朝ご飯は　たまに　パンと　紅茶(こう)だけです。→　朝ご飯は　パンと　紅茶(こう)だけのことが
　　　　　　　　　　　　　　　　　　　　　　　　あります。

7. 初級(しょきゅう)の　クラスは　時々　十四、五人　→　初級(しょきゅう)の　クラスは　十四、五人のことが
　　　です。　　　　　　　　　　　　　　　　　　　　あります。

13.7.7 Transformation Drill

1. ひとりで　辞書を　<u>引きなさい。</u>　　　　→　ひとりで　辞書を　<u>引いてごらんなさい。</u>

2. あなたの　知っている　音と　訓(くん)を　　→　あなたの　知っている　音と　訓(くん)を
　　　ならべなさい。　　　　　　　　　　　　　　　ならべてごらんなさい。

3. 日本語で　一から　百まで　数(かぞ)えなさい。→　日本語で　一から　百まで　数(かぞ)えて
　　　　　　　　　　　　　　　　　　　　　　　　ごらんなさい。

4. この　文を　英語に　訳しなさい。　　　　→　この　文を　英語に　訳してごらん
　　　　　　　　　　　　　　　　　　　　　　　　なさい。

5. この　字の　〈へん〉を　見つけ　　　　　→　この　字の　〈へん〉を　見つけて
　　　なさい。　　　　　　　　　　　　　　　　　ごらんなさい。

6. わからなければ、先生に　聞きなさい。　　　→　　わからなければ、先生に　聞いてごらん
　　　　　　　　　　　　　　　　　　　　　　　　　　　なさい。

7. あの　食堂で　アルバイトしなさい。　　　→　　あの　食堂で　アルバイトしてごらん
　　　　　　　　　　　　　　　　　　　　　　　　　　　なさい。

13.7.8　Transformation Drill

1. 母が、自分で　きっぷを　買いなさいと　→　母が、自分で　きっぷを　買うように
　　言ったんです。　　　　　　　　　　　　　　　言ったんです。

2. 辞書を　もっと　引いてごらんなさいと　→　辞書を　もっと　引くように　言われ
　　言われました。　　　　　　　　　　　　　　ました。

3. 先生が、行く　場所を　早く　　　　　　→　先生が、行く　場所を　早く
　　決めなさいと　おっしゃいました。　　　　　決めるように　おっしゃいました。

4. 試合の　時、もっと　がんばれと　　　　→　試合の　時、もっと　がんばるように
　　言われました。　　　　　　　　　　　　　　言われました。

5. 次の　駅で　乗りかえてくださいと　　　→　次の　駅で　乗りかえるように
　　駅員が　言った。　　　　　　　　　　　　　駅員が　言った。

6. 私の　意見に　はんたいしないでと　　　→　私の　意見に　はんたいしないように
　　頼みました。　　　　　　　　　　　　　　　頼みました。

7. 台所を　あまり　よごさないで　　　　　→　台所を　あまり　よごさないように
　　くださいと　頼まれました。　　　　　　　　頼まれました。

13.7.9　Substitution Drill

小学生にさえ　意味が　わかるはずです。

1. 一郎君　　　　　　　　　　　　……　一郎君にさえ　意味が　わかるはずです。

2. 使い方が　わからないんです　……　一郎君にさえ　使い方が　わからないんです。

3. できましたよ　　　　　　　　……　一郎君にさえ　できましたよ。

4. 訳せますよ　　　　　　　　　……　一郎君にさえ　訳せますよ。

5. 子ども　　　　　　　　　　　……　子どもにさえ　訳せますよ。

6. 一年生　　　　　　　　　　　……　一年生にさえ　訳せますよ。

7. やさしすぎます　　　　　　　……　一年生にさえ　やさしすぎます。

13.7.10 Transformation Drill

1. これは 高くて、ぼくには 買え
   ません。　　　　　　　　　　⟶　これは あまり 高くて、ぼくには
   　　　　　　　　　　　　　　　　　　　買えません。

2. 子どもは おかしを 食べたので、⟶　子どもは おかしを あまり 食べた
   おなかが いたくなりました。　　　　ので、おなかが いたくなりました。

3. 試験が むずかしく、困ってしまった。⟶　試験が あまり むずかしく、困って
   　　　　　　　　　　　　　　　　　　　しまった。

4. 事務所が しずかなので、だれも　⟶　事務所が あまり しずかなので、
   いないと 思いました。　　　　　　　だれも いないと 思いました。

5. あれは 忙しい アルバイトだから、⟶　あれは あまり 忙しい アルバイト
   やめることに しました。　　　　　　だから、やめることに しました。

6. となりの へやが うるさくて、　⟶　となりの へやが あまり うるさくて、
   寝られないんです。　　　　　　　　　寝られないんです。

7. スミスさんの 日本語が じょうずな ⟶　スミスさんの 日本語が あまり
   ので、おどろきました。　　　　　　　じょうずなので、おどろきました。

8. 数が 多くて、数えられませんでした。⟶　数が あまり 多くて、数えられません
   　　　　　　　　　　　　　　　　　　　でした。

13.7.11 Substitution Drill

1. 使い方に なれるまで 大変ですね。

2. 大学を 卒業する　　　　　……　大学を 卒業するまで 大変ですね。

3. 仕事が 決まる　　　　　　……　仕事が 決まるまで 大変ですね。

4. いいのを えらぶ　　　　　……　いいのを えらぶまで 大変ですね。

5. くつが かわいてしまう　　……　くつが かわいてしまうまで 大変ですね。

6. むこうの 気候に なれる　……　むこうの 気候に なれるまで 大変ですね。

7. 外国旅行は 出発する　　　……　外国旅行は 出発するまで 大変ですね。

8. 前のように やせる　　　　……　前のように やせるまで 大変ですね。

13.7.12 Response Drill

1. この 漢字は 習いましたか。

   はい　　　　　　　　　　　　……　はい、もう 習っています。

2. 私が 買うように 言った 辞書は 買いましたか。

   いいえ　　　　　　　　　　　……　いいえ、まだ 買っていません。

3. この　字の　画数が　いくつか　数えましたか。

いいえ　　　　　　　　　　　……　いいえ、まだ　数えていません。

4. 日本の　小説や　ずい筆は　読みましたか。

はい　　　　　　　　　　　　……　はい、もう　読んでいます。

5. あの　人と　テニスの　試合を　しましたか。

いいえ　　　　　　　　　　　……　いいえ、まだ　していません。

6. 美術館とか　いろいろな　所は　見学しましたか。

いいえ　　　　　　　　　　　……　いいえ、まだ　見学していません。

7. 日本の　工業について　レポートを　もう　書いたんですか。

いいえ　　　　　　　　　　　……　いいえ、まだ　書いていません。

13.7.13 Transformation Drill

1. 何か　食べる　物を　注文して　　　　　⟶　何か　食べる　物を　注文して
　　くれますか。　　　　　　　　　　　　　　もらえますか。

2. ちょっと　こちらへ　来て　　　　　　　⟶　ちょっと　こちらへ　来て
　　くださいませんか。　　　　　　　　　　　いただけませんか。

3. 辞書を　貸してくれますか。　　　　　　⟶　辞書を　貸してもらえますか。

4. さんせいの　方は　手を　上げて　　　　⟶　さんせいの　方は　手を　上げて
　　くださいますか。　　　　　　　　　　　　いただけますか。

5. 辞書の　使い方を　教えて　　　　　　　⟶　辞書の　使い方を　教えて
　　くださいませんか。　　　　　　　　　　　いただけませんか。

6. この　字を　もう一度　正しく　　　　　⟶　この　字を　もう一度　正しく
　　書いてくれませんか。　　　　　　　　　　書いてもらえませんか。

13.8　EXERCISES

13.8.1　日本語で　こたえなさい。

1. あなたは　辞書を　使うことが　ありますか。

2. どんな　辞書を　持っていますか。

3. どんな　場合に　辞書を　使いますか。

4. 英和と　和英の　辞書について　説明してごらんなさい。

5. 漢字の　辞書を　引く　時、まず　何から　始めますか。

13.8.2 次の　文を　日本語に　訳しなさい。

1. My parents told me to write a letter (to them) at least once a week.

2. The lake was so large that I got surprised.

3. It is necessary to practice it until one becomes good at it.

4. I asked a Japanese friend to translate the letter written in Japanese for me.

5. There are times when I use my *kan'ji* dictionary, but it is sometimes difficult to find classifiers.

6. I imagine that my son must have become accustomed to a new life in Japan.

13.8.3 次の　文を　英語に　訳しなさい。

1. あにに　少なくとも　二百ぐらい　漢字を　覚えたろうと　言われました。

2. 和英の　辞書が　必要なことが　あるので、一さつ　買うことに　しました。

3. この　漢字は　あまり　ふくざつで、何が　部首か　全然　わかりません。

4. 毎日　忙しくて、新聞を　読む　時間さえ　ありません。

5. まだ　習っていない　漢字の　意味を　調べるのには、この　辞書が　ないと、
困るでしょう。

13.8.4 文を　作りなさい。

1. つまり
2. たとえば
3. 少なくとも
4. あまり…　ので

13.8.5 次の　漢字の　部首を　見つけなさい。

1. 海
2. 行
3. 安
4. 館
5. 機
6. 研
7. 紙
8. 思
9. 時
10. 近

13.8.6 次の　漢字の　字画は　いくつですか。

1. 頼
2. 所
3. 遠
4. 鉄
5. 然
6. 高

13.8.7 言べんの　字を　いくつ　知っていますか。　書きなさい。

13.8.8 漢字で　書きなさい。

1. にほんごを　まなびはじめてから、にねんに　なる。
2. ただしい　じしょの　ひきかたを　おぼえることが　ひつようだ。
3. くるまの　うんてんを　れんしゅうしています。

4. <u>さけ</u>という <u>じ</u>は <u>ぜんぶで</u> <u>なん画</u>か 数えてごらんなさい。

5. これは おもしろい <u>かたち</u>の <u>さら</u>ですね。<u>しぜん</u>な <u>いろ</u>が きれいです。

6. <u>ごりょうしん</u>が とても <u>しんせつ</u>に してくださいました。

7. この <u>ぶん</u>を <u>わえい</u>の <u>じしょ</u>を つかって <u>やく</u>しなさい。

8. この <u>じ</u>の <u>いみ</u>は <u>ぜんぜん</u> わかりません。

13.8.9　読みなさい。

1. 引、強、弱	4. 車、転	7. 雨、両
2. 私、和、秋	5. 酒、湖	8. 話、訳
3. 今、全、合	6. 親、新	9. 練、紙

13.8.10 Describe the procedure for finding a *kan'ji* reading and meaning.

13.8.11 Use the *kan'ji* list in Lesson 14 of this volume and identify their classifiers.

13.8.12 In case you cannot find the pronunciation of a *kan'ji* by its classifier, what can you do next?

13.8.13 According to the sentences given, tell which *kan'ji* is the correct one.

1. Watashi wa maiasa okiru no ga *hayai* desu.

　　速い　　　　　　早い

2. Samui kara shatsu o *kinasai*.

　　着なさい　　来なさい

13.9　SITUATIONAL AND APPLICATION CONVERSATION

13.9.1 Mr. Roberts asks Miss Smith if she reads Japanese newspapers.

Miss Smith says that she sometimes does but that she must consult a *kan'ji* dictionary.

Mr. Roberts asks what kind of dictionary she is using.

Miss Smith answers that she bought the *Kan'ji Nyūmon* because she was told by her teacher to buy one.

13.9.2 Tell your classmates how to look up the character 近 or some others in a *kan'ji* dictionary.

13.9.3 Discuss with your friends the dictionary or dictionaries you own: kinds, usage, good points or weak points, etc.

13.10 READING COMPREHENSION

13.10.1

　日本語を　習い始めてから　もう　十か月に　なる。漢字は　今までに　三百あまり
習ったろうか。はじめは、会話を　習ったり　日本の　ことを　多く　知ったりするのは
おもしろいが、漢字の　勉強は　いやだと　思っていた。しかし、最近　漢字の　勉強が
おもしろくなり出した。それは、たくさんの　「へん」や　「かんむり」の　意味や　形が
わかってきて、漢字が　だんだん　覚えやすくなってきたからであろう。それに、このごろは
ひらがなばかりで　書いてある　文が　読みにくくなってきた。日本人の　友だちが、以前
ひらがなだけで　書かれた　私の　手紙を　読んで、読みにくいと　言っていたのを　思い出
した。

13.10.2

女子学生　「ねえ、この　字　どういう　意味?」

男子学生　「どれ? "金"へんに "同じ"? 見たことが　ないなあ。でも、ちょっと
　　　　　待って、調べてみるから。」

女子学生　「はじめ　金へんで　引くんでしょう?」

男子学生　「そうだよ。金へんは　八画だから、この　辺に　あると　思うけど…あ、
　　　　　あった。それで、"同じ"は　一、二、三、…六画だから、金へんの　六画で
　　　　　さがすと…。」

女子学生　「なかなか　見つからないのね。」

男子学生　「そんなこと　ないよ。ええと、295 ページか。…ほら、あったじゃないか。」

女子学生　「あ、本当。何て　書いてある?」

男子学生　「読み方は "ドウ"で、意味は　copperだって。」

LESSON 14
漢字の 話

14.1 PRESENTATION

　日本文化の 歴史は、 そのまま 日本語の 歴史でもある。 千数百年以上も 前に 中国文化が 日本に 紹介されたが、 その 時、 中国の 文字 ― 漢字 ― が とり 入れられ、 この 漢字から かたかなや ひらがなが 生まれた。 そして、 和語に 漢語が くわわり、 表現も ずっと ゆたかに なった。

　この ほか、 十六世紀の 中ごろから ポルトガルや オランダの 船が 日本へ 来始めると、 さまざまな 外国品が 輸入された。 それと 同時に、 ヨーロッパ語の 単語が 日本語風に 発音され、 日本語の 一部として 使われ出した。 たとえば、 「ガラス」（オランダ語）、 「パン」（ポルトガル語）、 「スープ」（英語）など たくさん ある。 このような 単語が 外来語と 呼ばれる ものである。

　漢字の むずかしさは、 一つの 漢字に 普通 二種類の 読み ― 音と 訓 ― が あり、 さらに 二つ以上の 音や 訓を 持つものも あることである。 たとえば、 「人」の 音は 「じん」と 「にん」であり、 訓読みは 「ひと」である。 このように、 漢字を 多く 知ると 同時に、 一つの 漢字の 読みを 多く 知っていることも 大切である。

14.2 KAN'JI STUDY

―― 漢字の 勉強 ――

(1)

橋本 「あなたたちの 学部では、 一、二年の 時に どういう 科目が 取れるん ですか。」

岡田 「政治学、 経済学、 社会学、 歴史、 文学、 美術、 教育学、 心理学、 地理、 数学、 哲学、 言語学、 それから、 専門科目です。」

橋本 「日本語科には 先生が 何人 いらっしゃるんですか。」

岡田 「教授が 二人、 助教授が 三人、 講師が 五人、 助手が 数人 います。」

(2)

弟 「お姉さん、 お母さんが 呼んでるよ。」

姉 「お母さん、 なあに？」

母　「弟や　妹たちを　午後　映画にでも　連れてってくれないかしら。　ちょっと
　　　大事な　会を　うちで　開くんだけど、　じゃますると　悪いから。」

姉　「いいわ。　公園へ　連れてって、　公園の　中を　歩いたり　走ったりして
　　　遊ばせるから。」

母　「じゃあ、　犬も　連れてったら？」

姉　「そう　するわ。」

(3)

杉山　「あなたの　お姉さんは　何を　していらっしゃるんですか。」

スミス「姉は　音楽家です。」

杉山　「じゃあ、　あなたも　画家だし、　あなたの　家族は　芸術家ばかり
　　　　なんですね。」

スミス「そうでもありませんよ。　父は　政治家ですし、　兄は　軍人ですから。」

14.3　VOCABULARY

Presentation

そのまま	sono mama	......	Adv.	as it is
数百	suuhyaku	......	N	several hundred
文字	moji	......	N	letter; character
とり入れられ	toriirerare	......	V + Dv	Stem form of *toriirerareru* – is introduced
和語	wago	......	N	original Japanese language or words (*wa* means Japan)
漢語	kan'go	......	N	Chinese word; word of Chinese origin
くわわり	kuwawari	......	V	Stem form of *kuwawaru* – is added (intransitive Verb)
ポルトガル	Porutogaru	......	N	Portugal
オランダ	Oran'da	......	N	Holland
外国品	gaikokuhin	......	N	foreign goods
同時に	dooji ni	......	Adv.	at the same time
ヨーロッパ語	yooroppago	......	N	European languages
単語	tan'go	......	N	word; vocabulary item
風	-fuu	......	Nd	style; way
発音され	hatsuon sare	......	V	Stem form of *hatsuon sareru* – is pronounced (passive of *hatsuon suru*)

発音	hatsuon	......	N	pronunciation
一部	ichibu	......	N	a part
オランダ語	oran'dago	......	N	the Dutch language
ポルトガル語	porutogarugo	......	N	the Portuguese language
外来語	gairaigo	......	N	foreign word; word of foreign origin (usually excludes Chinese words)
むずかしさ	muzukashisa	......	N	difficulty
読み	yomi	......	N	reading(s)
音	on	......	N	reading based on the original Chinese sounds
訓	kun	......	N	reading based on the Japanese meaning
同時	dooji	......	N	the same time

—— Kan'ji no Ben'kyoo ——

(1)

橋本	Hashimoto	......	N	family name
学部	gakubu	......	N	school or college of a university
科目	kamoku	......	N	course; subject
岡田	Okada	......	N	family name
政治学	seijigaku	......	N	politics
経済学	keizaigaku	......	N	economics
美術	bijutsu	......	N	fine arts
心理学	shin'rigaku	......	N	psychology
地理	chiri	......	N	geography
数学	suugaku	......	N	mathematics
言語学	gen'gogaku	......	N	linguistics
専門科目	sen'mon'kamoku	......	N	major subjects
科	-ka	......	Nd	course; major; department
助教授	jokyooju	......	N	associate or assistant professor
講師	kooshi	......	N	lecturer; instructor
助手	joshu	......	N	assistant

(3)

杉山	Sugiyama	......	N	family name
音楽家	on'gakka	......	N	musician

画家	gaka	......	N	painter; fine artist
芸術家	geijutsuka	......	N	artist
政治家	seijika	......	N	politician

14.4 KAN'JI (for passive learning)

14.4.a 同 [6.6.9] (1) DOO (5) 同時（に）

14.4.1 表 (1) HYOO (2) list; express; schedule; expose (3) classifier 主（衣 [cloth]） (4) 十 主 声 丰 表 表 (5) 代表的、時間表 [time table] (6) homonym 俵

14.4.2 現 (1) GEN (2) present; express (3) classifier 王 [jewelry] (4) 丨 王 現 (5) 表現、現金 [cash]、現代

14.4.3 船 (1) *fune* (2) boat; ship (3) classifier 舟 [ship] (4) 丿 几 月 舟 舮 船 (5) 小さな船

14.4.4 科 (1) KA (2) course; major (3) classifier 禾 [crop] (4) 禾 科 科 科 科 (5) 科目、教科書、日本語科、科学 [science]

14.4.b 美 [12.6.1, Vol. II] (1) BI (5) 美人、自然美

14.4.5 術 (1) JUTSU (2) art; magic (3) classifier 彳（行 [walk, road]） (4) 彳 什 休 術 術 (5) 美術、美術館、手術 [medical operation]

14.4.6 育 (1) IKU (2) raise; educate; bring up (3) classifier 亠（月 [body, flesh]） (4) 亠 云 育 (5) 教育

14.4.c 言 [2.6.9, Vol. III] (1) GEN (5) 言語、言語学、発言 [speak]

14.4.7 弟 (1) *otooto* (2) younger brother (3) classifier 弓 [bow] (4) ヽ ソ 半 弟 弟 弟 (5) 弟たち

14.4.8 姉 (1) *nee* (2) older sister (3) classifier 女 [woman] (4) 女 女 女 姉 姉 (5) お姉さん

14.4.d 姉 [14.4.8] (1) *ane* (5) 姉と弟

14.4.9 妹　　(1) *imooto*　　(2) younger sister　　(3) classifier 女 [woman]

（4) 女 妇 妹 妹　　(5) 姉妹

14.4.10 映　　(1) EI　　(2) reflect; project　　(3) classifier 日 [sun]

（4) 日 町 映 映　　(5) 映<ruby>画<rt>が</rt></ruby>

14.4.11 画　　(1) GA　　(2) picture　　(3) classifier 一

（4) 一 ㄇ 币 面 画 画　　(5) 映画、画家、日本画、洋画、はん画

14.4.12 連　　(1) *tsu(reru)*　　(2) take along　　(3) classifier 辶　　(4) 車 連

（5) 子どもを 連れて行く

14.4.13 走　　(1) *hashi(ru)*　　(2) run　　(3) forms the classifier 土 (走 [run])

（4) 土 キ キ 声 走　　(5) ろう下を 走らないでください

14.4.14 犬　　(1) *inu*　　(2) dog　　(3) forms the classifier 大 (犬 [dog])

（4) 大 犬　　(5) 犬の声、犬がなく

14.4.15 芸　　(1) GEI　　(2) arts　　(3) classifier ⺾　　(4) ⺾ 兰 芸

（5) 芸術、芸<ruby>人<rt>にん</rt></ruby> [entertainer]

14.4.16 兄　　(1) *ani*　　(2) older brother　　(3) classifier 儿　　(4) ロ ㇕ 兄

（5) 兄と弟　　(6) 儿 is the shape of a kneeling man's legs

14.4.17 軍　　(1) GUN　　(2) military　　(3) classifier 冖 (車 [car])　　(4) 冖 軍

（5) 軍人、<ruby>空<rt>くう</rt></ruby>軍 [air force]、<ruby>海<rt>かい</rt></ruby>軍 [navy]、<ruby>陸<rt>りく</rt></ruby>軍 [army]

14.5　EXERCISES

14.5.1 次の <ruby>質<rt>しつ</rt></ruby>問に　こたえなさい。

A. 1. 外来語、漢語、和語というのは　何ですか。説明してください。

2. あなたの　知っている　外来語を　言ってください。

3. あなたの　知っている　漢字の　中で、一つの　漢字に　音と　<ruby>訓<rt>くん</rt></ruby>が　ある　漢字の　<ruby>例<rt>れい</rt></ruby>を　五つ　言いなさい。

4. あなたは　漢字を　習う　時の　むずかしさは　何だと　思いますか。

5. ひらがなや　かたかなは　何から　作られましたか。

B. 1. あなたの　専門は　何ですか。

2. 今　どんな　<ruby>科目<rt>もく</rt></ruby>を　取っていますか。

3. どの　<ruby>科目<rt>もく</rt></ruby>が　最も　おもしろいですか。

4. ほかに　どんな　<ruby>科目<rt>もく</rt></ruby>を　勉強してみたいと　思いますか。どうしてですか。

14.5.2 漢字で　書きなさい。

    1. がいこくの　せいひんが　たくさん　ふねで　はいりました。

    2. あにが　あねと　おとうとを　よんでいます。

    3. ぼくが　べんきょうしたい　か目は　きょういくがく、しゃかいがく、

       びじゅつしで、せんもんは　げんごがくです。

    4. ごご、えいがへ　いもうとを　つれていった。

    5. おじは　ぐんじんで、おばは　がかです。

    6. いぬが　こうえんの　なかを　はしっています。

    7. 文じで　ひょうげんしてあります。

    8. どうぶつえんまで　あるきましょうか。

    9. げいじゅつに　きょうみを　もっていますか。

   10. せんそうと　どうじに　くにへ　かえった。

14.5.3 The following are the 119 *kan'ji* classifiers covered in the four volumes of this text. The meanings of classifiers (appearing in brackets in the Kan'ji section of the text) are tentative, random, and sometimes not necessarily accurate. Try to formulate at least one *kan'ji* using each of the classifiers listed. The roman numeral indicates the volume number and the arabic numbers indicate the lesson number. In designating a classifier for a *kan'ji*, Kikuya Nagasawa's *Meikai Kan'wa Jiten* is used.

(II 1)　一、口（四）、亠（六）、八、ノ（九）、十

(II 2)　大、子、宀（生）、日、木、イ（休）、月、車

(II 4)　水、彳（行）、土、目（見）、丷（半）、火、金

(II 5)　艹（花）、人、女（好）、戸（所）、矢（智）、小、山

(II 7)　門（間）、夕（外）、馬（駅）、凵（出）、口（中）

(II 8)　田（男）、扌（持）、亠（前）、言、禾（私）、貝（買）

(II 9)　夂（教）、牛（先）、卜（上）、羽、糸、ヨ（書）、宀（字）

(II 11)　釆（番）、北、阝*1（都）、立（新）、西

(II 12)　羊（美）、食、川、牜（物）、尸（屋）

(II 13)　雨、ナ（左）

(III 2)　方（旅）、辶（近）、冂（円）

(III 3)　氵（漢）、ク（勉）、弓（強）、宀（毎）

(III 4)　頁

(III 6)　米、广（度）、卓（朝）

(III 7)　阝*2（院）、厂（歴）、長、川（州）、夂（冬）

(III 8)　主（青）、几（風）、竹

(III 9) 母、白（的）、士（賣）

(III 11) ネ（社）、⺍（覚）

(III 12) 耂（考）、走（起）、牛

(III 13) 七（切）、尹（君）、忄（忙）

(IV 2) 里（黒）、飛

(IV 3) 疒（病）、匸（医）、ン（次）、豆（頭）

(IV 4) 鳥（島）、共（黄）、夫（春）、心（悪）、酉（配）

(IV 6) 二（元）

(IV 7) 工、⺍（業）、癶（発）、戈（戦）、爫（受）、ム（台）

(IV 8) 魚、王（理）、鳥、皿、止（歩）

(IV 9) 歹（残）、阝（興）、石（研）

(IV 11) 比（皆）、隹（集）

(IV 12) 欠（歌）、耳

(IV 13) 舌（辞）、夕（然）、开（形）

*₁ 阝 = right side of *kan'ji*

*₂ 阝 = left side of *kan'ji*

14.5.4 Indicate the pronunciation of the following *kan'ji* on the right and match each with the appropriate pronunciation of the *kan'ji* from the column on the left.

1. 青 せい		a. 棺
2. 生 せい		b. 時
3. 寺 じ		c. 牲
4. 官 かん		d. 清
5. 反 はん		e. 悟
6. 吾 ご		f. 胴
7. 同 どう		g. 飯
8. 交 こう		h. 姓
		i. 持
		j. 館
		k. 校

14.5.5 次の　漢字を　読んだり、書いたり、意味を　言ったりして　練習しなさい。

行く、来る、帰る、出る、出かける、入る、上がる、上げる、下げる、歩く、

走る、乗る、急ぐ、運転する、旅行する、出張する、案内する、連れて行く

食べる、飲む、食事する

言う、話す、表現する、呼ぶ、質問する、聞く、発音する、声を出す、命令する、
頼む、電話する

思う、考える、決める 、決まる、思い出す、気にする、気をつける、心配する、
安心する、困る

見る、見せる、見つかる、見つける、見物する、見学する

教える、知らせる、知る、習う、勉強する、研究する、覚える、調べる、
専攻する、書く、読む、練習する

修理する、世話する、作る、料理する、手つだう、協力する、洗う、使う、
持つ、取る、取り入れる、入れる、開く、開ける、閉める、出す、送る、
取りけす、残る、住む、待つ、会う、着る、に合う、合わせる、治す

遊ぶ、楽しむ、歌う、泳ぐ、休む、寝る、昼寝する、起きる、働く、勤める

降る、晴れる、曇る、風がふく

借りる、貸す、払う、売る、買う、注文する、受ける、輸入する、輸出する、
紹介する

始まる、始める、終わる、終える、卒業する、生まれる、死ぬ、発達する、
起こる、変わる、変える、変化する

新しい、古い、近い、遠い、高い、安い、低い、広い、多い、少ない、大きい、
小さい、明るい、暗い、早い、速い、美しい、楽しい、長い、深い、若い、悪い、
重い、強い、弱い、忙しい

好き、大好き、大変、大事、大切、必要、現代的、便利、不便、自由、完全、
変、急、急速、有名、元気、文化的、近代的、代表的、歴史的、自然的、本格的、
医者、かんご婦、学者、記者、政治家、専門家、軍人、音楽家、芸術家、小説家、
ずい筆家、画家、美術家

学長、学部長、教授、助教授、講師、助手、校長、先生

大学生、高校生、中学生、小学生、学生、卒業生、(大学)院生

社長、重役、部長、課長、社員、秘書、事務員、工場長、工具、駅長、駅員、
図書館長、図書館員、銀行員、会社員、店員、給仕、ゆうびん局員

家族、父、母、兄、姉、妹、弟、主人、家内、子ども、赤ちゃん、夫婦、友だち、
男、女、お客様、皆さん、人々、病人、年取った人、外国人、米国人、英国人、
日本人、国民

田中、広田、内田、戸田、吉田、山田、山口、山崎、山本、松本、中島、中村、野村、

木村、佐々木、鈴木、木下、杉山、林、小林、森、青木、高木、井上、石井、
石川、大川、小川、谷川、池田、清水、小山、高橋、橋本、岡田、渡辺、原、
伊藤、加藤、斎藤、安藤

海、海岸、湖、川、山、火山、島、道、田、畑、世界、国、州、町、村、
外国

公園、動物園、美術館、図書館、学校、大学、高校、中学校、小学校、大学院、
学部、病院、医院、大使館、駅、バス停、映画館、銀行、ゆうびん局、会社、
事務所、工場、店、食堂、きっさ店、旅館、薬屋、肉屋、米屋、本屋、新聞屋

教室、研究室、図書室、学長室、学部長室

家、客間、台所、居間、風呂場、ろう下、お手洗い、地下室、日本間、洋間、
茶の間、食堂

地下、入口、出口、窓、屋根、建物、所、場所

左、右、上、下、外、中、中心、こっちの方、その辺、東、西、南、北

本州、四国、九州、北海道、日本、中国、英国、米国、東洋、西洋、関西、関東、
東京、京都、大阪、横浜、広島、鎌倉、川崎、長崎、奈良、日光、上野、神田、
新宿、富士山

朝、昼、夕方、晩、夜、夕べ、今晩

今週、来週、先週、週末

今月、来月、先月、何月

来年、きょ年

春、夏、秋、冬

日曜日、月曜日、火曜日、水曜日、木曜日、金曜日、土曜日

午前、午後

一時、二時半、四時十九分

一日、二日、三日、四日、五日、六日、七日、八日、九日、十日、十二日、
二十日、二十四日、二十九日、三十日、三十一日

一月、二月、三月、四月、五月、六月、七月、八月、九月、十月、十一月、十二月

毎朝、毎晩、毎週、毎月、毎年、毎日

今、最近、昔、前、最後、終わり、以前、以後

時代、現代、近代、明治時代、江戸時代、戦後、戦前

五分、三時間、四日、二週間、六か月、五年

休み、夏休み、お正月、たんじょう日、結婚記念日

前、時、間、場合

哲学、文学、美術、芸術、音楽、歴史学、経済学、政治学、地理学、社会学、

宗教学、教育学、数学、医学、心理学、英語学、言語学、日本語学、専門科目

乗り物、地下鉄、電車、汽車、急行、普通、飛行機、船、自動車、車、自転車

食べ物、食料、牛肉、ぶた肉、鳥、魚、貝、ご飯、お米、くだ物、塩、西洋料理、

日本料理、中国料理

飲み物、水、お湯、お茶、紅茶、牛乳

色、赤、青、黒、白、茶色、黄色、緑色

宗教、仏教、神道、キリスト教、神様、教会、神社、寺、祭り

体、頭、顔、目、口、鼻、耳、手、足

鉄、金、銀、石、石炭、石油

花、木、竹、物、皿、お金、薬、着物、洋服、水着、くつ下、絵、はん画、紙、

黒板、えん筆、本、さんこう書、教科書、資料、辞書、絵本、新聞、手紙、速達、

切手、地図、表、小説、ずい筆、日記

文字、漢字、当用漢字、教育漢字、言語、敬語、ことば使い、意味、単語、音、

訓読み、発音、外来語、漢語、和語、英語、宿題、問題、会話、授業、講義、

専門、名前、例、返事

産物、原料、電気、製品、品物、外国品、機械、電話

生活、洋風、日本風、和風、活動、交際、仕事、計画、制度、運動、試合、会、

映画、音楽会、行事、条件、地位

文化、交通、産業、農業、工業、社会、教育、住まい、人口、自然、四季、

変化、事故

天気、気候、空、雲、雨、雪、風、台風、降る、晴れる、曇る、予報、地震

以上、以下、以外、以内、以前、以後

数、番号、数百年、数度、数回、数人、数千円、数台、一回、一番、七度五分

第二次、二番線

自分で、特に、全部、一部、全然

本当に、前もって、最も、同時に、同じ、次、普通

14.6 KAN'JI LIST

The following list consists of the *kan'ji* and their readings that have been introduced in Volumes II, III, and IV. A small number above certain *kan'ji* indicates that those *kan'ji* were first introduced with other readings in the section indicated by the number. *Kan'ji* in Lesson 14 of Volume IV have not been included here.

(A)

a(garu) (geru)	上 [9.6.4, II]	12.6.d	IV
a(keru)	開	2.6.2	IV
a(u)	会	8.6.10	III
a(u)	合	4.6.6	III
ai	合 [4.6.6, III]	13.6.b	IV
aida	間 [7.6.3, II]	7.6.b	III
aji	味	7.6.8	III
aka(i)	赤	2.6.9	IV
aka(rui)	明 [11.6.5, III]	12.6.a	IV
aki	秋	4.6.2	IV
ame	雨	11.6.9	III
AN	安 [12.6.11, III]	3.6.a	IV
ao(i)	青	8.6.2	III
ara(u)	洗	6.6.9	III
aru(ku)	歩	8.6.13	IV
asa	朝	6.6.5	III
ashi	足	2.6.7	III
aso(bu)	遊	11.6.10	IV
atama	頭	3.6.8	IV
atara(shii)	新	11.6.8	II
ato	後	13.6.5	III
atsu(maru) (meru)	集	11.6.13	IV

(B)

ba	場	9.6.9	III
BAN	番	11.6.1	II
BAN	晩	12.6.10	III
BEI	米	6.6.2	III
BEN	勉	3.6.5	III
BEN	便	11.6.6	IV
BU	部	13.6.1	III
BUN	文	8.6.7	II
BUN	聞 [7.6.7, II]	3.6.c	III

BUTSU [BUT-]	仏	6.6.1	IV
BUTSU	物 12.6.8, II	8.6.a	IV
BYOO	病	3.6.1	IV
(C)			
CHA	茶	13.6.10	III
CHI	地	9.6.10	III
chichi	父	9.6.4	III
chii(sai)	小	5.6.9	II
chika(i)	近	2.6.6	III
CHOO	長 7.6.4, III	13.6.a	III
CHUU	中 7.6.9, II	12.6.c	II
(D)			
-da	田	13.6.5, 2.6.c	II, III
da(su)	出 7.6.8, II	13.6.d	III
DAI	大	2.6.1	II
DAI	題	4.6.4	III
DAI	代	7.6.3	IV
DAI [TAI]	台	7.6.12	IV
de(ru)	出	7.6.8	II
DEN	電	13.6.3	II
DO	土	4.6.4	II
DO	度	6.6.4	III
DOO	動	13.6.4	II
(E)			
E	絵	9.6.6	III
EI	英	11.6.11	III
EKI	駅	7.6.6	II
EN	円	2.6.10	III
EN	園	12.6.14	IV
(F)			
fu(ru)	降	12.6.4	IV
fuka(i)	深	6.6.4	IV

FUN [-PUN]	分	4.6.6	II
furu(i)	古	11.6.7	II
futa(tsu)	二	1.6.2	II
FUU	風	8.6.7	III
fuyu	冬	7.6.7	III
(G)			
GAI	外	7.6.4	II
GAKU	学	2.6.2	II
GAKU	楽	4.6.12	IV
-GATSU	月	2.6.8	II
GEN	元	6.6.13	IV
GETSU	月 2.6.8, II	4.6.b	II
GIN	銀	8.6.9	III
GO	五	1.6.5	II
GO	語	9.6.1	II
GO	後 13.6.5, III	2.6.a	IV
GO	午	2.6.6	IV
GYOO	業	7.6.2	IV
GYUU	牛	12.6.7	III
(H)			
HACHI	八	1.6.8	II
haha	母	9.6.3	III
HAI [-PAI]	配	4.6.10	IV
hai(ru)	入 13.6.8, II	7.6.a	III
haji(maru) (meru)	始	9.6.1	IV
HAN	飯	12.6.6	III
HAN	半	4.6.7	II
hana	花	5.6.1	II
hana(su)	話	3.6.4	III
hara(u)	払	8.6.10	IV
haru	春	4.6.8	IV
hatara(ku)	働	4.6.7	III

HATSU [HAT-] [-PATSU]	発	7.6.4	IV
haya(i)	早	6.6.8	III
haya(i)	速	9.6.2	IV
HEN	辺	4.6.5	IV
HEN	変 [11.6.7, III]	13.6.c	III
hi [-bi]	日 [2.6.5, II]	4.6.a	II
HI	飛	2.6.7	IV
hi(ku)	引	13.6.2	IV
hidari	左	13.6.6	II
higashi	東 [7.6.1, II]	11.6.b	II
hiku(i)	低	3.6.10	IV
HIN	品	7.6.11	IV
hira(ku)	開 [2.6.2, IV]	11.6.a	IV
hiro(i)	広	8.6.4	III
hiru	昼	6.6.10	III
hito	人	5.6.2	II
hito(tsu)	一	1.6.1	II
HITSU [-PITSU]	筆	12.6.1	IV
HITSU	必	13.6.3	IV
HON [-BON] [-PON]	本	2.6.6	II
HOO	方	4.6.5	III
HYAKU [-BYAKU] [-PYAKU]	百	1.6.11	II

(I)

I	医	3.6.2	IV
I	以	9.6.5	IV
I	意	11.6.11	IV
I	位	13.6.3	III
i(ku)	行	4.6.3	II
i(ru)	入	13.6.8	II

ka(u)	買	8.6.10	II
kaa	母 9.6.3, III	9.6.b	III
kae(ru)	帰	7.6.6	III
KAI	界	11.6.2	III
KAI	会 8.6.10, III	11.6.a	III
KAI	回	3.6.12	IV
KAI	海 8.6.1, IV	11.6.c	IV
kai	貝	8.6.4	IV
kami	紙	9.6.6	II
KAN	間	7.6.3	II
KAN	館	2.6.5	III
KAN	漢	3.6.1	III
kane	金 4.6.10, II	2.6.b	IV
kan'ga(eru)	考	12.6.2	III
kao	顔	12.6.3	IV
karada	体	12.6.10	IV
-kata [-gata]	方 4.6.5, III	6.6.b	III
katachi	形	13.6.11	IV
KATSU	活	6.6.3	IV
kawa	川	12.6.3	II
kaze	風 8.6.7, III	12.6.b	IV
kazu	数	3.6.3	IV
KEN	研	9.6.11	IV
KEN	見 4.6.5, II	11.6.d	IV
KI	気	5.6.5	II
KI	機	2.6.8	IV
KI	汽	4.6.3	IV
KI	黄	4.6.6	IV
KI	記	12.6.2	IV
ki	木 4.6.9, II	8.6.a	III
ki(ku)	聞	7.6.7	II
ki(masu)	来	8.6.4	II
ki(maru) (meru)	決	11.6.12	IV

KYOO	教	9.6.2	II
KYOO	強	3.6.6	III
KYOO	興	9.6.8	IV
KYUU	九	1.6.9	II
KYUU	急	12.6.4	III
KYUU	究	9.6.12	IV

(M)

ma	間 ^{7.6.3, II}	8.6.b	III
ma(tsu)	待	12.6.6	II
machi	町	13.6.2	II
mado	窓	4.6.4	IV
mae	前	8.6.5	II
MAI	毎	3.6.8	III
MAN	万	1.6.13	II
mana(bu)	学 ^{2.6.2, II}	13.6.a	IV
me	目	11.6.2	II
MEI	明	11.6.5	III
MI	味 ^{7.6.8, III}	9.6.b	IV
mi(ru)	見	4.6.5	II
michi	道	6.6.6	IV
migi	右	13.6.7	II
mimi	耳	12.6.8	IV
mina	皆	11.6.3	IV
minami	南	11.6.4	II
mise	店	9.6.8	III
mit(tsu)	三	1.6.3	II
mizu	水 ^{4.6.1, II}	4.6.c	III
mizuumi	湖	11.6.8	IV
mo(tsu)	持	8.6.2	II
MOKU	木	4.6.9	II
MON	問	4.6.3	III
MON	門	9.6.13	IV

ON	音		4.6.11	IV
ona(ji)	同		6.6.9	IV
on'na	女		8.6.3	II
oo(i)	多		11.6.6	II
oo(kii)	大 [2.6.1, II]		5.6.a	II
oshi(eru)	教 [9.6.2, II]		13.6.b	II
otoko	男		8.6.1	II
oyo(gu)	泳		11.6.9	IV

(R)

RAI	来 [8.6.4, II]		2.6.b	III
REKI	歴		7.6.2	III
REN	練		13.6.9	IV
RI	理		8.6.7	IV
RI	利		11.6.7	IV
ROKU	六		1.6.6	II
RYO	旅		2.6.1	III
RYOO	料		8.6.6	IV
RYOO	両		13.6.13	IV

(S)

sa(garu) (geru)	下 [9.6.10, II]		12.6.e	IV
SAI	最		6.6.10	IV
sakana	魚		8.6.3	IV
sake	酒		13.6.12	IV
sama	様		2.6.3	IV
SAN	三		1.6.3	II
SAN	産		9.6.7	IV
sara	皿		8.6.12	IV
SE	世		11.6.1	III
SEI	生		2.6.3	II
SEI	製		7.6.10	IV
SEI	西 [11.6.9, II]		9.6.a	IV
SEKI	石 [3.6.9, III]		4.6.a	IV
SEN [-ZEN]	千		1.6.12	II

SEN	先	9.6.3	II
SEN	戦	7.6.6	IV
SEN	専	9.6.4	IV
SETSU	説	11.6.4	III
SETSU	切	12.6.4	III
SHA	車 2.6.9, II	13.6.a	II
SHA [-JA]	社	11.6.6	III
SHA	者	3.6.7	IV
SHI	四	1.6.4	II
SHI	仕	13.6.8	III
SHI	史	7.6.3	III
SHI	死	12.6.12	IV
shi(meru)	閉	2.6.10	IV
shi(ru) (raseru)	知	5.6.7	II
SHICHI	七	1.6.7	II
shima	島	4.6.1	IV
SHIN [-JIN]	神	6.6.2	IV
SHIN	新 11.6.8, II	3.6.b	III
SHIN	心	3.6.4	IV
SHIN	親	13.6.14	IV
shio	塩	8.6.9	IV
shira(beru)	調	11.6.3	III
shiro(i)	白	2.6.11	IV
shita	下	9.6.10	II
SHITSU	室	11.6.4	IV
SHO	書 9.6.8, II	9.6.b	II
SHO [-JO]	所 5.6.6, II	4.6.b	III
SHOKU	食 12.6.2, II	12.6.b	II
SHOO	小 5.6.9, II	3.6.a	III
SHOO	正	9.6.1	III
SHU	主	8.6.3	III
SHUU	週	3.6.7	III
SHUU	州	7.6.5	III

SHUU	習 9.6.5, II	13.6.d	IV
SOO	争	7.6.7	IV
sora	空	12.6.5	IV
soto	外 7.6.4, II	9.6.c	II
SOTSU	卒	11.6.2	IV
su(ki)	好	5.6.3	II
su(mu)	住	6.6.1	III
SUI	水	4.6.1	II
suku(nai)	少	11.6.10	II
SUU	数 3.6.3, IV	7.6.b	IV

(T)

ta	田	13.6.5	II
ta(beru)	食	12.6.2	II
tada(shii)	正 9.6.1, III	13.6.c	IV
TAI	大 2.6.1, II	13.6.b	III
taka(i)	高	6.6.3	III
take	竹	8.6.8	III
tano(mu)	頼	2.6.1	IV
tano(shii)	楽 4.6.12, IV	6.6.a	IV
TATSU	達	7.6.5	IV
te	手	4.6.10	III
TEKI	的	9.6.5	III
TEN	天	5.6.4	II
TEN	店 9.6.8, III	9.6.d	III
TEN	転	13.6.10	IV
tera	寺	2.6.4	III
TETSU	鉄	8.6.1	III
TO	都	11.6.5	II
to(ru)	取	6.6.6	III
toki	時 2.6.10, II	4.6.a	III
tokoro	所	5.6.6	II
TOKU	特	6.6.5	IV

tomo	友	2.6.8	III
TOO	東	7.6.1	II
TOO	当	8.6.6	III
too	十	1.6.10	II
too	父 9.6.4, III	9.6.e	III
too(i)	遠	11.6.5	IV
tori	鳥	8.6.11	IV
toshi	年 2.6.4, II	12.6.a	II
tsugi	次	3.6.6	IV
tsuka(u)	使	3.6.2	III
tsuku(ru)	作	12.6.5	II
tsuto(meru)	勤	7.6.13	IV
TSUU	通	6.6.12	IV
tsuyo(i)	強 3.6.6, III	12.6.c	IV
(U)			
u(keru)	受	7.6.8	IV
u(ru)	売	9.6.7	III
u(mareru)	生 2.6.3, II	7.6.d	III
ue	上	9.6.4	II
umi	海	8.6.1	IV
UN	運	11.6.1	IV
uta; uta(u)	歌	12.6.7	IV
utsuku(shii)	美	12.6.1	II
(W)			
WA	話 3.6.4, III	6.6.a	III
WA	和	13.6.6	IV
waka(i)	若	4.6.8	III
waru(i)	悪	4.6.9	IV
watakushi	私	8.6.9	II
(Y)			
ya	屋	12.6.9	II

LESSON 15
REVIEW AND APPLICATION

15.1 PATTERNS

15.1.1 Interrogative Noun

a. Interrogative Noun + *ka* "some ～"

何	か	（が）	たりないようです
		（を）	えらんでください
だれ どなた	か	と	いっしょに　さんかします
		に	そうだんすることに　します
		（を）	行かせましょう
いつ	か	の	問題について　また　話し合うんですか
		（は）	日本へ　行けるでしょう
どこ	か	で	ビールでも　飲みませんか
		の	ガラス工場へ　見学に　行ったそうです
		へ	ピクニックに　行こうと　しています
		から	来た　鳥が　教室に　入りました
どっち どちら	か	の	本が　山田教授のです
		（が）	使えないはずです
		に	れんらくしてください
いくつ	か	（の）	例を　あげてごらんなさい
		の	漢字の　説明を　しました
いくら	か		お金が　残ったら、おごってあげよう
何	か		めずらしい　おみやげを　見つけたら、買っておいてください 変な　鳥が　むこうの　方に　いるようですね
だれ どなた	か		はんたいする　人が　いると　困ります できる　人は　読んだり　訳したりしてください

いつ	か	仕事が ひまな 時に 秘書に 調べさせましょう 急に 戦争が 起こるかもしれません
どこ	か	広い 所に 行きたいなあ 小さい 村を おとずれたい
どっち どちら	か	必要な 方を えらんでください いいのに 早く 決めましょう

b. Interrogative Noun + *mo* "(not) any ～"

何		も	食べたり 飲んだりしたくないんです はんたいするわけが ないです
だれ どなた		も	けいさつに 知らせなかったようです 漢字の 辞書の 引き方を 知りません 日本人の 友だちが いません
	に	も	本当の 意味が わからなかったらしいです
いつ		も	つごうが よくない 日ばかりです 日曜日は 勉強しないことに しています
どこ	へ	も	出かける 計画は ありません
			行かないで、へやに 残っていなさい
	に		とまらないで、すぐ 帰って来たんです
			よくなかったろうと 兄に 言われました
どっち どちら	から	も	ほしくないし、必要でもないです
			電話も 手紙も 来ないと 心配です
			むずかしい ことばで、言いにくいです
いくつ		も	覚えていません 持っていません
いくら		も	払えないんです

c. Interrogative Noun + *demo* "any ～"

何		でも	いいから、好きな 物を えらびなさい
			わからない 問題は 質問したほうが いいですよ
だれ		でも	学生なら、クラブ活動に さんかできます
どなた			なれている 人に 説明させましょう
			中級に 入れるわけではありません
	に		教えるわけには いかないんです
いつ		でも	テニスコートが ぬれていない 時に 練習しましょう
			つごうの いい 午後に いらっしゃいませんか
どこ		でも	あなたの 見学したい 所へ 案内します
	へ		行ってみたい 気が します
	に		あると、便利なんですけど
	から		美しい けしきが 見られます
どっち		でも	君が 使っていないのを 貸してくれ
どちら	の		けっこうだと 思います
いくつ			残っている 物を 全部 いただきます
いくら		でも	払ってくれませんか
	の		一万円以下なら 買えます
どんな	の	でも	いいから 見せてください

15.1.2 TAROO form

父が 新しい 計画は もう 決まったろう	
先生が 島田君は はんたいだったろう	
主人が わたしに かばんが 重かったろう	と　言いました
ポール君が ぼくに 貸した 本は おもしろかったろう	聞きました
教授が あの 辺は 火山が 多く、あまり きれい じゃなかったろう	

雨が 降りやんだろう	と　兄が 聞いています
友子さんは がっかりしたろう	母が 心配しています

医者は　病気が　治って　安心したろう	ぼくに　言いました
部長の　家は　駅から　遠かったろう	課長に　聞かれました
弟は　夕べ　おそくまで　起きていたから、 　きょうは　ねむかったろう	と　思います
山本さんは　雨に　降られて　大変だったろう	みんなは　言った

15.1.3　Change of state *-te kuru, -te iku*

だんだん　空が　曇って	
東の　空が　晴れて	
夕方から　雨が　降って	
昔の　ことを　思い出して	
最近　すこし　ふとって	きます
病気で　どんどん　やせて	きました
雨が　降り出して、テニスコートが　ぬれて	
おなかが　すいてくるし、のども　かわいて	
長い　時間　ゴルフを　して、つかれて	
七月に　なると、ずっと　あつくなって	

ことば使いは　時代によって　変わって	
空が　晴れて	
戦争で　人が　おおぜい　死んで	
工業が　どんどん　発達して、生活が　ゆたかに　なって	いきます
かれらは　大きな　仕事を　どんどん　なしとげて	いくでしょう
一つずつ　計画を　決めて	
さくらの　花が　だんだん　ちって	
天気が　よくなったので、ぬれた　道が　かわいて	

15.1.4　TA form of Verb equivalent to *-te iru*

ぬれている	コート	→	ぬれた	コートでは　試合が 　できません
よごれている	車	→	よごれた	車を　運転するのは　いや です

つかれている	時	つかれた	時は すぐ 寝なさい
死んでいる	ねこ	この 死んだ	ねこは だれのですか
困っている	問題	これは とても 困った	問題です
やせている	人	あの やせた	人は おじです
ふとっている	体 →	あんなに ふとった	体では 大変でしょう
こわれている	皿	こわれた	皿は むこうへ 持って 行きなさい
晴れている	空	晴れた	空は 青くて きれいだ
なれている	人	なれた	人に はじめに やって もらいましょう

15.1.5 TE form of motion Verb + *iru*

学校へ 行った	兄は 学校へ 行って	
買い物に 出かけた	姉は 買い物に 出かけて	
急行は もう 出た →	急行は もう 出て	います いました
うちへ 帰った	お姉さんは うちへ 帰って	
事務所へ 来た	お客さんが 事務所へ 来て	

15.1.6 *koto ga aru* "there are times when"

わたしは 主人は お兄さんは 岡田さんは	外国へ 出張する 友だちの 名前を まちがえる ほん訳を 頼まれる 朝ご飯を 食べない 会社へ 行かない	
中級は 助手が 教える 公園の さくらは 三月に さく ここからは 晴れた 日に 山が 見える 一年じゅう 雪が 降らない 時間によって とても 忙しい お金が 全然 ない あの 医者の ことば使いは しつれいな 人によって ダンスが 好きじゃない		ことが あります

15.1.7 Question

伊藤さんは　会社を　やめる

あなたの　お母さんは　がっかりする

橋本さんは　映画を　見ない

きのう　経済学の　試験が　あった

妹さんたちを　公園へ　連れて行かなかった   のではありませんか

あの　人の　意見は　正しい   んじゃないですか

初級の　英語は　おもしろくない   んじゃない?

この　とけいは　スイス製な

君の　兄さんは　会社員な

この　ことばは　英語じゃない

ポール君の　お父さんは　軍人だった

15.1.8 TE form of Verb + *aru*

黒板に　字が　書いて

ビールが　買って

パンクは　なおして   あります

ドアは　開けて   ありません

宿題が　やって   ない（です）

この　小説は　英語に　訳して

ここの　お皿は　洗って

15.1.9 "tell someone to do ～" "tell someone not to do ～"

早く　起きる

皆が　行ける　所を　えらぶ

できるだけ　正しく　訳す

もっと　よく　辞書を　引く

―――――――――――――――――

なるべく　はんたいしない

あまり　がっかりしない

いやな　ことは　思い出さない

大きな　声で　話さない

ように　 言ってください

言われました

話しておきました

頼む

おねがいします

15.1.10 "it is because ~ that ~"

かれに　お金を　貸す		かれが　困っている
この　辺に　住みたい		交通が　便利だ
歌を　歌わない		声が　悪い
働きに　行かれない	のは	体が　弱い	からです
試合が　なくなった		雨が　降った
てるてるぼうずを　下げた		雨が　降りそうだった

15.1.11 Compound Verb

a. "start doing"

強い　風が　ふき	
つめたい　雨が　降り	
北海道は　もう　雪が　降り	出します
子どもたちが　歌を　歌い	出しました
杉山さんが　じょうずな　フランス語で　話し	
花が　もう　ちり	

b. "stop doing"

赤ちゃんが　なき	
雪が　やっと　（降り）	やみます
空が　晴れて、風が（ふき）	やみました

15.1.12 Causal clause "so ~ that ~"

	心配して、	夜　寝られないんです
	働いて、	病気に　なりました
	忙しくて、	昼ご飯を　食べる　時間が　なかったんです
あまり あんまり	へやが　あつくて、	勉強が　できません
	しずかで、	るすだと　思いました
	中が　よごれていたので、	びっくりしました
	練習したので、	つかれました
	試験が　悪かったので、	がっかりしてしまったんです

あまり	暗いので、	何も　見えません
あんまり	びんぼうなので、	お米が　買えないそうです

15.2　OTHERS

15.2.1　*toka* "and/or"

山		湖の　ある　所へ　行きたいです
えびフライ		てんぷらを　おごってもらいました
本		ざっしなら、デパートでも　買えますよ
"へん"	とか	"かまえ"は　見つけにくいですか
仏教		神道について　話してください
地震		台風の　被害が　大きかったんです
政治学		経済学を　学びました

15.2.2　*sae* "even"

初級の　クラスの　学生		この　ことばを　知っていますよ
あいかわらず　忙しくて、新聞		読む　時間が　ないんです
ぼくは　まだ　ひらがな		覚えていないんです
本が　きらいで、小説	さえ	読まないそうです
これなら、高校生に		わかるはずです
両親から		何も　知らせてもらわなかったのです
明治時代に		たくさん　ありました
近くの　公園へ		行ったことが　ないんです

15.3　REVIEW DRILLS

15.3.1　Substitution and Transformation Drill

1. A:　先生に　レポートを　書くように　言われましたか。

　　B:　ええ。でも、もう　レポートは　書いてあります。

　　A:　そうですか。むずかしかったんじゃないですか。

　　B:　ええ、むずかしかったんです。

1. 辞書を　買う、高かった
2. 宿題を　やる、大変だった
3. 漢字を　書く、多かった
4. 窓を　開ける、あつかった
5. 手紙を　訳す、訳しにくかった

2. A: さむくなってきましたね。

   B: そうですね。これから　もっと　さむくなるでしょうか。

   A: これ以上　あまり　さむくならないと　思いますけど。

   B: そうだと　いいんですけどねえ。

     1. あつくなる
     2. 風が　強くなる
     3. 曇る
     4. 台風が　ひどくなる
     5. さむくなる

3. A: どうして　仕事を　やめたんですか。

   B: あんまり　つまらなかったので、やめたんです。

   A: 仕事を　やめたのは　つまらなかったからですか。

   B: ええ、そうなんです。

     1. 運動を　やめる、練習が　きびしい
     2. クラブに　入る、おもしろそうだ
     3. その　計画に　はんたいする、ひどい　計画だ
     4. ドアを　閉める、外が　うるさい

4. A: ロシア語を　習いましたか。

   B: いいえ、習いませんでした。

   A: どうして　習わなかったんですか。

   B: ロシア語を　習わなかったのは　むずかしそうだったからです。

     1. 試合に　出る、かぜを　引く
     2. 教室に　残る、急いでいる
     3. 辞書を　買う、どれが　いいか　わからない
     4. ピクニックに　さんかする、さそわれない

5. A: どこかへ　行きませんか。

   B: いいですね。どこが　いいかしら？

   A: どこでも　いいですけど、日光なんか　いいんじゃないですか。

   B: いいですねえ。

     1. 何か　飲む、ビール
     2. だれか　さそう、みち子さん
     3. いつか　みんなで　集まる、今度の　日曜日
     4. どれか　買う、こういう　形
     5. どこかの　クラブに　さんかする、テニス・クラブ

15.4 REVIEW EXERCISES

15.4.1 ＿＿に ひらがなを 入れなさい。一つの ＿＿に ひらがなが 一つ 入ります。

1. どこ＿＿ ＿＿ 適当(てき)な 場所を えらんでください。

2. あの 医者は おじの 友だちのような 気＿＿ します。

3. 日記に どんな こと＿＿ 書いてありますか。

4. 事務(む)所に だれ＿＿ いないので、困りました。

5. よし子さん＿＿ ダンスパーティー＿＿ ＿＿ 映画(えいが)に さそうつもりです。

6. 何＿＿ おもしろそうな 話題が あったら、話してください。

7. どこを 見学する＿＿ まだ 決まらないんです。

8. 漢字は もちろん まだ 習っていない＿＿、かたかな＿＿ ＿＿ まだなん です。

15.4.2 Select the appropriate word for each of the blanks.

1. （　　　　　　　） むずかしかったので、（　　　　　　　） こたえられなかったん です。
   〈ほとんど、なるべく、とにかく〉

2. （　　　　　　　） 練習したのに、試合(し)が なくなったんです。
   〈とにかく、なるべく、せっかく〉

3. （　　　　　　　） ひらがなだけは 早く 書けるように 覚えてください。
   〈少なくとも、多くとも、しばらく〉

4. かれの 家が （　　　　　　　） りっぱだったので、びっくりしてしまった。
   〈ますます、あまり、さっそく〉

5. むずかしそうですね。でも、（　　　　　　　） やってみましょう。
   〈せっかく、とにかく、多くとも〉

15.4.3 Connect each of the A-group expressions with an appropriate B-group expression and give the English equivalent.

A	B
何も	遠い 所へ 行きたいなあ。
どっちか	おもしろい 話は ないかな。
どこか	漢字を 知っている 人は 教えてあげてください。
だれも	自分の したことを 覚えてないんですか。

何か　　　　　　　　正しい　方を　えらんでください。

だれか　　　　　　　ひまな　時には　まいります。

いつでも　　　　　　教室に　残っている　学生は　いません。

　　　　　　　　　　おいしい　店へ　行こうよ。

15.4.4 次の　ことばを　使って、文を　作りなさい。

1. ～(する)ことが　あります　　　　4. ～てある
2. ～ように（言う）　　　　　　　　5. ～のは　～からだ
3. ～てくる　　　　　　　　　　　　6. ～たあと

15.4.5 Circle the correct one.

1. 日本では　現代(げん)でも　昔のように　かたなを　使うことが $\begin{cases} しますか。 \\ ありますか。 \\ なりますか。 \end{cases}$

2. 歴史を $\begin{cases} 勉強する \\ 勉強した \\ 勉強して \end{cases}$ 後で、どんな　授業を　取るつもりですか。

3. だいぶ　さむくなって $\begin{cases} いきます \\ きました \end{cases}$ が、皆様　お元気ですか。

4. 手紙に　何が　書いて $\begin{cases} いました \\ ありました \\ いきました \end{cases}$ か。

5. ひとりでは $\begin{cases} 行かない \\ 行き \\ 行く \end{cases}$ ように　頼んだんですが。

6. かれが　ふとっている $\begin{cases} の \\ こと \end{cases}$ は　運動を　ほとんど　しない $\begin{cases} ので \\ から \end{cases}$ であろう。

7. $\begin{cases} 何か \\ 何も \\ 何でも \end{cases}$ わからないことが　ありますか。あったら、$\begin{cases} 何か \\ 何も \\ 何でも \end{cases}$ 質問(しつ)してください。

15.4.6 意味を　言いなさい。

1. 空が　曇ってきたから、雨が　降り出すかもしれない。あした　雨だと
　　がっかりだなあ。

2. 新しい　計画を　作るたびに、だれか　はんたいする　人が　いるので、
　　困ります。

3. 子どもが　急に　なき出したので、おどろきましたが、おかしを　やると、すぐ
　　なきやみました。おなかが　すいていたようです。

4. 変だなあ、さっきまで　ここに　あったのに。どこへ　行っちゃったんだろう？

5. みのる君に　おくれないように　言ってくれませんか。もう　急行の　きっぷが
　　買ってあるから、十分以上　待つわけには　いかないって。

6. ぼくは　込んだ　電車じゃ　行く　気が　しないから、やめようかな。

15.4.7 Write the reading for each word and match related words in A and B groups:

A		B	
歩く（　　　）＿＿＿		1. 心配する（　　　）	
終わる（　　　）＿＿＿		2. 起きる（　　　）	
西洋（　　　）＿＿＿		3. 始まる（　　　）	
遠い（　　　）＿＿＿		4. 貸す（　　　）	
安心する（　　　）＿＿＿		5. 大学（　　　）	
明るい（　　　）＿＿＿		6. 昼（　　　）	
寝る（　　　）＿＿＿		7. 製品（　　　）	
形（　　　）＿＿＿		8. 熱（　　　）	
借りる（　　　）＿＿＿		9. 走る（　　　）	
病気（　　　）＿＿＿		10. 弱い（　　　）	
午前（　　　）＿＿＿		11. 暗い（　　　）	
教授（　　　）＿＿＿		12. 色（　　　）	
夜（　　　）＿＿＿		13. 東洋（　　　）	
強い（　　　）＿＿＿		14. 午後（　　　）	
工場（　　　）＿＿＿		15. 近い（　　　）	

15.4.8 日本語で　こたえなさい。

 A. 1. 漢字は　全部で　いくつぐらい　読んだり　書いたりできますか。

   2. 漢字の　読み方を　知りたい　場合、辞書の　引き方を　知っていなければ
    なりません。引き方を　説明してごらんなさい。

   3. この　日本語「四」が　終わったら、何か　ほかの　クラスを　取りたいと
    考えていますか。

   4. 日本語の　むずかしさは　どこに　ありますか。どういう　勉強の　し方が
    いいと　思いますか。

   5. 日本語で　使われる　外来語(foreign loan words)の　うち、英語から
    とり入れられた　ものには　どんなのが　ありますか。知っているのを
    ならべなさい。

   6. 英語の　なかの　外来語の　例（れい）を　あげなさい。

 B. 1. 今週の　日曜日（よう）、何を　しようと　思いますか。

   2. あなたは　祭り（まつ）を　見に　行ったり、寺を　見物したりすることが
    ありますか。今までに　どんな　所へ　行きましたか。

   3. 何か　活動に　さんかしていますか。していたら、その　活動について
    話してください。

15.5 MIKE HARRISON SERIES (6)

——マイク・ハリソン、スポーツを　する——

15.5.1 ——友だちの　佐藤（さとう）に　会う——

佐藤（さとう） 「どう? その　後。」

マイク 「ちょっと　調子（ちょうし）が　悪くて。」

佐藤（さとう） 「仕事が　忙しすぎるんじゃないの? 」

マイク 「そんなことは　ないけど、それより　日本に　来てから　運動不足（ぶそく）らしいん
  ですよ。」

佐藤（さとう） 「それは　いけないなあ。運動を　していた　人が　急に　しなくなると、体に
  よくないよ。何か　スポーツを　始めたら? 」

マイク 「でも、なかなか　機会が　なくて。」

佐藤（さとう） 「前は　何を　やっていたの? 」

マイク 「水泳（えい）、テニス、バスケット、何でも　やってたけど。」

佐藤（さとう） 「そう?　ぼくの　いとこが　入ってる　テニス・クラブが　あるんだけど、

入会金は　安いし、そんなに　込んでないようだよ。テニスでも　やったら　どう？
もし　よかったら　紹介するけど。」
マイク　「一度　会って　話を　聞こうかな。」
佐藤　「それが　いいよ。じゃあ、今晩でも　れんらくするから。」

15.5.2　──きっさ店で、マイク　佐藤たちに　会う──
マイク　「おそくなって　すみません。」
佐藤　「いや。ぼくたちも　今　来たところなんだ。こっち　ぼくの　いとこの
　　　　よし子さん。こちら　マイクさん。」
マイク　「はじめまして。」
よし子　「はじめまして。どうぞ　よろしく。」
佐藤　「まず、何か　注文しよう。マイクは　何？」
マイク　「ぼくは　アメリカン。」
よし子　「あたしは　コーヒーと　スパゲティ・ミートソース。」
佐藤　「すごい　食欲だなあ。」
よし子　「だって、お昼を　食べてないのよ。」
佐藤　「ふとるよ。」
よし子　「いじわるね。」
マイク　「それで、よし子さんは　毎週　プレーしていらっしゃるんですか。」
よし子　「毎週　かならずというわけではないけど、少くとも　月に　三回は　やって
　　　　います。」
マイク　「いいですね。」
よし子　「マイクさんも　テニスを　なさりたいとか。」
マイク　「ええ、日本に　来てから　ほとんど　何も　スポーツを　やってないので、何か
　　　　やらないと　調子が　出なくて。」
よし子　「わたしの　クラブに　入ろうと　思えば、すぐ　入れるはずですけど、一度
　　　　ビジターとして　いらっしゃいませんか。それで、気に　入ったら　入会すれば
　　　　いいんじゃないですか。」
マイク　「そう　できますか。」
よし子　「ええ、どうぞ。あしたの　土曜も　わたし　行きますけど。」
佐藤　「さっそく　行ってみたら？　ぼくも　行こうかな。」
マイク　「いいですね。じゃあ、よし子さん　よろしく。」

15.5.3　——土曜日、テニスの　後——

佐藤　　「ああ、つかれた。」

マイク　「ひさしぶりで　つかれたけど、気持が　いいです。」

よし子　「マイクさん、とても　じょうずだわ。わたしなんか　相手じゃ　つまらない
　　　　　でしょう？　じょうずな　男の人が　いれば　よかったんだけど。」

マイク　「そんなことは　ないですよ。でも、女の人の　方が　多いですね。いつも　こんな
　　　　　ですか。」

よし子　「日によって　ちがいますけど、男の人は　ゴルフを　することが　多いから
　　　　　でしょう。それで、入会は　どう　なさいますか。」

マイク　「入ろうと　思ってますけど。」

よし子　「そうですか。じゃあ、後で　いっしょに　受付へ　行きましょうか。」

マイク　「お願いします。」

よし子　「その　前に、コートが　あいているから、もう　ちょっと　プレーしませんか。」

マイク　「やりましょう。佐藤さんは？」

佐藤　　「ぼくは　もう　だめだ。ここから　見てるよ。」

マイク　「じゃあ。」

15.5.4 New Vocabulary (for passive learning)

1.

その後	sono go	......	after that; since then
運動不足	un'doo-busoku	......	lack or insufficiency of physical exercise
機会	kikai	......	chance; opportunity
水泳	suiei	......	swimming
バスケット	basuketto	......	basketball
いとこ	itoko	......	cousin
入会金	nyuukaikin	......	initiation fee

2.

アメリカン	amerikan	......	American coffee
スパゲティ・ミートソース	supageti miitosoosu	......	spaghetti with meat sauce
食欲	shokuyoku	......	appetite
いじわる	ijiwaru	......	spiteful
プレーする	puree suru	......	play
とか	toka	......	(I heard) ～ and such

ビジター	bijitaa	......	visitor
気に 入る	ki-ni-iru	......	like
入会する	nyuukai suru	......	become a member
3. ひさしぶり	hisashiburi	......	after a long absence
受付	uketsuke	......	information office
あいている	aite iru	......	is not occupied; is vacant

APPENDIX I
ABBREVIATIONS

A	......	Adjective	*karui, nakattari, sabishikattaroo*
Adv.	......	Adverb	*kesshite, shibaraku*
B	......	Base	*yasashi(soo da), ik(eru)*
C	......	Copula	*desu, da, dattari, dattaroo*
D	......	Derivative	
Da	......	adjectival Derivative	*-rashii, -nai, -tai*
Dv	......	verbal Derivative	*-mase, -reru, -rareru, -seru, -saseru*
E	......	Predicate Extender	*(-te) aru, (-te) oru, (-te) kure, (-te) kuru*
I	......	Inflection	*(hik)u, (hido)i*
N	......	Noun	
Na	......	adjectival Noun	*kawaisoo, kan'zen*
Nd	......	dependent Noun	*yoo, wake, tokoro, -dai, -fiito*
Ni	......	interrogative Noun	*dare (demo), nani (ka)*
N	......	ordinary Noun	*jisho, kumo, kaban, onaji*
NM	......	Noun Modifier	*onaji yoo na (kuruma)*
P	......	Predicate	
PC	......	Pre-Copula	*n, no*
PM	......	Predicate Modifier	(Adverb, time Noun, N + R, number)
PN	......	Pre-Noun	*don'na, dooiu*
R	......	Relational	
Rc	......	clause Relational	*to, shi, kara*
Rp	......	phrase Relational	*sae, toka, bakari*
S	......	Sentence	
SI	......	Sentence Interjective	*are, eeto*
SP	......	Sentence Particle	*kana, kashira, naa*
V	......	Verb	*sasou, mieru, dekiru*

APPENDIX II
SENTENCE STRUCTURE
PHRASE STRUCTURE

$$S = SI + PM \left\{ \begin{array}{l} (NM)^{*1} \left\{ \begin{array}{l} PN \\ N + (R)^{*2} \\ Adv.^{*3} \\ P^{*4} \end{array} \right\}^{*5} + N + (R) \\ (Adv.) + Adv. + (R) \\ P^{*6} + (R) \end{array} \right\} //P \left\{ \left\{ \begin{array}{l} V\{ B + I + D\} \\ A\{ B + I + D\} \\ (NM) + N + (R) + C \end{array} \right\} + (R) + (E)^{*7} + (PC)^{*8} + (C)^{*9} \right\} + SP$$

[*1] (NM) = NM optional

[*2] (R) = R optional

[*3] Adv. is only followed by Na such as *kirei*, adverbially used N such as *san'nin*, *kyoo*, or place N such as *ushiro*, *ue*.

[*4] limited to final-clause Predicate such as *iku*, *itta*.

[*5] ( ) = specification or limitation

[*6] limited to TE, KU, TARI, Stem forms. R is obligatory for TARI, Stem forms, but optional for TE, KU forms.

[*7] (E) = E optional

[*8] (PC) = PC optional

[*9] (C) = C optional

APPENDIX III
RELATIONALS

Relational		Lesson	Functions	Example Sentences
bakari	Rp	4	limitation [nothing but; only]	*Hatake bakari miemasu ne.*
demo	Rp	8	suggestion made at random [or something; or somewhere; etc.]	*Koohii demo nomimashoo ka?*
demo	Rp	4	[even]	*Kodomo demo dekimasu.*
demo	Rp	11	after an interrogative word [any ~]	*Nan demo arimasu.*
ka	Rp	11	after an interrogative word [some ~; any ~]	*Doko ka e ikimashoo.*
kara	Rp	4	[through; via]	*Mado kara yoku goran nasai.*
koso	Rp	3	emphatic	*Kon'do koso isshooken'mei yarimasu.*
made	Rc	4	[until]	*Kaeru made wa shin'pai desu.*
mo	Rp	11	after an interrogative word and in negation [(not) any ~]	*Donata ni mo aimasen deshita.*
ni	Rp	3	actor in passive [by]	*Doroboo ni toraremashita.*
ni	Rp	8	person who is made to do	*Musume ni tetsudawaseyoo.*
ni	Rp	8	addition [and; what's more]	*Suupu ni ebi furai o kudasai.*
o	Rp	8	person who is made to do (intransitive Verb)	*Kodomo o ikasetai n desu.*
sae	Rp	13	extreme [even]	*Kaze ga fuite, ame sae furihajimeta.*
shi	Rc	6	addition [in addition; what's more]	*Nodo ga itai shi, netsu mo aru n desu.*
to	Rc	7	[when; if; whenever]	*Haru ni naru to, Nihon de wa yoku kaze ga fukimasu.*
toka	Rp	11	[and; or]	*Tenisu toka pin'pon no yoo na un'doo ga suki desu.*

APPENDIX IV
CONJUGATION TABLE
FORM

This appendix includes all the Verbs, Adjectives, adjectival and verbal Derivatives, adjectival Nouns plus the Copula that have been introduced from Vol. I to Vol. IV. Numbers in this appendix refer to lessons of Vol. IV in which the words first occur. Words without a number are those introduced in Vol. I, II, or III. See Appendix IV of Vol. III for those words.

1. Verb

a. Vowel Verb

ageru		iru		kowareru		nureru	3	taberu	
ageru	11	kaeru		kuraberu		oboeru		tariru	3
akeru		kakeru		kureru		okiru		tateru	
atsumeru	9	kan'gaeru		machigaeru		okureru		toriireru	4
awaseru		kan'jiru	12	makaseru	7	oriru		tsukareru	3
awaseru	12	kariru		mieru	4	oshieru		tsureru	
dekakeru		kazoeru	13	miru		otozureru		tsutomeru	
dekiru		kikoeru	4	miseru		sageru	12	ukeru	4
deru		kimeru	9	mitsukeru	13	sashiageru		umareru	
deru	2	ki-o-tsukeru		mukaeru		shimeru		wasureru	
fueru		kireru		nareru	13	shiraberu		yameru	
hajimeru		kiru		nashitogeru	9	shiraseru		yaseru	12
hareru	12	kotaeru		neru		sugiru		yogoreru	
ireru									

Conjugation

Neutral Form							Plain Form				
Stem Form	Base Form	TE Form	BA Form	TARI Form	TARA Form	Pre-Nai Form	Dictionary Form	TA Form	OO Form	TAROO Form	Imperative Form
age(masu)	age	agete	agereba	agetari	agetara	age(nai)	ageru	ageta	ageyoo	agetaroo	agero
i(masu)	i	ite	ireba	itari	itara	i(nai)	iru	ita	iyoo	itaroo	iro

b. Consonant Verb

Group 1   /r/ group

agaru		hakaru	3	*kudasaru		nokoru		shiru	
agaru	12	hashiru		kumoru	12	noru		suwaru	
aru		*irassharu		magaru		odoru	6	tomaru	
atsumaru	9	iru	2	mairu	8	ogoru	8	toru	
chiru	12	kaeru		mitsukaru		okoru		tsukuru	
furu		kakaru		nakunaru	12	okuru		uru	
futoru	12	kawaru		naoru		oru	2	wakaru	
gan'baru		kimaru	9	naosu	3	*ossharu		yaru	
hairu		ki-ni-naru		naru		owaru			
hajimaru		komaru		*nasaru	2	sagaru	12		

*The Stem forms of these Verbs and *gozaru* are different from those of other Verbs: *r* before *i* is omitted.

Group 2   /w/ group

ajiwau		harau	4	kayou		omou		tetsudau	
arau		iu		morau		osou	4	tsukau	
au		kamau		narau		sasou	11	ukagau	
chigau		kau		niau		suu		utau	6

Group 3   /t/ group

butsu 3	matsu	motsu	tatsu

Group 4   /k/ group

aruku	hiku 3; 13	kawaku 8	odoroku	tsuzuku 4
fuku 12	hiraku 2	kiku	saku	
haku	iku	migaku	suku	
hataraku	itadaku	naku 12	tsuku	
hiku	kaku	ochitsuku	tsuku 6	

Group 5   /s/ group

dasu	kaesu	naosu 3	torikesu
dasu 12	kasu	nobasu	watasu
hanasu 2	kowasu	omoidasu 11	yakusu 13
itasu 2	naosu	sagasu	yogosu

Group 6   /m/ group

komu	nusumu 3	sumu 7	tanoshimu 6	yasumu
nomu	sumu	tanomu	yamu 12	yomu

Group 7   /b/ group

asobu	erabu 11	manabu 13	narabu 13	yobu

Group 8   /g/ group

isogu	nugu	oyogu

Group 9   /n/ group

shinu 2

Conjugation

Neutral Form							
Group	Stem Form	Base Form	TE Form	BA Form	TARI Form	TARA Form	Pre-Nai Form
1	ogori(masu)	ogor	ogotte	ogoreba	ogottari	ogottara	ogora(nai)
2	sasoi(masu)	saso(w)	sasotte	sasoeba	sasottari	sasottara	sasowa(nai)
3	buchi(masu)	but	butte	buteba	buttari	buttara	buta(nai)
4	hiraki(masu)	hirak	hiraite	hirakeba	hiraitari	hiraitara	hiraka(nai)
5	kowashi(masu)	kowas	kowashite	kowaseba	kowashitari	kowashitara	kowasa(nai)
6	tanomi(masu)	tanom	tanon'de	tanomeba	tanon'dari	tanon'dara	tanoma(nai)
7	erabi(masu)	erab	eran'de	erabeba	eran'dari	eran'dara	eraba(nai)
8	isogi(masu)	isog	isoide	isogeba	isoidari	isoidara	isoga(nai)
9	shini(masu)	shin	shin'de	shineba	shin'dari	shin'dara	shina(nai)

Plain Form					
Group	Dictionary Form	TA Form	OO Form	TAROO Form	Imperative Form
1	ogoru	ogotta	ogoroo	ogottaroo	ogore
2	sasou	sasotta	sasoo	sasottaroo	sasoe
3	butsu	butta	butoo	buttaroo	bute
4	hiraku	hiraita	hirakoo	hiraitaroo	hirake
5	kowasu	kowashita	kowasoo	kowashitaroo	kowase
6	tanomu	tanon'da	tanomoo	tanon'daroo	tanome

Plain Form				
Group	Dictionary Form	TA Form	OO Form	TAROO Form	Imperative Form
7	erabu	eran'da	eraboo	eran'daroo	erabe
8	isogu	isoida	isogoo	isoidaroo	isoge
9	shinu	shin'da	shino	shin'daroo	shine

c. Irregular Verb

kuru	gakkari suru	ken'butsu suru	san'po suru	shuuri suru
suru	gochisoo suru	ken'gaku suru 11	san'sei suru 11	soodan suru 9
*aisatsu (o) suru 12	han'tai suru 11	ken'kyuu suru	sen'koo suru	sotsugyoo suru
an'nai suru 8	hattatsu suru 3	ki-ni-suru	setsumei suru	un'ten suru
an'shin suru	hirune suru	kyooryoku suru	shigoto suru	yooi suru 2
arubaito suru	hon'yaku suru 13	meirei suru 2	shin'pai suru 3	yoyaku suru
ben'kyoo suru	hyoogen suru 2	pan'ku suru	shitaku suru	yunyuu suru 7
bikkuri suru 12	kaimono suru	ren'raku suru 7	shitsumon suru	yushutsu suru 7
chuumon suru 8	kan'sha suru	ren'shuu suru	shokuji suru	zan'gyoo suru 3
chuusha suru 3	keikaku suru 11	ryokoo suru	shookai suru	
den'wa suru	keiken suru	ryoori suru	shuppatsu suru 2	
en'ryo suru 8	kekkon suru	san'ka suru 11	shutchoo suru 2	

*O is optional before *suru*. Many Verbs formulated on the basis of a Noun plus *suru* have this option.

Conjugation

Neutral Form							Plain Form				
Stem Form	Base Form	TE Form	BA Form	TARI Form	TARA Form	Pre-Nai Form	Dictionary Form	TA Form	TAROO Form	OO Form	Imperative Form
ki(masu)	k	kite	kureba	kitari	kitara	ko(nai)	kuru	kita	kitaroo	koyoo	koi
shi(masu)	s	shite	sureba	shitari	shitara	shi(nai)	suru	shita	shitaroo	shiyoo	shiro

2. Adjective

abunai 3	hikui	kurushii	ookii	tsumetai
akai	hiroi	kuwashii	oshii 6	tsuyoi 9
akarui	hoshii	mazui	osoi	ureshii
amai	hosonagai	mezurashii 8	sabishii 6	urusai
aoi	ii	mijikai	samui	utsukushii
aoi 12	isogashii	mushiatsui	semai	wakai
atarashii	itai	muzukashii	shiroi	warui
atatakai	karai	nagai	subarashii	yasashii
atsui	karui 6	nai	sugoi	yasui
chairoi	kawaii	natsukashii 6	sukunai	yoi
chiisai	kibishii	nemui	suppai	yoroshii
chikai	kiiroi	nikui	suzushii 13	yowai 9
fukai 4	kitanai	oishii	tadashii 13	
furui	kitsui	okashii	takai	
hayai	kowai 4	omoi 6	tanoshii	
hazukashii	kurai	omoshiroi	tooi	
hidoi 7	kuroi	ooi	tsumaranai	

Conjugation

Plain Form			Neutral Form					
Dictionary Form	TA Form	TAROO Form	TE Form	KU Form	BA Form	TARI Form	TARA Form	Base Form
abunai	abunakatta	abunakattaroo	abunakute	abunaku	abunakereba	abunakattari	abunakattara	abuna

3. Adjectival Derivative

	Plain Form		Neutral Form					
Dictionary Form	TA Form	TAROO Form	TE Form	KU Form	BA Form	TARI Form	TARA Form	Base Form
-nai	-nakatta	-nakattaroo	-nakute	-naku	-nakereba	-nakattari	-nakattara	-na
-rashii*	-rashikatta	-rashikattaroo	-rashikute	-rashiku	-rashikereba	-rashikattari	-rashikattara	-rashi
-tai	-takatta	-takattaroo	-takute	-taku	-takereba	-takattari	-takattara	-ta

*-Rashii in this book was introduced with no conjugation as shown above.

4. Verbal Derivative

	Plain Form				Neutral Form						
Dictionary Form	TA Form	OO Form	TAROO Form	Imperative Form	Stem Form	Base Form	TE Form	BA Form	TARI Form	TARA Form	Pre-Nai Form
-garu	-gatta	(-garoo)*	-gattaroo	(-gare)*	-gari	-gar	-gatte	-gareba	-gattari	-gattara	-gara(nai)
-reru	-reta	-reyoo	-retaroo	-rero	-re	-re	-rete	-rereba	-retari	-retara	-re(nai)
-rareru	-rareta	-rareyoo	-raretaroo	-rarero	-rare	-rare	-rarete	-rarereba	-raretari	-raretara	-rare(nai)
-seru	-seta	-seyoo	-setaroo	-sero	-se	-se	-sete	-sereba	-setari	-setara	-se(nai)
-saseru	-saseta	-saseyoo	-sasetaroo	-sasero	-sase	-sase	-sasete	-sasereba	-sasetari	-sasetara	-sase(nai)

*These forms are not used today.

Normal Form				
Dictionary Form	Stem Form	TA Form	OO Form	Imperative Form
-masu	-mase(n)	-mashita	-mashoo	-mase

5. Copula

Normal Form			Neutral Form					Plain Form			
Dictionary Form	TA Form	OO Form	TE Form	NA* Form	BA Form	TARI Form	TARA Form	Dictionary Form	TA Form	OO Form	TAROO Form
desu	deshita	deshoo	de	na	nara(ba)	dattari	dattara	da	datta	daroo	dattaroo

*Na form is used mainly with adjectival Nouns such as follow:

ben'ri		gen'ki		jiyuu		nigiyaka	suki
bin'boo	13	hen		joozu		nihon'teki	taihen
bun'kateki		heta		kan'tan		raku	taisetsu
daiji	3	hima		kan'zen	3	rekishiteki	teinei
daijoobu		hitsuyoo		kawaisoo	3	rippa	tekitoo
daikirai		hon'kakuteki	9	keizaiteki		sakan	tokui
daisuki		in'shooteki		kin'daiteki	7	samazama	11	tooyooteki
dame		ippan'teki		kirai		shin'pai	yutaka
den'tooteki		iroiro		kirei		shin'setsu	yuumei
fuben		iya		kyuu	2	shitsurei	
fukuzatsu		jama		kyuusoku	7	shizuka	

APPENDIX V
PRESENTATION AND DIALOG
ROMANIZATION AND ENGLISH EQUIVALENT

2.1 —— Iroiro na Hyoogen ——

Nihon'go de wa, hito ni mono o tanomu toki ya meirei suru toki ni, iroiro na hyoogen o tsukau Tatoeba, eigo no "Don't open it" to iu bun wa, "Akenaide kudasai," "Akenaide kure," "Akenaide," "Akeru na" nado to hyoogen suru koto ga dekiru.

—— Various Expressions ——

The Japanese use various expressions when asking someone to do something or when giving an order. For example, the English sentence "Don't open it" can be expressed *Akenaide kudasai, Akenaide kure, Akenaide, Akeru na*, etc.

2.2

Buchoo no Okusan:	Moshi moshi, An'doo no kanai de gozaimasu ga, shujin orimasu ka/
Hisho:	Buchoo no okusama de irasshaimasu ka/Buchoo wa ima Yamada kachoo to ohanashi o nasatte imasu. Shooshoo omachi kudasaimase.

....

Buchoo:	Moshi moshi.
Okusan:	A, anata. Rusu no aida ni, anata kara den'wa ga attatte kiita n desu kedo, nan no yoo desu no/
Buchoo:	Jitsu wa, kyuu ni kyoo kara futsuka made Oosaka e shutchoo shiro to iu meirei ga deta n da. Hon'too wa shachoo ga ikareru hazu datta n da kedo, hoka no kai ni derareru koto ni natta n da yo.
Okusan:	Maa, soo. Sore de, ichido uchi e kaette irassharu no/
Buchoo:	Un, kigae ga iru node kaeru kedo, yukkuri shite iru hima ga nai n da. Dakara, iru mono o kuroi kaban ni irete oite kurenai ka/
Okusan:	Kuroi kaban desu ne/Hitsuyoo na mono yooi shite okimasu. Shuppatsu wa nan'ji desu ka/
Buchoo:	Gogo niji no hikooki na n da kedo, uchi ni wa ichijimae ni tsuku to omou yo.
Okusan:	Wakarimashita.
Buchoo:	Jaa, tanomu yo.

Wife of the Dept. Head:	Hello, this is Mrs. Andō. Is my husband in?
Secretary:	Mrs. Andō? He is now talking with Section Chief Yamada. Would you please wait for a minute?

. . . .

Mr. Andō:	Hello …
Wife:	Hi, honey; I heard that there was a phone call from you while I was out. What do you want with me?
Mr. Andō:	The fact is, I suddenly got an order to take an official trip to Ōsaka today through the second. Originally the president was supposed to go there, but it has been decided that he will attend another meeting.
Wife:	Oh, is that right? Then, are you coming back once (before leaving for Ōsaka)?
Mr. Andō:	Yeah, I'm coming home because I need spare clothes, but I don't have time to stay long. So, will you have the necessary things put in the black bag?
Wife:	The black bag? I will have the necessary things ready. What time are you setting out (for Ōsaka)?
Mr. Andō:	I'm going to take the fourteen-hour flight, and I hope I will be home before one o'clock.
Wife:	All right.
Mr. Andō:	OK, please do so.

3.1 —— Byooki ——

Nihon no igaku ga kanari hattatsu shite iru koto wa yoku shirarete iru Shikashi, byooin, kan'gofu nado no kazu wa mada mada tarinai Mata, byoonin ga an'shin shite byooki o naosu koto ga dekiru shakai hoshoo seido mo kan'zen de wa nai.

—— Disease ——

It is well known that medical science in Japan has been well developed. However, the number of hospitals, nurses, and the like is not yet sufficient. Besides, a social security system under which sick persons may be helped without any anxiety has not been completely established.

3.2 —— Saitoo iin de ——

Kan'gofu:	Tsugi no kata, doozo.
Hirota:	Hai. A, doomo, sen'sei.
Isha:	Yaa, Hirota san. Doo shita n desu ka/
Hirota:	Kesa kara, atama ga itakute, doomo kibun ga yoku nai n desu. Kaze o hiita rashii n desu.
Isha:	Nodo o mimashoo…. Akaku natte imasu ne. Kaze desu ne.
Hirota:	Yappari soo desu ka. Kinoo tsukarete ita noni, kachoo ni tanomarete, yoru osoku made zan'gyoo shita n desu. Sono ue, kaeri ni wa ame ni furarete, sukkari nurete shimatta n desu.
Isha:	Oyaoya. Yuube wa kanari zaazaa furimashita kara ne/(kan'gofu ni) Dewa, Yamaguchi kun, Hirota san no netsu o hakatte.

326

Kan'gofu: Hai.... San'juu shichido nibu desu.

Isha: Aa, soo. Netsu ga hikui kara, shin'pai wa nai desu ne. Chuusha o shite okimashoo. Sore kara, kusuri o agemasu kara, ichinichi ni san'kai non'de kudasai.

Hirota: Doomo arigatoo gozaimashita. Itsumo kanai ni hatarakisugi da to iwarete imasu. Kon'do koso yukkuri neru koto ni shimasu.

Isha: Sore ga ichiban desu ne. Odaiji ni

—— At Dr. Saitō's office ——

Nurse: Next, please.
Hirota: Yes. Hello, Doctor.
Doctor: Oh, Mr. Hirota. What's the matter with you?
Hirota: Since this morning I have had a headache and don't feel well. It seems to me that I have caught a cold.
Doctor: Let me check your throat. ... It's red. You have a cold.
Hirota: That's what I thought. Although I was tired yesterday, I was asked by the section chief to do overtime work till late at night. Besides, it rained on me on my way home and I was all wet.
Doctor: Oh, dear. It rained quite heavily last night, didn't it?
(*To the nurse*) Well, Miss Yamaguchi, take Mr. Hirota's temperature.
Nurse: Yes, sir. ... It's 37.2.
Doctor: Thank you. Since your temperature is low, you need not worry. I'll give you a shot. And I'll give you medicine; please take it three times a day.
Hirota: Thank you very much. My wife always tells me that I am overworking. I'll have a good rest this time for sure.
Doctor: That's the best thing (for you to do). Take care of yourself.

4.1   —— Nihon no Shizen ——

Nihon wa yama ga ookute, ta ya hatake ga sukunai shimaguni de aru. Sekitan ya sekiyu nado shigen mo kesshite yutaka da to wa ienai. Shikamo, kazan ga ookute, jishin ga shibashiba okoru. Natsu kara aki ni kakete wa yoku taifuu ni osowareru.

Nihon'jin no seikaku wa kooiu shizen to fukai kan'kei ga aru ka mo shirenai.

—— Nature in Japan ——

Japan is an island country where mountains are numerous and irrigated and cultivated fields are scarce. We can never say that resources such as coal and petroleum are abundant. Furthermore, there are numerous volcanos, and earthquakes occur frequently. During the summer through the fall Japan is attacked by frequent typhoons.

The character of the Japanese people might have a deep relation with these features of nature.

4.2   —— Kisha no naka de ——

Ogawa: Han'furii san, kotchi no mado kara chotto goran nasai. Dan'dan'batake ga miete, ii keshiki desu yo.

Han'furii:	Aa, kono hen wa zutto mikan no hatake bakari tsuzuite iru n desu ne. Kiiroku natta mikan ga kirei desu nee.
Ogawa:	Shin'bun ni yoru to, haru to natsu no ten'ki ga warukatta node, itsumo no yoo ni takusan toreru ka doo ka wakaranai soo desu yo/
Han'furii:	Soo wa omoemasen kedo nee ...
Ogawa:	Aki ni natte kara, ten'ki ga tsuzuita kara, omotta yori ii ka mo shiremasen ne.
Han'furii:	Tokoro de, moo taifuu wa konai deshoo ne/Kono natsu wa taifuu bakari de, hon'too ni iya ni narimashita.
Ogawa:	Moo daijoobu deshoo. Demo, ichido taifuu ni osowarereba, noogyoo wa ookina higai o ukemasu kara ne. Okome demo mikan demo toriireru made wa shin'pai desu.
Han'furii:	Boku mo kono natsu hajimete taifuu no kowasa o shirimashita.

—— On the train ——

Ogawa:	Look through this side's window for a moment, Mr. Humphrey. You can see terraced fields and it's nice scenery.
Humphrey:	Oh, I see nothing but tangerine fields around here. How beautiful those yellow tangerines are!
Ogawa:	According to the newspaper, it is said that they don't know whether they can have a good harvest as usual or not because of the bad weather during the spring and the summer.
Humphrey:	I hardly think so.
Ogawa:	We may have a better harvest than we think, as the good weather has continued since the fall.
Humphrey:	By the way, typhoons won't be coming any more, will they? We had typhoons one after another this summer, and I was entirely tired of them.
Ogawa:	I hope we are all right now. But once we are attacked by a typhoon, our agriculture will get widespread damage. So we can't be free from anxiety until the harvest is over, regardless of rice or tangerines.
Humphrey:	I experienced the dreadfulness of typhoons for the first time this summer.

6.1 —— Matsuri ——

Nihon'jin no shuukyoo ni wa bukkyoo to shin'too ga aru. Soshite, korera wa nihon'jin no seikatsu to kanari fukai kan'kei o motte ori, ima demo iroiro na gyooji to shite nokotte iru. Toku ni, shin'too no matsuri wa tanoshiku, kodomo no koro no natsukashii omoide no hitotsu de aru.

—— Festivals ——

Buddhism and Shinto are the religions of the Japanese people. And these religions have fairly deep relations with the life of the Japanese, and they remain as various (religious) events even now. Especially the Shinto festival is joyful and it is one of good memories of their childhood.

6.2 —— Michi de ——

Joon'zu: Sakki kara nigiyaka na on'gaku ya koe ga kikoeru shi, hito ga oozei ittari kitari shite iru shi, nani ga aru no kashira.

Shimada: Omatsuri desu yo. Isoganai kara, chotto itte mimashoo ka.

Joon'zu: Omatsuri desu ka. Omoshirosoo desu ne.... A, are wa/

Shimada: Omikoshi desu. Kotchi e kisoo da kara, kono hen de mattemashoo.... A, kita, kita.

Joon'zu: Kazari ga ippai tsuite ite, omosoo desu ne. Omosa wa dono kurai aru no kashira.

Shimada: Yoku shiranai kedo, sen'kiro gurai kana/

Joon'zu: Min'na onaji kimono o kiteru n desu ne.

Shimada: Aa, happi desu ne/Saikin wa soroi no happi o kitari, rippa na omikoshi o tsukuttari shite, zuibun sakan ni narimashita ne.

Joon'zu: Mae wa chigatta n desu ka/

Shimada: Ee, kootsuu no jama ni naru to itte, omikoshi mo nai shi, sabishii omatsuri o shita toki mo atta n desu yo.

—— On the street ——

Miss Jones: I have been able to hear cheerful music and voices for some time; what's more, many people are coming and going; I wonder what's happening?

Mr. Shimada: It is a festival. Shall we go and see it as we are not in a hurry?

Miss Jones: Festival! Sounds interesting.... Oh, what's that over there?

Mr. Shimada: That is an *omikoshi*. It seems to be coming this way, so let's wait for it around here.... Oh, here it comes.

Miss Jones: There are a lot of decorations attached to it, and it looks heavy. I wonder how much it will weigh?

Mr. Shimada: I don't really know, but I presume it weighs about one thousand kilograms.

Miss Jones: Everybody wears the same kind of *kimono*, doesn't he?

Mr. Shimada: Oh, yes, a "happy" coat. Recently people wear the uniform "happy" coat, and make a fine *omikoshi*; festivals have become very vigorous.

Miss Jones: Was it different before?

Mr. Shimada: Yes, there was the age when we had desolate festivals without *omikoshi* being carried in the streets, it being said that they interfered with traffic.

7.1 —— Nihon no Koogyoo ——

Nihon de wa kin'daiteki na koogyoo wa Meiji jidai ni natte hattatsu shihajimeta. Meiji no owari goro kara, suudo no sen'soo ni yotte sara ni hattatsu shita ga, dainiji sekai taisen de Nihon no koogyoo wa hidoi son'gai o uketa. Shikashi, sen'soo ga sumu to, kyuusoku ni hattatsu shi, sen'zen ijoo no koogyookoku ni natta.

—— Manufacturing Industry in Japan ——

Modern manufacturing industry in Japan began its development during the Meiji era. From late in the Meiji era, Japanese industry further developed as a result of several wars, but it received serious damage from World War II. After the war ended, however, industry began to develop rapidly and Japan became a more industrialized nation than it was before the war.

7.2 —— Den'sha no naka de ——

Moogan: Komimasu ne.

Nomura: Choodo shigoto ga owatte, kooin'tachi ga kaeru tokoro deshoo.

Moogan: Kono hen made kuru to, hoton'do koojoo bakari desu ne/

Nomura: Ee, kono hen wa Nihon no koogyoo no chuushin no hitotsu desu kara.

Moogan: Koogyoo to ieba, Nihon ni wa ii den'ki seihin ga ooi desu ne. Jitsu wa, yasukute ii rajikase ga attara, nidai kaoo to omotte iru n desu. Kuni no otooto mo hoshigatte iru shi.

Nomura: Soo da! Tomodachi ga den'ki seihin no kaisha ni tsutomete imasu. Yokattara, yasuku kaeru ka doo ka kiite agemashoo.

Moogan: Onegai shimasu. Boku no kuni mo Nihon kara rajikase ya bideo nan'ka yunyuu shite iru kedo, mukoo de kau to takai n desu yo.

Nomura: Soo desu ka. Jaa, kyoo kaettara sassoku den'wa de ren'raku shite mimasu yo. Ikura gurai dattara ii n desu ka/

Moogan: Nedan wa Nomura san ni makasemasu. Nomura san ga yasui to omottara, sore de ii desu.

—— In the train ——

Mr. Morgan: It's getting crowded, isn't it?

Mr. Nomura: I presume that factory workers are on their way home after just having finished their work.

Mr. Morgan: Coming to this area, we see almost nothing but factories, don't we?

Mr. Nomura: Yes, that is because this area is one of the industrial centers of Japan.

Mr. Morgan: Speaking of industry, there are a lot of good electric goods in Japan. The fact is, I am thinking of buying two radio casette tape recorders if there are good and inexpensive ones. My younger brother at home also wants to have one.

Mr. Nomura: Oh, yes! One of my friends is working for an electric goods company. I'll ask him if he can buy them for you at a low price or not, if you want (me to do it).

Mr. Morgan: Yes, I do. My country is also importing radio casette tape recorders and video tape recorders and the like from Japan, but they are expensive if we buy them there, you know.

Mr. Nomura: Really? Well, I'll try to contact him on the phone immediately after going home today. How much would be good for you?

Mr. Morgan: I'll leave the price to you, Mr. Nomura. If you think it reasonable, that'll be fine with me.

8.1   —— Nihon'jin no Shokuseikatsu ——

Umi no san'butsu no yutaka na Nihon de wa, mukashi kara sakana ya kai o omo ni tabe, Meiji ni natte, yatto gyuuniku ya butaniku ga nihon'jin no shokuseikatsu ni toriirerareta.

Mukashi ni kuraberu to, nihon'jin no shokuseikatsu wa zuibun kawari, shurui ga fueta. Gen'dai no Nihon hodo iroiro na ryoori ga taberareru kuni wa mezurashii ni chigai nai.

—— Eating Habits of the Japanese People ——

In Japan where sea products are abundant, people have been eating mainly fish and shellfish since the old times, and finally in the Meiji era beef and pork were introduced into the Japanese people's dietary life.

In comparison with the old times, the Japanese people's eating habits have been changing a great deal, and the kinds of food have increased. Countries like modern Japan where various kinds of food can be eaten must be rare.

8.2

Ishida:	Onaka ga sukimashita ne. Shokuji demo shimashoo ka.
Yamazaki:	Ii desu ne. Doko ni hairimasu ka/
Ishida:	Ii tokoro ni an'nai shimasu yo. Kyoo wa boku ga gochisoo shimasu.
Yamazaki:	Iya, sore wa ikemasen. Warikan ni shimashoo.
Ishida:	Maa, soo iwanaide, kyoo wa boku ni ogorasete kudasai.
Yamazaki:	Soo desu ka/ Jaa, en'ryo shinaide, gochisoo ni narimasu.

. . . .

Kyuuji:	Irasshaimase. Ima sugu menyuu o omochi shimasu.... Omatase shimashita. Nan ni nasaimasu ka/
Ishida:	Yamazaki san, suki na mono o chuumon shite kudasai. Bifuteki demo doo desu ka/ Koko no bifuteki wa hyooban ga ii n desu yo/
Yamazaki:	Bifuteki da to chotto oosugiru node, ebi furai ni suupu o itadakimasu. Sore to pan ni shimasu.
Ishida:	Boku wa bifuteki Isogasete warui kedo, hayaku shite kuremasen ka/
Kyuuji:	Hai, narubeku hayaku itashimasu. Raisu to pan to, dochira o omochi shimashoo ka.
Ishida:	Pan to raisu o hitotsu zutsu.
Kyuuji:	Kashikomarimashita.

. . . .

Yamazaki:	Ishida san, shio totte kudasai.
Ishida:	Are, nai desu ne. Kyuuji ni motte kosasemashoo. (Kyuuji ni) Shio ga nai n da kedo...
Kyuuji:	Doomo mooshiwake gozaimasen. Sugu motte mairimasu.

Mr. Ishida:	I'm hungry, how about you? Shall we have dinner or something?
Mr. Yamazaki:	All right. Where shall we go in?
Mr. Ishida:	I'll take you to a good place. I'll treat you today.
Mr. Yamazaki:	Oh no, please don't do that. Let's go dutch.
Mr. Ishida:	No, no, don't say that. Please let me treat you today.
Mr. Yamazaki:	All right. Then, I'll accept your treat with pleasure.

. . . .

Waiter:	Welcome, sirs. I'll bring a menu to you right away, sir. ... I'm sorry to have kept you waiting. What would you like to have?
Mr. Ishida:	Mr. Yamazaki, please order anything you like. How about beefsteak or something like that? This restaurant's beefsteak is very popular.
Mr. Yamazaki:	Beefsteak is a little heavy for me. I'll have fried prawns and soup. And I'll have bread.
Mr. Ishida:	A beefsteak for me, please. Sorry for making you rush, but please prepare them quickly.
Waiter:	Yes, we'll do it as soon as possible. Which shall I bring you, rice or bread?
Mr. Ishida:	One each of bread and rice, please.
Waiter:	Yes, sir.

. . . .

Mr. Yamazaki:	Mr. Ishida, please pass me the salt.
Mr. Ishida:	Oh, there is no salt! I'll have the waiter bring it here. (*To the waiter*) We don't have any salt ...
Waiter:	I'm very sorry. I'll bring it for you in a moment.

9.1 —— Nihon no Rekishi ——

Sekai no hoka no kuniguni to onaji yoo ni, Nihon no rekishi mo gaikoku kara tsuyoi eikyoo o uketa. Mazu, Edo jidai made wa Chuugoku no eikyoo ga ookikatta.

Seiyoo to no kootsuu wa juurokuseiki ni hajimatta ga, hon'kakuteki ni natta no wa Meiji jidai de aru. Sono go, wazuka hyakunen amari no aida ni, Nihon wa kin'daika o nashitogeta ga, sono hayasa wa sekai ni mo rei ga nai to iwarete iru

—— History of Japan ——

The history of Japan has been strongly influenced by foreign countries, as the histories of other countries in the world have been. First of all, China was a great influence until the Edo era.

Communication with Western countries started in the sixteenth century, but it took on a real shape in the Meiji era. Since then, in a period of barely over a hundred years, Japan has achieved modernization. It is said that its speed of modernization is unprecedented in the world.

9.2

Shizuko:	Tanikawa sen'sei no rekishi no jugyoo, aikawarazu omoshiroi wa ne.
Jon:	Boku mo sen'sei no koogi o kiku tabi ni, masumasu rekishi ga suki ni naru n desu.
Shizuko:	Jon san wa rekishi o sen'koo suru tsumori/
Jon:	Mada kimeta wake de wa nai desu. Sen'sei ni soodan shite kara, kimeyoo to omotte.

Shizuko: Kon'do no rekishi no repooto, dooiu koto ni tsuite kaku ka kimeta no/

Jon: Meiji igo no Nihon ni tsuite kakoo to omotte iru n desu. Nihon no yoo ni, furui bun'ka ga nokotte ite, kin'dai san'gyoo no hattatsu shite iru kuni ni kyoomi ga aru node.

Shizuko: Shiryoo wa aru no/ Kaku yori shiryoo o atsumeru hoo ga taihen deshoo/

Jon: Hoton'do toshokan ni aru yoo desu. Sore de, nai no dake Tanikawa sen'sei kara kariyoo to omotte iru n desu kedo.

Shizuko: Sen'sei, kashite kudasaru kashira.

Jon: Nagai aida kariru wake ni wa ikanai daroo kedo, shigonichi nara kashite moraeru to omoimasu.

Shizuko: Soo ne. Tanikawa sen'sei, ima rooka ni irassharu yoo da kara, tanon'de mitara/

Shizuko: Professor Tanikawa's history class is interesting as usual, isn't it?
John: Every time I attend his lecture, I'm more and more interested in Japanese history.
Shizuko: John, are you going to major in history?
John: It's not that I have decided to major in it yet. I'm planning to decide after consulting with the professor.
Shizuko: Did you decide what subject you are writing on for the history paper this time?
John: I'm thinking of writing about Japan after Meiji. I'm interested in a country like Japan, where an old culture still exists and yet modern industry has developed.
Shizuko: Do you have the materials? Isn't it harder to gather materials than to write a paper?
John: Almost all the materials I need seem to be in the library. So, I am thinking of borrowing from Professor Tanikawa only those which are not in the library.
Shizuko: I wonder if he will lend them to you.
John: I don't think I'll be able to borrow them for a long period, but I guess I can if it is for four or five days.
Shizuko: Yeah. Why don't you ask Professor Tanikawa right now since he is in the hall?

11.1 —— Gakusei Seikatsu ——

Nihon no gakusei wa yoku kurasu, zemi, kurabu no nakama de ryokoo shitari, kon'pa o hiraitari, un'doo o shitari suru.

Gakusei seikatsu no naka de, mottomo tanoshiku, sotsugyoo shita ato mo omoidasareru no wa, kooiu samazama na gyooji ya kurabu katsudoo, tomodachi to no koosai nado de aroo.

—— Student Life ——

Japanese students often do things like traveling, holding parties, playing sports, and so forth among friends in their class, seminar, and club.

Through one's student life the things that are the most pleasant and that are recalled even after one's graduation would be these various kinds of events, club activities, associations with friends, and the like.

11.2 —— Ninen'sei no kurasu de ——

Gakusei (1): Minasan, kaeranaide, shibaraku kyooshitsu ni nokotte ite kudasai. Kokuban ni kaite aru yoo ni, tsugi no doyoobi ni kurasu de doko ka e pikunikku ni ikoo to iu keikaku ga aru n desu ga, doo deshoo ka.

Gakusei (2): Min'na de mada doko e mo itta koto ga nai kara, ii to omoimasu.

Gakusei (3): Doko ka amari tooku nai tokoro e iku no nara, san'sei desu.

Gakusei (2): Boku mo. Dare demo san'ka dekiru yoo na, chikakute ben'ri na tokoro nara, doko demo ii n ja nai desu ka/

Gakusei (3): Dekitara, mizuumi toka kawa toka kaigan o eran'dara ii to omou kedo. Min'na de oyoidari, geemu o shite ason'dari, uta o utattari dekite omoshiroi n ja nai kashira.

Gakusei (2): San'sei Hayashi sen'sei mo sasottara doo desu ka/

Gakusei (3): Ii to omoimasu.

Gakusei (1): Dare ka hoka no iken no hito wa te o agete kudasai. Dare mo han'tai suru hito wa imasen ne/Dewa, daitai kimarimashita ne/

Gakusei (2): Kyoo kite inai hito ga imasu kedo.

Gakusei (1): Mada iku basho toka atsumaru jikan ga kimete nai node, ashita moo ichido hanashiaitai to omoimasu.

Gakusei (2): Jaa, kitenai Satoo san'tachi ni wa boku kara ren'raku shite okimasu.

—— In the sophomore class ——

Student (1): Everyone, please don't go home; stay in the classroom for a while. As is written on the blackboard, there is a plan for our class' going on a picnic somewhere next Saturday. What do you think?

Student (2): We haven't been anywhere all together, so I think it is a good idea.

Student (3): I agree, if we go to some place that is not so far from here.

Student (2): Me too. Don't you think that any place would be all right if the place is near here and convenient so that anyone can participate?

Student (3): If possible, it will be nice to choose a lake or a river or a beach or something like that. Wouldn't you think that it's fun to go there because we all can do things like swimming, playing games, singing songs together?

Student (2): I agree. How about inviting Professor Hayashi too?

Student (3): I think that's nice.

Student (1): If there is anyone who has a different opinion, please raise a hand. There is nobody who objects to this, is there? Well, then, this matter has been almost decided, hasn't it?

Student (2): There are some who are not here today.

Student (1): Since the place to go and the time to meet haven't been settled yet, we would like to talk about these matters once more tomorrow.

Student (2): Then, I'll inform Mr. Satō and others who are not here of this plan.

12.1 —— Nihon'jin to Kikoo ——

Nihon'jin ni yotte kakareta shoosetsu, zuihitsu, tegami, nikki nado ni wa, taitei shiki no hen'ka ya ten'ki no koto ga kaite ari, haiku ni wa kisetsu no kotoba ga nakereba naranai. Mata, kao o awaseru to, "Yoku furimasu ne" toka "Atsuku natta ne" toka aisatsu suru.

Kono yoo ni, kikoo no hen'ka ya ten'ki no koto o itsumo wadai ni suru no wa nihon'jin ga shizen no hen'ka o kan'jiyasui kara de aroo.

—— The Japanese and the Climate ——

In most of the novels, essays, letters, diaries, and the like written by Japanese people, the change of four seasons and weather are referred to and there must be a season word in *haiku*. Also, when they see each other, they greet saying something like "It is raining a lot, isn't it?" or "It's gotten hot, hasn't it?"

Thus, the reason why the Japanese always talk about the change of climate and the weather is that they are sensitive to the change of nature.

12.2

Toda: Sakki made sora ga akarukatta noni, kumotte kita yoo ne.

Shimizu: Hon'too da. Kaze mo dan'dan tsuyoku natte kita shi, ame ga furidashisoo da ne. Ashita ame ni furareru to, komaru n da kedo naa.

Toda: Dooshite son'na ni komatta kao o shite iru no/Nani ka aru no/ashita

Shimizu: Un, ashita wa taisetsu na tenisu no shiai na n da. Ame de shiai ga nakunattara gakkari da naa. Sekkaku chooshi ga agatte kita noni ...

Toda: "Teru-teru-boozu" o sagete, "teru-teru-boozu" no uta demo utattara doo/

Shimizu: Joodan ja nai yo. Demo, soo demo shitai ki ga suru kedo ...

Toda: Ten'ki yohoo ja furutte iwanakatta kara, ashita ni nareba harete kuru n ja nai kashira.

Shimizu: Soo nara ii kedo. Nureta kooto ja yarinikui kara, tonikaku futte hoshiku nai naa.

Miss Toda: The sky was light a while ago, but it looks like it's getting cloudy.

Mr. Shimizu: That's right. The wind has gradually become violent, and it looks like it's starting to rain. I don't know what to do if it should rain tomorrow.

Miss Toda: Why do you have such a troubled look? Do you have anything to do tomorrow?

Mr. Shimizu: Yeah, I have an important tennis game tomorrow. It would be disappointing should the game be canceled because of rain! After all, I am now in better condition,

Miss Toda: Why don't you hang a *teru-teru-bōzu* doll and sing the song of *teru-teru-bōzu*?

Mr. Shimizu: No joking! But I feel like doing something like that.

Miss Toda: The (radio) weather forecaster didn't say it would rain, so it'll become fair tomorrow, I hope.

Mr. Shimizu: I hope so. It's hard to play on a wet tennis court, so I hope it won't rain anyway.

13.1 —— Jisho no Hikikata ——

Nihon'go o manabu baai, shokyuu de wa jisho wa toku ni hitsuyoo nai. Shikashi, chuukyuu ya jookyuu ni naru to, kan'ji no jisho to kotoba no jisho to sukunaku tomo nishurui no jisho ga hitsuyoo ni natte kuru. Hon'yaku no tame ni wa, eiwa ya waei no jisho sae hoshiku naru.

Kan'ji no jisho o hiku toki, "hen" toka "kan'muri" toka "kamae" nado no bushu ga wakareba, ato wa wariai kan'tan de aru. Kono bushu ga hayaku mitsukerareru koto to, jikaku ga tadashiku kazoerareru koto ga mottomo taisetsu na koto de aru.

—— How to Use Dictionaries ——

In the case of studying the Japanese language, dictionaries are not particularly necessary in elementary classes. However, when it comes to intermediate and advanced classes, at least two kinds of dictionaries, a *kan'ji* dictionary and a vocabulary dictionary, become a necessity. For translation one would like to have the English-Japanese and the Japanese-English dictionaries.

It is comparatively simple to look up Chinese characters in a *kan'ji* dictionary, once classifiers such as *hen, kan'muri, kamae,* and the like are found. To be able to find these classifiers quickly and to be able to count the number of strokes correctly are the most important things.

13.2

Gakusei: Sen'sei, mae sen'sei wa kan'ji no jisho o kau yoo ni osshaimashita ne/

Sen'sei: Ee. Katta n desu ka/

Gakusei: Hai. Demo, amari setsumei ga fukuzatsu de, tsukaikata ga zen'zen wakaranai n desu. Oshiete itadakemasu ka/

Sen'sei: Jisho no tsukaikata wa mada ren'shuu shite nakatta desu ne. Oshiete agemashoo.

Gakusei: Tatoeba, kono ji na n desu kedo …

Sen'sei: Aa, jiten'sha no ten desu ne. Kore wa hidarigawa no kuruma ga "hen" desu. Kuruma wa nanakaku desu kara, bushu no hyoo no nanakaku no tokoro de kuruma o mitsukeru n desu.

Gakusei: A, arimashita.

Sen'sei: Atta deshoo/Soko ni peejisuu ga kaite arimasu kara, sono peeji o hiraku to, kurumahen no ji ga zen'bu naran'de imasu. Ten to iu ji no, "hen" o totta nokori no bubun wa yon'kaku desu kara, yon'kaku no tokoro o sagaseba, ten ga mitsukarimasu. Kore de daitai wakattaroo to omoimasu ga.

Gakusei: Nareru made taihen desu ne.

Sen'sei: Soo, kihon ni naru katachi, tsumari bushu o shiranai to, nani kara hajimetara ii no ka wakaranai koto ga arimasu kara, kore o takusan oboete oita hoo ga ii desu ne. Jaa, kon'do wa sake to iu ji o hitori de hiite goran nasai.

Gakusei: Hai, yatte mimasu.

Student: Sir, you told us to buy a *kan'ji* dictionary before, didn't you?

Teacher: Yes. Did you buy one?

Student: Yes. But the explanation (of how to use it) is so complicated that I don't know how to use it at all. Would you show me (how to use it)?

Teacher: You haven't practiced how to use a (*kan'ji*) dictionary yet, have you? I'll show you.

Student: For example, (I'd like to look up) this character ...

Teacher: Oh, it's *ten* as in *jiten'sha*. The left side of this character, *kuruma*, is *hen*. *Kuruma* has seven strokes, so you try to find *kuruma* from among the seven-stroke characters in the classifier list.

Student: Oh, I've found it.

Teacher: You found it, didn't you? The page number is written there. If you open the dictionary to that page, there are all the characters with the *kurumahen* classifier listed. The rest of the character *ten*, after taking away the *kurumahen*, consists of four strokes; if you look for *ten* in the four-stroke section, you can find it. I suppose you've gotten a rough idea with this (explanation).

Student: It seems a nuisance until I get accustomed to it.

Teacher: Uh huh, if you are not familiar with the basic forms, that is, classifiers, you sometimes don't know what you should start with. So you'd better memorize the classifiers, as many as possible. Now, this time look up the character *sake* by yourself.

Student: Yes, I'll try.

14.1 —— Kan'ji no Hanashi ——

Nihon bun'ka no rekishi wa, sono mama nihon'go no rekishi de mo aru. Sen suuhyakunen ijoo mo mae ni Chuugoku bun'ka ga Nihon ni shookai sareta ga, sono toki, Chuugoku no moji—kan'ji—ga toriirerare, kono kan'ji kara katakana ya hiragana ga umareta Soshite, wago ni kan'go ga kuwawari, hyoogen mo zutto yutaka ni natta.

Kono hoka, juurokuseiki no naka goro kara Porutogaru ya Oran'da no fune ga Nihon e kihajimeru to, samazama na gaikokuhin ga yunyuu sareta Sore to dooji ni, yooroppago no tan'go ga nihon'gofuu ni hatsuon sare, nihon'go no ichibu to shite tsukawaredashita. Tatoeba, "garasu" (oran'dago), "pan" (porutogarugo), "suupu" (eigo) nado takusan aru. Kono yoo na tan'go ga gairaigo to yobareru mono de aru.

Kan'ji no muzukashisa wa, hitotsu no kan'ji ni futsuu nishurui no yomi—on to kun—ga ari, sara ni, futatsu ijoo no on ya kun o motsu mono mo aru koto de aru. Tatoeba, 人 no on wa "jin" to "nin" de ari, kun yomi wa "hito" de aru. Kono yoo ni, kan'ji o ooku shiru to dooji ni, hitotsu no kan'ji no yomi o ooku shitte iru koto mo taisetsu de aru.

—— The Story of *Kan'ji* ——

The history of Japanese culture is also the history of the Japanese language as it is. More than one thousand and several hundred years ago Chinese culture was introduced into Japan. At that time Chinese characters—*kan'ji*—were adopted, and *katakana* and *hiragana*, based upon these *kan'ji*, were produced. And Chinese words have been added to the original Japanese words; thus Japanese expressions have become much more rich.

Besides this, when Portuguese and Dutch ships began visiting Japan in the middle of the sixteenth century, various foreign goods were imported. At the same time, vocabulary items of European languages were pronounced in Japanese style and came to be used as part of the Japanese language. For instance, there are many words such as *garasu* (Dutch), *pan* (Portuguese), *sūpu* (English). Vocabulary items like these were called *gairaigo* [words of foreign origin].

The difficulties of *kan'ji* exist in that there are normally two kinds of readings—*on* and *kun*—for a *kan'ji*, and furthermore there are even some *kan'ji* that have more than two *on* or *kun* readings. For example, the *on* readings of 人 are *jin* and *nin*, and its *kun* reading is *hito*. This being so, it is important for us to know as many readings as possible of a *kan'ji*, as well as knowing many *kan'ji*.

14.2   (1)

Hashimoto: Anatatachi no gakubu de wa, ichininen no toki ni dooiu kamoku ga toreru n desu ka/

Okada: Seijigaku, keizaigaku, shakaigaku, rekishi, bun'gaku, bijutsu, kyooikugaku, shin'ri-gaku, chiri, suugaku, tetsugaku, gen'gogaku, sore kara, sen'mon kamoku desu.

Hashimoto: Nihon'goka ni wa sen'sei ga nan'nin irassharu n desu ka/

Okada: Kyooju ga futari, jokyooju ga san'nin, kooshi ga gonin, joshu ga suunin imasu.

(2)

Otooto: Oneesan, okaasan ga yon'deru yo

Ane: Okaasan, naani/

Haha: Otooto ya imoototachi o gogo eiga ni demo tsuretette kurenai kashira. Chotto daiji na kai o uchi de hiraku n da kedo, jama suru to warui kara.

Ane: Ii wa. Kooen e tsuretette, kooen no naka o aruitari hashittari shite asobaseru kara.

Haha: Jaa, inu mo tsuretettara/

Ane: Soo suru wa.

(3)

Sugiyama: Anata no oneesan wa nani o shite irassharu n desu ka/

Sumisu: Ane wa on'gakka desu.

Sugiyama: Jaa, anata mo gaka da shi, anata no kazoku wa geijutsuka bakari na n desu ne.

Sumisu: Soo de mo arimasen yo. Chichi wa seijika desu shi, ani wa gun'jin desu kara.

(1)

Mr. Hashimoto:	What courses can you take when you are a freshman or a sophomore in your school (of arts)?
Mr. Okada:	We can take politics, economics, sociology, history, literature, fine arts, education, psychology, geography, mathematics, philosophy, linguistics, and our major courses.
Mr. Hashimoto:	How many teachers are there in the faculty of the Japanese department?
Mr. Okada:	There are two professors, three assistant professors, five lecturers, and several assistants.

(2)

Younger brother:	Sister, mother is calling you.
Older sister:	What is it, Mother?
Mother:	I wonder if you could take your younger brother(s) and sister(s) out to a movie or something this afternoon. I am having a party at home …
Older sister:	OK, Mother. I'll take them to the park and let them play in the park, walking and running.
Mother:	Then how about taking the dog with you?
Older sister:	OK. I'll do that.

(3)

Sugiyama:	What is your older sister doing?
Smith:	My older sister is a musician.
Sugiyama:	And you are a painter, so your family are all artists, aren't they?
Smith:	Not really. My father is a politician and my older brother is in the military.

APPENDIX VI
GLOSSARY

(A)

aaiu	ああいう	PN	9	that kind of ～ (see 9.4.12)
abunai	あぶない	A	3	is dangerous
agaru	上がる	V	12	go up; rise
ageru	上げる	V	11	raise; hold up
aikawarazu	あいかわらず	Adv.	9	as usual
aisatsu	あいさつ	N	12	greeting
aisatsu suru	あいさつする	V	12	greet
-amari	あまり	Nd	9	a little more than ～ (see 9.4.4)
amari	あまり	Adv.	13	so ... that (see 13.4.6)
An'doo	安藤	N	2	family name
an'mari	あんまり	Adv.	13	so ... that (see 13.4.6)
an'nai	案内	N	8	guide
an'nai suru	案内する	V	8	take someone to a place; guide
aoi	青い	A	12	is pale
are	あれ	SI	8	oh?
arera	あれら	N	6	those things
aru	ある	E	11	after the TE form of a Verb (see 11.4.5)
ato	後	N	11	afterward; later; after (see 11.4.2)
atsumaru	集まる	V	9	get together; be collected (intransitive Verb)
atsumeru	集める	V	9	gather; collect (transitive Verb)
awaseru	合わせる	V	12	bring together (*kao o awaseru* means "see each other")

(B)

baai	場合	N	13	case; occasion
bakari	ばかり	R	4	only; just; nothing but (see 4.4.8)
bideo	ビデオ	N	7	video tape recorder
bikkuri suru	びっくりする	V	12	get surprised (colloquial equivalent for *odoroku*)

bin'boo	びんぼう	Na	13	poor; poverty
booeki	貿易	N	7	foreign trade
-bu	分	Nd	3	counter for one-tenth of a degree (see 3.4.9)
bubun	部分	N	13	part; portion
bukkyoo	仏教	N	6	Buddhism
bun	文	N	2	sentence
bushu	部首	N	13	classifier
butaniku	ぶた肉	N	8	pork
butsu	ぶつ	V	3	beat
byoonin	病人	N	3	sick person; a patient

(C)

(ni) chigai nai	（に）ちがいない	V + E	8	must (be) (see 8.4.3)
chiru	ちる	V	12	fall; scatter (intransitive Verb)
chooshi	調子	N	12	condition
chuukyuu	中級	N	13	intermediate level
chuumon	注文	N	8	order
chuumon suru	注文する	V	8	order
chuusha	注射	N	3	shot; injection
chuusha suru	注射する	V	3	give a shot
chuushin	中心	N	7	center; core

(D)

-dai	台	Nd	7	counter for TV sets, automobiles, machines, pianos, etc. (see 7.4.7)
daiji	大事	Na	3	important; valuable
dainiji sekai taisen	第二次世界大戦	N	7	the Second World War
dan'dan'batake	だんだん畑	N	4	terraced fields
dan'su	ダンス	N	11	dance
dare demo	だれでも	Ni + R	11	anybody (see 11.4.8)
dare ka	だれか	Ni + R	11	someone (see 11.4.6)
dare mo	だれも	Ni + R	11	(not) anyone (see 11.4.7)
dasu	出す	V	12	start (doing); begin (doing) (compound component) (see 12.4.6)

dattara	だったら	C	7	if it were such and such (TARA form of *da*) (see 7.4.6)
dattari	だったり	C	6	TARI form of *da* (see 6.4.6)
dattaroo	だったろう	C	13	TAROO form of Copula *da* (see 13.4.9)
de aroo	であろう	C + E	11	OO form of *de aru* (see 11.4.3)
deeto	デート	N	11	date
de gozaimasu	でございます	C + E	2	copular expression used for honorific purposes (see 2.4.3)
de irasshaimasu	でいらっしゃいます	C + E	2	copular expression used for honorific purposes (see 2.4.3)
demo	でも	R	4, 11	even (see 4.4.11); *demo* after an interrogative Noun (see 11.4.8)
demo	でも	R	8	or something; or somewhere; or someone; etc. (see 8.4.5)
den'ki	電気	N	7	electricity
deru	出る	V	2	come out; is issued; appear; attend
-do	度	Nd	3	counter for degrees (see 3.4.9)
doko demo	どこでも	Ni + R	11	anywhere (see 11.4.8)
doko ka	どこか	Ni + R	11	somewhere; anywhere (see 11.4.6)
doko (e) mo	どこ(へ)も	Ni + R	11	(not) anywhere (see 11.4.7)
dooiu	どういう	PN	9	what kind of ~ (see 9.4.12)
doroboo	どろぼう	N	3	thief

(E)

ebi	えび	N	8	prawn, lobster; shrimp
Edo	江戸	N	9	the old name of Tōkyō
eiwa	英和	N	13	English-Japanese (dictionary)
en'ryo	えんりょ	N	8	reserve; hesitation
en'ryo suru	えんりょする	V	8	have reservations; hesitate
erabu	えらぶ	V	11	choose; select
-eru	える	Dv	4	potential Derivative (see 4.4.2)

(F)

-fiito	フィート	Nd	6	feet
fukai	深い	A	4	is deep
fuku	ふく	V	12	blow (intransitive Verb)

furai	フライ	N	8	fried food
futoru	ふとる	V	12	get fat
(G)				
gakkari	がっかり	N	12	disappointment (colloquial) (see 12.4.12)
-garu	がる	Dv	7	(see 7.4.8)
-gawa	がわ	Nd	13	side
geemu	ゲーム	N	11	game
gen'dai	現代	N	8	present age
goran nasai	ごらんなさい	N + V	4	look; see (see 4.4.6)
goran nasai	ごらんなさい	E	13	equivalent for *minasai* after TE form (see 13.4.12)
-guramu	グラム	Nd	6	gram
gyooji	行事	N	6	event
gyuuniku	牛肉	N	8	beef
(H)				
haiku	俳句	N	12	*haiku*; 5-7-5-syllabled Japanese poem
hakaru	はかる	V	3	measure
hana	はな	N	3	nose
Han'furii	ハンフリー	N	4	Humphrey
han'tai	はんたい	N	11	opposition; dissent; negative
han'tai suru	はんたいする	V	11	oppose; (say) against
happi	はっぴ	N	6	"happy" coat
harau	払う	V	4	pay
hareru	晴れる	V	12	become fair; clear up
hatake	畑	N	4	farm; cultivated field
hattatsu	発達	N	3	development
hattatsu suru	発達する	V	3	develop; progress (intransitive Verb)
hayasa	速さ	N	9	speed
hen	へん	N	13	(see 13.4.4)
hen'ka	変化	N	12	change; variation
hidoi	ひどい	A	7	is cruel; is serious; is harsh; is hard
higai	ひがい	N	4	damage; harm
hiku	引く	V	3, 13	draw; pull; look up

hiraku	開く	V	2	hold (a meeting); open
Hirota	広田	N	3	family name
hisho	秘書	N	2	secretary
hitori de	ひとりで	Adv.	8	alone; by oneself
hon'kakuteki	本格的	Na	9	full-scale; real; earnest
Hon'kon	ほんこん	N	4	Hong Kong
hon'yaku	ほん訳	N	13	translation
hon'yaku suru	ほん訳する	V	13	translate
hoshoo	保障	N	3	security
hoton'do	ほとんど	Adv.	7	almost
hyoo	表	N	13	list; table
hyooban	ひょうばん	N	8	reputation
hyoogen	表現	N	2	expression
hyoogen suru	表現する	V	2	express

(I)

igai	以外	N	7	except; other than (see 7.4.3)
igaku	医学	N	3	medical science
igo	以後	N	9	after; post- ~ (see 9.4.14)
iin	医院	N	3	medical office
ijoo	以上	N	7	above; more than (see 7.4.3)
ika	以下	N	7	below; less than (see 7.4.3)
iken	意見	N	11	opinion
iki	行き	N	3	(on one's) way to ~ (see 3.4.7)
iku	いく	E	12	(see 12.4.5)
inai	以内	N	7	within
-in'chi	インチ	Nd	6	inch
ippai	いっぱい	Adv.	6	a lot; full
iru	いる	V	2	need (intransitive Verb) ("need ~" is ~ *ga iru*) (see 2.4.15)
Ishida	石田	N	8	family name
itasu	いたす	V	2	do (polite equivalent of *suru*) (see 2.4.7)
izen	以前	N	9	before; pre- ~ (see 9.4.14)

(J)

jidai	時代	N	7	era; time; age
jikaku	字画	N	13	number of strokes
jishin	地震	N	4	earthquake
Jon	ジョン	N	9	John
joodan	じょうだん	N	12	joke
jookyuu	上級	N	13	advanced level
jugyoo	授業	N	9	class; instruction

(K)

ka	か	R	11	after an interrogative Verb (see 11.4.6)
kaeri	帰り	N	3	(on one's) way back (opp. *iki* "(on one's) way (to)") (see 3.4.7)
kai	会	N	2	meeting
-kai	回	Nd	3	time(s)
kai	貝	N	8	shellfish; sea shell
kaigan	海岸	N	11	beach; seashore
-kaku	画	Nd	13	counter for strokes
kamae	かまえ	N	13	(see 13.4.4)
kana	かな	SP	6	I wonder (if) ... (see 6.4.7)
kanemochi	金持ち	N	13	the rich
kan'gofu	かんご婦	N	3	nurse
kan'jiru	感じる	V	12	feel; is sensitive
kan'kei	関係	N	4	relation; connection
kan'muri	かんむり	N	13	(see 13.4.4)
kan'zen	完全	Na	3	complete; perfect
kao	顔	N	12	face
kara	から	R	4	through; via (see 4.4.5)
karada	体	N	12	body; construction
kare	かれ	N	6	he
karera	かれら	N	6	they (people) (usually male)
karui	かるい	A	6	is light
kashira	かしら	SP	6	I wonder (if) ... (see 6.4.7)
katsudoo	活動	N	11	activity
kawaisoo	かわいそう	Na	3	pitiful; poor

kazan	火山	N	4	volcano
kazari	かざり	N	6	decoration
kaze	かぜ	N	3	(a) cold
kaze	風	N	12	wind
kazoeru	数える	V	13	count
keikaku	計画	N	11	plan
keikaku suru	計画する	V	11	plan
keikan	けいかん	N	2	policeman
keisatsu	けいさつ	N	7	police
ken'gaku	見学	N	11	observation study; field trip
ken'gaku suru	見学する	V	11	visit someplace for study
kesshite	けっして	Adv.	4	(not) by any means; never (always used in negation)
ki	気	N	12	mind; spirit (see 12.4.15)
kigae	着がえ	N	2	spare clothes
kihon	基本	N	13	basis
kikai	機械	N	7	machine
kikoeru	聞こえる	V	4	can be heard (see 4.4.2)
kimaru	決まる	V	9	is determined; is decided (intransitive Verb (see 9.4.9)
kimeru	決める	V	9	decide (transitive Verb) (see 9.4.9)
kin'dai	近代	N	9	modern age (cf. As far as Japan is concerned, *kin'dai* covers the period from the Meiji era to the present while *gen'dai* covers the period after the Second World War.)
kin'daika	近代化	N	9	modernization
kin'daiteki	近代的	Na	7	modern
kirisutokyoo	キリスト教	N	6	Christianity
-kiro(guramu)	キログラム	Nd	6	kilogram (see 6.4.10)
koe	声	N	4	voice
(o)kome	(お)米	N	4	rice
kon'pa	コンパ	N	11	party (usually students') (originated from "company")
koogi	講義	N	9	lecture
koogyoo	工業	N	7	manufacturing industry

kooiu	こういう	PN	9	this kind of ～ (see 9.4.12)
koojoo	工場	N	7	factory (工場 may also be read *kooba*.)
koosai	交際	N	11	association
kooto	コート	N	12	(tennis) court
korera	これら	N	6	these (see 6.4.2)
-koro	ころ	Nd	6	(approximate) time
koshoo	こしょう	N	8	pepper
koso	こそ	R	3	used to emphasize the preceding word (see 3.4.10)
kowai	こわい	A	4	is fearful
kuchi	口	N	3	mouth
kumo	雲	N	12	cloud
kumoru	曇る	V	12	get cloudy
kun	訓	N	13	reading based on the Japanese meaning
kurabu	クラブ	N	11	club; society
kuru	くる	E	12	has come to such and such a state (see 12.4.5)
kyooju	教授	N	12	professor
kyookai	教会	N	6	church
kyuu	急	Na	2	urgent; sudden
kyuuji	給仕	N	8	waiter
kyuusoku	急速	Na	7	rapid

(M)

maa	まあ	SI	8	used to stop someone
made	まで	Rc	4	until (see 4.4.12)
maikon	マイコン	N	7	personal computer; microcomputer
mairu	まいる	E	8	polite equivalent of *kuru* and *iku* (see 8.4.17)
mairu	まいる	V	8	polite equivalent of *kuru* and *iku* (see 8.4.17)
makaseru	まかせる	V	7	leave (it to someone)
manabu	学ぶ	V	13	study
-mase	ませ	Dv	2	imperative form of *-masu* (see 2.4.9)

masumasu	ますます	Adv.	9	more and more
matchi	マッチ	N	8	a match
matsuri	祭り	N	6	festival
Meiji	明治	N	7	Meiji (name of the emperor who reigned 1868 through 1912)
meirei	命令	N	2	order; command
meirei suru	命令する	V	2	order; give a command; direct
menyuu	メニュー	N	8	menu
mezurashii	めずらしい	A	8	is rare
midori(iro)	みどり(色)	N	2	green
mieru	見える	V	4	can see (see 4.4.2)
mikan	みかん	N	4	tangerine; mandarin orange
mimi	耳	N	3	ear
mina(san)	皆(さん)	N	11	everybody; (you) all (*Min'na* is used to refer to one's in-group members or in informal speech and is never followed by -*san*. *Mina* may or may not be followed by -*san*, but it should be followed by -*san* when it is addressed to a group of people.)
mitsukeru	見つける	V	13	find; discover (transitive Verb) (cf. *mitsukaru*)
mizuumi	湖	N	11	lake (lit. "freshwater sea")
mo	も	R	11	after an interrogative Noun (see 11.4.7)
Moogan	モーガン	N	7	Morgan
Mooshiwake gozaimasen.	もうしわけ ございません。	(exp.)	8	I am sorry. (lit. There is no excuse.)

(N)

na	な	SP	2	means "prohibition" when used after the Dictionary form of a Verb (see 2.4.2)
naa	なあ	SP	12	exclamatory Sentence Particle (see 12.4.8)
-naide	ないで	Da	8	without (doing); instead of (doing) (see 8.4.7)
nakama	なかま	N	11	associate; fellow; partner; companion

naku	なく	V	12	cry; mew; twitter
nakunaru	なくなる	V	12	disappear; run out
nan demo	何でも	Ni + R	11	anything
nani ka	何か	Ni + R	11	something
nani mo	何も	Ni + R	11	(not) anything
-nan'ka	なんか	Nd	7	colloquial equivalent of -*nado* – and the like (see 7.4.10)
naosu	治す	V	3	cure; heal
narabu	ならぶ	V	13	line up; is listed; is in a row (intransitive Verb)
nareru	なれる	V	13	get accustomed; is tame (~ *ni nareru* "get accustomed to ~") (see 13.4.10)
narubeku	なるべく	Adv.	8	if possible
nasaru	なさる	V	2	polite equivalent of *suru* "do" (see 2.4.7)
nashitogeru	なしとげる	V	9	achieve; complete
natsukashii	なつかしい	A	6	is dear
nedan	ねだん	N	7	price
netsu	熱	N	3	temperature; fever (~*ga aru* or *nai*; ~ *ga takai* or *hikui*)
ni	に	R	3	by (see 3.4.2)
ni	に	R	8	used after a person who is made to do (see 8.4.8)
ni	に	R	8	and; in addition (see 8.4.14)
ni kakete	にかけて	R + V	4	through ~ (see 4.4.3)
nikki	日記	N	12	diary
ni yoru to	によると	R + V + R	4	according to ~
ni yotte	によって	R + V	12	by (see 12.4.2)
nodo	のど	N	3	throat
nokori	残り	N	13	the rest; the remainder
Nomura	野村	N	7	family name
noogyoo	農業	N	4	agriculture
nureru	ぬれる	V	3	get wet
nusumu	ぬすむ	V	3	steal; rob
nyaanyaa	ニャーニャー	Adv.	3	mew-mew

(O)

o	を	R	8	used after a person who is made to do (see 8.4.8)
Odaiji ni.	お大事に。	(exp.)	3	Please take good care of yourself. (said to a sick person) (see 3.4.12)
odoru	おどる	V	6	dance
Ogawa	小川	N	4	family name
ogoru	おごる	V	8	treat someone to food; one pays for someone else's food, drinks, movies, etc.
omikoshi	おみこし	N	6	portable shrine
omoi	重い	A	6	is heavy; is serious
omoidasu	思い出す	V	11	recall
omoide	思い出	N	6	memory
omosa	重さ	N	6	weight
on	音	N	13	reading based on the original Chinese sounds
onaka	おなか	N	3	stomach; belly
ooku tomo	多くとも	Adv.	13	at most (see 13.4.2)
oru	おる	V	2	humble equivalent of *iru* (see 2.4.4)
oru	おる	E	6	(see 6.4.3)
osou	おそう	V	4	attack; hit
owari	終わり	N	7	end
oyaoya	おやおや	SI	3	my goodness

(P)

pikunikku	ピクニック	N	11	picnic
-pon'do	ポンド	Nd	6	pound

(R)

raisu	ライス	N	8	rice
rajikase	ラジカセ	N	7	radio casette tape recorder
-rareru	られる	Dv	2	Derivative used to show politeness and/or respect (see 2.4.12)
-rareru	られる	Dv	3	passive Derivative (see 3.4.2)
-rareru	られる	Dv	4	potential Derivation (see 4.4.2)

rei	例<ruby>れい</ruby>	N	9	precedent; example
ren'raku	れんらく	N	7	contact
ren'raku suru	れんらくする	V	7	contact
-reru	れる	Dv	2	Derivative used to show politeness and/or respect (see 2.4.12)
-reru	れる	Dv	3	passive Derivative (see 3.4.2)
rooka	ろう下	N	9	narrow hall; corridor
ryooriten	料理店	N	8	restaurant

(S)

-sa	さ	(suffix)	4	turns the preceding Adjective into a Noun (see 4.4.13)
sabishii	さびしい	A	6	is lonely; is lonesome; is deserted; is sad
sae	さえ	R	13	even (see 13.4.3)
sagaru	下がる	V	12	hang down; go down (intransitive Verb)
sageru	下げる	V	12	hang; lower; bring down (intransitive Verb)
Saitoo	斉藤	N	3	family name
samazama	さまざま	Na	11	various kinds
san'butsu	産物	N	8	product of a district
san'gyoo	産業	N	9	industry
san'ka	さんか	N	11	participation
san'ka suru	さんかする	V	11	participate; join (~ ni san'ka suru) (intransitive Verb)
san'sei	さんせい	N	11	approval; consent; agreement
san'sei suru	さんせいする	V	11	agree; approve; consent; support
sara ni	さらに	Adv.	7	more and more; furthermore
-saseru	させる	Dv	8	causative Derivative (see 8.4.8)
sasou	さそう	V	11	invite someone to do
sassoku	さっそく	Adv.	7	instantly; quickly
Satoo	佐藤	N	11	family name
satoo	さとう	N	8	sugar
seido	制度	N	3	system
seihin	製品	N	7	manufactured goods

seikaku	性格	N	4	character; personality
-seiki	世紀	Nd	9	century
sekitan	石炭	N	4	coal
sekiyu	石油	N	4	petroleum
sekkaku	せっかく	Adv.	12	with much trouble; specially (see 12.4.13)
sen'zen	戦前	N	7	prewar
-seru	せる	Dv	8	causative Derivative – make someone do such and such (see 8.4.8)
shi	し	Rc	6	what's more; in addition (see 6.4.5)
shiai	試合	N	12	(sport) game; match
shibafu	しばふ	N	2	grass; lawn
shibashiba	しばしば	Adv.	4	often; frequently (formal equivalent of *yoku*)
shigen	資源	N	4	resources
shiki	四季	N	12	four seasons
Shimada	島田	N	6	family name
shimaguni	島国	N	4	island country
Shimizu	清水	N	12	family name
shin'too	神道	N	6	Shinto
shinu	死ぬ	V	2	die
shio	しお	N	8	salt
shirenai	しれない	E	4	(see 4.4.4)
shiryoo	資料	N	9	data; research material; reference
shizen	自然	N	4	nature
Shizuko	しず子	N	9	girl's first name
shokuryoo	食料	N	4	food; materials to eat
shokuseikatsu	食生活	N	8	eating habits; dietary life
shokyuu	初級	N	13	elementary level
shoosetsu	小説	N	12	novel
shooshoo	しょうしょう	Adv.	2	formal equivalent of *chotto* "a while"; "a little" (see 2.4.8)
shuppatsu	出発	N	2	departure; setting out
shuppatsu suru	出発する	V	2	depart; set out

shurui	種類	N	8	kinds
-shurui	種類	Nd	13	kinds; sorts
shutchoo	出張	N	2	official trip; business trip
shutchoo suru	出張する	V	2	take an official trip
shuukyoo	宗教	N	6	religion
son'gai	そん害	N	7	loss; damage; harm
sono ue	そのうえ	SI	3	in addition to; what is more
-soo	そう	Nd	6	look (like); appear; sound (see 6.4.8)
soodan	そうだん	N	9	consultation
soodan suru	そうだんする	V	9	consult (~ *ni soodan suru* "consult with ~")
sooiu	そういう	PN	9	that kind of ~ (see 9.4.12)
sora	空	N	12	sky
sorera	それら	N	6	those things (see 6.4.2)
soroi	そろい	N	6	the same; uniform
sukkari	すっかり	Adv.	3	completely; thoroughly
sukunaku tomo	少くとも	Adv.	13	at least (see 13.4.2)
sumu	すむ	V	7	end; is over (intransitive Verb)
suru	する	E	6	used after the TARI form (see 6.4.6)
-suu	数	Nd	13	number
suudo	数度	N	7	several times (*suu-* means "several" before a counter)
suupaa	スーパー	N	4	supermarket
suupu	スープ	N	8	soup
(T)				
ta	田	N	4	rice paddy; irrigated rice field
tabi	たび	Nd	9	every time (see 9.4.8)
tadashii	正しい	A	13	is correct; is right
taifuu	台風	N	4	typhoon
Tanikawa	谷川	N	9	family name
tanoshimu	楽しむ	V	6	enjoy
tariru	たりる	V	3	is enough; is sufficient (intransitive Verb)
tatoeba	たとえば	SI	2	for example

-ten	点 (てん)	Nd	9	counter for marks; points
teru-teru-boozu	てるてるぼうず	N	12	(see 12.4.14)
to	と	Rc	7	when; if; whenever (see 7.4.2)
Toda	戸田 (とだ)	N	12	family name
toka	とか	R	11	and/or (see 11.4.10)
tokoro	ところ	Nd	7	moment; occasion (see 7.4.4)
tonari	となり	N	3	next (to someone or something); next door
tonikaku	とにかく	Adv.	12	anyway
toriireru	取り入れる	V	4	crop; gather in; take in; harvest
tsukareru	つかれる	V	3	get tired
tsuku	つく	V	6	is attached
tsumari	つまり	SI	13	that is; in other words
tsuyoi	強い	A	9	is strong
tsuzuku	つづく	V	4	continue; follow (intransitive Verb)

(U)

ukeru	受ける	V	4	receive; get; is given
un'doo	運動	N	11	sport
uta	歌	N	11	song
utau	歌う	V	6	sing

(W)

wadai	話題	N	12	topic
waei	和英	N	13	Japanese-English (dictionary)
wake	わけ	Nd	9	reason; circumstance; meaning (see 9.4.10)
wan'wan	ワンワン	Adv.	3	bow-wow
warikan	わりかん	N	8	dutch treat; each person pays for his own food, drinks, movies, etc.
wazuka	わずか	Adv.	9	only; barely; merely

(Y)

yakusu	訳す	V	13	render; translate
Yamaguchi	山口	N	3	family name
Yamazaki	山崎 (ざき)	N	8	family name

yamu	やむ	V	12	stop; cease (intransitive Verb) (see 12.4.6)
yasai	やさい	N	4	vegetables
yaseru	やせる	V	12	get thin
yatto	やっと	Adv.	8	at last; finally
yohoo	予報	N	12	forecasting; predict
yoo	用	N	2	business to do; things to do
yoo	よう	Nd	9, 13	like; as; as if; so that; way (see 9.4.2) (see 13.4.5)
yooi	用意	N	2	preparations
yooi suru	用意する	V	2	prepare; get ready for
yowai	弱い	A	9	is weak
yunyuu	輸入	N	7	import
yunyuu suru	輸入する	V	7	import
yushutsu	輸出	N	7	export
yushutsu suru	輸出する	V	7	export
yuube	夕べ	N	3	last night; evening

(Z)

zaazaa	ザーザー	Adv.	3	onomatopoeia for heavy rainfall (see 3.4.8)
zan'gyoo	残業	N	3	overtime work
zan'gyoo suru	残業する	V	3	do overtime work
zemi	ゼミ	N	11	seminar
zuihitsu	ずい筆	N	12	essay
zutto	ずっと	Adv.	4	consecutively; throughout; all during

APPENDIX VII
INDEX TO NOTES